This bo

17 FEB 2000

Macmillan Master Series

Accounting
Advanced English Language
Advanced Pure Mathematics
Arabic
Banking
Basic Management
Biology
British Politics
Business Administration
Business Communication
C Programming
C++ Programming
Chemistry
COBOL Programming
Communication
Counselling Skills
Database Design
Economic and Social History
Economics
Electrical Engineering
Electronic and Electrical
  Calculations
Electronics
English Grammar
English Language
English Literature
Fashion Styling
French
French 2
German
Global Information Systems

Internet
Italian
Italian 2
Java
Marketing
Mathematics
Mathematics for Electrical and
  Electronic Engineering
Microsoft Office
Microsoft Windows, Novell
  NetWare and UNIX
Modern British History
Modern European History
Modern World History
Networks
Pascal and Delphi
Programming
Philosophy
Photography
Physics
Psychology
Shakespeare
Social Welfare
Sociology
Spanish
Spanish 2
Statistics
Systems Analysis and Design
Visual Basic
World Religions

Macmillan Master Series
Series Standing Order ISBN 0–333–69343–4
(*outside North America only*)

You can receive future titles in this series as they are published by placing
a standing order. Please contact your bookseller or, in case of difficulty,
write to us at the address below with your name and address, the title of
the series and the ISBN quoted above.

Customer Services Department, Macmillan Distribution Ltd
Houndmills, Basingstoke, Hampshire RG21 6XS, England

Mastering
Economics
Fifth Edition

Jack Harvey

MACMILLAN

First edition 1984
Second edition 1985
Reprinted twice
Third edition 1989
Reprinted once
Fourth edition 1994
Reprinted three times
Fifth edition 2000

Published by
MACMILLAN PRESS LTD
Houndmills, Basingstoke, Hampshire RG21 6XS
and London
Companies and representatives
throughout the world

ISBN 0–333–77924–X

A catalogue record for this book is available from the British Library.

This book is printed on paper suitable for recycling and made from fully managed and sustained forest sources.

10 9 8 7 6 5 4 3 2 1
09 08 07 06 05 04 03 02 01 00

Printed in Great Britain by
Creative Print & Design (Wales), Ebbw Uale

20 00000 239

Contents

List of Tables	x
List of Figures	xi
Preface to the First Edition	xiv
Preface to the Fifth Edition	xv
Acknowledgements	xvi

Part I   Introduction

1 **Solving the problem of scarcity** — 3
    1.1 The economic problem — 3
    1.2 Economic systems — 4
    1.3 The market economy — 5
    1.4 The command economy — 7
    1.5 Britain's mixed economy — 9
    1.6 The limitations of economics — 9

Part II   Private-sector production

2 **The operation of the free market** — 13
    2.1 Markets — 13
    2.2 Forces determining price — 17
    2.3 The determination of price: market clearing — 23
    2.4 Changes in the conditions of demand and supply — 24
    2.5 Functions of price in the market economy — 25
    2.6 Further applications — 29

3 **Demand** — 32
    3.1 The marginal-utility theory — 32
    3.2 Price elasticity of demand — 35
    3.3 Income-elasticity of demand — 38
    3.4 Cross-elasticity of demand — 38

4 **Supply: (i) the structure of industry** — 41
    4.1 The role of the firm — 41
    4.2 What to produce — 43
    4.3 The legal form of the firm — 44
    4.4 Raising the necessary capital — 48
    4.5 The division of labour — 52
    4.6 The advantages of large-scale production — 53
    4.7 The size of firms — 56
    4.8 The location of production — 58
    4.9 The distribution of goods to the consumer — 60

5 Supply: (ii) costs and profitability   68
   5.1 Combining resources   68
   5.2 The costs of production   71
   5.3 How much to produce: output of the firm under perfect
        competition   76
   5.4 The industry's supply curve   81
   5.5 Elasticity of supply   82

Part III Factors of production and their rewards

6 The determination of factor rewards   89
   6.1 Introduction   89
   6.2 The theoretical determination of factor rewards   90

7 Labour and wages   95
   7.1 The workforce of the UK   95
   7.2 The nature of the labour force   96
   7.3 Methods of rewarding labour   98
   7.4 The determination of the wage-rate in a particular industry,
        occupation or locality   100
   7.5 Trade unions: the process of collective bargaining   104
   7.6 The government and wages   111

8 Capital, land and entrepreneurship   113
   8.1 Capital   113
   8.2 Interest   115
   8.3 Land and rent   116
   8.4 Entrepreneurship   122
   8.5 Profit   123

Part IV The government and the allocation of resources

9 Making the most of limited resources   129
   9.1 An analysis of the problem   129
   9.2 Factors determining the position of the PPC   130
   9.3 The shape of the PPC   132
   9.4 The conditions for a country to obtain maximum satisfaction
        from its limited resources   132

10 Monopoly and imperfect competition   136
   10.1 Deviations from perfect competition   136
   10.2 Monopoly   137
   10.3 The control of monopoly   142
   10.4 Discriminating monopoly   147
   10.5 Monopolistic competition: imperfect competition with
         many firms   149
   10.6 Oligopoly: imperfect competition with few firms   152
   10.7 Pricing policy in the real world   153

11 The provision of goods and services by the public sector   156
    11.1 The case for public sector provision   156
    11.2 Accountability v. economic efficiency   157
    11.3 The problem of assessing needs   158
    11.4 Pricing policy in the public sector   159
    11.5 The nationalised industries and privatisation   161

Part V The environment

12 Externalities and cost–benefit analysis   169
    12.1 Externalities   169
    12.2 Possible methods of dealing with externalities   170
    12.3 Why cost–benefit analysis (CBA)?   171
    12.4 Difficulties of CBA   172
    12.5 An assessment of CBA   173

13 Protecting the environment   175
    13.1 Economic aspects of the environment   175
    13.2 Conservation   176
    13.3 Maintaining a renewable stock of fish   177
    13.4 Preserving an historic building   179
    13.5 Pollution   182
    13.6 Road traffic   187
    13.7 Concluding observations   196

Part VI Money and financial institutions

14 Money and financial markets   201
    14.1 Money   201
    14.2 The provision of liquid capital   203
    14.3 Money markets   203
    14.4 The capital market   208
    14.5 Markets in securities: the Stock Exchange   211

15 Clearing banks   216
    15.1 Types of banks in the UK   216
    15.2 The creation of credit   217
    15.3 Bank lending   220
    15.4 Modification of the cash-ratio approach   223
    15.5 The effects of recent increased competition   223

16 The Bank of England   225
    16.1 Functions of the Bank of England   225
    16.2 Responsibility for operating monetary policy   227

Part VII The government's overall management of the economy

17 Outline of government management policy   231
    17.1 The government's macro objectives   231

17.2 Differences in the method of analysis 232
17.3 The government and the distribution of income 234

18 Measuring the level of activity: national income calculations 236
18.1 The principle of national income calculations 236
18.2 National income calculations in practice 237
18.3 Uses of national income statistics 243

19 Unemployment 248
19.1 The nature of unemployment 248
19.2 Causes of unemployment 249

20 The level of output and aggregate demand: the Keynesian approach to full employment 252
20.1 The link between spending and production 252
20.2 Reasons for changes in aggregate demand 254
20.3 Consumption spending 256
20.4 Investment spending 259
20.5 The effect on the level of income of changes in investment 262
20.6 Leaks and injections in general 263
20.7 Aggregate demand and full employment policy 264

21 The relationship of the price level and the level of employment 268
21.1 The development of 'full employment' theory 268
21.2 AD and AS curves 268
21.3 A first step towards an explanation of inflation 270
21.4 Monetarism 272

22 Government policy to control inflation 276
22.1 Introduction 276
22.2 Measuring changes in the value of money 276
22.3 Why control inflation? 279
22.4 Post-war demand management in the UK 280
22.5 The implementation of monetarism by the Thatcher government 282
22.6 Subsequent policy misjudgements 286

23 Balanced regional development 290
23.1 The nature of the problem 290
23.2 Workers to the work 293
23.3 Work to the workers 294
23.4 Regional policy in the context of the EU 297

24 Growth 299
24.1 The nature of growth 299
24.2 Achieving growth 300
24.3 The government and growth 303

25 Public finance 305
25.1 The distribution of income 305
25.2 Government revenue and expenditure 305

25.3	The modern approach to taxation	308
25.4	The structure of taxation	310
25.5	The advantages and disadvantages of direct taxes	312
25.6	The advantages and disadvantages of indirect taxes	314
25.7	The incidence of taxation	317

Part VIII   International trade

26 The nature of international trade — 327

26.1	How international trade arises	327
26.2	The advantages of international trade	327
26.3	What determines the rate at which goods are traded internationally?	330
26.4	The pattern of the UK's overseas trade	333
26.5	Free trade and protection	336

27 Foreign currency exchange rates — 342

27.1	The determination of exchange rates	342
27.2	What are the main underlying influences on the demand for and supply of foreign currency?	343

28 Balance-of-payments stability — 346

28.1	The nature of imports and exports	346
28.2	The balance-of-payments accounts	348
28.3	The correction of a balance-of-payments disequilibrium	352
28.4	Reducing expenditure on imports: deflation	352
28.5	Expenditure-switching by exchange rate depreciation	354
28.6	Managed flexibility	357

29 The European Union — 360

29.1	Background to the European Union (EU)	360
29.2	The institutions of the EU	361
29.3	The establishment of a common market	362
29.4	The Single Market 1993	364
29.5	Advantages for the UK of belonging to the EU	365
29.6	Problems facing the UK as a member of the EU	366
29.7	The Exchange Rate Mechanism (ERM)	369
29.8	Economic and Monetary Union (EMU): the single currency	371

Answers to self-test questions	376
Index	392

◼◪ List of tables

2.1 Demand schedule for No-Such Market for the week ending 30
January 1999 18
2.2 An increase in demand 19
2.3 Supply schedule for No-Such Market for the week ending 30
January 1999 21
2.4 An increase in supply in the spring 22
3.1 Elasticity of demand and total outlay 36
4.1 Size of manufacturing establishments in the UK, 1996 57
5.1 Variations in output of potatoes resulting from a change in labour
employed 69
5.2 Costs, revenue and profits of Rollermowers 74
5.3 Short-period supply schedule 82
7.1 Workforce in employment in the UK 96
7.2 The industrial distribution of employees 96
10.1 Costs, revenue and profits of Airborne Mowers 140
18.1 Calculations of Gross National Product of the UK, 1996 239
20.1 Investment in the UK 1997: Gross Fixed Capital Formation, £mn. 260
22.1 The £'s falling purchasing power 1526–1996 277
23.1 Percentage rate of unemployment by Government Office Region,
October 1998 291
26.1 The terms of trade of the UK, 1988–96 (base year 1990) 332
26.2 The UK's imports and exports 1996 334
26.3 Percentage distribution of the UK's trade between the EU and the
rest of the world, 1982 and 1996 335
28.1 The balance of payments of the UK, 1996 349

■ ⊻ List of figures

1.1	The flow of goods and resources in an economic system	5
1.2	The allocation of products and resources through the market economy	6
1.3	The allocation of resources and products through a command economy	8
2.1	Quantity demanded and price	19
2.2	Quantity supplied and price	21
2.3	The determination of equilibrium price	23
2.4	The effect on price of a change in the conditions of demand	25
2.5	The effect on price of a change in the conditions of supply	25
2.6	Excess demand for Cup Final tickets	27
2.7	The black-market price of Cup Final tickets	27
2.8	The effect on house prices of an increase in demand by owner-occupiers	28
2.9	The effect of a change in the conditions of supply on price and quantity traded	28
2.10	Stabilisation of the price of butter	29
2.11	Joint demand	30
2.12	Joint supply	30
2.13	The effect on quantity bought of a change in the tax on a good	31
3.1	Elasticity of demand	35
3.2	Cross-elasticity of demand	39
4.1	Economy in tools through specialisation	53
4.2	Economising in distribution through the wholesaler	61
5.1	The relationship between the number of labourers employed, average product and marginal product	70
5.2	The relationship between returns and costs	75
5.3	Cost curves	75
5.4	The firm's demand curve under perfect competition	76
5.5	The firm's demand curve under perfect and imperfect competition	77
5.6	The supply of a factor under perfect and imperfect competition	77
5.7	The equilibrium output of the firm under perfect competition	79
5.8	The short-period supply curve of the industry	81
5.9	The effect of competition on the super-normal profits and output of Rollermowers	82
5.10	Elasticity of supply	83
5.11	Extremes of elasticity of supply	83
5.12	Changes in the price of cane sugar over time in response to a change in demand	85
6.1	The firm's demand curve for labour	92

6.2	The determination of the price of a factor	92
7.1	The relationship between the wage-rate and hours worked	98
7.2	The effect on the wage-rate of a change in marginal revenue productivity	107
7.3	The effect on the wage-rate of trade-union restriction of the supply of labour	108
7.4	The relationship of substitutability between labour and land and numbers employed	109
7.5	The extent to which demand for the product contracts as a result of a wage increase	110
8.1	The effect of the price of a product on the rent of land	118
8.2	The determination of rent when land is fixed in supply	119
8.3	Economic rent	120
8.4	Economic rent and elasticity of supply	121
9.1	A production possibility curve	130
10.1	Market forms	137
10.2	Marginal revenue under conditions of perfect and imperfect competition	139
10.3	The equilibrium output of a monopolist	141
10.4	Output under perfect competition and monopoly	141
10.5	Monopoly and price control	145
10.6	Price and output under a contestable market	146
10.7	Receipts under perfect discrimination	148
10.8	The possibility of supply with price discrimination	149
10.9	Monopolistic competition: equilibrium of firms in the short and long periods	151
10.10	The product life-cycle	154
11.1	Increasing revenue by 'block pricing'	162
12.1	The external cost of nitrates applied to land	170
13.1	Over-fishing	178
13.2	Adjustments to the present value of a historic building for different uses	180
13.3	Changes in future relative prices of historic buildings and offices	181
13.4	Methods of preserving a historic building	182
13.5	Efficient output with external costs	184
13.6	Allowing for the external cost of congestion	191
13.7	The effect of high fixed costs on public transport	193
13.8	Difference in average costs per passenger mile of car, bus and rail transport	194
14.1	The provision of finance in the United Kingdom	204
14.2	A commercial bill of exchange	205
14.3	The capital market	209
15.1	How a bank creates credit	219
15.2	The nature and distribution of a bank's main assets	221
15.3	The pyramid of bank credit	222
18.1	The value of the total product equals the sum of values added by each firm	237

18.2   Summary of Gross National Product calculations   241
18.3   Gross National Product and National Income   242
18.4   Calculating personal disposable income from Gross National
       Product   244
19.1   The effect on employment of a wage increase in an export industry   250
20.1   The circular flow of income   253
20.2   The level of income maintained through investment   255
20.3   The relationship between consumption and income   257
20.4   The effect on income of an increase in the level of investment   263
20.5   Total leaks and injections   264
20.6   Achieving a full-employment aggregate demand by budgetary
       policy   265
21.1   The relationship of output and the price level to AD and AS   269
21.2   The Phillips curve   271
21.3   The inflationary process   272
21.4   The effect of inflation-expectations on the rate of unemployment   274
22.1   Monetary control alternatives   282
22.2   Supply-side policy   285
23.1   Assisted Areas, Great Britain: as defined by the Department of
       Trade and Industry at 1 August 1993   296
24.1   Economic growth   300
24.2   Factors leading to growth   301
25.1   Public money, 1999–2000 where it comes from and where it goes   306
25.2   The difference between regressive, proportional and progressive
       taxes   309
25.3   The diagrammatic representation of a tax on the supply side   319
25.4   The diagrammatic representation of a tax on the demand side   320
25.5   The relationship of elasticity of demand and production when a
       tax is imposed on a good   320
25.6   The relationship of elasticity of supply and production when a tax
       is imposed on a good   321
25.7   The diagrammatic representation of a subsidy   323
26.1   The principal exporters to and importers from the UK, 1996   335
27.1   The determination of exchange rates   343
28.1   How exports pay for imports   347
28.2   Achieving balance-of-payments equilibrium by deflation   354
29.1   The effect on supply of a guaranteed 'intervention' price   367

Preface to the first edition

Mastering Economics is written for those who are embarking on a study of economics. While its main aim is to cover basic examinations in schools and colleges, it will also meet the requirements of most professional syllabuses and will provide preliminary reading for university students.

For the general reader seeking guidance in understanding economic problems and policies, the book sets out the essential background and introduces in simple form the techniques used by economists.

Particular attention has been paid to current views regarding the defects of the 'laissez-faire' system in solving the economic problem, the role the government can play in a 'mixed' economy, and the increase in the importance of the public sector over the past thirty-five years – subjects which are inclined to be glossed over in elementary texts.

I would like to thank Andrew Leake, senior economics master at Latymer Upper School, and David Whitehead, lecturer in education at the University of London, who read the original typescript and made many helpful suggestions.

JACK HARVEY

◼ ⊻ Preface to the fifth edition

Tables and facts have been brought up to date and the text revised to cover changes in the working of institutions and developments in economic policy over recent years.

As regards particular topics, this new edition discusses the problem of road traffic in the environment, the Public Finance Initiative as a follow-up to privatisation, changes in the functions of the Bank of England, developments in regional policy and the pros and cons of the European Union's single currency.

To reinforce this edition's emphasis on explaining the role of government in a market economy, some additional elementary theory has been introduced. Furthermore, the order of certain chapters has been rearranged so that, as far as possible, relevant simple theory precedes its application in the formulation of government policy. This approach is illustrated in particular in Chapters 21 and 22 which deal with the control of inflation.

Each chapter begins with a statement of its objectives and concludes with a few self-test questions. These are designed to indicate whether the preceding text has been fully understood and to encourage the student to think further on the issues raised. In general, questions need answers only in one or two words or in note form, and can eventually be compared with those given at the end of the book.

In emphasing the role of the government in pursuing its economic aims, we must always remember that it is continually making subjective decisions since objectives other than increases in the national product have to be taken into account. This is particularly evident as regards the decision as to whether the UK should adopt the single currency and enter fully into Economic and Monetary Union (EMU), for the economic gain has to be weighed against constitutional drawbacks which might follow (Chapter 29). Similarly while measurement of the national product is concerned with wealth, this omits many aspects of life which are central to a people's real happiness (Chapter 18, question 5).

JACK HARVEY

◼◪ Acknowledgements

The author and publishers wish to thank the Office for National Statistics for permission to reproduce extracts from official publications, and the Bank of England for permission to quote from its *Fact Sheets*.

 **Part I**

Introduction

▪ ⌄ ▪ Solving the problem of scarcity

Objectives

1 To describe how the 'economic problem' arises
2 To examine the respective strengths and weaknesses of the market and command economies
3 To indicate the objectives of Britain's 'middle way' approach
4 To suggest how the economist can contribute to solving the problem of scarcity

1.1 The economic problem

(a) Wants and limited resources

Have you been window-shopping lately, gazing longingly at the various goods on display? If only you had the means to buy them! This is the *economic problem* – unlimited wants, very limited means. You just can't get a quart out of a pint pot.

While we can never completely overcome the difficulty, we can, by 'economising', make the most of what we have. Thus the housewife buys that assortment of goods which will give maximum satisfaction from her limited housekeeping allowance. Similarly, the student strives to make his grant go as far as possible. And the businessman takes decisions which will achieve the maximum return on capital. The government, too, has to plan its spending in order to make the most of the funds at its disposal.

(b) Opportunity cost

Thus economics is concerned with the problem of choice – the decisions forced upon us by the smallness of our resources compared with our wants. But choice involves sacrifice. If the newspaper boy spends his earnings on a football, he will have to postpone buying the table-tennis bat he also wants. The schoolgirl who works in a store on a Saturday has to forgo the game of tennis she would otherwise have played. When the farmer sows a field with wheat, he accepts that he will have to go without the barley it could have grown.

Because resources are limited, having 'this' means going without 'that'; or, as the Yorkshireman says, 'There's no owt for nowt in this world'. We speak, therefore, of *opportunity cost* – the cost of something in terms of the best alternative gone without.

Usually economising does not mean a complete rejection of one good in favour of another, but rather deciding to have a little bit more of one and a little less of the other. In short, as we shall see, it involves choice at the *margin*.

(c) 'Free' and 'scarce' goods

Few goods are so plentiful that nobody will give anything for them. Air is one of the few exceptions. In some years, too, there is such an abundant apple harvest that a farmer says, 'Help yourself'. Such goods are termed 'free' goods. But most goods are 'scarce' – they can be obtained only by going without something else. With these goods we have to economise, so they are referred to as 'economic goods'. They are the subject-matter of economics – the study of how people allocate their limited resources to provide for their wants. It is against this backcloth of limited resources that all economic decisions by consumers and firms have to be made.

1.2 Economic systems

(a) The role of the economic system

In primitive economies, the individual uses his resources directly to provide what he wants. Thus Robinson Crusoe had to decide how much time to spend hunting, fishing, growing corn and relaxing in the sun according to the strength of his preferences for meat, fish, bread and leisure. Similarly, in a subsistence economy the farmer's output is mainly for his own family's needs.

Today, however, decisions as to what shall be produced are linked only indirectly with the actual consumer. Man now specialises in production, obtaining the variety of goods he wants by exchange. Thus, on the one hand, we have what we will call 'households', the units which both consume goods and services and supply the resources, such as labour, to produce them. On the other hand, we have 'firms', the organisations which decide what goods and services to produce, and use accordingly the resources supplied by households (Figure 1.1).

But if the greatest possible satisfaction is to be obtained from limited resources there must be a link between households and firms. Put briefly, the following questions have to be answered:

(i) *What* goods and services shall firms produce?
(ii) *How much* of each good and service shall be produced?
(iii) *How* shall the goods and services be produced?
(iv) How shall products be *divided* between households?

To solve these problems we need an economic system to provide the link between households and firms.

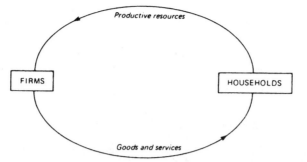

Figure 1.1 The flow of goods and resources in an economic system

(b) Different forms of economic system

Man's first exchanges were quite simple: there was a direct swap of one good for another – a 'market' was established (see p. 13). Eventually a 'go-between' – money – was developed, allowing goods to be 'priced' and sold more easily. The subsistence economy had now evolved into the *market economy*, where answers to the above questions follow from people's decisions in the market.

In contrast to the market economy, there is the *command* or *centrally directed economy*, where the state decides what to produce, directs the factors of production accordingly and distributes what is produced with the emphasis being 'to each according to his need' rather than on financial ability to pay.

Our task now is to examine in turn the respective strengths of these two systems.

1.3 The market economy

(a) Outline of the market mechanism

In the market economy, emphasis is laid on the freedom of the individual, both as a consumer and as the owner of resources.

As a consumer he expresses his choice of goods through the price he is willing to pay for them. As the owner of resources used in production (usually his own labour) he seeks to obtain as large a reward as possible. If consumers want more of the good than is being supplied at the current price, this is indicated by their 'bidding-up' the price. This increases the profits of firms and the earnings of factors producing that good. As a result, resources are attracted into the industry, and supply expands. On the other hand, if consumers do not want a particular good, its price falls, producers make a loss, and resources leave the industry.

The *price system* therefore indicates the wishes of consumers and allocates the community's productive resources accordingly (Figure 1.2). There is no direction of labour; people are free to work wherever they choose.

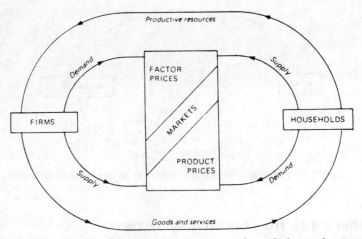

Figure 1.2   The allocation of products and resources through the market economy

(b) Defects of the market economy

In practice the market economy does not work quite so smoothly as this. Nor are its results entirely satisfactory. We speak of 'market failure'.

First, the *competition* upon which the efficiency of the market economy depends *may break down*. An employer may be the only buyer of a certain type of labour in a locality. If so, he is in a strong position when negotiating rates of pay with individual workers. The state may therefore have to intervene, e.g. by stipulating a minimum wage. Similarly, on the selling side, one seller may be able to exclude competitors. This puts the consumer in a weak position because he cannot take his custom elsewhere (see Chapter 10).

Second, some vital *community goods*, such as defence, police, justice and national parks, cannot be adequately provided through the market. This is mainly because it would be impossible to charge a price since 'free-riders' cannot be excluded (see p. 156).

Third, *consumers' choice* may be distorted by extensive persuasive advertising, sometimes of goods, e.g. cigarettes, injurious to health.

Fourth, *competition itself may sometimes lead to inefficiency.* Small units may not be able to secure the advantages of large-scale production. Duplication of research and competitive advertising may waste resources. Uncertainty as to rivals' plans may hold back investment.

Fifth, in practice the price mechanism may function sluggishly, through *imperfect knowledge* or *immobility of factors of production* (see pp. 137–8). As a result, supply is slow to respond to changes in demand.

Sixth, the private-profit motive does not always ensure that *society's* well-being (as distinct from the sum total of *private* wealth) will be maximised. There may be 'spillover' benefits or costs (often referred to as *externalities*). Thus, in providing a car park, a supermarket attracts customers; but there is an additional benefit in that it reduces congestion for all road users. On the other hand there may be *external costs*. A manufacturer does not consider the soot which falls from his factory chimney onto nearby washing-lines; but, although not a cost to him, it is one to the surrounding community (see Chapter 12).

Seventh, in a market economy where individuals decide what to produce, resources may remain *unemployed* because firms as a whole consider that profit prospects are poor or the demand for exports falls (see Chapter 19).

Lastly, the consumers with the most money have the greatest pull in the market. As a result, resources may be devoted to producing luxuries for the rich to the exclusion of necessities for the poor. While this is really brought about by the unequal distribution of wealth and income rather than by the market system, the fact is that the latter tends to produce, and even accentuate, such inequality. Efficiency is achieved through the profit motive: owners of factors of production sell them at the highest possible price, while firms keep production costs as low as they can in order to obtain the highest profit margin.

Factor earnings decide who is to receive the goods produced. If firms produce better goods or improve efficiency, or if workers make a greater effort, they receive a high reward, giving them more spending power to obtain goods in the market.

In this way the price system acts, as it were, like a marvellous computer, registering people's preferences for different goods, transmitting those preferences to firms, moving resources to produce the goods, and deciding who shall obtain the final products. Thus, through the motivation of private enterprise, the four problems inherent in economising are solved automatically.

1.4 The command economy

(a) Central decision-making

With the command economy, the decisions regarding what? how much? how? and for whom? are taken by an all-powerful planning authority. It estimates the assortment of goods which it considers people want and directs resources into producing them. It also decides how the goods produced shall be distributed among the community with the emphasis on 'to each according to his need' rather than on financial ability to pay (Figure 1.3). Thus economic efficiency largely depends upon how accurately wants are estimated and resources allocated.

(b) Merits of the command economy

The merits claimed for the command economy correspond closely to the defects of the market economy. The central planning authority can: (i) allow for the uneven distribution of wealth when planning what to produce and in rewarding the producers; (ii) ensure that adequate resources are devoted to community, public and merit goods; (iii) eliminate the inefficiencies resulting from competition; (iv) use its monopoly powers in the interests of the community, e.g. by securing the advantages of large-scale production, rather than restricting output to maximise profits; (v) use advertising to inform rather than simply to

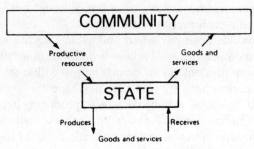

Figure 1.3 The allocation of resources and products through a command economy

persuade or 'brain-wash'; (vi) allow for external costs and benefits when deciding what and how much to produce; and (vii) employ workers in order to keep them occupied although to do so may be unprofitable in the narrow sense.

(c) Defects of the command economy

Nevertheless the command economy has inherent defects which lay it open to criticism on both economic and political grounds.

First, estimating the satisfaction derived by individuals from consuming different goods is impossible – although some help might be obtained by introducing a modified market system, where changes in prices signal changes in wants.

Second, many officials are required to estimate wants and to direct factors of production. Inasmuch as such officials are not needed in a market economy they represent wasted factors of production. Moreover, the use of officials may lead to bureaucracy – excessive form-filling, 'red tape', slowness in coming to decisions and an impersonal approach to consumers. At times, too, officialdom has been accompanied by corruption.

Third, even when wants have been decided upon, difficulties of co-ordination arise. On the one hand, wants have to be dovetailed and awarded priorities. On the other, factors have to be combined in the best proportions. Usually plans are co-ordinated through numerous committees, directed at the top by a central planning committee whose members are primarily politicians.

Fourth, it is argued that state ownership of resources, by reducing personal incentives, diminishes effort and initiative. Direction of labour may mean that people are dissatisfied with their jobs; officials may play for safety in their policies. Thus production may be less than under private enterprise.

Fifth, and probably most important, there is the political danger. Once individuals have given power to the state to decide what is good for them and to direct all factors of production, it may eventually seize absolute political power. Thus the ultimate choice between a market economy and a command economy (in their extreme forms) really hinges on whether people prefer to run the risk of dictatorship or to accept the defects of the market economy which allows them to choose their own jobs.

1.5 Britain's mixed economy

(a) The 'middle way'

Fortunately a community does not have to make a complete choice between these two extremes. Instead it can compromise by having a market economy where the government takes an active part in overcoming its defects.

Thus, in an attempt to get the best of both worlds the UK has a 'mixed economy' consisting of, a 'private sector' and a 'public sector'.

The *private sector*, covering those firms which are privately owned, is responsible for three-quarters of national production. Here decisions are taken in response to price signals, the outstanding merit of the market economy.

The *'public sector'* includes government departments, local authorities, government agencies, such as the Forestry Commission and the Post Office, and supervisory bodies, such as the Environment Agency. All are distinguished by the fact that their capital is publicly owned and their policies can be influenced through the ultimate supply of funds by the government. Thus the existence of the public sector enables the government to exercise an important measure of control over the economy. Moreover, decisions on what to produce can be based on need rather than demand (see p. 158).

(b) The role of the government

The first part of this book is concerned mainly with the private sector: how goods and resources are allocated through markets, and how producers, the owners of resources, are rewarded. Attention is then directed to how the market economy can, given certain conditions, achieve an efficient allocation of resources. The recognition that in practice these conditions do not hold, e.g. because not all goods can be priced in the market or because externalities are important, leads to a consideration of the ways in which the government can intervene to improve the market's allocation.

Above all, the government must be concerned with the inherent instability of the market economy, as reflected in cyclical booms and recessions. This is taken up in Part VII which outlines the development of economic theory as the basis of government policy.

1.6 The limitations of economics

(a) Welfare and wealth

The economist who is concerned with human welfare must recognise that in the last resort people do not want goods as such, but simply the satisfaction they obtain when consuming those goods. Yet it is quite impossible to measure satisfaction. It is probable, for instance, that a schoolgirl derives more enjoyment from £55 spent on a new tennis racket than a millionaire does from £55 spent on a dinner. Yet we can never be sure – satisfaction, like love or pain, is a personal feeling which cannot be measured objectively. This means that government policy on redistribution of income rests on subjective judgements (see p. 234).

So the economist, working on the principle that two loaves are better than one, measures the output of goods and services and declares that any increase over a given period of time indicates an increase in welfare. Nevertheless, as we see in Chapter 18, this approach is only an approximation, and its limitations have to be constantly borne in mind.

(b) The role of economics

In practice many economic decisions involve subjective judgements; that is, they cannot be made solely by an objective appraisal of the facts but depend to some extent on personal views in interpreting facts. Indeed the relative size of the public sector and the extent to which the government interferes with the operations of firms in the private sector are determined largely by the political philosophy of the elected government.

The economist tries to be as objective as possible, establishing principles which, given certain conditions, show how the economy works and can be used to predict the likely results of policies.

Decision-makers may brush these principles to one side, either because facts necessary for a complete answer are not available or because different weight is given to assumptions. But at least economics provides a reminder of where objectivity ends and subjectivity begins.

QUESTIONS

1 What, in the last resort, has a millionaire to economise in?

2 'Many policy objectives rest upon *normative statements*. For example, a government may consider imposing taxes to achieve *equity*. But economics cannot judge whether equity is a worthwhile objective.

   However, economics can analyse all possible options so that policy-makers can decide on the best instruments to achieve their objectives.'
   (a) Define phrases italicised.
   (b) What contribution could economics make to the policy of achieving equity through taxation?

Part II

Private-sector production

■Ⅴ 2 The operation of the free market

Objectives

1 To define a 'market'
2 To explain how the interaction of demand and supply determines a 'market clearing' price
3 To show how the conditions of demand and supply can change
4 To analyse how such changes affect the market price
5 To derive the functions of the 'price system'

2.1 Markets

(a) Value and price

In the market economy a want is significant only when a person is prepared to give up something in order to satisfy it. As the strength of the different wants varies, so will the amounts which people are willing to give up. In other words, different goods have different *values*, value being the *rate* at which a particular good or service will exchange for others. In modern economic systems the values of goods are expressed in terms of money, as *prices*.

Changes in *relative* prices, if supply conditions have not changed, indicate a relative shift in the importance of the goods concerned. Thus price changes signal changes in what people want. We must therefore examine the mechanism by which these signals are flashed up. We begin by looking at the *market*.

(b) What is a market?

'I am offered £1,050 for this heifer. No more offers? For the last time of asking, any advance of £1,050? Going at £1,050, going, gone.' Down comes the hammer. 'Sold at £1,050 to Mr Giles on my right.'

This is the local cattle-market. On his stand above the cattle-ring is the auctioneer. Inside the ring, a black-and-white heifer is appraised by local farmers and dealers. Some are buyers, some sellers. The market fixes the price at which those who want something can obtain it from those who have it to sell.

Note that it is only exchange value which is significant here. The farmer selling the heifer may have felt that it ought to have made more than £1,050. Or, as it was the first calf reared by his son, it may have had great 'sentimental value' to him. Such considerations, however, mean little in the market economy.

Of course, prices are not always fixed by auction. This is the method usually employed where there are many buyers but the seller only comes to the market infrequently, or wishes to dispose of his goods quickly. If there are few buyers and sellers, e.g. in the purchase of a house or a second-hand car, the final price may be arrived at by 'higgling' – the seller meeting the prospective buyer personally and bargaining with him.

But where goods are in constant demand the above methods take too long. Thus most goods, such as foodstuffs, clothing and household utensils are given a definite price by the shopkeeper. But buyers will still influence this price. If it is too high, the market will not be cleared; if it is too low, the shopkeeper's stocks will run out.

A market need not be formal or held in a particular place. Secondhand cars are often bought and sold through newspaper advertisements. Secondhand furniture may be disposed of by a card in a local shop window. Foreign currency, gold, base metals, raw cotton and other goods which can be accurately described are dealt in over the telephone.

However, in studying the market economy it is essential to understand how price is determined. Since this is done in the market, we can define the market simply as *all those buyers and sellers of a good who influence its price*. Within the market there is a tendency for the same price, allowing for costs of transport, to be established for the same commodity.

(c) World markets

Today modern transport allows many commodities to have a world market – a price change in one part of the world affects the price in the rest of the world. Examples of such commodities are wheat, coffee, oils, basic raw materials (such as cotton and rubber), gold, silver and base metals. What conditions must a commodity fulfil to obtain a world market?

First, there must be a wide demand. The basic necessities of life (e.g. wheat, vegetable oils, wool, cotton) answer this requirement. In contrast, such goods as national costumes, books translated into little-used languages and postcards of local views have only a local demand.

Second, commodities must be capable of being transported. Land and buildings are almost impossible to transport. Personal services are limited by the distance the consumer can travel. Labour, too, is particularly immobile, especially when it comes to moving to a different country (see Chapter 7). Furthermore, governments may, by import taxes and quotas, effectively prevent the entry of certain commodities into the country.

Third, the costs of transport must be small in relation to the value of the commodity. Thus the market for diamonds is worldwide, whereas that for bricks is local. Similarly wheat and oil are cheap to transport compared with coal because they are more easily handled – although, as sea transport is relatively cheap, coal mined near the coast can be sent long distances.

Last, the commodity must be durable. Goods which perish quickly, such as milk, bread, fresh cream and strawberries, cannot be sent long distances. Nevertheless, modern developments, such as refrigeration, canning and air freight transport, are extending the market even for these goods.

(d) Perfect and imperfect markets

In any market the price of the commodity in one part affects its price in another part. Hence the same price tends to be established. Where price differences are eliminated quickly, we say the market is a 'perfect' market. (Note that this is not quite the same as 'perfect competition' – see Chapter 5).

For a market to be perfect certain conditions have to be fulfilled. First, buyers and sellers must have exact knowledge of the prices being paid elsewhere in the market. The development of communications, particularly telecommunications and the internet, has facilitated this. Second, both buyers and sellers must base their actions solely on price, and not favour one particular person out of loyalty or mere inertia. Thus, if one seller puts up the price of his good, his customers immediately go to another who is cheaper. Alternatively, if he lowers his price, customers will so flock to him that he would sell out quickly unless he raises his prices to that asked elsewhere.

Examples of perfect markets are the precious-stones market of Hatton Garden in London, and above all the organised produce markets and the stock exchange (see below). In these markets the two essential conditions are fulfilled, for prices are watched closely by professional dealers. As a result of their operations, variations in price are quickly eliminated.

But such conditions are rarely satisfied in other markets. Buyers and sellers neither have perfect knowledge nor act solely on the basis of price. The ordinary housewife, for instance, cannot afford the time to go from one shop to another in order to compare the prices of her everyday purchases, though she is usually much more careful when spending on the more expensive goods bought at infrequent intervals. Similarly, shopkeepers do not always know what competing shopkeepers are charging for their goods. Moreover, purchasers may be influenced by considerations other than price. Thus they may continue to deal with one particular trader, even though he is charging a slightly higher price, because he has given them good service in the past. Finally, although two goods may be virtually the same physically, by 'product differentiation' and advertising the merits of his own brand a producer may convince the consumer of its superiority. Such 'persuasive' advertising, which accounts for over a half of present advertising expenditure, makes the market less perfect, and must be contrasted with 'informative' advertising, which increases knowledge and thus helps to make the market more perfect.

Where price differences persist, markets are said to be 'imperfect'. As we have already hinted, such markets are often found in retailing.

(e) Organised produce markets

As explained above, the market for certain commodities is worldwide. Moreover, many of these commodities are in constant demand, either as basic raw materials or as main foods or beverages for a large section of the world's people. They therefore figure prominently in international trade, and are the subject of the following discussion.

England's foreign trade began with the export of raw wool in the thirteenth century, and it was extended by the subsequent development of the chartered companies. These were based in London, and it was there that merchants gathered to buy and sell the produce which the companies' ships brought from abroad.

The big change, however, came about with the expansion of international trade following the industrial revolution. The UK became the greatest importing and exporting nation in the world. London, her chief port and commercial city, not only imported the goods which were required for the people of her own country but, assisted by the fact that British ships were the carriers of world trade, built up an important entrepôt business, acting as a go-between in the distribution of such commodities as tea, sugar, hides, skins and wool to many other countries, particularly those of western Europe.

Hence formal 'organised markets' developed. These markets are distinctive in that buying and selling takes place in a recognised building, business is governed by agreed rules and conventions, and often only certain persons are allowed to engage in transactions. They are thus a highly developed form of market. Today London has exchanges which trade in both spot and forward contracts in such commodities as gold and silver, petroleum, wool, tea, coffee, base metals (tin, copper, lead, aluminium, nickel and zinc), grain, and shipping freights. It must not be thought, however, that such organised produce markets exist only in London. Liverpool has exchanges for cotton, and most of the other large trading countries have exchanges too. Although today many of the goods go directly to other countries, the earnings of London dealers are part of the UK's income from 'invisible exports' (see p. 348).

Broadly speaking, organised markets fulfil three main functions. First, they enable manufacturers and wholesalers to obtain supplies of commodities easily, quickly and at the competitive market price. Because they are composed of specialist buyers and sellers, prices are sensitive to any change in demand and supply. Thus they are perfect markets.

Second, 'futures' dealings on these markets enable people to protect themselves from heavy losses through price changes. Thus a cotton grower prefers to know what price he will receive before his output is actually delivered to the market. On the other hand a cotton spinner has to protect himself from a rise in the price of raw cotton between the time he quotes a price for his yarn and the time of its actual manufacture. Where a good is bought today for delivery today, the deal is known as a 'spot' transaction and the price is the 'spot price'. With many goods, however, it is possible to buy today for delivery in the future. The good may not even be in stock, but the seller contracts to obtain and deliver it at the agreed time. The price agreed upon is the 'future' or 'forward' price. For a commodity to be dealt in on a futures market certain conditions must be fulfilled: (i) the commodity must be durable, thereby enabling stocks to be carried; (ii) the commodity must be described in terms of grades which are internationally uniform; (iii) dealings must be frequent enough to occupy professional dealers; and (iv) the commodity must be subject to price fluctuations.

In future dealings the dealer uses his expert knowledge to make a profit on what he considers will be the future price of the commodity. At any time a dealer will quote a price (according to the view he takes of the future movement of prices) at which he is prepared to buy or sell at some future date. Thus a cotton grower can cover himself against a possible fall in price by selling his produce forward, while a cotton spinner can quote a weaver a price for yarn and guard himself against loss by buying the raw cotton forward.

Such dealing usually performs the third function of organised markets – evening out price fluctuations. At a time when an increase in supply would cause the price to fall considerably, the dealer adds his demand to the normal demand in order to build up his stocks, and thereby keeps the price up. On the other hand, when the good is in short supply he releases stocks and so prevents a violent rise in price. The difficulty is that speculation on the future price may dominate the real forces which influence it, prices fluctuating violently in response to changes in optimism and pessimism.

2.2 Forces determining price

(a) Demand and supply

'That animal was cheap', remarks Phil Archer as the auctioneer's hammer falls. 'And no wonder', replies Brian Aldridge. 'This has been a long winter. We're now in the middle of April, and the grass is hardly growing. Hay's running short, and breeders are being forced to sell sooner than expected. Old Giles is about the only farmer who'll take the risk of buying extra cattle.'

What can we learn from Brian Aldridge's observations? Simply that the £1,050 at which the heifer was sold was not really determined by the final bid. The real factors producing the relatively low price were the reluctance of farmers to buy and the number of young animals being offered for sale. In short, the price was determined by the interaction of the forces of demand and supply. We shall look at each in turn.

(b) Preliminary assumptions

First, we examine how these forces work in an imaginary market – for eggs. To simplify, we shall assume that:

(i) All eggs are exactly the same in size and quality.
(ii) There are no transport costs within the market.
(iii) The market consists of so many small buyers and sellers that there is keen competition.
(iv) It is a perfect market – price differences are quickly eliminated because buyers and sellers (1) have complete knowledge of prices and conditions in other parts of the market, and (2) act solely on the basis of price.

(v) There is no interference by the government in the operation of market forces, e.g. by price control, regulating supply, etc.

(c) Demand

Demand in economics is the desire for something *plus* the willingness and ability to pay a certain price in order to possess it. More specifically, it is how much of a good people in the market will buy at a given price over a certain period of time.

It is helpful if we separate the factors affecting demand into (i) price, and (ii) the conditions of demand.

(i) Price (the conditions of demand remaining unchanged)

Normally a person will demand more of a good the lower its price. This is because, once you have some units of a good, you have partly satisfied your want and so will only buy more at a lower price. This conforms to our everyday observations. 'Winter sale, prices slashed' announce the shops when they wish to clear their stocks of clothing.

We can draw up a table showing how many eggs a person would be willing to buy at different prices. If they are very expensive, other foodstuffs will, as far as possible, be substituted; if they are cheap, people may even buy them to pickle. By adding up the demand from all buyers of eggs in the market at different prices over a given period of time, it is possible to obtain a *market demand schedule* (Table 2.1).

Note that this schedule does not tell us anything about the actual market price or how much is in fact sold. It is an 'if' schedule. All it says is: '*If* the price is so much, then this quantity will be demanded.' Plotting this schedule on a graph, and assuming that demand can be obtained for intermediary prices, gives the demand curve *D* in Figure 2.1.

(ii) The conditions of demand

Something may occur to cause housewives to demand more eggs at a given price. In other words, the demand schedule alters. Suppose, for instance, farmers unite in an advertising campaign describing tasty egg dishes. As a result more eggs are demanded at all prices (Table 2.2).

Table 2.1 Demand schedule for No Such Market for the week ending 30 January 1999

Price (pence per egg)	Eggs demanded* (thousands)
12	3
10	9
8	15
6	20
4	25
2	35

* what buyers would take at each price.

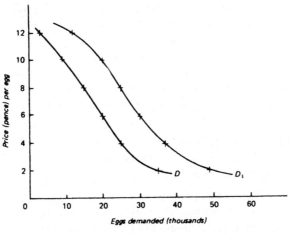

Figure 2.1 Quantity demanded and price

Table 2.2 An increase in demand

Price (pence per egg)	Eggs demanded (thousands)
12	12
10	20
8	25
6	30
4	37
2	49

Plotting this revised demand schedule gives curve D_1 to the right of D. Had conditions so changed that demand decreased, the new demand curve would have been to the left.

The influence of both (i) price, and (ii) the conditions of demand, on the quantity demanded is thus shown on the graph. The former determines the shape of the demand curve – its slope downwards from left to right. The latter determines the position between the axes – an increase in demand shifting the curve to the right, a decrease to the left. For clarity's sake, a change in demand resulting from a change in price will in future be referred to as an *extension* or *contraction* of demand; a change in demand due to new conditions of demand will be described as an *increase* or *decrease* in demand.

Conditions of demand may change in a *short* period of time through:

(1) A change in the price of other goods
Goods compete for our limited income and are thus, to some extent, substitutes for each other. When the prices of other goods fall, the particular good under discussion becomes relatively dearer and therefore less of it is demanded. When the prices of other goods rise, it becomes relatively cheaper, and so more of it is demanded.

But the effect on the demand for a particular good is more pronounced when the price of a close *substitute* changes. Suppose that fried tomatoes are an alternative to eggs for breakfast. If the price of tomatoes falls, housewives will tend to buy them rather than eggs. Thus, although there has been no initial increase in the price of eggs, demand for them has decreased. Similarly, where goods are *complements*, a change in the price of one good has a pronounced effect on the demand for the other. For example, a fall in the price of cars results in more cars being purchased, leading eventually to an increase in the demand for petrol and tyres.

(2) A change in tastes and fashion
A campaign advertising eggs would increase demand; a scare that eggs were the source of infection would decrease it.

(3) Expectations of future price changes or shortages
The fear that the price of eggs may rise considerably next week will induce people to increase their demand now in order to have eggs in stock.

(4) Government policy
A selective tax on eggs paid by the consumer would raise the price and lead to a decrease in demand; a rebate paid to the consumer would have the opposite effect (see p. 31 and pp. 320–2).

Over a *longer* period the conditions of demand may change through:

(5) A change in real income
If there were an all-round increase in real income (that is, money income adjusted for any change in the price level) people could afford more eggs, and demand would probably increase. Or it might now be possible to afford mushrooms for breakfast, and these would take the place of eggs.

(6) Greater equality in the distribution of wealth
The wealth of a country may be so distributed that there are a few exceptionally rich people whereas the remainder are exceedingly poor. If many poor people felt they could not afford eggs, greater equality of wealth would be likely to increase the demand for eggs.

(7) A change in the size and composition of the population
Additional people coming into the market will, with their extra income, increase demand, especially if eggs figure prominently in their diets.

(d) Supply

Supply in economics refers to how much of a good will be offered for sale at a given price over a given period of time. As with demand, this quantity depends on (i) the price of the good, and (ii) the conditions of supply.

(i) Price (the conditions of supply remaining unchanged)

Normally more of a good will be supplied the higher its price. The real reason for this is explained in Chapter 3. But even a brief consideration of how the individual farmer reacts to a change in price will show that it is likely to be true. If the price of eggs is high, he will probably consume fewer himself in order to send as many as possible to market. Moreover, the higher price allows him to give his chickens more food so that they can lay a few extra eggs. When we extend our analysis to the market supply it is obvious that a higher price for eggs enables farmers – including the less efficient – to produce more.

Hence we are able to draw up a *market supply schedule* – the total number of eggs supplied at different prices by all the sellers in the market over a given period of time (Table 2.3).

Once again it must be noted that this is an 'if' schedule, for all it says is: '*If* the price is so much, then this quantity will be offered for sale.'

We can plot this schedule (Figure 2.2); assuming supply for all intermediate prices, a supply curve *S* is obtained.

However, there is a fundamental difference between demand and supply. Whereas demand can respond almost immediately to a change in price, a period of time must usually elapse before supply can be fully adjusted. For the first day or two the only way in which the farmer can send more eggs to market is by eating fewer himself. By the end of the week he may have increased output by giving the hens more food or by leaving the light on in the hen-house all night; the higher price covers the extra cost. But to obtain any sizeable increase the farmer must

Table 2.3 Supply schedule for No Such Market for the week ending 30 January 1999

Price (pence per egg)	Eggs supplied* (thousands)
12	40
10	32
8	25
6	20
4	13
2	7

* what sellers would offer at each price.

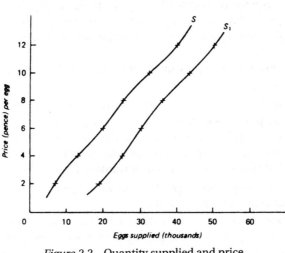

Figure 2.2 Quantity supplied and price

Table 2.4   An increase in supply in the spring

Price (pence per egg)	Eggs supplied (thousands)
12	50
10	43
8	36
6	30
4	25
2	19

add to his hens; if all farmers are following the same policy, this will take about five months, the period required to rear laying hens from chicks.

These different period of time are dealt with more fully in Chapter 5.

(ii) The conditions of supply

The number of eggs supplied may change even though there has been no alteration in the price. In the spring, for instance, chickens lay more eggs than in winter. Thus more eggs will be supplied at all prices in the spring, and fewer in winter, as shown in Table 2.4.

Table 2.4 shows that, compared with winter when only 25,000 eggs were supplied at 8p each (Table 2.2), during the spring 36,000 were supplied. Or, looked at in another way, 25,000 eggs can be supplied in the spring at 4p each compared with 8p in the winter. When plotted, the revised supply schedule gives a curve S_1 to the right of the old one. Had supply decreased, the new supply curve would have been to the left.

Like demand, therefore, supply is influenced by both (i) price, and (ii) the conditions of supply. The former determines the shape of the curve – its upward slope from left to right. The latter determines its position between the axes – an increase in supply shifts the curve to the right, a decrease to the left. To distinguish between the two we shall refer to a change in supply resulting from a change in the price of a commodity as an *extension* or *contraction* of supply; a change in supply due to new conditions of supply will be described as an *increase* or *decrease* in supply.

In general, conditions of supply may change fairly quickly through:

(1) Price expectations

Where a commodity is durable and the relative cost of storage low, e.g. gold, wheat, antiques, price expectations can, as with consumers' demand, affect supply. Thus if the price is expected to rise, stocks will be held or even augmented. If the price is expected to fall, stocks will be depleted. Supplies of perishable goods such as eggs are at a disadvantage here.

(2) A change in the prices of other goods, especially when it is easy to shift resources and the good in question is in 'joint supply'

Suppose, for instance, that there is a considerable increase in the price of chicken meat, including boiling fowls. It may pay the farmer to cull more of his older hens. Thus fewer eggs are supplied at the old price.

(3) A change in the prices of factors of production
A fall in the cost of pullets or of their food would reduce the cost of producing eggs. As a result more eggs could be supplied at the old price, or – looked at in another way – the original quantity could be produced at a lower price per egg. A rise in the wages of workers on chicken farms would have the opposite effect.

(4) Changes resulting from nature
(e.g. the weather, floods, drought, pest) and from *abnormal circumstances* (e.g. war, fire, political events).

(5) Government policy
A tax on the output of eggs or an increase in employers' national insurance contributions would result in fewer eggs being offered for sale at the old price. That is, the supply curve moves to the left. On the other hand a subsidy, by decreasing costs, would move the supply curve to the right (see p. 322).

Other changes in supply take longer, occurring through:

(6) Improved techniques
Technical improvements reduce costs of production, shifting the supply curve to the right. Thus improved automatic feeding devices might be developed, or selective breeding produce hens which lay more eggs.

(7) The discovery of new sources or raw materials, or the exhaustion of existing sources

(8) The entry of new firms into the industry

2.3 The determination of price: market clearing

The demand and supply curves can be combined in a single diagram (Figure 2.3).
Let us see how this analysis helps as a first approach to understanding how the market is cleared. The assumptions we have made so far are:

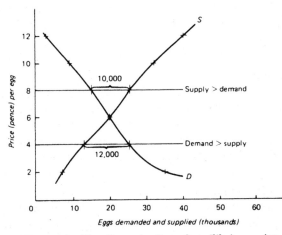

Figure 2.3 The determination of equilibrium price

(i) Many buyers and sellers.

(ii) Keen competition between buyers, between sellers, and between buyers and sellers.

(iii) More will be demanded at a lower price than at a higher price.

(iv) Less will be supplied at a lower price than at a higher.

Given assumptions (iii) and (iv), the two curves slope in opposite directions. Thus they cut at a single point – in our example, where the price is 6p. It can be predicted that in No-Such Market, where these conditions of demand and supply exist, the price of eggs will move towards and eventually settle at 6p. This is the *market clearing* or *equilibrium* price.

This proposition can be proved as follows. Suppose that initially the price of eggs is fixed at 8p. Here 15,000 will be demanded but 25,000 supplied. There is thus an excess supply of 10,000. But some sellers will want to get rid of their surplus supplies, and therefore reduce the price being asked. As this happens some supplies are withdrawn from a market, and there is an extension of demand. This continues until a price of 6p is reached, when 20,000 eggs are both demanded and offered for sale. Thus 6p is the only price at which there is harmony between buyers and sellers: given existing demand and supply, the market is 'cleared'.

Similarly, if the initial price is 4p, 25,000 will be demanded, but only 13,000 offered for sale. Housewives queue to buy eggs, and sellers see that their supplies will quickly run out. Competition among buyers will force up the price. As this happens, more eggs are supplied to the market, and there is a contraction of demand. This continues until a price of 6p is reached, when demand equals supply at 20,000 eggs.

2.4 Changes in the conditions of demand and supply

The equilibrium price will persist until there is a change in the conditions of either demand or supply.

Let us begin with our market price of 6p. Suppose tastes alter, and people eat more eggs. The conditions of demand have now changed, and the demand curve shifts to the right from D to D_1 (Figure 2.4).

At the original price of 6p we now have an excess of demand over supply – 30,000 eggs are demanded, but only 20,000 are supplied. As explained in the previous section, competition between buyers will now force up the price to 8p, where 25,000 eggs are both demanded and supplied.

Similarly a decrease in demand – resulting, for instance, from a significant fall in the price of tomatoes – would cause the curve to shift to the left and the price of eggs to fall.

Alternatively a change may occur in the conditions of supply. At any given price more eggs can be produced during the spring, when the supply curve shifts to the right from S to S_1 (Figure 2.5).

At the original price of 6p we now have an excess of supply over demand –

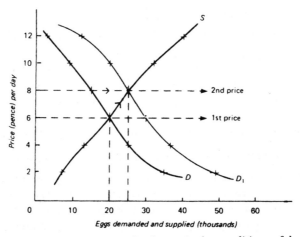

Figure 2.4   The effect on price of a change in the conditions of demand

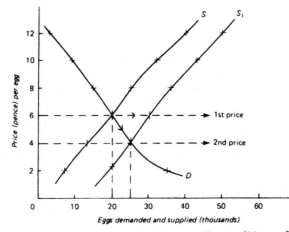

Figure 2.5   The effect on price of a change in the conditions of supply.

30,000 eggs are supplied, but only 20,000 are demanded. Here competition amongst sellers will mean that the price falls to 4p, where 25,000 eggs are both demanded and supplied.

2.5 Functions of price in the market economy

Our analysis can be applied to practical problems, especially those relating to government policy. First, however, we use it to examine the role of price in the market economy.

In a free market, price both indicates and motivates.

(a) Price 'rations out' scarce goods

At any one time the supply of a good is relatively fixed. It therefore has to be apportioned among the many people wanting it. This is done by adjusting price. As price rises, demand contracts; as it falls, demand expands. At the equilibrium price demand just equals the supply. Should supply increase, the total quantity can still be disposed of by lowering the price; should supply decrease, the price would have to be raised.

We can illustrate how price works by considering two current problems:

(i) Who shall be allowed to park his car in a congested area?

Car parking is causing traffic congestion in the centre of Barthem City. This is because it costs motorists nothing to park their cars at the kerbside. The council decides to restrict parking to one side of the road and to 800 one-hour only places, each with a parking meter. The demand schedule for one-hour parking is estimated to be as follows:

Price (pence)	Demand
60	450
40	800
20	1,200
0	1,800

The council therefore fixes a charge of 40p.

This introduction of parking meters: (1) makes parkers pay for the space they occupy; (2) bars the all-day parker by limiting meter time to one hour; (3) forces the all-day parker and those who will not pay 40p to travel by public transport or to park off the street or out of the city centre; (4) causes the demand for off-street parking to increase, thereby encouraging firms to expand supply; (5) helps to relieve congestion by limiting parking to one side of the street or prohibiting it in busy roads.

(ii) Why do ticket touts obtain such high prices for Cup Final tickets?

To ensure that the regular football supporter can afford a Cup Final ticket, prices are fixed by the Football Association. Let us simplify by assuming that the FA has one price, £10 for the 100,000 tickets, but that a free-market price would be £30. In Figure 2.6, when the price is £30 demand equals the available supply, but at the controlled price of £10 demand exceeds supply by 150,000.

But some tickets are obtained by touts, who re-sell at a profit in a free market where demand and supply determine price. Keen club supporters, not lucky enough to have been allocated a ticket, are willing to pay more than £10. As the price rises, some people possessing tickets may be induced to sell them to the touts. Thus the demand and supply curves are roughly as shown in Figure 2.7, giving a 'spiv-market' price of £100.

An important conclusion can be drawn from this example: where price is controlled below the market price, only some form of rationing can ensure that everybody gets a share of the limited supply. Normally this is achieved by the FA, which, after allocating a certain number of tickets to each finalist, limits each affiliated club to approximately two. One alternative would simply be a 'first

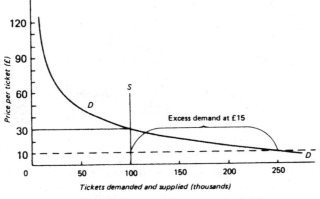

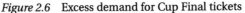

Figure 2.6 Excess demand for Cup Final tickets

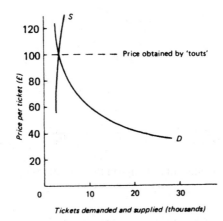

Figure 2.7 The black-market price of Cup Final tickets

come, first served' method of distribution, penalising those who could not queue and increasing the scope for tout activity.

(b) Price indicates changes in wants

Prices are the signals by which households indicate the extent to which different goods are wanted, and any changes in those wants.

Consider how the demand for owner-occupied houses in south-east England has increased over the long-term through the pressure of population, higher real income, tax concessions, etc. As a result, prices have risen from OP to OP_1 (Figure 2.8).

(c) Price induces supply to respond to changes in demand

When demand increases, price rises and supply extends; when demand decreases, price falls and supply contracts. Thus in Figure 2.8 the increase in price

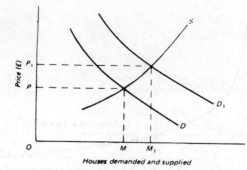

Figure 2.8 The effect on house prices of an increase in demand by owner-occupiers

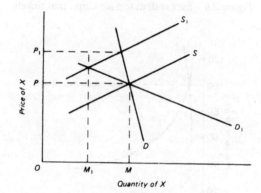

Figure 2.9 The effect of a change in the conditions of supply on price and quantity traded

has made it profitable for extra houses MM_1 to be supplied by new building, by transferring houses from the rented sector, etc.

(d) Price indicates changes in the conditions upon which goods can be supplied

If the cost of producing a given commodity rises, this should be signalled to consumers, who can then decide to what extent they are prepared to pay these higher costs by going without other goods. Again this is achieved through price. Assume in Figure 2.9 that the cost of producing good X has increased because raw materials have risen in price. Where demand is depicted by D, most consumers pay the higher costs (price rises by PP_1) rather than do without the good. Where demand is depicted by D_1, consumers tend to go without the good as its price rises (demand falls by MM_1), substituting other goods for it.

(e) Price rewards the factors of production

Payments for factors of production give their owners spending power. The relative size of this spending power determines the division (usually termed 'distribution') of the cake produced. If the price of a good rises, producers can afford to offer higher rewards in order to attract factors from other uses.

2.6 Further applications

(a) How can the government stabilise commodity prices?

The government can use a stockpile in order to stabilise the price of basic commodities where demand or supply fluctuates.

In Figure 2.10, it is assumed that the demand for butter remains constant, but that the conditions of supply change from one period to another. S_1 is the supply curve for period 1, S_2 for period 2 and S_3 for period 3. The government has a stockpile by means of which it stabilises the price of butter at OP a tonne. This it does by adding MM_2 to the stockpile in period 2 and withdrawing M_4M in period 3.

(b) How would an increase in the demand for cars affect the price of tyres?

Cars and tyres are 'jointly demanded'. With such goods prices move in the same direction. This can be seen in Figure 2.11. The increased demand for cars leads to an increased demand for tyres, and the prices of both rise.

(c) How would an increase in the price of petrol affect the price of paraffin?

Petrol and paraffin are 'jointly supplied': increased production of one automatically increases production of the other. Suppose that demand for petrol increases but that there is no change in the demand for paraffin. The price of petrol rises from OP to OP_1, and supply expands from OM to OM_1 (Figure 2.12). But this means that the supply of paraffin increases, although there has been no

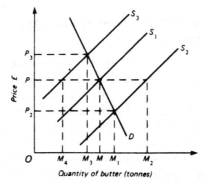

Figure 2.10   Stabilisation of the price of butter

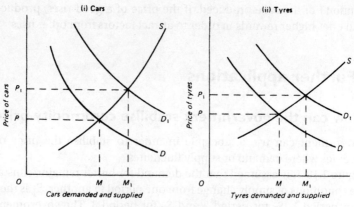

Figure 2.11   Joint demand

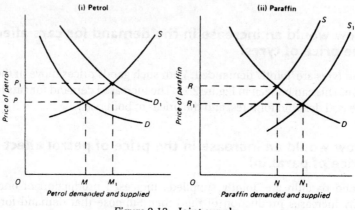

Figure 2.12   Joint supply

change in price. Thus the supply curve for paraffin moves from S to S_1, and the price of paraffin falls from OR to OR_1.

(d) How could the government secure greater use of unleaded petrol?

Here the government must operate to alter the relative prices of leaded and unleaded petrol by increasing the tax on the former and reducing it on the latter. The effect is shown in Figure 2.13. Because of the increased tax on leaded petrol, demand decreases at all prices, the demand curve now being D_1 instead of D. Price, including the higher tax rises from OP to OP_1, and the amount sold contracts by MM_1 (Fig. (i)).

In contrast, the reduced tax on unleaded petrol allows the same amount to be obtained at a lower price, as shown by the higher demand curve, D_1. Price falls to OP_1 and the amount sold expands by MM_1 (Fig. (ii)).

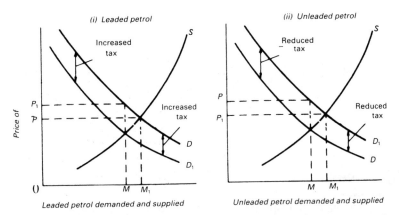

(i) Leaded petrol

Increased tax

Increased tax

Price of

Leaded petrol demanded and supplied

(ii) Unleaded petrol

Reduced tax

Reduced tax

Unleaded petrol demanded and supplied

Figure 2.13 The effect on quantity bought of a change in the tax on a good

QUESTIONS

1 Why do improved communications help to remove market imperfections?

2 In a market economy, an increase in the demand for a good is usually indicated by a rise in its price. Can you think of four alternative signals which may in practice exist for certain goods?

3 Account for the 'black market' in Wimbledon tennis tickets.

4 How could the government use the price mechanism to:
   (a) encourage goods to travel by rail rather than by road?
   (b) influence people to build garages in order to take their cars off the streets at night?

■ ☑ **3** Demand

Objectives

1 To explain the response of demand to a change in price
2 To define 'elasticity of demand'
3 To show how 'elasticity of demand' can be measured
4 To indicate practical applications of the term

3.1 The marginal-utility theory

Our assumption in Chapter 2 that more of a good will be demanded the lower its price was based solely on our everyday observations. However, by examining a little more closely how the individual consumer 'economises', we can explain why this is normally so. We shall use the marginal-utility theory.

(a) Preliminary assumptions

(i) Our consumer is a housewife.
(ii) She has a limited housekeeping allowance per week.
(iii) She acts so as to obtain the maximum satisfaction from her limited income.
(iv) During the period of time under consideration, income, tastes and the other conditions of demand do not change.
(v) She knows how much satisfaction each unit of a good will give.
(vi) She is one of a large number of buyers and her demand does not directly affect the price of the good.

(b) Questions to be answered

Three basic questions have to be answered. First, what conditions will hold when the consumer has obtained the maximum satisfaction from her limited resources? In other words, what are the equilibrium conditions? Second, how does she achieve this equilibrium? Third, what happens when the equilibrium is disturbed by a price change? We deal with each in turn.

(i) The equilibrium condition

Our housewife will be in equilibrium when she would not switch a single penny of her expenditure on one good to another.

We can be more explicit by introducing the term 'utility'. In economics this simply means that a good has the power to satisfy a want, irrespective of whether it is useful. Note, too, that we cannot measure utility objectively; like fear, it is purely subjective to the individual.

However, our housewife knows in her own mind how much satisfaction each good affords her. She is in equilibrium, therefore, when she has obtained the greatest possible utility from her income: that is, *she maximises total utility*.

She achieves this by careful allocation of her spending – say between cheese and margarine. All the time she is asking: 'If I spend a penny more on cheese, will I obtain more or less utility than if I spent the penny on margarine?' Only when the satisfaction she obtains from the last penny spent on cheese (in the sense of the penny she only just decided to spend) is equal to that from the last penny spent on margarine will she be in equilibrium. That is, her spending adjustments take place at the margin.

Note that we did *not* say that she obtained the same utility from the last pound of cheese as she obtained from the last pound of margarine. If, for instance, a pound of cheese were four times as expensive as a pound of margarine, that would obviously be unreasonable; we would expect four times the amount of utility.

Sometimes, however, we cannot buy goods in 'pennyworths' – the good is 'lumpy' and we have to take a whole 'lump' of it or nothing at all. Can we restate our equilibrium condition to allow for this? Yes, but first we must define more carefully the concept of the margin and what we mean by 'marginal utility'.

Each small addition to a given supply of a good is called the *marginal increment*, and the utility derived from this increment is known as the *marginal utility*. Our original condition of equilibrium can therefore be stated in general terms:

$$\frac{\text{The marginal utility of 1p}}{\text{spent on good } A} = \frac{\text{The marginal utility of 1p}}{\text{spent on good } B}$$

But the marginal utility of 1p spent on good A depends on how much of a unit of good A you get for 1p. Thus:

$$\frac{\text{The marginal utility of 1p}}{\text{spent on good } A} = \frac{\text{The marginal utility of one unit of good } A}{\text{The number of pence it costs to buy a unit of good } A}$$

Similarly with good B. Thus our original equilibrium condition can be rewritten as:

$$\frac{\text{The marginal utility of one unit of good } A}{\text{Price of a unit of } A \text{ in pence}} = \frac{\text{The marginal utility of one unit of good } A}{\text{Price of a unit of } B \text{ in pence}}$$

That is:

$$\frac{\text{Marginal utility of good } A}{\text{Price of } A} = \frac{\text{Marginal utility of good } B}{\text{Price of } B}$$

The argument can be extended to cover more than two goods.

(ii) How does the consumer achieve this equilibrium?

The question must now be asked: how can our housewife arrange that the utility of the last penny spent on different goods is the same? The answer is to be found in the so-called *law of diminishing marginal utility*. Although wants vary considerably in their nature, they all possess the underlying characteristic that in a given period they can be satisfied fairly quickly. Thus, if a boy drinks lemonade to quench his thirst, the first glass will yield him a great amount of satisfaction. Indeed, the second glass may be equally satisfying. But it is doubtful whether he will relish the third glass to the same extent. If he continues to drink the lemonade, there will come a time when a glass gives him no additional satisfaction whatsoever and, in fact, it might be that he would be better off without it – there is a 'disutility'. We can therefore state a general rule that the utility derived from any given addition to a consumer's stock of a good will *eventually* decline.

This means that our housewife can arrange that equal utility is derived from the last penny spent on each good by varying the quantity she buys. If she buys more of a good, the stock of other goods remaining fixed, its marginal utility relative to other goods falls. Similarly, if she reduces the quantity she buys, the marginal utility of the good relative to other goods rises. She makes such marginal adjustments until she is in equilibrium.

(iii) What happens when the equilibrium is disturbed by a price change?

Suppose the price of cheese falls from 230p to 210p per pound while the prices of other goods remain unchanged. How will this affect her demand for cheese? We can proceed in either of two ways:

(1) The fall in the price of cheese will enable her to obtain more cheese than before for every penny, including the last, which she was spending on it. More cheese usually implies greater satisfaction. The last penny spent on cheese, therefore, now yields greater satisfaction than the last penny being spent on other goods. Hence she reduces the utility obtained from the last penny spent on cheese by buying more cheese.

(2) The alternative form of the equilibrium condition is:

$$\frac{\text{The marginal utility of the last 1 lb of cheese}}{\text{Price of 1 lb of cheese}} = \frac{\text{The marginal utility of one unit of good } B}{\text{Price of one unit of good } B}$$

A fall in the price of cheese destroys this relationship; the marginal utility of cheese to its price is now higher than with goods *B*, *C*, etc. To restore the equilibrium relationship, the marginal utility of cheese must be decreased. Hence our housewife buys more cheese.

The reasons for this expansion in the demand for cheese can be analysed more closely. A reduction in the price of cheese means that our housewife is now able to purchase all the cheese she had before and still have money left over. This is an *income* effect of a price fall – she can now buy more of all goods, not only of cheese. But, in addition to this income effect, more cheese will tend to be bought because of a 'substitution effect'. At the margin this means than a penny spent on cheese will now yield more satisfaction that a penny spent on other foods. Thus cheese is substituted for other foods. If cheese is a good substitute, marginal utility will diminish comparatively slowly as the consumption of it increases. A given price fall, therefore, will lead to a considerable increase in the quantity of cheese demanded.

Although we have explained the behaviour of only one consumer, it is reasonable to expect other buyers in the market to act similarly. Since the *market-demand curve* is made up of the demand schedules of all the individual purchasers, we can conclude that more of a good will be demanded the lower its price.

3.2 Price elasticity of demand

(a) Measurement of elasticity of demand

Consider Figure 3.1. At price OP, demand for both commodities A and B is OM. But when the price of both falls by PP_1, demand for A expands by only MM_1, whereas that for B expands by MM_2. Responsiveness of demand to a change in price is of obvious importance to a firm which has some control over the price it charges. In economic terms it is interested in its 'price-elasticity of demand'.

Elasticity of demand always refers to the elasticity at a particular price, and in what follows when we talk about 'elasticity', it will be assumed that there is some price in mind.

Elasticity of demand is defined by comparing the rate at which demand expands to the rate at which price falls. Using this definition, elasticity of demand can be measured in two ways. One is direct, showing the degree of elasticity: the other is indirect, merely indicating whether the demand for the good is elastic or inelastic.

(i) *Elasticity of demand is the proportionate change in the amount demanded in response to a small change in price divided by the proportionate change in price.* That is:

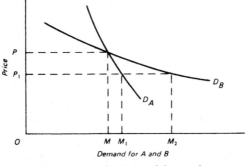

Figure 3.1   Elasticity of demand

$$\text{Elasticity of demand} = \frac{\text{Proportionate change in demand}}{\text{Proportionate change in price}}$$

$$= \frac{\dfrac{\text{Change in quantity demanded}}{\text{Original quantity demanded}}}{\dfrac{\text{Change in price}}{\text{Original price}}}$$

$$= \frac{\dfrac{\text{New quantity} - \text{Old quantity}}{\text{Old quantity}}}{\dfrac{\text{New price} - \text{Old price}}{\text{Old price}}}$$

We can illustrate by an example from the demand schedule, Table 2.1 (see p. 18). When price falls from 10p to 8p, demand for eggs expands from 9,000 to 15,000. Elasticity of demand is thus equal to

$$\frac{\dfrac{6,000}{9,000}}{\dfrac{2}{10}} = \frac{\dfrac{2}{3}}{\dfrac{1}{5}} = 3\frac{1}{3}$$

Similarly, for a rise in price from 8p to 10p, elasticity of demand equals $1\frac{3}{8}$. The difference in the two results occurs because we are measuring from different prices and for a relatively large change. (It should also be noted that it is conventional to ignore the minus sign which results from the fact that the typical demand curve has a negative slope.)

(ii) If the proportionate expansion in demand is greater than the proportionate fall in price, the total amount spent on the good will increase. In other words, *demand is elastic when, in response to a fall in price, total outlay increases; or, in response to a rise in price, total outlay decreases. Similarly demand is inelastic when, in response to a fall in price, total outlay decreases; or, in response to a rise in price, total outlay increases.* Elasticity of demand is equal to unity when, as price changes, total outlay remains the same. Thus using the same demand schedule, we have Table 3.1.

Between 8p and 6p, elasticity of demand equals unity.

Table 3.1 Elasticity of demand and total outlay

Price of eggs (pence)	Demand (thousands)	Total outlay (pence)	
10	9	90,000	} Elastic demand
8	15	120,000	
6	20	120,000	} Inelastic demand
4	25	100,000	

(b) Factors determining elasticity of demand

(i) The availability of substitutes at the ruling market price

As a good falls in price, it becomes cheaper relative to other goods. People are induced to buy more of it to replace goods which are now relatively dearer. How far they can carry out this replacement will depend upon the extent to which the good in question is, in their own minds, a substitute for the other goods. Goods within a particular class are easily substituted for one another. Beef is a substitute for lamb. Thus, if the price of beef falls, people will buy more beef and less lamb. Between one class and another, however, substitution is more difficult. If the price of meat in general falls, there will be a slight tendency to buy more meat and less fish, but this tendency will be very limited because meat is not nearly so perfect a substitute for fish as beef is for lamb.

The success of supermarkets has been based on the high elasticity of demand for their products; people switch to them when prices of processed goods are reduced, for they can recognise the packages and tins as being almost perfect substitutes for those being sold at higher prices by other retailers.

(ii) The number of possible substitute uses

Where a good can be substituted for another good, its demand tends to be elastic. And the more goods it can be substituted for, so the more will demand for it extend as its price falls. Thus reductions in the price of plastics have led to large extensions of demand as they have been substituted for materials used in such articles as enamel bowls, galvanised buckets, paper wrappings, glass garden cloches, wooden toys and tin containers.

(iii) The proportion of income spent on a good

When only a very small proportion of a person's income is spent on a good, as for example with pepper, salt, shoe-polish, newspapers and toothpaste, no great effort is made to look for substitutes when its price rises. Demand for such goods, therefore, is relatively inelastic.

On the other hand, when the expenditure on a good is fairly large – as, for example, with meat – a rise in price would provide considerable incentive to find substitutes.

(iv) The period of time

Since it takes time to find substitutes or to change spending habits, elasticity may be greater the longer the period of time under review. In practice many firms try to overcome the ignorance or conservatism of consumers by advertising, giving free samples or making special offers.

(v) The possibility of new purchasers

In discussing the possibility of substitution above, we have looked at elasticity of demand solely from the point of view of the individual consumer. But when we are considering market demand we must allow for the fact that, as price falls, new consumers will be induced to buy the good. In fact, with goods such as cars, video recorders, washing-machines, etc., of which most people require only one, it is the fall in price bringing the good within reach of new consumers which leads to the increase in demand. Hence a fall in price which induces people in a numerous income group to buy will produce a big elasticity of demand.

(c) Uses of the concept of elasticity of demand

The concept of the elasticity of demand figures prominently in both the economist's theoretical analysis (see p. 76) and in the practical decisions of the businessman and government.

Thus a trade union will find it more difficult to obtain a wage increase for its members without creating unemployment where the elasticity of demand for the product made is high (see p. 110)

A rail operator, too, has to consider elasticity of demand when fixing fares. Should they, for example, raise fares in order to reduce losses? If, at existing fares, the demand is relatively elastic, then a fare increase would mean that total revenue would fall. Losses would only be reduced if operating costs (through carrying fewer passengers) fell more than revenue. Indeed, consideration could be given to reducing fares, since the extra revenue might cover any additional cost of running more trains.

Finally, the Chancellor of the Exchequer must take account of elasticity of demand when imposing a selective tax on a particular good. The demand may be so elastic that the increase in price might cause such a falling-off in sales that the total tax received is less than it originally was.

3.3 Income-elasticity of demand

An increase in real income usually increases the demand for goods, but to a varying degree. Thus it is possible to speak of *income-elasticity of demand* – the proportionate change in demand divided by the proportionate change in real income which has brought it about. If demand increases 20 per cent, for instance, as a result of a 10 per cent increase in real income, income-elasticity of demand equals 2. Which goods have a high income-elasticity of demand depends upon current living standards. In Western Europe today it is demand for such goods as cars, dishwashers, central-heating appliances and personal services which expands most as income increases. In contrast, necessities, such as salt and soap, have a low income-elasticity of demand.

3.4 Cross-elasticity of demand

When we refer to 'elasticity of demand' without qualification, we are speaking, as above, of what is more precisely '*own-price* elasticity of demand'. But where two goods are related, e.g. as substitutes or complements, a change in the price of one

Cross-elasticity

Complementarity ◀——————————⊖——————————➕➤ Substitutability

Figure 3.2   Cross-elasticity of demand

will lead to a change in demand for the other. Thus a rise in the price of oil leads to an increase in the demand for coal, while a fall in the price of video recorders leads to an increased demand for video tapes.

The extent to which the demand for a good changes in response to a price change of another good is known as *cross-elasticity of demand*:

$$\frac{\text{Cross-elasticity}}{\text{of demand}} = \frac{\text{Percentage change in the quantity demanded of good } X}{\text{Percentage change in the price of good } Y}$$

With substitutes, cross-elasticity is positive. For example, an increase in the price of *Y* would lead to an increase in the demand for *X* (as with oil and coal in the example above). With complements, cross-elasticity is negative, since a fall in the price of *Y* leads to a rise in the demand for *X* (as with video recorders and tapes above). The closer the substitutes or complements, the larger will be the figure for cross-elasticity. A cross-elasticity near zero signifies that there is little relationship between the two goods (Figure 3.2).

QUESTIONS

I   What well-known proverb refers indirectly to people making marginal decisions?

2   By referring to the diagram:
    (a) Write down the elasticity of demand when:
        (i) price rises from Op to Op_1;
        (ii) price falls from Op_1 to Op.
    (b) Explain why you think the demand for *X* is elastic or inelastic between prices Op and Op_1.

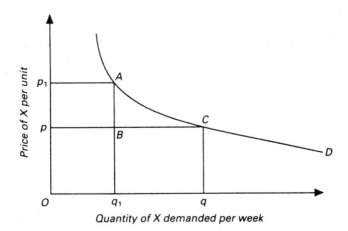

Quantity of X demanded per week

3 If the demand for agricultural products is inelastic, what effect will a fall in their price have on farmers' incomes?

4 South West Trains has to allocate its scarce resources, e.g. limited track capacity, according to market demand. For return journeys between Southampton and London, the fares are:

before	8.40 am	£34
after	8.40 am	£15.60.

(a) How does the concept of elasticity of demand help to explain the difference in fares?

(b) What are the two essentials for South West Trains ability to charge different prices?

■ ⊻ 4 Supply: (i) the structure of industry

Objectives

1 To define 'production' and 'the firm'
2 To examine how the objectives of the firm are related to 'profit'
3 To consider the firm's most important pre-production decisions

4.1 The role of the firm

(a) The meaning of 'production'

Early economists considered that only work in the extractive industries (agriculture, mining and fishing) was productive. In his *Wealth of Nations* in 1776 Adam Smith added manufacturing, but he was specific in excluding workers who merely rendered services.

This was illogical. People work, and production takes place, in order to satisfy wants. Consequently people who render services must be regarded as being productive. The soldier, actor and footballer are all satisfying wants. Similarly, in a factory, the clerk who calculates the wages is just as productive as the man who makes the nuts and bolts. All are helping to produce the final product, a good satisfying wants.

Wants can take different forms. Most people like a newspaper to read at the breakfast-table; thus the boy who takes it from the shop to the customer's letter-box is productive. Most people, too, prefer to buy their potatoes weekly; thus the farmer or merchant who stores them through the winter is satisfying the wants of consumers, and is similarly productive. Utility is created by changing not only the *form* of our scarce resources, but also their *place* and *time*.

For certain purposes it may still be useful to classify industries broadly. *Primary industries* cover the first steps in the productive process – agriculture, fishing, mining and oil-prospecting. *Secondary industries* use the raw materials of the extractive industries to manufacture their own products – flour, clothing, tinned salmon, steel girders, petrol and so on. *Tertiary industries* are concerned with the provision of services – transport, communications, distribution, commerce, government, and professional and other services.

(b) The objectives of the firm

In a market economy a firm has to cover its costs if it is to stay in business. Thus regard must be paid to 'profitability'.

But in practice are firms always single-minded in seeking to *maximise money profits*? The answer is no; there is a range of possible objectives.

Personal motives may be important, especially where the manager is also the owner of the firm. Thus emphasis may be placed on good labour relations, the welfare of the workers, the desire for power, political influence, public esteem or simply 'a quiet life'. To cover such objectives profit would have to be interpreted in a wider sense than 'money profit'.

With major companies there is in practice a gap between the ownership and administration. The business is run by professional managers, and is too complex for shareholders to be able to exert effective control. This applies even to the institutional shareholders, who avoid being directly involved in the running of the business. Thus the motives of the full-time executive managers tend to override the shareholders' desire for maximum return on capital invested. Managers may be anxious for the security of their own jobs and, instead of taking the calculated risks necessary to earn maximum profits, may tend to play for safety. More likely, they will be motivated by personal desires for status. Provided they achieve a level of profit which keeps shareholders content, their positions and salaries can be enhanced by expanding the firm to where it *maximises sales* rather than profits. Alternatively, the rate of growth may be maximised.

Even when there is an emphasis on money profit, a firm may stress its long-term position rather than immediate maximum profit. Security of future profits may be the dominating motive for mergers and takeovers as an alternative to developing new products and techniques. Moreover, where there is an element of monopoly, a firm can follow its own pricing policy rather than have it determined by competitive market conditions (see Chapter 5). In such circumstances it may not adjust prices to short-term changes in demand and supply conditions. For one thing, there are the administrative costs of printing and distributing new price lists. For another, frequent changes in price tend to offend retailers and customers.

Again, a firm enjoying a degree of monopoly has always to assess what effect the pursuit of maximum profit may have on its overall position in the long term. Will a high price attract new entrants or encourage the development of a rival product? Will it lead to adverse publicity and eventually to government intervention by a reference to the Office of Fair Trading?

Finally, a firm has often to modify its objectives in deference to government policy. Thus it may be expected to follow government guidelines regarding wage increases, to have regard to the environment in the disposal of its waste products and even to retain surplus workers for a time rather than add to an already high level of unemployment.

Yet, while we must take account of these other objectives, our analysis cannot proceed far if any are seen as the main motive force of the firm. In any case they merely supplement the profit objective, for profits have to be made if the firm is to survive. Thus it is useful to start with the broad assumption that firms seek to maximise profits. We can then establish principles concerning how resources should be combined and what output should be produced.

(c) The decisions of the firm

To achieve its objective of maximising profit, a firm has to assess the demand of potential customers for its product and produce that output which secures the greatest difference between total revenue and total cost. Moreover, the cost of producing this given output must be the lowest possible.

This means that the firm has to answer the following questions:

(i) What goods shall it produce?
(ii) What shall be its legal form?
(iii) How shall it raise the necessary capital?
(iv) What techniques shall be adopted, and what shall be the scale of operations?
(v) Where shall production be located?
(vi) How shall goods be distributed to the consumer?
(vii) How shall resources be combined?
(viii) What shall be the size of output?
(ix) How shall it deal with its employees?

We consider the first six problems in the remainder of this chapter; the rest are examined in Chapters 5 and 7.

4.2 What to produce

(a) The first approach

Other things being equal, a firm will produce those goods which enable it to make the greatest return on capital. However, in practice, this usually means that it has to choose a line of production within the limited range of its specialist knowledge. Let us assume that the firm is manufacturing light farm machines and that it is contemplating producing lawnmowers.

Since it is likely that some firms are already producing lawnmowers, the market economy throws up two guidelines. First, there is the current price of mowers. The firm would have to estimate its own costs for producing similar mowers, the number it could expect to sell at this price, and its likely profits, and thus calculate the return on capital employed. Second, the accounts of companies have to be filed with the Registrar of Companies, and the profit earned by public companies is publicised in the financial pages of leading newspapers and specialist journals. If existing producers of lawnmowers were shown to be earning a high rate of profit, the prospects for a new competitor would look favourable.

(b) Market research

Where the proposed market is new or different from that for existing products, the above indicators are not so useful. Here the firm must fall back on some form of market research.

Initially, it may be producing similar goods, e.g. light agricultural machinery, and some indications of potential demand may come from wholesalers, retailers or even customers in conversation with the firm's representatives. Such suggestions can be cross-checked with those of other distributors (see p. 62).

Where the reaction is generally favourable, more thorough market research can be carried out, probably through a specialist market-research organisation. Market research can cover desk research, field studies and test marketing.

Desk research examines the broad determinants of the potential demand by using (i) published material, e.g. government statistics, and (ii) the firm's own sales records. As we saw in Chapter 2, these determinants are price and the various conditions of demand. More specialist facts could be obtained from relevant periodicals and trade journals, e.g. *Gardeners' World* (where circulation figures indicate the number of keen gardeners). Membership figures for the Royal Horticultural Society could also be used.

More precise information on potential sales necessitates a planned consumer-orientated *market-research programme* in potential markets. This would cover many aspects of market behaviour, particularly consumer reaction to the product – especially with regard to its quality, packaging, delivery dates and after-sales service, and to price cuts.

Before a national or major sales campaign is undertaken, some form of *test marketing* would probably be carried out so that modifications could be made to correct any deficiencies. For instance, such a test might reveal that certain features of the product were unnecessary, thus permitting greater standardisation. Moreover, not all potential customers have identical preferences. The firm would therefore consider (i) a 'marketing mix' – producing different models at different prices – and (ii) varying sales methods and channels of distribution (see below).

4.3 The legal form of the firm

In the private sector a firm can trade as a sole proprietor, partnership, private company, public company or co-operative society. For a new firm the choice is really between the first three, the actual decision largely resting on whether freedom from control by the Registrar of Companies compensates for unlimited liability. The legal form hardly affects its ability to raise capital for, unless it is an offshoot of a large parent company, it has to be fairly successful before outsiders can be induced to subscribe capital for large-scale development.

(i) The sole proprietor

The sole proprietor is the oldest form of business organisation. Even today, from the point of view of numbers, small firms predominate, but in their total productive capacity they are far less important than companies (see Table 4.1, p. 57). Such one-person firms range from the window-cleaner working on his own account to the farmer, shopkeeper and builder who employ other workers and may even own many separate units. Nevertheless these businesses all share the characteristic of being owned and controlled by a single person. This person decides the policy of the firm, and alone takes the profits or bears losses. This makes for energy, efficiency and careful attention to detail. In addition, the only accounts which have to be submitted are to the Inland Revenue for income-tax assessment and to the Customs and Excise Department if registered for VAT. No corporation tax is payable.

However, the sole proprietor suffers from five main disadvantages. First, such a firm can only develop slowly, because sources of capital are limited. The success of the venture, especially in its early stages, depends mainly on the person in charge, and nobody is likely to provide capital unless there is that confidence in the proprietor which comes from personal contact. Hence the main source of capital is the owner's savings together with such additional sums as can be borrowed from relatives, close friends, a bank, or perhaps the Rural Development Commission. In time, development may be financed by ploughing back profits, but this will probably be a slow process and sole traders generally remain comparatively small.

Second, in the event of failure, not only the assets of the business, but also the private assets and property of the proprietor can be claimed by creditors. In short, there is no limited liability.

Third, where profits are high, income tax paid on annual profits may be larger than a company's corporation tax. This is because income may be taxed at a high marginal rate of tax, whereas corporation tax is only 20% if a company's profits are less than £300,000 (with some marginal relief up to £1,500,000). Less tax leaves more funds for investing in the business.

Fourth, it is more difficult to transfer part of a business than to transfer shares in a company.

Fifth, there is a lack of continuity; on the retirement or death of the owner, a one-man firm may cease to function.

Because of these disadvantages, sole proprietors are mainly confined to businesses which are just setting up and also to certain industries, such as agriculture and retailing, where requirements of management make the small technical unit desirable.

(ii) The partnership

More capital is available when persons join together in a 'partnership', though normally not more than twenty may do so. Each partner provides a part of the capital and shares the profits on an agreed basis. Yet the amount of capital which can be raised in this way is still inadequate for large-scale business. Thus partnerships remain relatively small, predominating in retailing, insurance broking and underwriting, and among professional people (doctors, surveyors, consulting engineers and lawyers), where the capital provided is not so much in the form of money as in experience and skill, each partner probably specialising in a particular branch.

Nor is the partnership without its snags. The risk inherent in unlimited liability is increased because all partners are liable for the firm's debts, irrespective of the amount of capital which each has invested. Only if a partner takes no share in the management of the firm, and there is at least one ordinary partner, can he enjoy limited liability. Second, since any action taken by one partner is legally binding on the others, not only must each partner have complete confidence in his fellows, but the risk inherent in unlimited liability increases with the number of partners. Finally, at any time one partner may give notice to end the partnership, and it is automatically dissolved upon the death or bankruptcy of a partner. To preserve the business, surviving partners may be put to great expense and trouble in buying the partner's share or finding a purchaser acceptable to everyone.

(iii) The joint-stock company

The joint-stock company dates from Tudor times, when England's foreign trade began to expand. Instead of a trading ship's being owned by one person, it was financed by a number of people who bought 'shares' in a company formed for the purpose. However, since they enjoyed no limited liability, people were reluctant to join such companies: by purchasing only one share a person risked not only the money he had invested, but all his private assets, should the company be forced into liquidation. This made it impossible to adopt the technique of spreading risks by investing in a number of companies.

The industrial revolution, with the introduction of machines and factory organisation, made it essential that more capital should be available to industry. So, in order to induce small savers to invest, parliament granted limited liability in 1855.

Today the joint-stock company is the most important form of business organisation. The advantages it enjoys over the partnership are limited liability, continuity, the availability of capital (since investors can spread their risks and sell their shares easily) and, should the need arise, ease of expansion. Indeed, some kinds of businesses, e.g. aircraft production, could not be operated on a small scale. Here firms have to start as joint-stock companies, being either sponsored by important interests or developed as subsidiaries of existing large firms.

Against these advantages, however, certain disadvantages, which could add to costs, have to be considered. Even small companies have to file with the Registrar of Companies a balance sheet and an Annual Return giving the names of the directors and secretary, while companies with a turnover above £350,000 have to submit audited accounts. Furthermore, any assets of the company which have been built up over the years will increase the value of the original shares (usually owned by a family), so that when the time comes to wind up the company, e.g. because of retirement, this increase may be subject to capital gains tax. Finally, if the company is expanded by the issue of more shares, the original owners may lose control or even be subject to a takeover bid.

Each company has to submit to the Registrar of Companies its:

(i) *Memorandom of Association,* giving its name, the address of its registered office, the amount of the authorised capital it can raise and the objects of its activities, (usually affording it as wide a scope as possible); and

(ii) *Articles of Association,* containing the rules and regulations which govern how it will be run as regards the issue of shares, the company's borrowing powers, the election of officers, the powers of directors and the frequency of meetings.

Joint-stock companies are of two main kinds, private and public.

(1) The private company

A private company is simply a company that is not a public company and the formalities involved in its formation are few and inexpensive.

While conferring limited liability, it allows the business to be privately owned and managed. It is thus particularly suitable for either a medium-sized commercial or industrial organisation not requiring finance from the public, or for a speculative venture where a small group of people wishes to try out an idea and is prepared to back it financially to a definite limit before floating a public company. While private companies are considerably more numerous than public companies, their average capital is much smaller.

(2) The public company

When a large amount of capital is required, the first step is usually to form a public company. This must have at least two shareholders, an authorised minimum capital of £50,000 (a quarter of which is paid up) and carry the designation 'public limited company' – abbreviated to Plc – after its name. But it is the second step which is really important – getting its shares 'quoted' on the Stock Exchange or the Alternative Investment Market (AIM) (see p. 213). This entails an exhaustive examination of the company's affairs which have to be advertised very fully in at least two leading London newspapers.

(iv) Co-operative societies

Although there were many co-operative societies in operation before the Rochdale Pioneers of 1844, it was these twenty-eight workers who started the modern co-operative movement. By subscribing a few pence per week they accumulated an initial capital of £28, with which they rented a store and started trading with small stocks of flour, oatmeal, sugar, butter and candles. Profits were distributed to members in proportion to their purchases. In 1991 there were 65 retail co-operative societies in the UK, with an aggregate membership of over 8 million. Turnover was £7.3 bn, making these societies Britain's biggest retailer. In addition, these retail societies largely provide the capital and control the operations of the Co-operative Wholesale Society.

The minimum shareholding in a retail co-operative society is usually £1. Only if a full share is held does a member enjoy voting rights, but each member has only one vote irrespective of the number of shares held. Some societies still distribute profits as a dividend in proportion to the value of the member's purchases as recorded at check-out through a numbered plastic card. Others use the National Dividend Stamp scheme run by the Co-operative Wholesale Society. Stamps are given to customers in proportion to their purchasers, and a book of stamps can be redeemed for cash, goods or a deposit in a share account, in which case a bonus is usually added.

In the main, however, it is price cuts which have allowed co-operative shops to compete with supermarkets and stores.

Co-operative societies described above are organised directly by consumers and are therefore called 'consumer co-operative societies'. Producers have also formed 'producer co-operative societies' e.g. the Meriden motorcycle workers' co-operative, which was established with government aid when its firm was threatened with closure. A highly successful retail co-operative is the John Lewis Partnership; and building societies can be regarded as 'co-operative' ventures.

Producer co-operatives are chiefly important in agriculture, particularly where production is carried on by small farmers, as in Denmark, New Zealand and Spain. Their main function is to market their produce and to purchase inputs. In comparison they have been slow to develop in the UK, but they could in future become more prominent, e.g. in the selling of milk, as the government has now wound up the Marketing Boards (except for the British Wool Marketing Board, which collects and sells the British wool clip).

4.4 Raising the necessary capital

(a) The need for liquid capital

In order to employ factors of production, a firm has to have finance. This is usually divided into (i) working capital and (ii) fixed capital.

(i) *Working capital* is for purchasing 'single-use' factors – labour, raw materials, petrol, stationery, fertilisers, etc. – more or less the factors we refer to in Chapter 5 as 'variable factors'. Finance for working capital can be obtained from a variety of sources: banks, trade credit, finance companies, factor houses (which discount outstanding invoices), tax reserves, intercompany finance, advance deposits from customers and the government (e.g. through the Business Start-up Scheme which on conditions provides an allowance of £40 per week for a year when starting a new business).

(ii) *Fixed capital* covers factors which are used many times – factories, machines, land, lorries, etc. Some finance for fixed capital is therefore required initially for advance payments on factory buildings, machinery and so on before the firm is earning revenue, though it is possible to convert fixed capital into working capital by renting buildings, hiring plant and vehicles or by leasing or buying on deferred payments through a finance company. Normally, fixed-capital requirements are larger than those for working capital. Moreover, lenders recognise that they part with their money for a longer period and accept a greater risk. Thus finance for fixed capital tends to be more difficult to raise than for working capital, unless the business starts as an off-shoot of a parent company.

(b) The long-term capital of a company

The *long-term finance* of a company is obtained in four main ways: (a) selling 'shares' in the company; (b) borrowing; (c) obtaining a government grant or loan; (d) retaining profits.

(i) Shares

A 'share' is exactly what the name implies – a participation in the provision of the capital. Shares may be issued in various units, usually from 5p upwards, purchasers deciding how many they want. Such an investment, however, involves two main risks. First, profits may be disappointing, and the price of the share may fall. Second, share prices in general may be falling just when the owner wishes to sell. To minimise these risks, investors usually have a portfolio of different shares, debentures and government bonds.

(1) Ordinary shares

The dividend paid to the ordinary shareholder depends mainly upon the profitability of the company. However, the ordinary shareholder's dividend ranks last in order of priority, and if the company should be forced into liquidation the ordinary shareholder is repaid only after other creditors have been paid in full. Thus the ordinary share is termed 'risk capital'. In return each ordinary shareholder has a say in the running of the company, voting according to the number of shares held. At a general meeting directors are appointed or removed, changes made in the company's methods of raising capital and conducting business, and auditors appointed. Thus, because they take the major risks and decisions regarding the policy of the company, the ordinary shareholders are the real 'entrepreneurs'. In practice, however, their rights are rarely exercised. Usually few shareholders take the trouble to attend meetings, while unless the company is large the directors may control a high proportion of the shares and so be in strong position. Indeed this may be achieved by making all new shares 'non-voting "A" shares'. Thus directors tend to be self-perpetuating.

(2) Preference shares

If investors prefer a slightly reduced risk, they can buy preference shares. Here the dividend is fixed at a given percentage and paid before the ordinary shareholder. Should the company be forced into liquidation, the preference shareholder usually ranks above the ordinary shareholder when it comes to the redemption of capital. Preference shares may be 'cumulative': if the company cannot pay a dividend one year, arrears may be made up in succeeding years before ordinary shareholders receive any dividend.

Since 1965 preference shares have lost popularity because of their unfavourable tax treatment (see below).

(ii) Borrowing

Long-term loans are usually obtained by issuing 'debentures', redeemable after a specified period but bearing a fixed rate of interest. Since this is a first charge on the company's profit, the risk to the investor's income is not so high. Moreover, should the company fail, debenture-holders are paid first. In fact 'mortgage debentures' are secured on a definite asset of the company. Should the company be unable to meet its interest charges or to redeem the loan when due, the debenture-holders can force it into liquidation.

Thus the purchaser of a debenture takes less risk should the company fail. But because he is merely lending money he enjoys no ownership rights of voting on management and policy. On the other hand, a company whose profits are subject to frequent and violent fluctuations is not well-placed to raise capital through debentures. The method is best suited to a company making a stable profit (adequate to cover the interest payments) and possessing assets, such as land and buildings, which would show little depreciation were the company to go into liquidation.

A company having a large proportion of fixed-interest loans to ordinary shares is said to be 'highly geared'. Such a company will be able to pay high dividends when profits are good, but unable to make a distribution when profits are low. Where profits are expected to rise in the future, therefore, a company may prefer to raise capital for expansion by issuing debentures if the cost of doing so is not too high. But it is the present-day corporation tax which provides the main impulse in this direction. Debenture interest (but not preference-share interest) is an accepted cost for the purpose of calculating tax. Thus it reduces taxable profits. On the other hand, if finance is raised by shares, there is no prior interest charge, and profits (which are subject to tax) are higher by that amount. This tax advantage has, since the introduction of corporation tax in 1965, led companies to finance capital expansion as far as possible by fixed-interest loans. A compromise is the convertible bond which affords the lender an equity interest by giving him the right to convert his loan at a future date into shares at a stipulated price. Preference shares are now rarely issued.

(iii) Government grants and loans

Grants and loans are available for venture capital (see below), to firms setting up in Assisted Areas (see p. 295), and also to farmers on a percentage basis for expenditure on certain improvements, e.g. woodland and hedge-planting, slurry disposal.

(iv) Retained profits

Not all profits are distributed to shareholders. In addition to providing for depreciation and for a contingency fund, profits will be regarded by a successful company as its major source of capital for future expansion.

(c) Financing the expansion of a company

Because the shares of a *private company* are illiquid in that they cannot be offered for sale by public issue, a difficult stage in its growth may be reached when its capital is in the region of £250,000. The gap can be bridged in four main ways. First, as part of the government's desire to encourage growth of the economy through the development of small businesses, banks and other institutions have been more willing to provide medium-term loans especially as, under the Loan Guarantee Scheme, the Department of Industry guarantees 80 per cent of loans up to £75,000. Second, a stockbroker may effect a 'private placing' of shares or debentures with a life insurance company or an investment trust, who are usually in a position to ignore the disadvantages of holding securities of private companies. Third, help might be obtained from the new issue market, where both issuing houses and merchant bankers assist firms to raise capital, even providing some themselves. Fourth, new 'venture' capital companies (including specialist arms of the clearing banks) now provide medium and long-term equity financing for new and developing businesses. And, to encourage the provision of such funds for small unlisted firms, it has been possible since 1996 to form venture capital trusts.

When a large amount of capital is required, it is usually necessary for a company to 'go public' with its shares quoted on the Stock Exchange or the AIM (see p. 213). The capital required can then be raised by a 'placing', an 'offer for sale' or a 'public issue by prospectus'.

The first is the usual method when under £15 million is required, for the costs of underwriting and administration are less. An issuing house, licensed dealer or investment company agrees to sell blocks of the shares direct to institutions and persons who it knows are likely to be interested in them.

For larger amounts an offer for sale is a likely method. The shares are sold *en bloc* to an issuing house, which then offers them for sale by advertisement similar to a public issue.

For more than £50 million, a public issue by prospectus can be employed. Here the company's object is to obtain in single day the capital it requires. Hence it must advertise well and price its shares a little on the cheap side. The advertisement is in the form of a prospectus which sets out the business, history and prospects of the company together with its financial standing and the security offered.

In practice, the sale is usually conducted through an *issuing house*, which advises on the terms of the issue. It will also arrange to have the issue underwritten: that is, it will find a number of institutions, such as merchant bankers, which, in return for a small commission, will take whatever part of the issue is left unsold. However, such underwriters do not have to rely entirely on permanent investors to buy the securities on the day of issue, for speculators, known as 'stags', are usually operating, and they buy the shares hoping to resell them quickly at a small profit. Furthermore, where a company is raising additional capital, existing shareholders are now usually given the right to purchase new shares through a *rights issue* in proportion to shares already held and usually at a favourable price.

4.5 The division of labour

(a) Advantages of specialisation

In organising production, the firm will have to consider the advantages of specialisation, the fundamental principle of modern production. Here we examine it with particular reference to labour – although, as we shall see, it is equally applicable to machines, the distribution of goods, localities and even countries.

Where workers are organised so that each specialises on a particular task, increased production results. This is because:

(i) Each worker is employed in the job in which his or her superiority is most marked

Suppose that, in one day, Smith can plane the parts for 20 tables *or* cut the joints for 10, whereas Brown can either plane 10 tables *or* cut the joints for 20. If each does both jobs and spends one day on them, their combined production will be 15 tables planed *and* 15 table-joints cut. But Smith is better at planing, while Brown is better at cutting joints. If they specialise on what they can do best, their combined production will be 20 tables planed *and* 20 table joints cut – an increase in output of a third.

Even if, initially, workers were equally proficient at the different jobs, it might still pay to specialise, for the following reasons.

(ii) Practice makes perfect, and so particular skills are developed through repetition of the same job

(iii) Economy in tools allows specialised machinery to be used

This is illustrated in Figure 4.1, where in (b) division of labour has been introduced. Not only are specialised tools in constant use but their output is much greater. Thus division of labour sets free talented men for research – and allows their inventions to be used profitably.

(iv) Time is saved through not having to switch from one operation to another, e.g. in obtaining and replacing different tools

(v) Less time is taken in learning a particular job

(vi) The employer can estimate his costs of production and output more accurately

(b) Disadvantages of the division of labour

While the division of labour leads to lower costs of production, it may have disadvantages both for the worker and for society. The worker may find his job monotonous, and with some occupations such as paint-spraying there is a risk of occupational disease. Moreover, the skilled specialist may face redundancy if demand falls, while a strike by a few key workers can lead to widespread

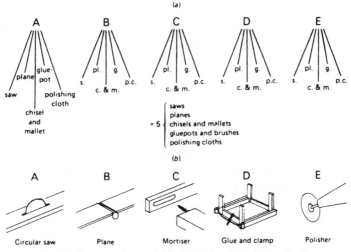

Figure 4.1   Economy in tools through specialisation

unemployment. Finally, standardised products tend to replace individual craft work.

(c) Limitations on the division of labour

Naturally the scope for the division of labour varies from one industry to another. Countries like Switzerland which have too few workers to permit much specialisation concentrate on manufacturing a narrow range of products. Again, in industries such as agriculture and building where the same operations are not taking place each day, many 'Jacks of all trades' are required. Moreover, an exchange system using money is essential: we must first unite in exchange before we can divide in production. Finally, the division of labour has to be related to current demand for the product. It is no use specialising in making something which nobody wants; conversely, minute division of labour is only possible when there is a large demand. The complex organisation of car production, for instance, rests on a mass demand for a standardised product made up from a multitude of small parts.

4.6 The advantages of large-scale production

As a firm's output increases, costs per unit may fall as a result of the advantages of large-scale production. These are often referred to as 'internal economies' to distinguish them from 'external economies', which arise indirectly from the growth of the *industry* (see p. 55).

(a) Internal economies

Internal economies are of five main kinds:

(i) Technical economies

In making a good, as distinct from distributing it, increased output permits more division of labour, greater specialisation of machines, the economy of large machines (e.g. a double-decker bus can carry twice as many passengers as a single-decker, though neither the initial cost nor running costs are doubled) and the linking of processes (e.g. in steel-making, where re-heating is avoided).

Generally technical economies fix the size of the unit actually producing, e.g. a supermarket, rather than the size of the firm, which may consist of many units, e.g. Tesco. Where technical economies are great, the size of the typical unit will tend to be large – as, for example, in the production of cars, sheet steel, gas and electricity. Where, however, increased output merely means duplicating and re-duplicating machines,the tendency will be for the unit to remain small. For instance, in farming at least one combine harvester is necessary for about 600 acres. Thus farms tend to remain small, for as yet there are no greater technical economies to be derived from large machines. Where few technical economies can be gained and yet the firm is large, consisting – as with chain stores – of many operating units, it is usually because other types of economy are possible, as follows.

(ii) Managerial economies

When output increases, division of labour can be applied to management. For example, in a shop owned and run by one man, the owner, although having the ability to order supplies, keep accounts and sell the goods, has yet to do such trivial jobs as sweeping the floor, weighing articles and packing parcels – tasks within the capability of a boy who has just left school. His sales, however, may not warrant employing a boy. The large business overcomes this difficulty: a brilliant organiser can devote all his time to organising, the routine jobs being left to lower-paid workers.

The function of management can itself be divided, e.g. into production, sales, transport and personnel. These departments may be further subdivided – sales, for instance, being split into sections for advertising, exports and customers' welfare.

(iii) Commercial economies

If a bulk order can be placed for materials and components, the supplier will usually quote a lower price per unit, since this enables him also to gain the advantages of large-scale production.

Economies can also be achieved in selling the product. If the sales staff are not being worked to capacity, the additional output can be sold at little extra cost. Similarly, administrative costs are spread. Indeed, the large firm often manu-factures many products, so that one acts as an advertisement for the others. Thus Hoover vacuum-cleaners advertise their washing-machines, dishwashers and steam-irons. In addition a large firm may be able to sell its by-products, something which might be unprofitable for a small firm.

Finally, when the business is sufficiently large, the division of labour can be introduced on the commercial side, with expert buyers and sellers being employed.

Such commercial economies represent real gains to the community, reducing prices through better use of resources. On the other hand, where a large firm uses its muscle to *force* suppliers into granting it favourable prices, it will simply result in higher prices to other buyers.

(iv) Financial economies

In raising finance for expansion the large firm is in a favourable position. It can, for instance, offer better security to bankers – and, because it is well-known, raise money at lower cost, since investors have confidence in and prefer shares which can be readily sold on the stock exchange.

(v) Risk-bearing economies

Here we can distinguish three sorts of risk. First, there are risks which can be insured against, enabling large and small firms alike to spread risks.

Second, certain businesses usually bear some risk themselves, saving some of the profits made by the insurance company. Here the large firm has a definite advantage. London Transport, for instance, can cover its own risks, while a large bank can call in funds from other branches when there is a run on the reserves in a particular locality.

The third kind of risk is one that cannot be reduced to a mathematical probability and thus cannot be insured against – risk arising from changes in demand for the product or in the supply of raw materials; this is usually referred to as risk arising from 'uncertainty'. To meet fluctuations in demand the large firm can diversify output (like British American Tobacco) or develop export markets. On the supply side, materials may be obtained from different sources to guard against crop failures, strikes, etc.

(b) External economies

While the firm can plan its internal economies, it can only *hope* to benefit from external economies which arise as the *industry* grows.

First, the concentration of similar firms in an area may produce mutual benefits: a skilled labour force; cooperation in common services such as marketing and research; better roads and social amenities; technical schools catering for the local industry; product reputation; ancillary firms supplying specialised machinery, collecting by-products, etc. The firm must take into account such economies when deciding where production shall take place, for the lower costs may outweigh any diseconomies which arise through traffic congestion, smoke, etc. (see p. 169).

Second, external economies can take the form of common information services provided either by associations of firms or even by the government.

Finally, as an industry grows in size, specialist firms may be established to provide components for all producers thereby extending economies of scale.

4.7 The size of firms

(a) Horizontal, vertical and lateral combination

The advantages of large-scale production provide firms with a strong impetus to combine.

Horizontal integration occurs where firms producing the same type of product combine. Thus Nestlé took over Rowntree, and Somerfield acquired Kwik Save.

Vertical integration is the amalgamation of firms engaged in the different stages of production of a good. It may be 'backward' towards the raw material, or 'forward' towards the finished product. Thus Britoil, an oil exploration company was taken over by BP.

Both the above can improve efficiency, thereby lowering costs per unit, and increasing profits. Thus horizontal integration can allow greater specialisation, commercial economies and a saving on administrative overheads. Vertical integration facilitates linked processes and reduces risk by increasing direct control over the supply and quality of raw materials and components. Moreover, all parts can be manufactured to an integrated design, and there is direct control over the distribution of the final product (see below).

Lateral integration occurs where a firm increases the range of its products. Concentration on one product may make a firm vulnerable to a change in fashion, a switch in government policy or a recession. Thus the firm diversifies, often by taking over other firms producing completely different products. For instance, P & O is engaged in shipping, cross-channel ferries, road transport and construction through its subsidiary companies.

Apart from increased efficiency and security of profits, integration may enhance a firm's prestige. One other aim, however, must not be overlooked – monopoly power. This is discussed in Chapter 10.

Integration may result from internal development or combining with existing firms either by merger or a takeover – when a company buys all the shares of a smaller firm and absorbs it completely – or by the formation of a holding company in which the parent company obtains enough shares to give it effective control, though the smaller company preserves its identity and enjoys considerable independence of action. Many large companies, e.g. Unilever, GEC and Great Universal Stores, hold such controlling interests in subsidiary companies.

(b) The predominance of the small firm

In spite of the advantages enjoyed by the large firm, we must not conclude that every firm has to be large to be competitive. Indeed the small firm still predominates in all forms of production. In agriculture two-thirds of all holdings are less than fifty hectares in size, while in retailing nearly nine-tenths of all firms consist of only one shop. Even more remarkably, the same is true of manufacturing where one would have thought that technical economies of scale would be all-important. Table 4.1, which covers the size of the establishment – the factory or workshop – in manufacturing, shows the small establishment is

Table 4.1 Size of manufacturing establishments in the UK, 1997

Employees	Number of establishments	Percentage of total establishments
1–9	127,295	69.6
10–99	47,255	25.8
100–999	8,045	4.4
Over 1,000	265	0.2
TOTAL	182,830	100

Source: Annual Abstract of Statistics.

also typical of manufacturing in the UK, with 95 per cent employing less than 100 people.

Any explanation of this predominance of the small firm has to deal with two salient facts: (i) small firms are especially important in certain industries, such as agriculture, retailing, building, and personal and professional services; (ii) variations in the size of firms exist even within the same industry. Both result from the nature of the conditions of demand and supply.

(i) Demand

Large-scale production may be only *technically* efficient; it is not *economically* efficient unless a large and regular demand justifies it.

The market may be small because demand is local (e.g. for personal services and the goods sold by the village store), or limited to a few articles of one pattern (e.g. for prestige luxury goods and highly specialised and individually designed machine-tools) or because transport costs are high (e.g. for bricks and perishable market-garden produce), or because product differentiation divides it artificially (see p. 78).

Where demand fluctuates (e.g. in construction), the overhead cost of idle specialised equipment is heavy – but the smaller the firm, the less the burden.

(ii) Supply

Even if demand is large, factors on the supply side may make for small firms. While in certain industries, e.g. retailing and building, it is possible to start with little capital, or be supported by franchising (e.g. McDonald's) or by jointing a wholesale chain (e.g. Spar), the difficulty of obtaining further funds and the taxation of profits are obstacles to expansion. Furthermore, government policy may give specific support to small companies, e.g. by a reduced rate of corporation tax. Alternatively, where vertical disintegration is possible, firms need not expand internally but simply employ specialist firms for advertising, research, supplying components and selling by-products. Important, too, is the fact that many small owners do not have the drive to expand or the ability to manage a large concern. Or, as in farming and retailing, they will work long hours (that is, accept a lower rate of profit) simply to be their own bosses.

Above all, as the size of the firm increases, management difficulties occur. If management is vested in heads of department, problems of co-ordination arise and rivalries develop. This means that one person must be in overall command – yet people with such capabilities are in very limited supply. In certain industries these difficulties may soon occur. Rapid decisions are required where demand changes quickly, e.g. in the fashion trades, or supply conditions alter, e.g. through the weather in agriculture. Or care may have to be given to the personal requirements of customers, e.g. in retailing and services. This may necessitate the close supervision of management, and thus the firm has to be small.

4.8 The location of production

In deciding where to produce, a firm has to weigh the advantages of a particular locality against the rent or land costs it will have to pay there compared with elsewhere.

(a) Location advantages

The advantages of production in a particular locality can be classified as: (i) natural, (ii) acquired and (iii) government-sponsored.

(i) Natural advantages

Costs are incurred both in assembling raw materials and in distributing the finished product. With some goods the weight of the raw materials is far greater than that of the finished product. This is particularly true where coal is used for heat and power, e.g. in iron and steel production.

Here transport costs are saved by producing where raw materials are found, e.g. on coal- and iron-ore fields, or where they are easily accessible, e.g. near a port.

On the other hand, in some industries the cost of transporting the finished product are greater than those of assembling the raw materials, e.g. with ice-cream, mineral waters, furniture and metal cans. With these it is cheaper for a firm to produce near the market for its goods. Thus Walls has ice-cream factories close to most large concentrations of population.

What is really important as regards transport costs is their ratio to the value of the product. Thus sand and gravel are excavated locally, whereas special types of brick are transported long distances.

Generally speaking, transport improvements and new developments (e.g. electrical power, lighter materials) have helped firms to move away from their sources of raw materials. The tendency now is, therefore, for firms to concentrate, not on the coalfields, but on the outskirts of areas of high population which provide both a supply of labour and a market for the finished good.

A river, estuary or coastal location may be essential when huge quantities of water are required by an industry (e.g. chemicals, atomic power), and this may also be important for waste disposal.

Besides accessibility to raw materials and nearness of markets, suitability of climate is a further natural advantage which may have to be considered when locating production. Indeed, in agriculture, it is usually decisive, provided soil conditions are not adverse.

Under 'natural advantages' we can also include an adequate supply of the type of labour required. Thus high technology industries have been attracted to the south-east of England by the skilled labour available, while the abundance of cheap labour has been important for the development of mass-production in Taiwan and Hong Kong.

(ii) Acquired advantages

Improved methods of production, the development of transport, inventions and new sources of power may alter the relative importance of natural advantages and so change an industry's location. Thus, as high-grade iron-ore fields have become exhausted and improved techniques have reduced coal consumption, it is now cheaper to transport the coal than the iron ore to produce pig-iron, and so the industry has shifted to the ports importing iron ore and to the low-grade iron-ore fields of the east Midlands. Similarly, improved transport may upset the relative pulls. Finally, new inventions, such as humidifiers and water-softeners (cotton and wool), can make an industry less dependent upon a particular locality.

Yet we must not over-stress the importance of the above changes. Even when natural factors have disappeared, an industry often remains in the same region because of the 'man-made' advantages it has acquired, e.g. steel, cotton. Such advantages were mentioned earlier when we studied external economies of concentration. A skilled labour force, communications, marketing and commercial organisations, nearby ancillary industries (to achieve economies of scale or to market by-products), training schools and a widespread reputation for the products of the region all help to lower the costs of production, thereby making the locality attractive to new firms.

(iii) Government-sponsored advantages

Unemployment in such highly localised industries as coal, cotton and ship-building, and environmental problems (traffic congestion, pollution, housing stress) in regions attracting new and expanding industries, have led the government to offer firms financial inducements to set up plants in Assisted Areas (see Chapter 23).

Such financial advantages have to be considered by a firm when deciding where to site its factory. But while government grants were a major inducement for Nissan to establish its car factory in Sunderland, the area's history of engineering skill, the availability of a large flat site and proximity to major port facilities for exporting all influenced the decision.

(b) The level of rents in different areas

Location advantages have to be weighed against the cost of land (or, where it is hired, rent). This cost varies from one locality to another and is determined by the market. Since other firms, possibly from other industries, may be looking for the same site advantages, competition will fix the price of land at the highest which the keenest firm is prepared to pay. This will be the firm which puts the greatest value on the land's advantages compared with those of land elsewhere. Thus, early in its history it seemed that the cotton industry might settle on Clydeside, for this had all the natural advantages of south-east Lancashire. But it also had advantages for producing iron and steel and for building ships, and in these her superiority was most marked. Thus shipbuilding firms were prepared to pay extra for this advantage. For cotton manufacturers this extra cost of a site on the Clyde exceeded any disadvantage of being in Lancashire. Thus shipbuilding firms settled along the Clyde, and cotton firms in Lancashire.

In the final analysis, therefore, it is not the absolute advantages of a district which decide where a firm locates, but the advantages relative to those of other districts. Thus an industry whose outlay on unskilled labour forms a high proportion of its production costs would, other things being equal, be able to bid more for land in an area of cheap labour than one whose spending on such labour was minimal. And in town centres we see the same principle at work – shops oust other businesses, and houses are converted into offices.

(c) Other influences on location

A firm will normally choose the site where the advantages are greatest compared with its cost. But even for a comparatively new industry, where natural advantages are important, we cannot assume that they will be decisive. Thus it is largely historical accident which accounts for the presence of the Rover plant at Cowley on the outskirts of Oxford, for the old school of William Morris came up for sale just as the production of cars at his original cycle works was being expanded.

Moreover, electricity has now practically eliminated dependence on a coalfield site. Yet firms may still go to the original areas because of the advantages acquired over time. Others may choose to be nearer their markets. Some 'foot-loose' firms have even located in certain districts, particularly south-east England, largely because the managing directors (or their wives) have preferred living there!

4.9 The distribution of goods to the consumer

(a) The scope of production

A manufacturer has to decide how to get his finished goods to the consumer. He may undertake the task himself. But if he does so, he must employ salesmen, run delivery transport, carry stocks, advertise his product, organise exports, advise customers, establish servicing centres and give credit. Experts for these highly specialised functions can only be employed if output is large enough. Moreover, the manufacturer's main ability lies in organising production rather than its distribution.

Thus the principle of the division of labour is usually applied. Just as the manufacturer buys raw materials and components from other producers, so specialist firms get his goods to the consumer – there is *forward* vertical *disintegration*. We will simplify our account of this selling process by grouping such firms into 'wholesalers' and 'retailers'.

(b) The wholesaler

The wholesaler buys goods in bulk from producers and sells them in small quantities to retailers. In doing so he helps production in a number of ways.

(i) He economises in distribution

Because shops usually stock a variety of goods, they can order supplies only in small quantities. Thus it is not economical for each producer to sell directly to them.

Figure 4.2 shows that, when four chocolate firms deliver in bulk to a wholesaler, the number of contacts and journeys is reduced from sixteen (a) to eight (b).

Particularly in agriculture, where the goods are perishable, the farmer finds it easier if, instead of trying to contact retailers himself, he delivers his produce to a wholesaler or commission salesman, for example at New Covent Garden, and leaves the actual selling to him.

Similarly, in the construction industry, where there are numerous small builders, it is easier for manufacturers to deliver through builders' merchants.

(ii) He keeps stocks

Consumers like the convenience of being able to obtain a good at a shop just when they require it. This means that stocks have to be held. Often, however, neither the producer nor the retailer has the necessary storage facilities or the extra capital required, and so it is left to the wholesaler.

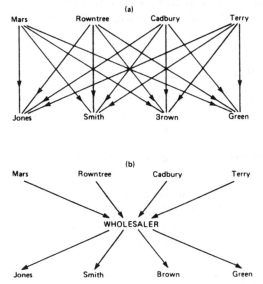

Figure 4.2 Economising in distribution through the wholesaler

In other ways, too, the costs of storage are removed from the producer or retailer. While loss through fire, flood or rats can be insured against, no insurance can be taken out to cover a fall in demand. Thus a wholesaler or dealer, who holds stocks of a good which is liable to go out of fashion, relieves manufacturers and retailers of that risk.

The holding of stocks is, in itself, a valuable economic function in that they help to even out fluctuations in price resulting from temporary fluctuations in demand or supply. Thus merchants replenish brick stocks during the winter, and run them during the rest of the year.

(iii) He arranges imports from abroad

Manufacturers could rarely be bothered to ship small parcels to individual retailers abroad or to undertake the currency and documentary arrangements. They prefer to deal with a wholesaler, an import merchant with established trade connections.

(iv) He carries out certain specialised functions

Not only does the wholesaler advertise goods but, in order to make selling easier, he may process goods – pasteurising milk, blending tea, refining sugar, and grading commodities such as wheat, cotton and wool tops.

(v) He is a channel for information and advice

Suggestions which customers make to the retailer are passed on to the wholesaler, who, if he sees that they reflect the general view, conveys them to the manufacturer. Thus the latter can improve his product and anticipate fashion changes.

(vi) He assists in the day-to-day maintenance of the good

With many products, particularly vehicles and machinery, the wholesaler relieves the manufacturer of the task of providing an efficient maintenance, repair and spare-part service.

(c) The retailer

The retailer performs the last stage of the productive process, for it is he who puts the goods in the hands of the actual consumer. His work is to have the right goods in the right place at the right time.

(i) He stocks small quantities of a variety of goods

What the 'right good' is depends on the customer, for different people have different tastes. It is therefore necessary to stock a variety of goods so that customers can choose and take delivery there and then. Thus the retail shop is basically a showroom, particularly where goods are bought infrequently.

The size of the stocks carried will depend on many factors: the popularity of the product, the possibility of obtaining further supplies quickly, the perishability of the good or the likelihood of its going out of fashion, the season, the possibility of future price changes and, above all, the cost (chiefly bank overdraft interest) of carrying stocks.

(ii) He takes the goods to where it is most convenient for the customer

Taking the goods to the customer usually means that the retailer sets up his shop within easy reach, e.g. in a town centre. However, with goods in every-day use, such as groceries, small shops are often dotted around residential districts. Where customers are very dispersed, the retailer may even be a 'travelling shop'.

While customers take most goods away with them, the retailer arranges delivery if transport is essential, e.g. for furniture, or if the customer likes the extra convenience of delivery, e.g. of the morning milk.

(iii) He performs special services for customers

In the course of his main business the retailer performs many services to build up customer goodwill. Where the good is not in stock he will order it, and in other matters where contact with the manufacturer is necessary he often acts for the customer, e.g. by returning the goods for repair.

With many goods, too, such as fishing tackle, photographic equipment, musical instruments and machinery, he can usually provide specialised advice.

Finally, goods may be sent on approval, or finance arranged through hire purchase, special credit accounts, etc.

(iv) He advises the wholesaler and manufacturer of customers' preferences

(d) Types of retail outlet

Retailing might be widely defined as including all shops, mail-order firms, garages, launderettes and betting shops, and indeed any business selling products or services to the consumer. However, it is usual to confine the meaning of 'retailing' to shops and mail-order outlets, as follows.

(i) Independents

These are mainly small shops with no branches, and they account for nearly two-fifths of total shop sales. Yet, in spite of their advantages of individual attention to customers, handy locations for quick shopping trips, and the willingness of owners to accept a lower return in order to be their own bosses, these independents have steadily lost ground to the larger stores.

A major bid to avert the decline has come through the voluntary chains, such as Spar, Mace and Wavy Line, of which about a third of the independents are members. While retaining their independence, members buy in bulk from wholesalers and use common advertising and display techniques.

A more recent development enabling an individual trader to set up in business is 'franchising', that is buying a concession from a major firm, e.g. Kentucky Fried Chicken, McDonalds, 'K' shoes. United Dairies. The concessionaire advises on obtaining finance and presenting the product in which he often establishes a brand name by advertising.

(ii) Multiples

These can be defined arbitrarily as organisations of ten or more shops. Some, such as Mothercare and Dixon's, sell a particular type of good. Others, such as Woolworth, Boots and Marks & Spencer, have a fairly extensive range of products. Together with the supermarkets they comprise about 50 per cent of the retail market.

Their chief advantages are economies of bulk-buying and centralised control, the elimination of the wholesaler, quick recognition through standardised shop-fronts, and a reputation established through brand names.

(iii) Supermarkets

These may be defined as self-service shops with a minimum selling area of 200 sq. metres, but the trend in recent years, especially among the multiple grocery companies, has been towards superstores (of at least 2,000 sq. metres) and hypermarkets (see below). While organisationally they would count as multiples, their share of the food trade warrants separate attention. In 1991 they accounted for half the grocery trade and over a third of retail food sales.

The field is led by the five major retail grocery chains: Tesco, Sainsbury, Safeway, Associated Dairies (ASDA), and Somerfield. Their strength lies in economies of scale, low labour costs, a clear and attractive display of merchandise, bulk buying and selling under their own label (e.g. Sainsbury cornflakes, Tesco coffee). As a result they have highly competitive prices and have gained ground rapidly.

Indeed, many of these self-service organisations have extended their activities beyond groceries to self-service of goods showing higher profit margins, e.g. clothing, hardware, cosmetics, pharmaceuticals, do-it-yourself and garden supplies.

(iv) Hypermarkets

Urban congestion, inadequate parking space and rising rents have made high street sites increasingly expensive. The answer to these problems has been the very large 'out-of-town' shopping centre or 'hypermarket', catering mainly for the car-borne weekly shopper.

(v) Department stores

Competition from multiples has forced department stores to alter somewhat their traditional pattern of having separate departments under the control of a responsible buyer, often described as 'many stores under one roof', in favour of bulk-buying by central office, more self-service, and extended credit facilities. As a result they have retained some 4 per cent of the retail market, but the modern development is towards covered shopping malls.

The main groups are House of Fraser, Debenhams, the John Lewis Partnership and Great Universal Stores.

(vi) Co-operatives (see pp. 47–8)

(vii) Mail order

Mail-order business, which accounts for nearly 3 per cent of the retail market, is particularly susceptible to higher postal charges.

The major companies, Great Universal Stores, Littlewoods Mail Order, Freemans and Empire Stores, sell by agency and illustrated catalogues, purchases usually being arranged through weekly interest-free payments. Over one-half of all sales are accounted for by women's clothing and household goods.

(e) Factors affecting the type of retail outlet

Over the last thirty years, the pattern of retailing has moved away from the small, independent shop towards the larger organisation, notably the multiples, supermarket chains and mail-order firms. This trend reflects a greater emphasis on competition through lower price rather than by better service.

The larger firms are in a strong position to cut prices. Not only do they obtain the advantages of large-scale production (particularly those of selling a whole range of goods and of buying in bulk), but they can use their bargaining strength to secure further price discounts from manufacturers. Indeed, the largest may force the manufacturer to supply goods under the retailer's 'own-brand' label at a price below that at which other retailers can buy the manufacturer's national brand. Moreover, since large retailers cater for a whole range of shopping, e.g. food, they can attract customers into stores by 'loss-leaders'.

Economic factors influencing this trend have been:

 (i) *Increased income*, which has led to a swing towards the more expensive processed foods and consumer durable goods and facilitated less frequent shopping trips.
 (ii) *An increase in car ownership*, which has enabled people to move from the city centre to the outer suburbs. Shops have followed, not only to be near their customers, but also to obtain larger sites with parking facilities, lower rents and less congestion. The car has also made customers more mobile, enabling them to travel to good shopping centres where they can purchase all their requirements at a single stop.
 (iii) *An increase in the number of married women gong to work*, which has promoted the demand for convenience foods and labour-saving devices. It has also led to the reduction of the number of shopping expeditions, a trend helped by the wider ownership of refrigerators and freezers.

These factors are likely to remain important in the future. It seems probable, therefore, that new supermarkets will take the form of discount stores or hypermarkets selling a wider range of products having a higher profit margin than groceries. Moreover, the more favourable response to recent planning applications is enabling new stores to be developed outside towns, while cash-and-carry warehouses are now available to consumers who can buy in quantity.

Such changes are likely to be at the expense of the medium-sized business, for the smaller local retailers offer 'convenience' services.

(f) The future of the middleman

Wholesalers and dealers who come between the manufacturer and the retailer or consumer are often referred to as 'middlemen'. They are frequently criticised on the grounds that they take too large a share of the selling price. It is argued that, if the manufacturer sold direct to consumers, prices could be reduced.

But, as we have seen, wholesalers relieve producers of essential functions, allowing them to obtain the advantages of specialisation in marketing products. Such forward vertical dis-integration is the cheapest way of getting goods to the consumer.

However, this does not mean that all criticism of middlemen is unjustified. Sometimes their profit margins are too high. This may occur through continuing with antiquated methods or by a single middleman's playing off one small producer, such as a farmer, against another (hence the formation of producers' co-operatives).

In recent years a tendency for the wholesaler to be eliminated has been due to: (i) the growth of large shops, which can order in bulk; (ii) the development of road transport, which reduces the necessity of holding large stocks; (iii) the desire of manufacturers to retain some control over retailing outlets in order to ensure that their products are pushed or a high standard of service, freshness, etc. is maintained; and (iv) the practice of branding many products, which eliminates many specialised functions. In other cases, however, the elimination of the wholesaler has been confined to sales of high-value goods, such as furniture and television sets; to circumstances where the producer and retailer are close together, as with the market gardener who supplies the local shop; and to cases where the manufacturer does his own retailing.

To some extent the wholesaler has responded to this challenge by developing in two main directions: (i) by establishing the cash-and-carry warehouse, sometimes called 'the retailers' supermarket'; and (ii) by becoming the organiser of a voluntary chain of retailers, who are supplied, and to some extent controlled, by him, e.g. Spar.

Selling direct to consumers by the manufacturer occurs chiefly where: (i) the manufacturer wishes to push his product (e.g. beer or footwear) or to ensure a standard of advice and service (e.g. sewing-machines); (ii) the personal-service element is important (e.g. made-to-measure clothing); (iii) the manufacturer is a small-scale producer-retailer, often selling a perishable good (e.g. cakes and pastries) or serving a local area (e.g. with printing); (iv) so wide a range of goods is produced that a whole chain of shops can be fully stocked (e.g. Whitbread ales, Thornton confectionery); or (v) the good is highly technical or made to individual specifications (e.g. machinery).

QUESTIONS

1 Why is the publisher of a book an 'entrepreneur'? Is the author a part-entrepreneur?

2 A public company requires finance to;
   (a) build a new factory
   (b) hold increased stocks

(c) maintain sales in a credit squeeze

(d) increase the rate of dividend to shareholders

Which one of the above would most likely be financed by:

    (i) current profits

    (ii) an overdraft from a commercial bank

    (iii) an issue of debentures

    (iv) increased trade credit?

3 Name four industries in which small firms are particularly numerous.

4 What functions of the retailer are performed by your local bookseller?

5 Why do antique shops tend to be found close together? Give two other examples.

◾▾ 5 Supply: (ii) costs and profitability

Objectives

1 To derive the guiding principle for the firm when combining resources
2 To explain how the difference between fixed and variable costs is important in both theoretical analysis and production decisions
3 To define 'perfect competition'
4 To show how the supply curve of the industry is derived from the combined output of its firms
5 To explain how 'super-normal' profit is eliminated in the long period under 'perfect competition'

5.1 Combining resources

(a) The problem of combining resources

In order to produce, the firm has to obtain and assemble resources – usually referred to as factors of production and classified as land, labour and capital (see p. 89). The problems peculiar to each of these three are considered in Chapters 6–8. Here we are concerned with the more general problem of how much of each a firm will hire. In other words, how will the firm allocate its spending in order to obtain the greatest possible output from a given outlay? For example, the same amount of concrete can be mixed by having many men with just a shovel apiece or by having only one man using a concrete-mixer. Can we discover any general principle governing the firm's decision? We can begin by seeing what happens to output when one factor is held fixed while the amount of another factor is increased.

(b) The law of diminishing (or non-proportional) returns

Assume: (i) production is by two factors only, land and labour; (ii) all units of the variable factor, labour, are equally efficient; (iii) there is no change in techniques or organisation.

Table 5.1 shows how the output of potatoes varies as more labourers work on a fixed amount of land. Until 3 men are employed, the marginal product of labour

Table 5.1 Variations in output of potatoes resulting from a change in labour employed

Number of men employed on the fixed unit of land	Total output	Output (50 kg bags) Average product	Marginal product
1	2	2.0	2
2	16	8.0	14
3	54	18.0	38
4	80	20.0	26
5	95	19.0	15
6	108	18.0	13
7	120	17.1	12
8	130	16.2	10
9	138	15.3	8
10	142	14.2	4
11	142	12.9	0

Notes:
(a) *Total output* is the total output (bags) from all factors employed.
(b) *Average product* refers to the average output per man. It therefore equals

$$\frac{\text{total output}}{\text{number of men employed}}$$

(c) *Marginal product* refers to the marginal output (bags) to labour, and equals the addition to total output which is obtained by increasing the labour force by one man. That is, marginal output equals total output of $(n + 1)$ men minus total output of n men.
(d) There is a fundamental relationship between average product and marginal product. Marginal product equals average product when the latter is at a maximum (Figure 5.1). This relationship is bound to occur. So long as the marginal product is greater than average product, the return to an additional labourer will raise the average product of all labourers employed. On the other hand, as soon as the marginal product falls below average product, the additional labourer will lower the average product. Hence when average product is neither rising nor falling, that is, at its maximum, it is because marginal product equals average product.
This relationship can be made clearer by a simple example. Suppose Atherton has played 20 innings and that his batting average is 60 runs. Now if in his next innings he scores more than 60, say 102, his average will increase – to 62. If, on the other hand, he scores less than 60, say 18, his average will fall to 58.

is increasing – the third labourer, for instance, adding 38 bags. Here there are really too few labourers for the given amount of land. Thereafter the marginal product falls, the fourth labourer adding only 26 bags, and so on; total output is still increasing, but at a diminishing rate. The maximum return per labourer occurs when there are 4 labourers to the plot. If we increase the number of labourers to eight, the maximum return per labourer can only be maintained by doubling the amount of land. When 11 labourers are employed they start to get in one another's way, and from then on total output is declining absolutely.

Again it must be emphasised that units of the variable factor are homogeneous. The marginal product of labour does not fall because less efficient labourers have to be employed. Diminishing returns are the result of more labourers being employed on a fixed amount of land.

Nor does the law formulate any *economic* theory; it merely states physical relationships. While the physical productivity of an extra labourer is important to

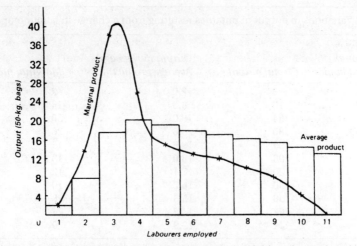

Figure 5.1   The relationship between the number of labourers employed, average product and marginal product

a farmer in deciding how many men to employ, it will not *determine* his decision. He must also know the relative costs of factors; that is, he requires economic data as well as technical facts.

(c) The practical applications of the law of diminishing returns

The law is significant both in our everyday life and in the theoretical analysis of the economist.

First, it helps to explain the low standard of living in many parts of the world, particularly the Far East. Increasing population is cultivating a fixed amount of land. Marginal product, and thus average product, are falling; so, therefore, is the average standard of living.

Second, it shows how a firm can adjust the marginal physical products of factors by altering the proportion in which they are combined. Thus few labourers to the plot gave a high return per labourer; after 4 labourers, the average product began to fall. So the law is often referred to as 'the law of varying proportions'. The firm will choose that combination of factors which yields the maximum output from a given outlay, as follows.

(d) The optimum combination of variable factors

So far we have assumed that there are just two factors, land and labour, and that land is fixed. But suppose that there is another variable factor, say capital. Now the farmer will have to decide how he will combine labour with capital.

How much of each he employs will depend upon its productivity relative to its price, since he will alter the combination until, for the last pound spent on both labour and capital, he obtains the same amount of product. Suppose, for instance, the last pound's worth of labour is yielding more potatoes than the last pound spent on capital. It will obviously pay the farmer to transfer this pound from capital to buying more labour, for this will increase his total physical yield.

But labour and capital are obtained in different units, their units being different in price. Thus we cannot directly compare the productivity of one man with that of one unit of capital, say a mechanical hoe; we must allow for their respective prices. If the cost of one man is only one-third of the cost of a mechanical hoe, then the marginal product of a man need only be one-third of the hoe's to give the same yield for a given expenditure. Thus the farmer will be in equilibrium in combining factors when:

$$\frac{\text{Marginal product of labour}}{\text{Price of labour}} = \frac{\text{Marginal product of capital}}{\text{Price of capital}}$$

A corollary of this is that, like the housewife in purchasing her goods, the firm will tend to buy more of a factor as its price falls, and less as it rises. Suppose the wage-rate rises but the marginal product of labour remains unchanged. The fundamental relationship stated above has now been destroyed. To restore the position it is necessary to raise the marginal product of labour and to lower that of capital by combining less labour with more capital: in short, a rise in wages without a corresponding increase in the productivity of labour will, other things being equal, tend to bring about the replacement of labour by machines (see p. 109).

5.2 The costs of production

(a) Opportunity costs and profit

Suppose a man sets himself up as a shopkeeper. He invests £6,000 of his savings in the business, and in the first year his receipts are £80,000 and his outgoings £44,000. The accountant would say that his profits over the year were £36,000. The economist, however, would disagree.

The reason for this is that the economist is not so much concerned with money costs as with 'opportunity cost' – what a factor could earn in its best alternative line of production. This concept of cost has a bearing on (i) the economist's concept of 'profit', and (ii) how long production should continue when total costs are not covered.

(b) 'Implicit costs'

The £44,000 money outgoings of the shopkeeper above can be regarded as 'explicit costs'. But when we look at costs as alternatives forgone we see immediately that the shopkeeper has certain 'implicit costs' – the rewards his own capital and labour could earn elsewhere. If, for instance, his capital could be invested at 8 per cent, there is an implicit cost of £480 a year. Similarly with his own labour. His next most profitable line, we will assume, is to be a shop manager earning £23,520 a year. Thus a total of £24,000 in implicit costs in addition to the explicit costs should be deducted from his receipts.

(c) Normal and super-normal profit

But we have not finished yet. The shopkeeper knows that, even in running a sweet-shop, some risk arises through uncertainty – a risk which he avoids if he merely works for somebody else. The shopkeeper must therefore anticipate at least a certain minimum profit, of say £4,000 a year, before he will start his own business. If he does not make this minimum profit, he feels he might as well go into some other line of business or become a paid shop manager. Thus another type of cost (which we call 'normal profit') has to be allowed for – the minimum return which keeps a firm in a particular industry after all other factors have been paid their opportunity cost. Normal profit is a cost because, if it is not met, the supply of entrepreneurship to that particular line of business dries up.

We have, therefore, the following costs: explicit costs, implicit costs and normal profit. Anything left over after all these costs have been met is 'super-normal' profit. In terms of our example, we have:

	£	£
Total revenue		80,000
Total costs: explicit	44,000	
implicit	24,000	
normal profit	4,000	
		72,000
Super-normal profit		8,000

(d) Fixed costs and variable costs

For the purposes of our analysis, we shall classify costs as either *fixed* or *variable*.

Fixed costs are those costs which do not vary in direct proportion to the firm's output. They are the costs of indivisible factors, e.g. buildings, machinery and vehicles. Even if there is no output fixed costs must be incurred, but for a time, as output expands, they remain the same.

Variable costs, on the other hand, are those costs which vary directly with output. They are the costs of the variable factors, e.g. operative labour, raw materials, fuel for running the machines, wear and tear on equipment. Where there is no output, variable costs are nil; as output increases so variable costs increase.

In practice it is difficult to draw an absolute line between fixed and variable costs: the difference really depends on the length of time involved. When current output is not profitable, the entrepreneur will have to contract production. At first overtime will cease; later, workers will be paid off. In time, more factors, e.g. salesmen, become variable, and if receipts still do not justify expenditure on them they too can be dismissed. A factor becomes variable when a decision has to be taken on whether it shall be replaced, for then its alternative uses have to be considered. Eventually machines need renewing; even they have become a variable cost. A decision may now be necessary to whether the business should continue.

The distinction between fixed and variable factors and costs is useful in two ways. First, in economic analysis it provides a means of distinguishing between differences in the conditions of supply which result from changes in the time period. The *short period* is defined as a period when there is at least one fixed factor. While, therefore, supply can be adjusted by labour working overtime and more raw materials being used, the time is too short for altering fixed plant and organisation. Thus the firm cannot achieve its best possible combination for a given output. In the *long period* all factors are variable; they can therefore be combined in the best possible way. Supply can now respond fully to a change in demand.

Second, as we shall see later, the distinction is fundamental when the firm is considering whether or not to continue producing. In the long period all costs of production, fixed and variable, must be covered if production is to continue. But in the short period fixed costs cannot be avoided by ceasing to produce; they have already been paid for, simply because it was necessary to have some 'lumpy' factors even before production could start. Only variable costs can be saved; and so, provided these are covered by receipts, the firm will continue to produce. Anything that it makes above such costs will help to recoup its fixed costs.

(e) Changes in costs as output expands

In discussing the law of diminishing returns we referred to quantities of factors and yields in physical terms. But in deciding how to maximise profit, the firm will be concerned with those quantities translated into money terms. It can then see directly the relationship between costs and receipts at different outputs and is thus able to decide what output will give the maximum profit (see Table 5.2). Our first task, therefore, is to consider how costs are likely to change as output increases. We shall assume perfect competition in buying factors of production – the demand of each firm is so small in relation to total supply that any change in demand will not directly affect the price of those factors.

In the short period there are, by definition, bound to be fixed factors. And when considering the law of diminishing returns we found that when a variable factor was added to a fixed factor the marginal product might increase for a time but would eventually diminish. How will this affect costs as output expands?

Let us assume that two factors are being used, one of them fixed. If each unit of the variable factor costs the same, but the output from additional units is increasing, the firm is obtaining an increasing amount of output for any given addition to expenditure. In other words the cost of each additional unit of output is falling as output expands. On the other hand, if the marginal product of the variable factor is diminishing, the cost of an additional unit of output is rising. This cost of an additional unit of output is known as *marginal cost* (MC).

The above conclusions are represented diagrammatically in Figure 5.2, where average product = total product of x units of the variable factor/x and average variable cost = total variable costs of n units of output/n.

Table 5.2   Costs, revenue and profits of Rollermowers (in £)

Output per week (units)	Fixed cost (FC)	Total Variable cost (TVC)	Total cost (TC)	Marginal cost (MC)	Average fixed cost (AFC)	Average variable cost (AVC)	Average total cost (ATC)	Total revenue (TR)	Profit, super-normal (TR−TC)
0	10,000								
				200					
10	10,000	2,000	12,000		1,000	200	1,200	4,500	−7,500
				140					
20	10,000	3,400	13,400		500	170	670	9,000	−4,400
				100					
30	10,000	4,400	14,400		333	146.7	480	13,500	−900
				100					
40	10,000	5,400	15,400		250	135	385	18,000	2,600
				135					
50	10,000	6,750	16,750		200	135	335	22,500	5,750
				185					
60	10,000	8,600	18,600		167	143.3	310	27,000	8,400
				240					
70	10,000	11,000	21,000		142.9	157.1	300	31,500	10,500
				300					
80	10,000	14,000	24,000		125	175	300	36,000	12,000
				390					
90	10,000	17,900	27,900		111.1	198.9	310	40,500	12,600
				510					
100	10,000	23,000	33,000		100	230	330	45,000	12,000
				660					
110	10,000	29,600	39,600		91.1	269.1	360	49,500	9,900
				840					
120	10,000	38,000	48,000		85	316.7	400	54,000	6,000

Notes:
(a) TC of n units = FC + VC of n units.
(b) MC is the extra cost involved in producing an additional unit of output. That is, MC of the nth unit = TC of n units – TC of n – 1 units. Here output is shown in units of 10, so that this difference in total costs has to be divided by 10.
(c) AFC of n units = $\dfrac{\text{FC}}{n}$.
(d) AVC of n units = $\dfrac{\text{TVC of } n \text{ units}}{n}$.
(e) ATC = $\dfrac{\text{TC of } n \text{ units}}{n}$.

(f) Costs schedules

Table 5.2 illustrates this relationship between output and costs. The figures, which have been kept as simple as possible, are for an imaginary firm, Rollermowers, manufacturer of lawnmowers. Fixed costs (FC) amount to £10,000, and, as variable factors are added, output expands. At first there is an increasing marginal product; as a result MC is falling. This has its effect on average total cost (ATC) until approximately 75 units are being produced. From then onwards, as the fixed factors are being worked more intensively, diminishing returns cause the ATC curve to rise. These figures can be plotted on a graph (Figure 5.3).

The following relationships between the curves should be noted:

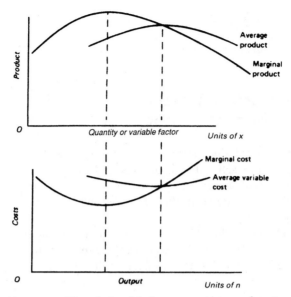

Figure 5.2 The relationship between returns and costs

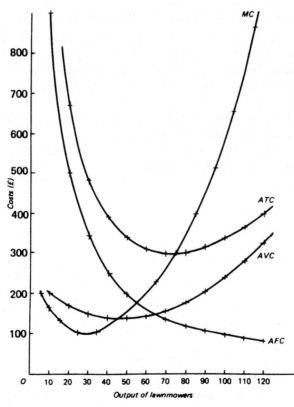

Figure 5.3 Cost curves

(i) AFC and AVC added vertically give ATC.

(ii) The MC curve cuts both the AVC and ATC curves when they are at a minimum, the same reason applying as in Table 5.1, note (d).

5.3 How much to produce: output of the firm under perfect competition

In order to ascertain whether a firm is maximising profits, we have to know (i) the price at which it can sell different outputs and the price at which it can buy different quantities of factors, and (ii) whether it is free to enter another industry where it can make higher profits. Both depend on the extent to which competition prevails.

First we shall assume that the conditions of 'perfect competition' – the highest form of competition – apply. Later we show how relaxing these conditions leads to imperfect competition, forms of which prevail in real life.

(a) The conditions necessary for perfect competition

For perfect competition to exist the following conditions must hold:

(i) A large number of relatively small sellers and buyers

If there are a large number of sellers relative to demand in the market, any one seller will know that, because he supplies so small a quantity of the total output, he can increase or decrease his output without having any significant effect on the market price of the product. In short he is a 'price-taker', and can sell any quantity at this price.

This is illustrated in Figure 5.4, where (a) shows market price *OP* determined by the demand for and supply of the goods of the industry as a whole. But the industry supply, we will assume, comes from a thousand producers, each of about the same size. Each producer therefore sells such a small proportion of the

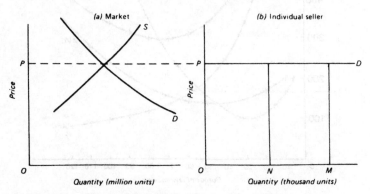

Figure 5.4   The firm's demand curve under perfect competition

total market supply that he can double his output from *ON* to *OM* or halve it from *OM* to *ON* without affecting the price – Figure 5.4b.

In other words, in perfect competition a seller is faced with an infinitely elastic demand curve for his product. If, in our example, he charges a higher price than *OP*, nobody will buy from him; if he charges less than *OP*, he will not be maximising his revenue, for he could have sold all his output at the higher price, *OP*.

In contrast, the producer in Figure 5.5b sells such a large proportion of the market supply that a change in his output affects the price he receives for his product. When he supplies *OM*, the price is *OP*. If he increases his supply to OM_1, the price falls to OP_1. Similarly, if he decreases his supply to OM_2, the price rises to OP_2. Alternatively a producer can decide on the price he charges, leaving it to the market to determine how much is sold at that price. But such a producer cannot fix both the price and quantity sold at the same time.

Similarly, on the buying side, purchasers of goods and of factors or production where there is perfect competition are faced with an infinitely elastic supply curve. For example, one producer can increase his demand for a factor of production but the price of the factor does not rise as a result (Figure 5.6a). Here the producer's demand is so small relative to the market supply that he can buy all the labour he requires at the prevailing market wage rate *OW*. On the other

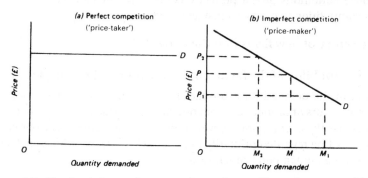

Figure 5.5   The firm's demand curve under perfect and imperfect competition

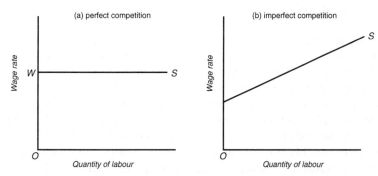

Figure 5.6   The supply of a factor under perfect and imperfect competition

hand, in (b) the producer employs such a large proportion of the market supply of labour that when he takes on more workers the wage rate rises.

(ii) Homogeneous product

Buyers must regard the product of one producer as being a perfect substitute for that of another, and purchase solely on the basis of price, switching to a competitor if one producer raises his price.

Such identity of product does not exist where there is a real or imaginary difference (e.g. a special wrapping or brand name) or where reasons other than price (e.g. goodwill) influence buyers. Here an individual producer can raise his price without necessarily losing all his customers. In short, product differentiation leads to some downward slope in the demand curve.

(iii) A perfect market, especially perfect knowledge of market conditions

There are two aspects of perfect knowledge:

 (i) sellers and buyers must know the prices being asked in other parts of the market, both product and factor, so that they can act accordingly;
(ii) in order to make free entry effective, a would-be producer must also know what profits are being made by existing producers.

The above conditions give a perfectly competitive market. For a situation of perfect competition to exist we must also have:

(iv) Free entry of new firms into the market

(v) Perfect mobility of the factors of production in the long period

A change in the demand for a product must, in the long period, result in the transfer of factors of production from one line of production to another.

In practice these conditions never apply simultaneously, and perfect competition must be regarded primarily as an analytical device which enables us to arrive at some fundamental conclusions.

(b) Maximising profit

Since the objective of the firm, we have assumed, is to maximise its profits, it will seek to produce that output where the difference between total revenue and total costs is greatest. The firm, therefore, will be concerned with two broad questions: (i) How much will it obtain by selling various quantities of its product? (ii) How much will it cost to produce these different quantities?

At first sight it may seem that maximum profit will occur at the minimum average cost output. But this is unlikely to be so. The real question which the entrepreneur will be continually asking is: 'If I produce another unit, will it cost me less or more than the extra revenue I shall receive from the sale of it?' That is, he concentrates his attention at the margin: if an extra unit of output is to be profitable, *marginal revenue* (the addition to total revenue received from it) must at least equal *marginal cost* (the cost of producing it).

Under perfect competition the firm will obtain the market price for its goods, whatever its output. In other words, marginal revenue (MR) equals price, with the price line horizontal (Figures 5.1 and 5.5). On the other hand, although under perfect competition the firm can buy increasing quantities of its factors at a given price, the MC curve eventually rises because of diminishing returns.

(c) The equilibrium output of Rollermowers

Let us return to our imaginary firm. Assume that the market price of mowers is £450. We can impose this MR curve on the cost curve diagram (Figure 5.7).

Now at any output where MR (price) is above MC, Rollermowers can increase profits by expanding output. Or, if MC is above MR, contracting output will increase profits. The equilibrium output, therefore, is where MR (price) equals MC, that is, 90 lawnmowers. Here average total cost is £310. Thus super-normal profit equals total receipts (£40,500) – total costs (£27,900) = £12,600 = shaded area *PDAC*.

But, for any output, current revenue must cover current costs. And while 'current revenue' is simply the number of goods currently produced times their price, 'current costs' depend as we have seen, on whether we are dealing with the short or the long period.

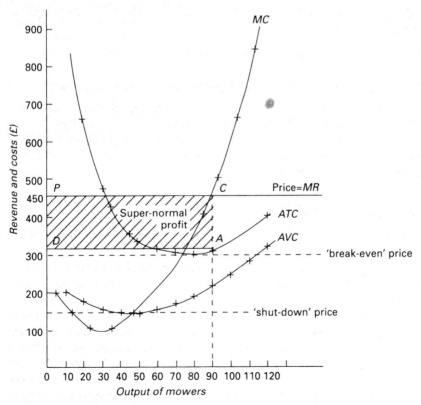

Figure 5.7 The equilibrium output of the firm under perfect competition

(d) The short-period 'shut-down' price

A firm will only *start* to produce if it expects total revenue to cover (i) the cost of fixed factors, (ii) the cost of variable factors, e.g. labour, raw materials, and (iii) normal profit.

We will imagine that the firm does think it can make a go of it. It buys highly specific machinery (fixed costs) which, we will assume for the sake of simplicity, has no value to any other firm, together with labour and raw materials (variable costs), and starts producing.

But as time goes by it finds that its original expectations are not being fulfilled. The price at which it can sell its good is lower than estimated. Although the cost of variable factors is being covered, the firm sees that, unless price rises the margin between the two is too small to provide sufficient cash to replace machines when they wear out. In other words the business as a whole will prove unprofitable.

But what will our firm save by stopping production forthwith? Obviously its variable costs, for these vary directly with output. But what of its machines, which, since they have no alternative use, have no resale price? These are fixed factors which have already been paid for, and ceasing to use them now cannot recoup past expenditure. Their opportunity cost is zero.

Consequently our firm takes a philosophic view of the situation. It has some perfectly good machines which, if used, will add nothing to costs. So, provided the cost of the variable factors is being covered, it goes on producing. Anything earned above such cost will help to recoup the cost of the fixed factors.

How can we tell if variable costs are being covered? Simply by looking at the AVC curve. If we take Rollermowers as an example, a price of £135 for a mower would just enable it to produce in the short period. Here MC would equal MR and, with an output of 45 units, TVC would just be covered. Any price lower than this, however, would mean that, for any output where MC = MR, total receipts (price times output) would be less than TVC (AVC times output). Rollermowers could not make a 'go' of it even in the short period; and so we can call £135 the 'shut-down' price.

(e) The firm's short-period supply curve

A firm's MC curve is its short-period supply curve. At any price below £135 per mower, Rollermowers will stop production, because TVC are not covered. At higher prices, however, it will produce an output where price equals MC, as follows:

Price (£)	Output (units)
135	45
185	55
240	65
300	75
390	85, and so on.

This schedule is graphed in Figure 5.8.

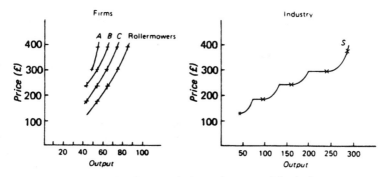

Figure 5.8 The short-period supply curve of the industry

5.4 The industry's supply curve

(a) The short-period supply curve

In the short period, no new firms can enter the industry because, by definition, they cannot obtain fixed factors. The supply curve of the industry, therefore, is obtained simply by adding the output of all existing firms at each given price.

Suppose, for the sake of simplicity, that the industry consists of four firms, the other three being less efficient than Rollermowers. Their outputs (starting from minimum AVC) are given under A, B and C in Table 5.3.

This is shown graphically in Figure 5.8. The MC curves of the four firms are summed horizontally to obtain the short-period supply curve of the industry. This rises from left to right, showing that more is supplied the higher the price.

It will be observed that the supply curve derived above is not smooth, but stepped. This is because we have taken only four firms. If there had been many firms, each differing only slightly in efficiency, we would have had a smoother curve.

(b) Supply in the long period

In the long period a firm will still produce where MR = MC, but total costs must be covered.

As regards the industry, however, any super-normal profits being made will attract new firms for these can now obtain plant. As a result, supply increases and the price of the product falls (in this case to £300), thereby eliminating super-normal profits. Moreover, competition forces all firms, both old and new, towards the most efficient size of 75 units producing capacity (Figure 5.9).

The above argument would produce a horizontal supply curve. In practice, however, it has to be modified. First, while there may be some external economies as the industry expands, there is a major diseconomy – higher rewards have to be paid to attract factors from other industries. Second, entrepreneurs are unlikely to be equally efficient in looking ahead when making their decisions, and some firms will always be doing better than others. The

Table 5.3 Short-period supply schedule

Price (£)	Output (units)			Rollermowers	Total
	Firm A	Firm B	Firm C		
135	–	–	–	45	45
185	–	–	45	55	100
240	–	45	55	65	165
300	50	55	65	75	245
390	55	65	75	85	280

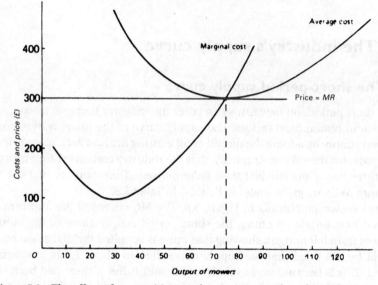

Figure 5.9 The effect of competition on the super-normal profits and output of Rollermowers

situation, therefore, is that even in the long period there is likely to be an upward-sloping supply curve. The extent to which this happens is indicated by elasticity of supply.

5.5 Elasticity of supply

(a) Definition

Consider Figure 5.10. For a rise in price from OP to OP_1, supply extends from OM to OM_1 with S_1 and to OM_2 with S_2. At price OP, therefore, S_2 is said to be more elastic than S_1.

More precisely, the elasticity of supply of a good at any price or at any output is the proportional change in the amount supplied in response to a small change in

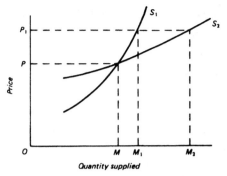

Figure 5.10   Elasticity of supply

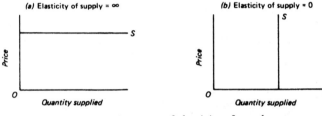

Figure 5.11   Extremes of elasticity of supply

price divided by the proportional change in price. In the supply schedule on p. 21, for instance, when the price of eggs rises from 10p to 12p supply expands from 32,000 to 40,000. Elasticity of supply is therefore equal to:

$$\frac{\dfrac{8}{32}}{\dfrac{2}{10}} = \frac{5}{4} = 1.25$$

As with elasticity of demand, we say that supply at a given price is elastic if elasticity is greater than 1, and that it is inelastic if elasticity is less than 1.
There are two significant limiting cases.

(i) Elasticity of supply equal to infinity

The main uses of this concept are: (1) where there is perfect competition in buying factors of production; and (2) where production takes place at constant cost. In both cases the supply the supply curve is horizontal – Figure 5.11a.

(ii) Supply absolutely inelastic

Here a good is fixed in supply whatever the price offered – Figure 5.11b. This applies to rare first editions and old masters, and by definition to fixed factors in the short period.

(b) Factors determining elasticity of supply

Elasticity of supply is determined by: (i) the period of time under consideration; (ii) the relationship between the individual firms' minimum-supply points; and (iii) the cost of attracting factors from alternative uses. We shall consider each in turn.

(i) Time

We distinguish three main periods:

(1) Momentary equilibrium
Here the supply is fixed, and elasticity of supply = 0. An example is Christmas trees on Christmas Eve. With many goods, some increase in supply can take place by drawing on stocks, utilising any spare capacity, or switching factors of production from one product to another (where a firm makes two or more different products).

(2) Short-period equilibrium
Usually varying supply requires a change in the factors of production employed. But this takes time – and the period differs for each factor. In the short period, as we have seen, it is possible to adjust supply only by altering the variable factors (raw materials, labour, etc.).

(3) Long-period equilibrium
Other factors – the fixed factors, e.g. land already sown and capital equipment – can be altered in the long period, allowing supply to adjust fully to a change in price. Thus elasticity is greater in the long period. For example, in Figure 5.10, S_1 could well represent the short-period supply curve, and S_2 the long.

(ii) The relationship between the firms' minimum-supply points

The supply curve is obtained by aggregating the supply of individual firms. If these firms each offer a supply to the market at more or less the same minimum price, supply will tend to be elastic at that price. Similarly, as price rises, the greater the number of firms coming in, the greater is the elasticity of supply.

(iii) The cost of attracting factors of production

In order to expand production additional factors have to be attracted from other industries. For an industry as a whole, this means that higher rewards will have to be paid. What we have to ask, therefore, is how much of a factor will be forthcoming in response to a given price rise. In other words, what is the elasticity of supply of factors of production? And, of greater significance, what influences determine this elasticity?

In answering this question we can first consider what happens when one particular industry, e.g. office-building, wishes to expand. Let us concentrate on one factor: labour. With increased demand for building labourers, wages rise. But they rise not only for the office-building industry but for all other industries employing such labourers – house-building, road-construction, public works, etc. How will it affect these industries?

First, they will try to substitute other factors, e.g. cement-mixers, bull-dozers, etc., for the labour which now costs more. Is such substitution physically possible? If so, is the supply of these alternative factors elastic, or will their prices rise sharply as demand increases? If physical substitution is fairly easy and the supply of alternative factors is elastic, it will mean that a small rise in wages will release much labour for the office-building industry.

Second, higher wages will lead to increased costs in building houses, constructing roads, etc. The supply curve of these products, therefore, moves to the left; and, the higher the proportion of wages to total costs, the further will it move. The extent to which this leads to a reduced production of these alternative goods, e.g. houses, will depend upon the elasticity of demand for them. If elasticity is high, the small rise in the price of houses will cause a considerable contraction of demand, and labour will be released for office-building. If, on the other hand, demand is inelastic, even a considerable rise in wages will have little effect on the output of houses, etc., and the increase in the supply of labour to office-building will be correspondingly small.

We see, therefore, that the two main influences affecting the elasticity of supply of a factor to a particular industry are (1) the extent to which other factors can be substituted, and (2) the elasticity of demand for the alternative goods it produces.

(c) Practical uses of the concept of elasticity of supply

(i) The elasticity of supply of a good is a major factor in determining how much its price will alter when there is a change in the conditions of demand

This can be seen by considering the likely effect on the price of cane sugar, in the short and long period, of an increase in the demand for sugar.

We can assume a fairly inelastic demand curve for sugar. The original price is OP (Figure 5.12). Demand then increases from D to D_1. The supply of cane sugar in the short run is inelastic, for supply can be expanded only by adding labour, fertilisers, etc. Price therefore increases to OP_1. But in the long period more land

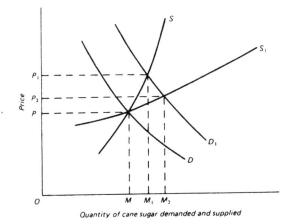

Figure 5.12 Changes in the price of cane sugar over time in response to a change in demand

can be planted with sugar-cane. Supply is now more elastic, and is represented by the curve S_1. The long-run price falls to OP_2.

(ii) The elasticity of supply is significant with regard to taxation

First, where the supply of a good is inelastic, the Chancellor of the Exchequer can impose a tax on the producer without its having a great effect on the amount of the good offered for sale. Suppose, for instance, that a man owns a field which is suitable only for sheep-grazing, and that the most any farmer will pay him for the use of this field is £10 a year, which the owner accepts. Now suppose that the government puts a tax of £5 a year on this type of land. This means that the owner will have to pay the tax out of his own pocket, for the farmer will pay no more, and the land cannot be put to any other use. In fact the government could tax almost all the rent away before it would make any difference to the number of sheep being grazed on it. However, if all the rent went on tax, the owner might leave the land standing idle (see p. 118).

Second, the relative elasticities of demand and supply determine the proportion of a selective indirect tax borne by the producer as compared with the consumer (see pp. 320–2).

QUESTIONS

1 Bearing in mind that MC is independent of the size of FC, will the equilibrium output of the firm be affected by:
  (a) a tax per unit of output?
  (b) a lump sum annual tax?

2 What four reasons can you advance to explain why the *long-period* supply curve of the industry should be upward-sloping?

Part III

The factors of production and their rewards

■ ☑ **6** The determination of factor rewards

Objectives

1 To identify the specific characteristic of a factor as a means of classification
2 To show how, given perfect competition, the reward of a factor is related to its productivity

6.1 Introduction

(a) Classification of factors of production

In order to examine the problems connected with employing resources it is helpful to classify them according to particular characteristics.

Land refers to the resources provided by nature, e.g. space, sunshine, rain and minerals, which are fixed in supply.

Labour refers to the effort, physical and mental, made by human beings in production. It is this 'human' element which distinguishes it from other factors, for it gives rise to problems regarding psychological attitudes and unemployment.

Capital as a factor of production consists of producer goods and stocks of consumer goods not yet in the hands of the consumer. While consumer goods directly satisfy consumers' wants, e.g. loaves, bicycles, TV sets, producer goods are only wanted for making consumer goods, e.g. buildings, machines, raw materials. Capital is treated as a separate factor of production in order to emphasise: (i) the increased production which results from using it, (ii) the sacrifice of present enjoyment which is necessary to obtain it (see Chapter 8), and (iii) the fluctuations of economic activity which may result from changes in its rate of accumulation (see Chapter 20).

Enterprise is the acceptance of the risks of uncertainty in production – risks which, as we saw earlier, cannot be insured against. They arise because the firm spends in advance on raw materials, labour and machines, and the extent to which such costs are covered depends on the demand for the product when it is sold. Tastes may have changed or a rival may be marketing the good at a lower price than anticipated. The reward for uncertainty-bearing is profit – unless it is negative: loss. Whoever accepts such a risk is a true entrepreneur – the farmer working on his own account, the person who buys ordinary shares in a company, or the citizen of a state, who ultimately has to bear any losses made by a nationalised industry.

(b) Sharing the national 'cake'

Factors of production co-operate together to produce the national product. How much of the cake each individual obtains depends upon (i) how much of the factors he owns, and (ii) the reward each factor receives.

Differences in individual incomes, therefore, depend upon both inequalities of ownership and inequalities in earnings. It is the latter which are the subject of this chapter.

(c) Factor rewards in a given industry, occupation or district

Here we are concerned solely with the reward to factors in a given industry, occupation or district. That is, we examine how the price of a factor service is determined in a particular market. Analysis by ordinary demand and supply curves is therefore possible. (Later, in Chapter 20, when we consider the economy as a whole, it is necessary to speak of labour, wages, capital, investment and the rate of interest in broad terms and to substitute a general (macro) approach for this particular micro analysis.)

6.2 The theoretical determination of factor rewards

The theory which follows applies to all resources. However, it is usually illustrated in terms of labour and the wage-rate, and we shall adopt this practice.

The wage-rate is the price of labour and, like other prices, it is determined in a free market by demand and supply.

(a) Demand

The demand for labour is made up of the individual demands of all the firms using it. It is a *derived demand* – the factor is not wanted for its own sake but simply for its contribution to the product it makes. The actual price which a firm is willing to pay for a worker depends upon the addition to receipts which will result.

We can be more precise by developing our analysis of the law of diminishing returns. Let us assume that (i) there is perfect competition in the market where the product is sold; (ii) there is perfect competition in buying labour – each firm is so small that it cannot, by varying its demand, alter the wage-rate which it has to pay; and (iii) in changing output, only the number of labourers employed is varied, other factors remaining fixed in supply.

The analysis of the law of diminishing returns (Chapter 5) was conducted in terms of physical yields – bags of potatoes. But when engaging labour, the firm is more interested in what the product sells for. What it asks, therefore, is how much will total receipts increase if an additional worker is employed? The value of this extra contribution is known as the *marginal revenue product* (MRP).

The MRP depends not only on the marginal physical product, but also on the price at which the product sells. Under perfect competition, the producer can sell any quantity at a given price. Hence the MRP is equal to the marginal physical product times the price of the product. Thus, by taking the marginal *physical* products of Table 5.1 and assuming that potatoes sell at £10 per bag, we can arrive at the MRP. For example, when 2 labourers are employed the marginal physical product is 14 bags, which at £10 a bag yields a total revenue of £140, and so on.

The farmer in our example will employ an extra worker so long as the MRP exceeds the cost, that is, the wage-rate. Thus, if the wage-rate were £130 per week, he would engage 6 workers because the value of the product of the sixth man was £130, and this just covered his wages. If fewer men, say 5, were employed, he could add more to receipts than to costs by taking on another worker, for the MRP of £150 would exceed the wage-rate (£130). On the other hand, if 7 men were employed, the farmer would be paying the seventh man £10 more than he contributed to receipts.

Of course it might be questioned whether the firm can always estimate the MRP of a factor of production. Thus, with certain workers, such as clerks, teachers and policemen, there is no definite physical product. How then can their marginal physical product, and thus the marginal revenue product, be measured? The answer is simply that it cannot be – but that does not alter the fact that, in practice, a firm behaving rationally and not 'empire-building' does proceed to engage workers as through it can so estimate.

The MRP at different wage-rates, therefore, gives the demand curve of the individual firm for labour (Figure 6.1). The *industry's demand curve* is the sum of the demands of the individual firms (curve *D*, Figure 6.2). This would be a simple horizontal addition if the price of the product remained unchanged. But it is much more realistic to assume that, as firms engage more labour, the extra output will lead to a fall in the price of the product. The result will be that the industry's demand curve for a factor will fall more steeply than the curve obtained by a straightforward addition of firms' marginal-revenue-product curves.

(b) Supply

The supply of labour will depend upon:

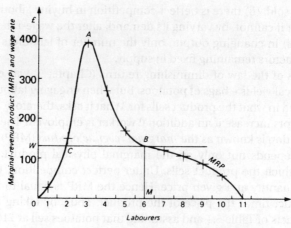

Figure 6.1 The firm's demand curve for labour

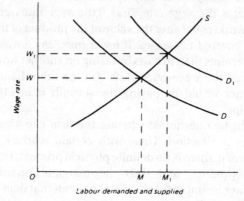

Figure 6.2 The determination of the price of a factor

(i) The response of existing labour to a higher wage rate

In the short period, an industry may find that a wage increase may result in *less* labour being supplied, the higher income enabling workers to enjoy more leisure, as happened in coal-mining. In the long period, however, higher wages should attract labour from other industries, occupations or localities, so that the long-period supply curve follows the shape of the *S* curve in Figure 6.2.

(ii) The cost of attracting workers from alternative uses or localities

In the long period, a higher wage will attract labour from other industries and occupations. The extent to which a given wage increase attracts workers depends upon the elasticity of demand for the products in these alternative sources. If demand is inelastic, higher wages can be offered to hold on to labour, and thus the supply of labour will expand little in response to the wage rise (see p. 107).

(iii) The mobility of labour

In the theoretical long period, a higher wage rate should attract labour from alternative uses or localities. But, because labour experiences particular difficulties in moving, the 'long period' is delayed indefinitely (see Chapter 7).

(c) Demand, supply, and the wage-rate

The reward of a factor, in this case the wage-rate, is determined by the interaction of demand and supply. Thus, in Figure 6.2, with demand curve D and supply curve S the wage rate is OW.

The wage-rate can rise through an increase in the MRP or a decrease in the supply of labour to the market. The MRP can rise through an increase in physical productivity or through a higher selling price of the product. Both would lead to a shift in the demand curve to the right, say from D to D_1 (Figure 6.2). As a result, the wage rate rises to OW_1 and the number of men employed increases from OM to OM_1. Higher labour productivity leads to higher employment, other things being equal. Similarly, a decrease in the supply of labour to a particular industry would have the effect of raising the wage-rate, but with fewer employed.

(d) The effect of imperfect competition on factor rewards

The above discussion assumed that there was perfect competition both in the sale of the product and in engaging factors of production. But in the real world such competition may not exist. If, for instance, the firm is selling its product under imperfect competition, the price received will fall as output increases. This means that the marginal revenue product of an extra labourer will be less than the marginal physical product multiplied by its price, since the lower price applies to all previous units produced. Similarly, a firm may be the only employer of a factor in a locality, so that, as this firm demands more, the factor price rises not only for the additional factor but for all previous factors. Thus the marginal cost of employing such factors is higher than their market price. In both instances the demand for the factor will be less than it would have been had competition prevailed.

Finally trade unions may exert a monopoly power in the sale of labour, a subject discussed in Chapter 7.

QUESTIONS

1 Upon what two elements does revenue productivity depend?

2 Given: (i) perfect competition; (ii) a 50 kg bag of potatoes sells for £10.
   (a) Complete the MRP schedule.
   (b) Calculate how many labourers will be employed when the wage-rate is £130 per week.

Number of labourers employed (1)	Marginal physical product (50 kg bags potatoes) (2)	Marginal-revenue product (£) (3)
1	2	
2	14	
3	38	
4	26	
5	15	
6	13	
7	12	
8	10	
9	8	

■ ☒ 7 Labour and wages

Objectives

1 To emphasise the special characteristics of labour
2 To consider different methods of rewarding workers
3 To explain why labour tends to be immobile
4 To analyse the determination of the wage–rate under perfect competition
5 To examine the strength of trade unions in collective bargaining
6 To suggest reasons for government interest in the process of wage negotiation

7.1 The workforce of the UK

Table 7.1 shows that in 1997 the UK had a workforce of nearly 26.5 million in employment. In addition, there were 1.5 million workers unemployed (as measured by the number of people claiming unemployment-related benefits), giving a total working population of around 28 million.

This represents an increase over the last 20 years of 2 million, of whom 1.5 million have been women. This influx of women has been brought about by the expansion of the service industries (Table 7.2) and the increase in part-time working. 45 per cent of women workers are part-time, compared with only 8 per cent of men, and today the activity rate of all women 16–60 years of age is 66 per cent, higher than all other countries except for Japan and the Scandinavian countries.

Over the last 20 years self-employment has also increased by 1.25 million (65 per cent), largely through the encouragement of the government. It occurs mostly in agriculture, construction, distribution, catering and professional services.

As regards the industrial distribution of employees (Table 7.2) the most significant change has been the increase in the service industries. This, however, is merely a reflection of a long-term trend. Thus, between 1975 and 1997 services increased from 52 per cent of all employees to 76 per cent, while in comparison and over the same period manufacturing has declined from 36 per cent to 18 per cent.

The basic reason for these changes bas been the increase in real income. As a result spending moves to those goods having a high income elasticity of demand.

Table 7.1 Workforce in employment in the UK (000s)

	1986	1991	1997
Employees in employment	21,377	22,250	22,791
Self-employed	2,792	3,413	3,338
HM Forces	322	297	210
Government-supported trainees	226	353	168
Total workforce in employment	24,717	26,313	26,507

Table 7.2 The industrial distribution of employees

	1991		1997	
	Thousands	*per cent*	*Thousands*	*per cent*
Service industries	16,187	72.8	17,263	75.8
Manufacturing	4,319	19.4	4,111	18.0
Other industries, including energy, water supply, agriculture and construction	1,744	7.8	1,417	6.2
Total all industries	22,250	100	22,791	100

Source: Annual Abstract of Statistics.

But the decrease in manufacturing has also been brought about by the uncompetitiveness of UK products in world markets, largely owing to the inability to contain wage costs relative to competitors. Technical advances and increased mechanisation also contributed (as also the decline in energy and agriculture). In contrast, services are more labour intensive although some – such as financial services, computers and telecommunications – have economised in labour employment.

7.2 The nature of the labour force

(a) Why labour is treated as a separate factor of production

Labour is the effort, both physical and mental, made by human beings in production. It is the 'human' element which is important.

Because people have feelings and emotions their response to economic forces is different from that of machines. First, whereas a machine which proves profitable can be reproduced fairly easily and quickly, the overall supply of labour does not depend upon its earnings. Other factors are more important in deciding how many children parents have. Second, the effort of labour is not determined solely by the reward offered. The method of payment may affect effort, while raising wages may result in less work being offered. Above all, a contented worker will produce more than an unhappy one; thus job satisfaction or loyalty to a firm, rather than a high rate of pay, may be decisive in inducing an employee to work overtime. Third, people have to go where the work is. But labour does not move readily, either occupationally or geographically, in response to job opportunities or the offer of a higher reward. Often such 'immobility' results from strong human contacts. Fourth, workers can combine together in trade unions. Finally, if unemployed for long periods, workers deteriorate physically and mentally.

Both firms and government must have policies which take account of these special characteristics. Training schemes are essential to improve the skill of workers and thus their productivity. Firms must pay particular attention to psychological and social factors in order to motivate workers, e.g. by profit-sharing schemes. Furthermore, they must endeavour to co-operate with the workers' trade-union representatives. Above all, firms have to comply with the constraints imposed by government policy (see pp. 111–12).

(b) The overall supply of labour

By the supply of labour we mean the number of hours of work offered. There are two separate problems to be considered: the total overall supply of labour available, and the supply of labour to a particular industry, occupation or locality. Here we consider the first.

The total supply of labour in an economy depends upon:

(i) The size of the population

The size of the population sets an obvious limit to the total supply of labour. But while it is influenced by economic factors, e.g. through their effect on the birth rate and immigration, it is doubtful, especially in more advanced economies, whether they are of paramount importance.

(ii) The proportion of the population which works

In Britain, the proportion of the population which works is 50 per cent of the total population (somewhat higher than most European countries). It is determined chiefly by:

(i) The numbers within the 16–65 age group.
(ii) The activity rates within this group, especially as regards young people and female workers. The tendency over the last twenty years has been for a higher proportion of young people to remain in further education, thus reducing their activity rate. On the other hand, higher proportion of women are now entering the working population. The expansion of the service and light

manufacturing industries has provided increased job opportunities for women, while the changed attitude to women workers is reflected in the Equal Pay Act 1970 and the Sex Discrimination Act 1975. Above all, the smaller family, the availability of crêches and school dinners, the development of part-time employment opportunities and new labour-saving domestic appliances have allowed married women to work.

(iii) The extent to which people over retiring age continue to work, something which is largely influenced by the level of pensions.

(iv) The numbers who can live on unearned incomes.

(v) The employment opportunities available – the tendency being for the working population to contract in a depression (mainly through withdrawal of married women).

(iii) The amount of work offered by each individual labourer

Higher rates of pay usually induce a person to work overtime, the increased reward encouraging a substitution of work for leisure. But this is not always so. In addition to the substitution effect, there is also the income effect, and the latter may outweigh the former (see p. 34). A higher wage rate enables the worker to maintain the existing material standard of living with less work, and extra leisure may be preferred to more goods. Thus while it is usual to depict the supply curve of labour as in Figure 7.1a, it is possible that, in the short period, it may follow the shape of the curve in Figure 7.1b.

Nevertheless, as we shall see, more significant than the overall supply of labour are the obstacles to mobility which divide up the labour market.

7.3 Methods of rewarding labour

(a) The wage-rate and earnings

Some people are self-employed – window-cleaners, plumbers, solicitors, etc. As such they are really entrepreneurs, securing the rewards when demand is high but accepting the risks of being unemployed or working for a low return.

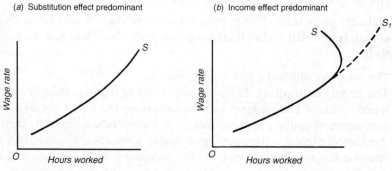

Figure 7.1 The relationship between the wage-rate and hours worked

Nevertheless, most workers contract out of risk, accepting a wage which is received whether or not the product of their labour is sold – although some element of risk-bearing may be incorporated in the wage agreement, e.g. by commission payments, bonus schemes, profit-sharing arrangements and the profit-related pay scheme introduced in 1986.

In what follows, reference will be mainly to the *wage-rate* – the sum of money which an employer contracts to pay a worker in return for services rendered. This definition includes salaries as well as wages, and makes no distinction between time- and piece-rates.

Earnings are what the worker actually receives in his pay-packet (his 'take-home' pay) *plus* deductions which have been made for national insurance, income tax, superannuation, etc. In practice earnings over a period often exceed the agreed wage-rate, additions being received for overtime working, piece-rates and bonus payments.

Where the nature of the work allows workers to be paid on a piece-rate basis as an alternative to time-rates, the firm has to consider their respective merits.

(b) Time-rates

Time-rates are more satisfactory than piece-rates where:

(i) A high quality of work is essential, e.g. computer programming.
(ii) The work cannot be speeded up, e.g. bus driving, milking cows.
(iii) There is no standard type of work, e.g. car repairs.
(iv) Care has to be taken of delicate machinery, e.g. hospital medical tests.
(v) Output cannot be easily measured, e.g. teaching, nursing.
(vi) Working long hours may undermine health, e.g. laundry work.
(vii) The labour is by nature a fixed factor which has to be engaged whatever the output, e.g. secretarial and selling staff.
(viii) Periods of temporary idleness necessarily occur, e.g. repair work.

On the other hand, time-rates have certain disadvantages:

(i) There is a lack of incentive for better workers.
(ii) Supervision of workers is usually necessary.
(iii) Agreements can be undermined by working to rule and 'go-slow' tactics.

(c) Piece-rates

Where output is both measurable and more or less proportionate to the amount of effort expended, piece-rates are possible. It is not essential that each individual worker's output can be measured exactly. So long as the output of the group can be assessed the worker can share in the group's earnings.

The advantages of piece-rates are:

(i) Effort is stimulated.
(ii) The more efficient workers obtain higher rewards.
(iii) Constant supervision and irksome time-keeping can be eliminated.
(iv) Interest is added to dull, routine work.

(v) Workers can proceed at their own pace.

(vi) A team spirit is developed where workers operate in small groups.

(vii) Workers are encouraged to suggest methods of improving production.

(viii) The employer's costing calculations are simplified.

(ix) Output is increased, and the more intensive use of capital equipment spreads overheads.

We see, therefore, that piece-rates have advantages for both employee and employer. Moreover, the lower prices which result benefit the community as a whole. Nevertheless, for the following reasons they are often disliked by trade unions:

(i) Workers may over-exert themselves.

(ii) Where piece-rates have to be varied according to local conditions or different circumstances, e.g. capital per employee, negotiations for a national wage-rate are difficult.

(iii) Variations in piece-rates from one place to another undermine union solidarity.

(iv) The union may lose control over the supply of labour, and this makes it difficult to take strike action or to apportion work in periods of unemployment.

(v) Piece-rates are subject to misunderstanding, e.g. a firm which instals a better machine may be accused of cutting the rate if it does not attribute all the increased output to the effort of labour.

(vi) Workers may resist being shifted from tasks in which they have acquired dexterity (and which therefore produce high piece earnings) even though the current needs of the factory organisation require such a transfer. Thus employers find that piece-rates lead to a loss of control over their employees, and many prefer to pay high time-rates to avoid this.

(d) Combined time- and piece-rates

When deciding the basis of the wage-rate, both employees and employers want certain guarantees. Workers have a minimum standard of living to maintain, and they desire protection against variations in output which lie outside their control, e.g. weather conditions. On the other hand, employers providing expensive equipment must ensure that it is used for a minimum period of time. Thus piece-rates are usually incorporated in a wider contract which provides for some basic wage and a stipulated minimum number of hours.

7.4 The determination of the wage-rate in a particular industry, occupation or locality

In theory, the wage-rate in a particular industry, occupation or locality will be determined as shown in Chapter 6 by demand and supply. Demand is shown by the MRP curve. Its position can shift with changes in: (a) the price of the final product, (b) the price of substitute or complementary factors, and (c) the productivity of labour (e.g. owing to a change in the amount of capital supplied). Supply depends upon the wage-rate offered compared with that in other industries.

In practice this merely provides a first approach. In the real world the actual wage-rate and conditions of employment are influenced by immobilities which split up supply, worker's psychological attitudes, imperfect competition in both the product and labour markets, the strength of the relevant trade union and government intervention.

Workers' resistance to a cut in the money wage-rate, their desire to preserve time-honoured wage differentials and notions regarding the status of their occupation all serve to prevent 'market clearing' with the workers preferring unemployment at least in the short run.

(a) The supply of labour

The main weakness of the MRP theory is that, in concentrating on what determines the demand for labour, it underplays conditions on the supply side.

The supply of labour to an industry depends on:

(i) The response of existing labour to a higher wage-rate

In the short period an industry may find that the supply curve of labour corresponds to curve S in Figure 7.1b. This was once the case in coal-mining, where, as wages have increased, miners preferred to enjoy more leisure. In the long period, however, higher wage-rates should attract labour from other industries, with the result that the long-period supply curve follows the dashed line, S_1.

(ii) The cost of attracting labour from alternative uses or localities

Unless there is unemployment, the supply of labour in a particular use can be expanded only by increasing the wage offered. This will attract labour of the same or of a nearly similar kind from other industries, occupations or localities. The extent to which this happens depends upon the elasticity of demand for the products in these alternative uses. If demand is inelastic, higher wages can be offered to hold on to labour, and thus the supply of labour will expand little in response to the wage rise (see p. 109).

(iii) The mobility of labour

A rise in the price of a factor should attract it from alternative uses or localities. This may take time, but it is achieved in the 'long period'. With labour, however, there are particular obstacles to moving, and these may mean that the long period is delayed indefinitely. Such obstacles provide frictions to the full and efficient operation of the price system.

Take the wages of plasterers, for instance. The demand for plasterers depends upon the price at which houses sell (a derived demand) and the productivity of plasterers. The supply of plasterers is the number offering their services at different wage-rates. This will vary with the length of time under consideration.

But in the long period more will be forthcoming the higher the wage-rate, since they will be attracted from lower-paid areas or occupations.

For example, if the conditions of demand and supply are different in different parts of the country, the wages of plasterers will differ. If there were perfect geographical mobility, plasterers would move from low-wage districts to high-wage districts, until eventually a common equilibrium wage-rate would be established. Similarly, where different wage-rates exist for different occupations, perfect occupational mobility would eventually eliminate these differences.

In practice, geographical and occupational mobility are not perfect, so that differences in wage-rates persist. A typist earns more in London than in Norwich; a doctor earns more than a docker. In short, immobilities result in the labour market's being divided into a number of separate smaller markets according to locality and occupation.

Thus differences in the wage-rates between occupations, or between localities for the same occupation, can frequently be explained by differences in the supply rather than by differences in demand. We are dealing not with one market for labour but with a number of fairly distinct markets.

(b) The immobility of labour

What are these major barriers? What are the causes of the 'immobility of labour', as it is usually termed?

Workers may be required: (i) to shift from one industry to another; (ii) to change occupation; (iii) to move home to a different district. Often conditions dictate that all three types of change take place at the same time, but this is not necessarily so. Each presents its own obstacles to workers in their efforts to change jobs.

(i) Obstacles between industries

Provided that it does not involve a change of occupation or district, a worker can usually move job from one industry to another fairly easily. Secretaries, lorry drivers and porters, for example, are found in most industries. But middle-aged and older workers may experience difficulty. Prejudice or tradition in certain industries may also prove to be obstacles. Women drivers, for instance, would find it difficult to become taxi drivers in London. Moreover, a worker's loyalty to a particular firm may prevent him or her from looking for another job, even though a cut in wages has been suffered (though obviously this does not apply if the worker is made redundant).

(ii) Obstacles to a change of occupation

In changing occupations, obstacles may be encountered in both moving out of the old occupation or in entering a new one. They arise because:

  (i) a high natural ability is required in certain occupations;
  (ii) training may be costly and take time;

(iii) stringent entry conditions are sometimes prescribed by trade unions and professional associations;

(iv) the new job may be repugnant; and, equally, some occupations, e.g. the Church, art and acting, are so pleasant that workers are not drawn into another occupation by the offer of a higher wage rate;

(v) through a high division of labour, only limited skills have been acquired;

(vi) workers may be reluctant or too old to learn a new job;

(vii) workers may prefer to remain unemployed rather than accept a wage below a 'recognised minimum' in an alternative occupation;

(viii) in spite of prohibiting legislation, there is discrimination on account of sex, colour, social class or religion;

(ix) workers are ignorant of wage-rates and opportunities in other occupations.

Of the above, the greatest obstacle to occupational mobility is natural ability. In this respect it should be noted that there can be more mobility between occupations, e.g. storeman and clerk, requiring the same level of innate ability than between doctors and dockers, where there are marked differences in the natural ability and training required. The first is sometimes termed 'horizontal' occupational mobility; the second, where there are non-competing groups of workers, 'vertical' mobility.

(iii) Obstacles to a change of district

When it comes to moving from one part of the country to another, workers have to overcome both real and psychological obstacles. These include:

(i) the costs of moving, which to many workers represent a considerable capital sum and are incurred even if workers own their own homes;

(ii) the difficulty of securing accommodation elsewhere on comparable terms, particularly for council and rent-controlled tenants but also for owner-occupiers having to move into the more expensive housing in southern England;

(iii) social ties of friends, clubs, Church, etc.;

(iv) family ties, such as the children's education;

(v) imperfect knowledge of vacancies or wages paid in other localities;

(vi) prejudice against certain parts of the country, e.g. people at present generally prefer to live in the south-east rather than in the industrial north.

Such immobility of labour means that wage-rates can often be more easily explained by supply conditions rather than by demand and is one of the major causes of unemployment. In Chapter 23, we consider some of the ways in which the government tries to reduce occupational and geographical immobility.

Imperfection in the labour market also arises where one firm is the major employer in a locality (see above). But mainly it is due to trade unions, which (through the closed shop) can establish what is virtually a monopoly in the supply of a given type of labour. We therefore analyse the economic background to trade-union activity with reference to its strength in negotiating wage increases.

7.5 Trade unions: the process of collective bargaining

It would be wrong to regard trade unions primarily as a disruptive influence in the economy. For one thing there must be a means by which workers can communicate with employers. For another, by making the worker more contented, they enhance productivity. We can summarise their most important functions as: (i) improving working conditions; (ii) providing educational, social and legal benefits for members; (iii) improving standards of work; (iv) obtaining pay increases; and (v) co-operating with governments in order to secure a workable economic policy and to improve working and living conditions generally. The remainder of this chapter is concerned with (iv).

(a) The process of collective bargaining

Collective bargaining is the settlement of conditions of employment by employers negotiating with the workers' trade unions. For its smooth working, certain conditions should be fulfilled. First, it must be pursued with good sense on both sides. This is enhanced where the industry has a tradition of good labour relations and where there is some accepted objective measure to which wage-rates can be linked (e.g. the Retail Prices Index, wage-rates paid in similar trades, the level of profits in the industry). Second, both sides should be represented by strong organisations. Where all employers are linked in an association, there is no fear of outsiders stealing a march by negotiating independent wage bargains, while, if the union can speak for all its members, employers know an agreement will be honoured. Unofficial stoppages damage the union's reputation, and to avoid them there must be regular contact between employer and union and prompt investigation of grievances on the shop-floor. Third, there must be an understood procedure for settling disputes. While this must not be so prolonged as to fray patience, it should exhaust all possibilities of reaching agreement before a strike or lock-out is called.

In short the procedure of collective bargaining covers (i) negotiation and (ii) the settlement of disputes.

(i) Negotiation

Broadly speaking the machinery for negotiation falls into three categories:

(1) Voluntary negotiation

Generally, the government has left it to the unions and employers' organisations to work out their own procedures, and today voluntary machinery covers nearly 48 per cent of the insured workers of the UK. Because union organisation varies, the recognised procedure differs between industries and trades.

(2) Joint Industrial Councils

Most industries have some national joint council or committee which, without outside assistance, thrashes out agreements. Usually it follows the system of Joint Industrial Councils, composed of representatives of employers and workers in the industry. These consider regularly such matters as the better use of the practical knowledge and experience of the work-people, general principles governing the conditions of employment, means of ensuring workers the greatest possible security of earnings and employment, methods of fixing and adjusting earnings, technical education and training, industrial research, improvement of processes and proposed legislation affecting the industry. Although Joint Industrial Councils are sponsored by the government, they are not forced upon any industry, and some important industries, such as iron and steel, engineering, shipbuilding and cotton, which had already developed their own procedure for negotiation, have not formed Joint Industrial Councils. Nevertheless, the tendency today is towards wage-rates being determined by local rather than by national agreements. Thus the government has not accepted the EU's Directive on Works Councils.

(3) Government appointed wage-fixing boards

In 1909 the government set up over 20 Trade Boards (renamed Wages Councils) to fix minimum wage-rates for the 'sweated' trades, such as retailing, catering, hair dressing and clothing manufacture. These were abolished in 1993.

However, the Agricultural Wages Board survived, largely because it was liked by employers. It consists of employers' and workers' representatives and some independent members, including the chairman. Each year it fixes minimum wage rates and holiday entitlements, and its orders are enforceable by law.

(ii) Settlement of disputes

Where the negotiating machinery fails to produce an agreement, it is a help if agreed procedures exist for ending the deadlock. Three methods can be employed: conciliation, arbitration or special inquiry.

(1) Conciliation

In 1974 the Secretary of State for Employment set up an *independent* Advisory, Conciliation and Arbitration Service (ACAS), controlled by a council whose members are experienced in industrial relations. When efforts to obtain settlement of a dispute through normal procedures have failed, ACAS can provide conciliation if the parties concerned agree.

(2) Arbitration

ACAS can, at the joint request of the parties to a dispute, appoint single arbitrators or boards of arbitration chosen from a register of people experienced in industrial relations to determine differences on the basis of agreed terms of reference.

Alternatively the Terms and Conditions of Employment Act 1959 allows claims that a particular employer is not observing the terms or conditions of employment established for the industry to be referred compulsorily to an industrial court for a legally binding award.

(3) Inquiry and investigation

The Secretary of State for Employment has legal power to inquire into the causes and circumstances of any trade dispute and, if he thinks fit, to appoint a court of inquiry with power to call for evidence. Such action, however, is chiefly a means of informing parliament and the public of the facts and causes of a major dispute, and is taken only when no agreed settlement seems possible.

The minister's power of inquiry also allows for less formal action, by way of setting up committees of investigation, when the public interest is not so general.

Neither a court of inquiry nor a committee of investigation is a conciliation or arbitration body, but both may make recommendations upon which a reasonable settlement of a dispute can be based.

(b) Trade union arguments for wage increases

A trade union is likely to base its claim for a wage increase on one or more of the following grounds.

(i) A rise in the cost of living

Because inflation reduces their real incomes, workers seek an increase in money wages. But difficulties have arisen. First, wage demands could become an annual event. Second, they were often pitched higher than the rate of inflation, thereby fuelling further inflation (see Chapter 22).

(ii) A higher wage-rate in comparable grades and occupations

The trouble here is that wage differentials are often ingrained in workers' attitudes, whereas they should reflect changes in the demand for and supply of particular types of labour. Furthermore, it is often difficult, indeed impossible, to assess 'comparability', e.g. between a social worker and a computer programmer. On the other hand, if there is a shortage of nurses in national health hospitals owing to the higher pay offered in private hospitals, there is a strong argument for increasing the wage of the state-paid nurse.

(iii) Profits have increased

Trade unions feel that they should share in extra profits and here they may be in a strong position (see pp. 109–11).

(iv) Productivity has increased

Where output per worker is increasing, there is a rise in the MRP curve, and firms can grant a wage increase (see below). But there may be difficulty in apportioning the increased productivity between the workers' efforts and investment in new machines, research, etc. Capital has to receive its share if investment is to continue.

(c) Trade union bargaining limitations

The question must now be answered – how, and to what extent, can trade unions secure increases in the wage rate for their members in conditions of free collective bargaining? We shall assume that the trade union is a 'closed shop' with 100 per cent membership, making it virtually a monopolist in selling its particular type of labour.

Broadly speaking, there are three ways in which a trade union can secure a wage increase:

(i) It can support measures which will increase the demand for labour

An increase in the demand for labour will come about if the MRP curve rises, either through an improvement in the physical productivity of the workers or through an increase in the price of the product.

The situation is illustrated in Figure 7.2. As marginal revenue productivity rises from MRP to MRP_1, wages of existing workers, ON, rise from OW to OW_1. Alternatively, if there were unemployment, extra men, NN_1, could be employed at the previous wage-rate.

(ii) It can restrict the supply of labour, allowing members to compete freely in fixing remuneration with employers

A trade union or professional association may be sufficiently strong to restrict entry by apprenticeship regulations (e.g. plumbers and electricians) or high professional qualifications (e.g. solicitors, doctors, accountants and surveyors). While a minimum wage-rate or scale of fees may be suggested, many members work on their own account and these are left to negotiate their own rewards.

We can therefore analyse this method of securing a wage increase by the simple demand-and-supply approach (Figure 7.3). If the trade union reduces the supply of workers in an occupation from S to S_1, the wage-rate rises from OW to OW_1.

(iii) It can fix a minimum wage-rate

Where wages are raised by restricting entry, the trade union does not have to worry about unemployed members. It works simply on the principle that, assuming demand remains unchanged, greater scarcity leads to a higher reward.

Most trade unions, however, are faced with a more difficult problem. While they may secure higher wage-rates for their members, their success may be double-edged if, as a result, many members are sacked. What we really have to ask, therefore, is: *Under what conditions can a trade union obtain higher wages for its members without decreasing the numbers employed?*

This means that we have to consider conditions of competition in both the product and factor markets. There are four main combinations:

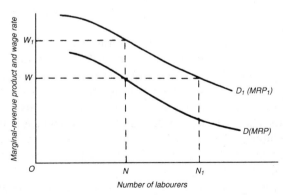

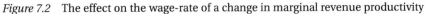

Figure 7.2 The effect on the wage-rate of a change in marginal revenue productivity

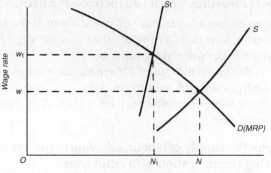

Figure 7.3 The effect on the wage-rate of trade-union restriction of the supply of labour

(1) Perfect competition in both selling the product and buying labour

In the short period, even if there is perfect competition, a firm may be making super-normal profits. Here a strong trade union could, by threatening to withhold all its labour, force the employer to increase wages to the point where the whole of his super-normal profits disappear.

But this could not be permanent. The long-period equilibrium position is one in which there are no super-normal profits and the wage rate is equal to the MRP. A higher wage will represent a rise in costs. Some employers will now be forced out of business (see p. 81) and remaining firms will have to reduce their demand for labour until once again the MC of labour (the wage rate) is equal to the marginal-revenue product. Thus, in Figure 7.3 we will assume that *OW* is the original wage rate fixed by competition and *ON* the number of men employed – the trade-union membership. Suppose the trade union stipulates a minimum wage of OW_1. In the long-period, employment will then be reduced to ON_1. Given a downward-sloping MRP curve, this will always be true. Where there is perfect competition both in selling the product and in buying labour, a trade union can successfully negotiate an increase in wages only if there has been increased productivity; any increase without this will merely lead to members becoming unemployed.

The amount of unemployment resulting from such a rise in wages depends upon the elasticity of demand for labour. This will vary according to:

(i) *The physical possibility of substituting alternative factors.* As the price of one factor rises, other factors become relatively cheaper and the tendency is to substitute them for the dearer factor. Thus, if wages rise, firms try to install more machinery and labour-saving devices; that is, they replace labour by capital. But because different factors are imperfect substitutes for each other, such substitution is limited physically. Indeed, if they have to be employed in fairly fixed proportions, little or no substitution is possible. As we saw in Chapter 5, the extent to which substitution can take place largely determines the elasticity of demand.

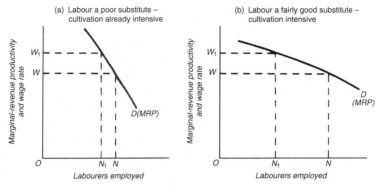

Figure 7.4   The relationship of substitutability between labour and land and numbers employed

The degree of substitution is shown by the slope of the MRP curve. Where labour is added to another factor, but is a poor substitute for it, marginal productivity falls steeply; where it is a fairly good substitute, marginal productivity falls more gently. Thus in Figure 7.4a, a labour is not a good substitute for land, and marginal-revenue productivity falls steeply as the number of men employed increases. Demand for labour is therefore inelastic, and a wage rise of WW_1 leads to only NN_1 extra men being unemployed. Compare this with Figure 7.4b, where labour and land are better substitutes. Here the same wage rise leads to a much larger number of men being unemployed.

It should be noted that, since the possibility of substitution increases over time, the longer the period under consideration, the greater will be the change in the labour force.

(ii) *The elasticity of supply of alternative factors.* Under conditions of perfect competition, the cost of a factor to an individual firm will not rise as the firm's demand for that factor increases (see p. 91). But when we are analysing a rise in the wage-rate of the workers of an *industry*, we must recognise that the whole industry will now be demanding the alternative factors in order to substitute them for labour. This increased demand will affect the price of the alternative factors, and a higher price will have to be paid in order to attract a greater supply. This increase in price of the alternative factors also limits the extent to which substitution is carried out. Thus if the supply of the alternative factor is perfectly elastic, only the physical considerations referred to above will affect the demand for it; if, on the other hand, supply is inelastic, then it is likely that the quick rise in its price will soon make it uneconomic to substitute it for labour. Once again, the elasticity of supply of the alternative factors will be greater the longer the period of time under consideration.

Where unemployed labour exists, two conditions prevail that make it difficult for a trade union to obtain a wage increase without reducing the level of employment: (i) a high degree of substitution existing between the union labour and the alternative factor, unemployed labour, particularly if the work performed is unskilled; (ii) an infinite elasticity of supply of the alternative factor, unemployed labour, at least for a time. Hence trade unions are relatively weaker in periods of unemployment.

(iii) *The proportion of labour costs to total costs.* The proportion of labour costs to total costs has two effects. First, if labour costs form only a small percentage of total costs, demand for labour will tend to be inelastic, for there is less urgency in seeking substitutes (see p. 37). Second, if labour costs form a small percentage of total costs, as in steel production, a rise in wages will produce only a small movement of the supply curve of the product to the left. The opposite applies in each case, e.g. with government services, which are labour intensive.

(iv) *The elasticity of demand for the final product.* The effect of a rise in the wage-rate will be to decrease the supply of a good at each price; that is, the supply curve moves to the left. Hence the market price of the good rises. We have to ask, therefore: 'How much will the demand for the good contract as a result of this rise in price?' Once again we are back to the practical application of elasticity of demand.

If demand is elastic (D_{el}), the quantity of the good demanded will contract considerably, from OM to OM_1 (Figure 7.5). This will mean a large reduction in the numbers employed. On the other hand, if demand is inelastic (D_{inel}), there will be no great contraction in the quantity demanded – only to OM_2. Here people are willing to pay a higher price for the good (OP_2), and this will cover the increase in wages. In other words, the marginal-revenue productivity of labour has risen.

Elasticity of demand depends mainly on the availability of substitutes. Thus demand in export markets is usually more elastic than in the home market, for with the former there are often many competing alternative sources of supply from firms in other countries. Consequently, if an industry sells a high percentage of its output abroad, e.g. electronic equipment and aero engines, the trade union is limited in its ability to secure a wage increase.

(2) Imperfect competition
If there is imperfect competition in selling the product or in hiring labour, the firm is likely to be making super-normal profits. Here it may be possible for

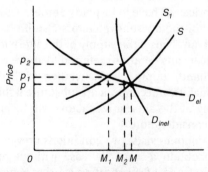

Figure 7.5 The extent to which demand for the product contracts as a result of a wage increase

the trade union to wring increased wages from the employer without loss of employment. Since it is a monopolist in the supply of labour, the union can insist that the firm shall employ *all* or none of its members at the new wage rate. Thus the firm may be forced to employ workers beyond the point where the MRP = MC. The difference would come from super-normal profits, with the firm working on the principle that 'half a loaf is better than no bread'.

In these circumstances there is a whole range of possible wage-rates between the minimum which workers will accept and the maximum which employers are prepared to give rather than lose all their labour. The success of the trade union will depend, therefore, upon (i) the extent to which it can maintain its monopoly position by preventing employers from engaging blacklegs – non-union workers, or other substitute labour – and (ii) the bargaining ability of its leaders relative to that of the employers. On the one side, the union leaders have to estimate how high they can push the wage rate without employers allowing a strike to take place; on the other, the employers must judge the lowest rate acceptable without a strike. As each is by no means certain of the other's strength, bluff will play a large part in the negotiations. Such factors as a large order-book for the firm's products, costly equipment's standing idle, a wealthy strike fund or increased profits, will obviously strengthen the union's hand. Considerations which could enlist public sympathy are a rise in the cost of living, a higher wage paid elsewhere in comparable occupations and an increase in productivity. Should a strike actually take place, it is usually because of mis-judgement by one side; it is doubtful whether either really gains in the long run by strike action. Thus the strike is a form of 'blood-letting', allowing one or both sides to reassess the position before further negotiations take place.

7.6 The government and wages

(a) Influence on wage determination

The government influences the wage-rate through: (i) its general minimum-wage regulation and its Agricultural Wages Board (see p. 105), (ii) the legal protection it affords to workers with regard to conditions of work, e.g. stipulating a written statement of the conditions of employment, prohibiting discrimination on account of sex or race, protecting employees against unfair dismissal, providing for redundancy payments and regulating conditions for health and safety at work; (iii) its efforts to break down illogicalities, etc. sanctioned by custom; (iv) guidelines for wage settlements which it may lay down from time to time in its efforts to combat inflation.

(b) Curbing trade-union power

With one main exception trade unions are similar to other pressure groups which seek to influence the government to further the interests of their particular causes. The exception is that trade unions can reinforce political means by economic sanctions. Moreover, in the case of key industries, just a small group of workers may, by strikes, go-slow tactics or working-to-rule, disrupt the whole economy.

Successive Conservative governments 1979–97 took the view, therefore, that to achieve the major role of stabilising the economy they could not allow policies to be undermined by trade unions misusing their current extensive legal advantages. Thus a succession of legislation progressively removed trade-union privileges.

In brief, the main changes effected are:

(i) Trade unions may be fined and their assets seized for offences committed by them or their members.
(ii) Before industrial action can be taken, approval must be obtained by means of a fully-postal ballot of its members, to be independently scrutinised.
(iii) Picketing by employees must be confined to their place of work.
(iv) Sympathetic strikes by workers not directly involved in the particular strike are illegal.
(v) A majority of members of a trade union must approve by secret ballot: (i) the setting up or continuance of a closed shop; (ii) any use of funds for any political purposes; (iii) the election of executive committees at least every five years.
(vi) Employers must be provided with at least 7 days' notice of official industrial action.
(vii) Union subscriptions can only be deducted from employees' pay with their express consent.

QUESTIONS

1 What makes the market for labour so imperfect?
2 Use demand-and-supply analysis to explain why a skilled worker earns more than an unskilled worker.
3 What are the disadvantages of tying wages to the cost of living?
4 What are the difficulties in applying the marginal-productivity theory to the determination of wage rates?

▣ Ⓥ 8 Capital, land and entrepreneurship

Objectives

1 To underline the importance of 'capital' in production
2 To explain why the return to 'land' typifies that of all fixed factors
3 To indicate the practical applications of the concept of 'economic rent'
4 To emphasise the distinction between normal and 'super-normal' profit in the functioning of the market economy

8.1 Capital

(a) What is capital?

A schoolteacher earns, say, £400 a week. She also has £1,300 in the National Savings Bank, yielding her £52 per annum interest (£1 a week). We can say, therefore, that her total income is £401 a week, or £10,852 per annum; her capital assets are £1,300.

Thus we see that, whereas *income* is a *flow of wealth* over a *period of time*, *capital* is a *stock of wealth* existing at any one *moment of time*.

This broad definition of capital, however, has slightly different meanings when used by different people. The ordinary individual, when speaking of his capital, would include his money assets, holdings of securities, and house, and possibly many durable goods, such as his car, television set, camcorder, etc. (sometimes referred to as 'consumer's capital'). The businessman would count not only his real assets (such as his factory, machinery, land and stocks of goods) but also any money reserves ('liquid capital') held in the bank, and titles to wealth (such as share certificates, tax-reserve certificates and government bonds).

But the economist considers capital chiefly as a form of wealth which contributes to production. In other words, he is concerned with capital as a *factor of production* – that is, as something real and not merely pieces of paper. It is the factory and machines, not the share certificates (the individual's entitlement to a part of the assets), which are vital to him.

This has two effects. First, in defining capital, he concentrates on producer goods and any stocks of finished consumer goods not yet in the hands of the final consumer. Second, in calculating the 'national capital', he has to be careful to avoid double-counting. Titles to capital – shares, bonds, savings certificates,

National Savings, Treasury Bills and other government securities – must be excluded. Share certificates merely represent the factories, machinery, etc., which have already been counted. Government debt refers to few real assets, for most has been expended on shell, ships, and aircraft in previous wars. The only exception regarding titles to wealth is where a share or bond is held by a foreign national, or conversely, where a British national holds a share or bond representing an asset in a foreign country. We then have to subtract the former and add the latter when calculating national capital. Foreign shares or bonds held by British nationals, for example, can always be sold to increase our real resources.

Naturally, 'social capital' (roads, schools, hospitals, municipal buildings, etc.) which belongs to the community at large is just as much capital as factories, offices, etc. And, in order to be consistent, owner-occupied houses have to be included, for they must be treated in the same way as houses owned by property companies.

(b) Capital as a factor of production

When the economist refers to 'capital', it is usually in the sense of *wealth which has been made by man for the production of further wealth*. This is because capital plays such an important part in increasing production and therefore in improving living standards. It is in this sense that the term is used from now on.

Increased production occurs because capital – tools, machines, irrigation works, communications, etc. – greatly assists people in their work. Indeed, with modern electronic equipment, machines often take over the work itself. As the use of capital increases, there are three possible gains. First, more current goods can be produced. Between 1987 and 1996 the output of agriculture increased by 19 per cent, although the number of employees *fell* by 21 per cent. There was thus an increased output per worker, due largely to more efficient machines and improved techniques resulting from capital investment in research. Second, instead of simply producing more current goods, people can be released to produce new goods. And, third, people can, as an alternative to more goods, enjoy increased leisure.

(c) The accumulation of capital

If capital is so important in adding to our well-being, why do we not have more of it? The answer is simply that we can accumulate capital only by postponing current consumption. In everyday language, more jam tomorrow means less jam today. The accumulation of capital represents an opportunity cost over time – consumption now or greater consumption later? A simple example will make this clear.

Suppose a peasant farmer has been tilling the ground with a primitive spade. By working 12 hours a day he can cultivate one hectare in a year. Obviously, if he had a plough which could be drawn by his oxen, it would help him considerably. How can be obtain it? Three ways are open to him:

(i) He could reduce the land he cultivates to $\frac{3}{4}$ hectare, using the 3 hours saved on tilling to make the plough.

(ii) He could reduce his leisure and sleeping time from 12 to 8 hours, using the extra 4 hours to make the plough.

(iii) He could decide not to consume some of the produce already harvested, exchanging it instead for the plough.

Whichever method is chosen entails some present sacrifice. With (i) and (iii) the farmer has less to eat, lowering his standard of living. With (ii) he has to go without some leisure. In short he has to draw in his belt or work harder. But the reward comes when he has the plough: with 12 hours' work a day he can now cultivate 2 hectares, thereby doubling his standard of living.

One other point emerges from this illustration: the more fertile his land, the easier it is for the farmer to increase his income. If, because of the poor type of soil, 16 hours were required to dig his 2 hectares, our farmer would have found it more difficult to obtain his plough. He could not reduce his consumption below the subsistence level; nor could he go without essential sleep. Similarly, countries with extremely low living-standards are in a vicious circle which can only be broken by economic aid from richer countries or by enforced five-year plans which ruthlessly cut current consumption, as in China and Cuba.

(d) Maintaining capital intact

Naturally our farmer will have to devote time to repairing the plough. So long as it is capable of cultivating 2 hectares, we can say that capital is being 'maintained intact'. If it is replaced by a better plough which allows more hectares to be cultivated, or another plough is added, capital is being 'accumulated'. Where capital is not maintained, it is being 'run down' or 'depreciated'.

In practice it is unusual for the same person to devote so much time to producing consumer goods and so much to the production of capital. Instead, production is organised by applying the principle of the division of labour – some people specialise in consumer goods and others in capital goods.

8.2 Interest

Investment, that is adding to capital goods or stocks, usually first involves obtaining liquid capital. Interest, expressed as a rate, is the price which has to be paid for this liquid capital. What we shall examine here is the rate of interest which has to be paid for liquid capital in a *particular* use or industry. We shall *not* discuss what determines the *general* level of interest in the economy.

The *demand for liquid capital* arises because it is necessary or advantageous to use capital in production. The farmer who sows his seed in the autumn and harvests his crop in the summer is using capital in the form of seed. Similarly, a manufacturer needs capital in the form of a factory and machines because it is cheaper to produce in this way.

Now, as we saw when examining the farmer's decision to make a plough, the accumulation of capital can come about only by postponing present consumption. This can be done directly by the producer himself. The farmer could have obtained his seed by putting aside a part of the previous year's harvest; the manufacturer can buy his machines by retaining, rather than distributing, some of his profits. However, such retentions may be inadequate for the capital needed. In this case, funds might be borrowed from other people who have saved.

The actual demand of the farmer or manufacturer would depend upon the marginal revenue productivity of such capital and the rate of interest. For instance, if the addition to profit which a farmer thinks will be received during the year for adding an extra ton of fertiliser costing £100 is £120, he would be willing to borrow the money for the fertiliser so long as the interest he had to pay was not more than £20 – that is, 20 per cent. The 'marginal-revenue-productivity-of-capital' curve will show the different amounts of capital which the farmer will find it profitable to borrow at different rates of interest.

The sum of the demand curves for liquid capital from all firms in an industry gives the demand curve for the industry, though some allowance should be made for a fall in the price of the good produced by the capital equipment (see p. 91).

The *supply* of liquid funds for a particular use can only be obtained by bidding them away from alternative uses. How much has to be paid for a given quantity relative to other uses will depend upon: (i) whether lenders consider more or less risk is involved; (ii) the period of the loan – people prefer to lend for a short period rather than a long one; and (iii) the elasticity of demand for other products employing capital.

Generally speaking, however, we can expect more liquid capital to be forthcoming the higher the rate of interest offered. We therefore have an upward-sloping supply curve, and the market rate of interest is fixed by the interaction of the demand and supply curves (as in Figure 6.2).

Once again, however, we must point out that this is only a partial explanation of the determination of a rate of interest. It does not tell us why, for instance, £10 million of liquid capital should be forthcoming at 10 per cent rather than 6 per cent or 14 per cent. This will depend upon the general level of interest rates. Today the short-term rate at least is decided by the Bank of England (see p. 287).

8.3 Land and rent

(a) The determination of 'commercial rent'

To the economist, the terms 'land' and 'rent' have a special meaning. This is just as well, for in everyday speech each can imply different things. Thus, if I buy land for farming it will probably include buildings, fences, a water supply and a drainage system all of which are really capital. Similarly, I can rent things other than land – a house, a television set, a telephone, building equipment, shooting rights, etc. Rent in this sense simply means a periodic payment for the use of something. It can be termed 'commercial rent'.

Usually, however, rent does refer to payment for the use of a piece of land, and before we consider 'land' and 'rent' in their special economic sense, we must ask what determines how much rent is paid to a landlord.

The problem is similar to the determination of the return on any factor service. The demand for land depends on its marginal revenue productivity, and the curve slopes downwards from left to right for the reasons given in Chapter 6.2. On the supply side, land, like labour, can usually be put to alternative uses – building factories or houses, growing wheat or barley, raising cattle or sheep, and so on. A given piece of land will be transferred to its most profitable use. If, for instance, the price of cattle rises and that of wheat falls, some land will be transferred from arable to pasture farming. Thus the supply curve for land in a particular use slopes upwards from left to right. The interaction of the demand and supply curves will give the rent actually paid (as in Figure 6.2).

Of course, this assumes (i) that the landlord can vary the rent charged any time the demand for and supply of his particular type of land alters, and (ii) that land can be transferred fairly quickly to a different use. The first assumption is complicated by the fact that rents are usually fixed for a period of years. Only when the contract expires is the landlord free to adjust the rent. The second assumption implies that we are concerned only with the long period in our analysis. But what of the short period, when land is a fixed factor? An analysis of this situation is basically what we are concerned with in the remainder of this chapter.

(b) Ricardo's views on 'land' and 'rent'

To explain the special meaning which economists today give to the terms 'land' and 'rent', we have to examine the views of Ricardo, an early-nineteenth-century economist. He was concerned not with the rent paid to land for a particular purpose, but with the rent paid to land as a whole. Moreover, he was referring to land in the economist's sense as the resources provided freely by nature (see p. 89) and as such, its total supply was fixed.

In this respect, he argued, land was different from the other factors of production, labour and capital, where more would be supplied the higher the price and, if no price at all were offered, there would be no supply. But with land as a whole – in the sense of space and natural resources – the same amount is available whatever the price offered. An increase in price cannot bring about an expansion of supply; and if the price fell to zero the same amount would still be available. Thus land as a whole has no supply price.

The return to land, therefore, was merely a 'residual' – the difference between, on the one hand, what was received for the product, and, on the other, the payments of wages and interest to labour and capital respectively. If the price received for the product was high, there would be more left over as rent; if the price was low, there would be less for rent. Rent did not determine the price of the good produced; instead, the opposite was true – rent was determined by price.

(c) The nature of the return to a fixed factor

Although there were certain blind spots in Ricardo's exposition of what determined price, he did point out an essential truth – that the return to a factor fixed in supply (that is, where supply is absolutely inelastic) will vary directly with variations in the price of the good produced by it. We can illustrate this more clearly by a simple example.

Let us assume: (i) a given plot of land on which only potatoes can be grown; (ii) that only land and labour are necessary to grow potatoes; and (iii) that the supply of labour for growing potatoes is perfectly elastic because only a small proportion of the total labour force is required.

The return to this plot of land will depend entirely on the price of potatoes. This can be seen from Figure 8.1. When the marginal revenue product of labour is shown by the curve QN, at a wage of OP, OM men are employed. The value of the total product is $OMNQ$; the wage-bill is $OMNP$ and the return of the plot of land PNQ. If now the price of potatoes increases, the marginal-revenue product of labour rises to Q_1N_1. OM_1 men are now employed at a wage-bill of OM_1N_1P. (Each worker still receives the same wage, OP, because the supply of this type of labour is perfectly elastic). But the return to the given plot of land has increased to PN_1Q_1. The opposite would apply if the price of potatoes fell.

Certain practical conclusions follow from the above analysis:

(i) Because the plot of land will grow only potatoes, it will be cultivated so long as the value of the total product is sufficient to pay the wage-bill. In other words, at the lower price a lump-sum tax on the plot up to QPN could be levied without affecting the output. This is the theoretical basis of the often-proposed tax on land.

(ii) The return to land as we have analysed it above – rent in its economic sense – is purely a surplus. It arose because, by definition, our plot of land was confined to one particular use – growing potatoes. The supply of this land offered for sale or hire will not be affected by a price, simply because

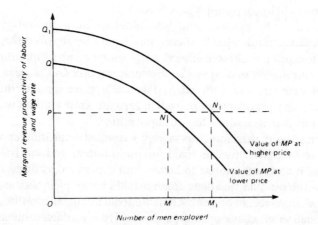

Figure 8.1   The effect of the price of a product on the rent of land

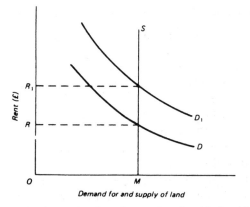

Figure 8.2   The determination of rent when land is fixed in supply

nobody has any other use for it. In short, it has no opportunity or transfer cost.

(iii) Once land has been built on, it is largely specific to a given use, and the return to the land and building will be dependent on future demand.

(iv) Because land is really space, it is impossible to increase the area of sites in city centers except by building upwards, e.g. as in Oxford Street and the City of London. Such fixity of supply means that rent is largely determined by current demand. Thus in Figure 8.2 it is assumed that the supply of land is fixed at *OM*.

This means that the rent is determined by demand: an increase from D to D_1 raises rent from *OR* to OR_1. For instance, rents in Oxford Street depend upon the demand for shops there (which in its turn depends upon people's spending) and rents in the City of London depend on the demand for offices three (which in turn depend upon the level of business activity).

(d) Economic rent

Economists have generalised Ricardo's concept of land to cover all factors which are fixed in supply. 'Economic rent' is the term used to describe *the earnings of any factor over and above its supply price.* Put in another way, it is any surplus over its transfer earnings – what it could obtain in its next most profitable use (its 'opportunity cost', in our earlier terminology). How this idea can be applied generally will now be explained.

The actual rate of return to a factor is the price per period of time at which it is selling its services. For example, the return to a plasterer is his wage, say £360 per week. But what is the opportunity cost? Simply what has to be paid to retain it in its present use – that is, sufficient to keep it from going to the best alternative use. Take our plasterer, for instance. His next-best occupation may simply be plasterer's labourer, earning £180 per week. He would offer his services as a plasterer, therefore, at anything above £180 per week.

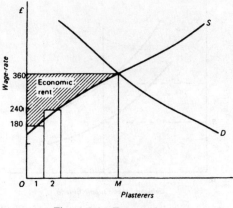

Figure 8.3 Economic rent

A second plasterer, however, may be a competent bricklayer, and as such earn £240 per week. He will only supply his services as a plasterer, therefore, if at least £240 per week is offered. And so we could go on. The supply curve of plasterers to the industry is thus an 'opportunity cost' curve (Figure 8.3).

If in Figure 8.3 we now insert the demand curve, we can obtain the current wage-rate to the industry, £360, when *OM* plasterers will be employed. But all plasterers receive this wage-rate. Thus the first plasterer receives an economic rent of £180, the second £120, and so on. The total economic rent received by plasterers as a whole is shown by the shaded area.

(e) What determines the size of economic rent?

The size of economic rent earned by a particular type of factor depends, on the one hand, on demand and, on the other, on the elasticity of supply of that factor and how the particular type of factor is defined.

(i) The elasticity of supply

Elasticity of supply is determined largely by the period of time under consideration and by immobilities, some of which cannot be eliminated even in the long period. Both will affect economic rent.

Let us assume that, in the short period, the supply of plasterers is fixed: there is insufficient time for them to move into alternative occupations or for others to move in. In short, there is no alternative occupation – they can either work as plasterers or not at all. Thus all their earnings are economic rent – Figure 8.4a.

In the long period, however, other occupations can be trained as plasterers, and existing plasterers can move elsewhere. Sufficient has to be paid – the opportunity cost – to retain plasterers. Thus we have a long-period supply curve of plasterers, and economic rent is smaller (Figure 8.4b).

If the supply of plasterers became perfectly elastic, economic rent would disappear (Figure 8.4c). Thus economic rent depends upon a less than perfectly elastic supply curve to the industry.

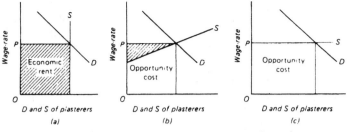

Figure 8.4 Economic rent and elasticity of supply

Sometimes the degree of immobility between different uses or occupations persists indefinitely. Building sites for offices in the City of London, for instance, earn rents far in excess of what they could obtain in their best alternative use, say for houses. Simply because such sites are very limited in supply, competition for office accommodation has forced up the rents of these sites far beyond the possible price which houses could offer. A large part of their earnings, therefore, is 'economic rent'.

Occasionally, too, we refer to the 'rent of ability'. Many footballers, pop singers, film stars, barristers and surgeons have talents which, to all intents and purposes, are unique, for they cannot be duplicated by training others. Their high earnings, therefore, are almost wholly in the nature of 'economic rent'.

(ii) The definition of an 'occupation', etc.

If we adopt a wide definition of our factor, e.g. land as a whole, the distinction is between employing it or idleness, and thus the whole of its earnings is economic rent. This is what Ricardo had in mind.

If, however, our definition is narrower, e.g. covering only land for a particular use, such as growing wheat, then the opportunity cost (e.g. growing barley) will be larger and the economic rent smaller. Similarly, we could distinguish between cabinet-makers and carpenters, surgeons and doctors, and so on. Each would give a smaller 'economic rent' than if the distinction were simply between cabinet-makers and labourers, surgeons and nurses, etc.

(f) Quasi-rent

For fixed factors, particularly capital equipment, what the firm has to pay to retain them will vary according to the period of time.

In the short period, capital equipment is, by definition, fixed in supply. There is no transfer price. More capital equipment cannot be added; nor can existing equipment be diminished. The firm will continue to work its capital equipment so long as total earnings just cover the cost of variable factors (see Chapter 5). Any earnings above variable costs will be in the nature of a residual which helps towards the cost of the fixed factors. The size of this residual depends upon the price at which the product sells.

This can be seen immediately if we refer back to Figure 5.7. Were the demand for mowers to increase, the price would rise, say to £600, and production would be expanded to the point where once again price equaled marginal cost – that is, to 100 units. The increased cost of such production would be equal to the increase in total cost – that is, £5,100. But total receipts would have increased by £19,500, and so the fixed factors earn an additional return – the increase in 'super-normal profit', equal to £14,400.

As time passes, however, we move into the long period. If the product has been selling at a high price, the high return to the capital equipment will induce firms to instal additional equipment. On the other hand, if the price of the product was low, existing capital equipment will either be transferred to its next most profitable use or, when it wears out, simply not be replaced. In the long period, therefore, earnings of fixed factors are, under perfect competition, equal to their transfer cost: economic rent is eliminated.

To distinguish between economic rent which is more or less permanent and that which disappears over time, the latter is often referred to as 'quasi-rent'. It is not a true rent, for the high return earned by such factors leads to an increase in their supply, and this eliminates the economic rent they earn. True rent refers only to factors which are fixed in supply; even if their earnings are high, identical factors are not forthcoming, and so economic rent persists.

8.4 Entrepreneurship

(a) The identity of entrepreneurship and risk-bearing

For production to take place, resources must be brought together and set to work. Whoever undertakes this task is often described as 'the entrepreneur'. Usually, however, economists give a narrower meaning to the term.

Organising production can be broken down into two parts. First, there is the task of co-ordination – setting the resources to work. Second, there is accepting the risk of buying factors to produce goods which will only be sold in the future – when receipts may not cover costs.

In practice it is not always easy to separate co-ordination and risk. A farmer, for instance, not only manages and runs his farm, but also accepts the risk involved in deciding what to produce. On the other hand, in a joint-stock company most co-ordination is left to a paid board of directors, with a manager under them. Here the risks of the business are borne by the ordinary shareholders. With a public sector agency, such as the Forestry Commission, they are carried by the taxpayers. Neither take a part in running the business, except remotely.

The function of co-ordination, therefore, can be fulfilled by a paid manager. In this respect, management is simply an exceptionally highly skilled form of labour. Thus we narrow our concept of enterprise to 'bearing those risks of the business associated with ownership'.

(b) The nature of risks

A business is always open to the risk of fire, accidents, burglary, storm damage, etc. But these risks are calculable. A mathematician can work out, for instance, the chances of a building's catching fire during the year. While he cannot say which building will be destroyed, he knows that on average, say, one out of every 10,000 will be. Such risks, therefore, can be insured against. They are then reduced to a normal cost – what the firm has to pay to contract out of the risk involved.

Certain risks, however, cannot be calculated according to the law of averages. Nobody, for instance, can forecast with certainty how many cold drinks will be sold in Britain next summer. That will depend on the weather. Similarly, it might be thought that a new 'mini' car will sell well. But again, there is a chance that it will not. The risk that demand will be different from that estimated cannot be reduced to a mathematical probability. Such a risk, therefore, cannot be insured against; it must be accepted by those persons whose money is tied up in producing goods for an uncertain demand.

These uninsurable risks are inherent in a dynamic economy. Modern methods of production take time. When an entrepreneur engages resources, therefore, it is an act of faith – faith in his estimate of the demand for the product some time ahead. But demand can never be completely certain. People have freedom of choice, and their tastes may change. Many of the factors affecting demand fluctuate even over a relatively short period of time. It is similar on the supply side. Techniques do not stand still; new methods discovered by a rival may mean that, by the time a firm's product comes on the market, it is undersold by a cheaper or better substitute.

Thus there is always some degree of uncertainty, and this involves risk. It is a risk which must be shouldered by those who back with their money the decision as to what shall be produced. The true entrepreneurs, therefore, are those who accept the risks of *uncertainty-bearing*.

8.5 Profit

(a) How profit differs in nature from other rewards

The reward of uncertainty-bearing is 'profit'. But profit differs from the earnings of other factors. First, it may be negative. Whereas wages, rent and interest are paid as part of a contract at the time of hiring, profits are received in the future, and then only if expected demand materialises. Thus its size is uncertain. Where the entrepreneur has been far too optimistic, a loss is made. Second, profit fluctuates more than other rewards, for it feels the immediate impact of booms and slumps. In a boom, profits rise faster than wages, while in a slump they fall more severely. Third, unlike wages, interest and commercial rent, which are contractual and certain payments, profit is simply a residual and variable.

(b) Differences in the meaning of the term 'profit'

It is essential to distinguish four different concepts of 'profit'.

(i) Profit in its everyday meaning

To the accountant, profit means simply the difference between total receipts and total costs (see p. 71). But, because the economist defines cost in terms of alternatives forgone, he would amend this idea of profit by deducting, first, the return which would have been received on capital had it been used elsewhere, and second, the value of the entrepreneur's skill in the best alternative line of business (see also p. 72).

(ii) Normal profit under perfect competition

Because uncertainty cannot be eliminated from a dynamic economy, there must be a return to induce people to bear uncertainty. This is true even in the long period. Thus there must be a rate of profit – the price which equates the demand for and supply of entrepreneurship. In the long period under perfect competition, any rent element from profit is eliminated. We then have normal profit – the cost which has to be met if the supply of uncertainty-bearing is to be maintained.

Two modifications should be noted. First, industries differ as regards the uncertainty involved. Where fashions or techniques change frequently, for instance, uncertainty is greater. Entrepreneurs in such riskier enterprises, therefore, require a higher level of normal profit. Second, the elimination of the rent element in profit in the long period is only possible if one assumes that entrepreneurs of equal ability are available. In practice this is not so. Thus there will always be some entrepreneurs earning a rent of ability (super-normal profit) even in the long period, simply because their forecast and decisions are more accurate.

(iii) Super-normal profit

Under perfect competition the entrepreneur is able to make super-normal profit for a period because new firms cannot enter the industry. Certain factors such as key workers and machines are for a time fixed in supply, and entrepreneurs already possessing them will make super-normal profit. In others words such profit is really the return to fixed factors in the short period; it is the 'quasi-rent' earned by such factors.

(iv) Monopoly profit

With monopoly, competitors can be excluded because certain factors, e.g. diamond-mines, know-how, patents and copyrights, are controlled by the monopolist (see Chapter 10). Even in the long period, competitors cannot engage such factors, and so super-normal profits persist. The profits of the monopolist, therefore, are closer to economic rent than to quasi-rent.

(c) The role of profit in the market economy

'Profit' tends to be an emotive word, and firms which make large profits are often frowned upon. But usually there is little justification for this, since it is through profits – and losses – that the market economy works. We must emphasise, however, that we are discussing only profits under competitive conditions. But, given such conditions, profit fulfills the following functions:

(i) Normal profit induces people to accept the risks of uncertainty

Because uncertainty is implicit in a dynamic economy, a reward – normal profit – is essential for entrepreneurs to undertake production. Thus normal profit is a cost, as essential as the payment of wages. The level will vary with the industry; thus it will be higher for oil exploration than for selling petrol.

(ii) Super-normal profit indicates whether an industry should expand or contract

When a firm produces a good which proves to be popular with consumers, it probably makes super-normal profit. This indicates that output should be expanded. On the other hand losses show that consumers do not want the good, and production should contract.

(iii) Super-normal profit encourages firms to increase production

Profits not only indicate that consumers want more of a good; they are also the inducement to firms to produce those goods. As we saw in Chapter 5, super-normal profits act as the spur for existing firms to increase capacity and for other firms to enter the industry. On the other hand, when losses are being incurred, firms go out of production and the industry contracts. Thus losses are as important as profits in the operation of the market economy.

(iv) Super-normal profit provides the resources for expansion

An industry making super-normal profit can secure the factors necessary to expand. First, profits can be ploughed back, while shareholders will respond to requests for further capital, usually through rights issues. New firms can enter the industry, because investors will subscribe to a company intending to operate where the level of profits is relatively high. Second, profits allow expanding firms to offer higher rewards to attract factors. In this way resources are moved according to the wishes of consumers.

(v) Super-normal profit encourages research, innovation and exploration

Research, e.g. for new drugs, and exploration, e.g. for oil, carry a high risk of failure and therefore of wasted capital expenditure. But the possibility of high returns if successful induces firms to engage in research, especially if new developments are protected for a period from competitors by patents.

(vi) Profits ensure that production is carried on by the most efficient firms

In a competitive industry the firm making the largest profit is the one whose costs are lowest. It will have an incentive to expand production and, if necessary, can afford to pay more for factors to do so. Less-efficient firms must copy its methods to retain factors. In any case the increased output of the more efficient firm will eventually lower the price of the product. As a result inefficient firms make losses: profits have become negative.

To sum up, profits and losses are the means by which the process of natural selection occurs in the market economy. Where there is competition it is wrong to regard profits as being somehow immoral. The exception is monopoly profits, which are not eliminated even in the long period. Entry into the industry is not free; consequently profits are not competed away. It may be that such monopoly profits stimulate research and allow an industry to expand. But where scarcity has been deliberately brought about, they simply represent an economic rent earned at the expense of consumers by the monopolist owners. Thus an efficient allocation of resources according to the wishes of consumers does not take place.

QUESTIONS

1 When Robinson Crusoe decides to make a net or the peasant farmer a plough, can they be *certain* of the yields from their investment? Give reasons.

2 Name five important public personalities whose earnings are largely in the nature of rent.

3 What is the advantage of levying a tax on a factor whose return is chiefly in the nature of economic rent? Name one practical difficulty.

4 A small farmer may well make less than he could earn as an employee.
   (a) Is his true profit positive or negative?
   (b) If negative, what is the compensation which makes him continue to farm on his own account?

5 What uncertainties are involved in launching a new soft drink on the market?

6 What are the six main disadvantages of taxing profits?

Part IV

The government and the allocation of resources

■ ⊻ 9 Making the most of limited resources

Objectives

1 To define the theoretical requirements for the efficient allocation of resources
2 To describe the factors which limit a country's possible output of goods and services
3 To explain the relationship of the use of a country's resources to the standard of living
4 To show how, under certain conditions, the market economy can achieve an efficient allocation of given resources
5 To indicate how the non-fulfilment of the required conditions leads to market failure and the possibility of government intervention

9.1 An analysis of the problem

(a) The 'production possibility curve' (PPC)

Although at any one time resources are limited, they have two important characteristics: (i) they are capable of alternative uses, and (ii) they can be increased over time. The first enables us to make the most of what we have; the second allows us to improve our lot. We can illustrate the situation as follows.

Suppose that country X produces only agricultural produce and manufactured goods and that it can, with given technology and all its resources fully employed, produce during a year the following alternative combinations (in unspecified units):

Agricultural produce	+	Manufactured goods
100		0
80		25
60		40
40		45
20		48
0		50

The table shows that, with its limited resources, country X can produce either

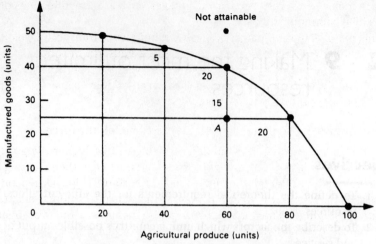

Figure 9.1 A production possibility curve

100 agricultural produce or 50 manufactured goods, or a combination of both. Any larger output is outside the curve and unattainable.

By plotting these alternative combinations we obtain a 'production possibility curve' (Figure 9.1).

An examination of the production possibility curve (PPC) raises four questions. First, what factors determine the distance of the PCC from the origin? Second, why is the PPC concave to the origin? Third, what conditions have to be fulfilled if country X is to obtain the maximum satisfaction from its limited resources? Fourth, can the PPC be eventually pushed further outward from the origin? We deal with each in turn.

9.2 Factors determining the position of the PPC

Since people can enjoy only what they produce with their limited resources, the production-possibility curve reflects the limit to their current material standard of living. Because income is not evenly distributed, however, what we are really considering is an average standard of living, usually measured by the national income per head of the population.

The factors which determine this can be classified as internal and external, the latter resulting from economic relationships with the rest of the world.

(a) Internal factors

(i) Original natural resources

Obviously, 'natural resources' cover such things as mineral deposits, sources of fuel and power, climate and the fertility of the soil and fisheries around the coast, but also included are geographical advantages, such as navigable rivers or lakes, which help communications.

While national output increases as new techniques or transport developments allow national resources to be exploited, the exhaustion of mineral resources works in the opposite direction. Moreover, where a country's economy is predominantly agricultural, variations in weather may cause its output to fluctuate from year to year.

(ii) The nature of the people, particularly of the labour force

Other things being equal, the standard of living will be higher the greater the proportion of workers to the total population and the longer their working hours.

But the quality of the labour force is also important. This will depend upon the basic characteristics of the people – their health, energy, adaptability, inventiveness, judgement and ability to organise themselves and to co-operate in production – together with the skills they have acquired through education and training.

(iii) Capital equipment

The effectiveness of natural resources and of labour depends almost entirely upon capital equipment. Thus machinery is necessary to extract oil and minerals, a turbine generator to harness a waterfall, and hotels to exploit Spanish sun and beaches. Similarly, the output of workers varies almost in direct proportion to the capital equipment and power at their disposal. Indeed, the most important single cause of material progress is investment, the addition to capital.

(iv) The organisation of resources

To achieve the maximum output from scarce factors of production, they must be organised efficiently. Have we the correct proportion of machinery to each worker? Is the production of the particular good being carried on in the best possible locality? Could the factors be better deployed within the factory? Such questions face those organising production.

(v) Knowledge of techniques

Technical knowledge is acquired through capital expenditure on research and invention. Further capital expenditure is necessary to develop and utilise discoveries, e.g. of nuclear energy and electonics (see Chapter 24).

(vi) Political organisation

A stable government promotes confidence, thereby encouraging saving and investment in long-term capital projects.

(b) External factors

(vii) Foreign loans and investments

A net income from foreign investments means that a country obtains goods or services from other countries without having to give goods and services in return, and vice versa. Generally speaking, welfare from this source is only likely to fluctuate over a long period.

(viii) The terms of trade

In the short run, fluctuations in the terms of trade can change material welfare, especially if the country has, like the UK, a high level of imports and exports.

By the *terms of trade* we mean the quantity of another country's products which a nation gets in exchange for a given quantity of its own products. Thus, if the terms of trade move in a nation's favour, it means that it gets a larger quantity of imports for a given quantity of its own exports. This happens because the prices of the goods that are imported have fallen relative to the prices of those exported (see Chapter 26).

(ix) Gifts from abroad

Aid to countries for purposes of economic development and defence improve the standard of living of the receiving countries.

9.3 The shape of the PPC

As resources are transferred to manufacturing from agriculture, an ever increasing quantity of manufactured goods has to be given up to obtain an extra 20 units of agricultural produce. For instance, when 40 agricultural units are produced, the opportunity cost of an extra 20 is only 5 manufactured goods, whereas when production is 60 agricultural units the opportunity cost of a further 20 is 15 manufactured goods.

The reason is that resources are not equally suited to producing agricultural produce and manufactured goods. For instance, factory workers would need training in farm work, while land, tractors, etc. would have to be worked more intensively. The result is that the PPC is concave to the origin.

9.4 The conditions for a country to obtain maximum satisfaction from its limited resources

(a) Basic requirements

The PPC suggests that, in order to obtain as high a standard of living as possible, country X must be concerned with:

(i) The allocation of resources

Because resources can be used in alternative ways, it is necessary to choose between manufactured goods and agricultural produce. The particular combination chosen should be the one which affords the community maximum satisfaction.

(ii) The full employment of resources

While it is impossible to produce a combination of agricultural produce and manufactured goods which lies to the right of the curve, any assortment on the origin side means that country X is not maximising its output because some resources are idle. A combination of goods on the production possibility curve can be obtained only if there is full employment.

(iii) The growth of resources

While at any given time, country X cannot do better than produce a combination which lies on its current PPC, over lime it can, by investing some resources in capital equipment, research, etc., push the PPC outwards so that a larger assortment of both agricultural produce and manufactured goods can be obtained.

We discuss (i) below and in Chapters 9–13; (ii) is covered in Chapters 17–23, and (iii) in Chapter 24.

(b) Efficiency in the allocation of resources

Efficiency in the allocation of resources is achieved when society has so allocated its limited resources that the maximum possible satisfaction is obtained. To ensure that no reshuffling of resources will increase satisfaction, there must be exchange efficiency, technical efficiency and economic efficiency. Let us examine what each involves and how the market economy can, given certain conditions, bring about all three simultaneously.

(i)   *Exchange efficiency* means that no overall gain in satisfaction can be obtained by an exchange of goods between persons. In the market economy this requirement is achieved by consumers relating their preferences to market prices. As we saw in Chapter 3, there is equilibrium within and between markets when all consumers have arranged their purchases so that:

$$\frac{\text{Marginal utility of good } A}{\text{Price of } A} = \frac{MU \text{ of good } B}{P_B} \quad \text{(and so on),}$$

$$\text{which can be rewritten:} \frac{MU_A}{MU_B} = \frac{P_A}{P_B}. \tag{1}$$

But since in competitive markets there is a *single price* for each good, it follows that each consumer will buy that quantity of the good which will make the marginal utility obtained from it equal to that obtained by other consumers. Should, for instance, one consumer have a higher marginal utility for good A, he will demand more of A and less of other goods, i.e. he offers 'other goods' in exchange for good A. As a result, an adjustment in the set of relative prices takes place until all consumers are in equilibrium.

(ii)   *Technical efficiency in production* means that no increase in output can be obtained by producers substituting one factor for another or reorganising the scale of production.

In the market economy individual producers combine resources to obtain maximum output of a given good from a limited budget. As we saw in Chapter 6, each producer employs that quantity of a factor where:

$$\frac{\text{marginal physical product of factor } M}{\text{Price of factor } M} = \frac{MPP_N}{P_N},$$

which can be rewritten: $\dfrac{MPP_M}{MPP_N} = \dfrac{P_M}{P_N}$. (2)

Since there is only one price at which one factor exchanges for another and each producer seeks to obtain the maximum profit from his limited resources, it follows that in equilibrium the marginal physical product of a factor is the same in all lines of production. If the marginal product is higher in one particular line, producers there will demand more of that factor, substituting it for other factors. As a result the relative factor prices change until the equilibrium condition is fulfilled.

(iii) *Economic efficiency* means that, out of the various total combinations of goods which can be obtained from society's limited resources, that particular assortment is produced which affords the greatest possible satisfaction. In short, supply must be related to demand.

In the market economy a network of relative prices is established which link individual preferences with the conditions of supply, as follows.

Given perfect competition (see p. 76) and no external costs or benefits, the opportunity cost of producing an additional unit of a good is reflected in money terms by marginal cost. Thus the production of good A will be where (i) $P_A = MC_A$; and of good B, where (ii) $P_B = MC_B$. By dividing (i) by (ii) we have:

$$\frac{P_A}{P_B} = \frac{MC_A}{MC_B}.$$ (3)

That is, the relative prices of A and B are equal to their relative marginal costs, the opportunity cost of supplying an addition unit.

We can now marry equations (1) and (3):

$$\frac{MU_A}{MU_B} = \frac{P_A}{P_B} = \frac{MC_A}{MC_B}.$$

Therefore,

$$\frac{MU_A}{MU_B} = \frac{MC_A}{MC_B}.$$

That is, the extent to which people prefer one good to another is equal to the relative cost of supplying those goods. Thus efficiency in the allocation of resources is achieved through the system of relative prices established in the market economy.

(c) Market failure and the role of government

Unfortunately the above conclusion is weakened by the fact that it is achieved only by a failure to specify the important underlying assumptions that:

(i) all the requirements of perfect competition (pp. 76–8) are fulfilled;
(ii) all goods can be priced in the market;

(iii) there are no external benefits and costs;

(iv) economic activity maintains a sustainable environment.

This leads to an examination of how the government can take measures to offset the defects of the market mechanism in allocating resources (Chapters 10–12).

One further point needs to be emphasised. The above analysis assumes that consumers and producers have perfect knowledge on which to base their decisions. This is not always so, because economic conditions are constantly changing and in doing so generate changes elsewhere. As a result, expectations of the future which are embodied in current decision-making may prove erroneous. This can lead to the underemployment of resources; that is, production is at some point on the origin side of the PPC. To combat this, the government has to undertake overall management of the economy. This is the subject-matter of Chapters 17–25.

Yet, in spite of its defects, an economy based on private incentives and competitive markets has proved to be the most successful in allocating current resources and pushing the PPC outwards. Thus, in general, government policy seeks to retain as far as possible the market mechanism, limiting interference to the minimum necessary to remedy its defects.

QUESTIONS

1 What is the difference between technical efficiency and economic efficiency?

2 From the point of view of economic efficiency, what is a major omission of consumers and producers maximising their own private benefits and profits?

3 In what ways should government policy be concerned with the production possibility curve?

4 In taking measures to improve economic efficiency, what other important consideration must the government bear in mind?

5 (a) If the government wishes to reduce the consumption of cigarettes and considers the elasticity of demand to be very low, what policy should it adopt?

(b) *Ought* the government to try to 'correct' consumer preferences in this way?

■ ✓ 10 Monopoly and imperfect competition

Objectives

1 To show how monopoly and imperfect competition may occur
2 To analyse the pros and cons of monopoly and its variants
3 To examine the difficulties and possible methods of government interference

10.1 Deviations from perfect competition

(a) How imperfect competition arises

Chapter 5, section 5.3(a), lists the conditions which must be fulfilled to achieve perfect competition:

(i) many small buyers and sellers;
(ii) homogeneous product;
(iii) perfect knowledge;
(iv) free entry to or withdrawal from the market;
(v) perfect mobility of the factors of production in the long period.

In the real world, however, these conditions may not hold. For instance:

(i) A seller may be so large that the quantity he supplies affects the price.
(ii) Products may not be homogeneous, because product differentiation or goodwill allow a producer to raise his price somewhat while still retaining some customers.
(iii) Lack of knowledge, barriers to entry or immobility of factors of production result in imperfect elasticity of demand or supply.

Thus some form of 'imperfect competition' results: a firm when selling its product is faced with a downward-sloping demand curve or, when buying a factor, with an upward-sloping supply curve.

(b) Forms of imperfect competition

There are many 'shades' of imperfect competition. At one extreme we have a single producer of a product, e.g. British Oxygen; at the other, the only difference

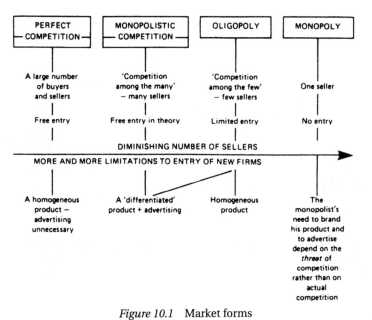

Figure 10.1 Market forms

from perfect competition is that firms each produce a slightly different brand, e.g. toothpaste. The first situation we call 'monopoly', the second 'monopolistic competition'. In between we can have just a few sellers of the same or of a slightly different product – 'oligopoly'. In this case, each seller has to take into account the reactions of rivals to his own pricing policy. The broad market forms are summarised in Figure 10.1.

10.2 Monopoly

(a) Foundations of monopoly power

While to some extent all goods are substitutes for each other, there may be essential characteristics in a good or group of goods which give rise to gaps in the chain of substitution. If one producer can so exclude competitors that he controls the supply of a good, he can be said to be a 'monopolist' – a single seller.

In real life there is seldom complete monopoly. But one producer may dominate the supply of a good or group of goods. In the UK any firm which accounts for a quarter (in value) of market sales is considered to be a monopoly (see p. 144).

Possible sources of a monopolist's power to exclude competitors are:

(i) Immobility of the factors of production

Such immobility means that existing suppliers cannot be challenged by new entrants. It may arise through:

(i) *Legal prohibition of new entrants* – as with certain public utility undertakings, where many firms would create technical difficulties, e.g. natural gas transmission, letter delivery (Post Office).

(ii) *Patents, copyrights and trademarks*, where the object is to promote invention and the development of new ideas.

(iii) *Government policy of establishing single buying and selling agencies*, e.g. the Post Office letter service.

(iv) *Control of the source of supply by one firm*, e.g. diamonds (De Beer), white salt (ICI and British Salt), mineral springs, a secret recipe (Kentucky Fried Chicken), specialist workers (e.g. dress-designers), trade unions and professional associations.

(v) *Restrictions on imports*, by tariffs, quotas, health controls, etc.

(ii) Ignorance

A monopoly may persist largely through the ignorance of possible competitors. They may not know about the super-normal profits being made by the existing firm, or they may be unable to acquire the necessary know-how, e.g. for involved technical processes.

(iii) Indivisibilities

Whereas the original firm may have been able to build up its size gradually, new firms may find it difficult to raise the large capital required to produce on a scale which is cost-competitive, e.g. with cars, drugs, computers.

In some cases, too, the efficient scale of plant may be so large relative to the market that there is only room for one firm. These 'natural' monopolies cover many of the public utilities, e.g. gas supply, water, electricity generation, but given certain conditions, there are possibilities of making such markets 'contestable' (see p. 145).

(iv) A deliberate policy of excluding competitors

Restriction of competition falls into two main groups. On the one hand, we have the sources of monopoly power described so far. These have, as it were, resulted indirectly rather than from any deliberate action by producers. Such 'spontaneous' monopolies must be contrasted with 'deliberate' monopolies – those which are created specifically to restrict supply (e.g. OPEC).

Deliberate action to exclude competitors takes various forms. Firms producing or selling the same good may combine, or a competitor may be subject to a takeover bid. Monopolies are often formed in the sale of services. Trade unions are primarily combinations of workers formed with the object of obtaining higher wages (see Chapter 7). Certain professions, such as medicine and the law, have their own associations which regulate qualifications for entry, professional conduct, and often the fees to be charged.

Some practices designed to exclude competitors are highly questionable – vicious temporary price-cutting, collusion in submitting tenders, collective boycotts, intimidation of rivals' customers by threats to cut off the supply of another vital product, etc.

As we see later (p. 142), it is essential to distinguish between the two types when formulating policy.

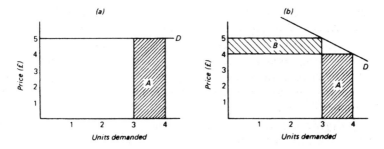

Figure 10.2 Marginal revenue under conditions of perfect and imperfect competition

(b) The effect of the downward-sloping demand curve on marginal revenue

Consider Figure 10.2. In (a) the producer is selling under conditions of perfect competition. His marginal revenue is equal to the full price, since all units sell at this. Thus, for the fourth unit, MR is the shaded area *A*.

In (b), however, the producer is selling under conditions of imperfect competition. If he wishes to sell a fourth unit, he must lower his price from £5 to £4. But this lower price applies not only to the fourth unit but also to the first three units. Thus his net addition to receipts is equal to what he gets for the fourth unit, *A*, less what he loses on the three previous units, *B*. Under imperfect competition, therefore, MR is always less than price at any given output.

(c) The relationship between the costs, revenue and output of a monopolist

Let us consider another imaginary manufacturer of lawnmowers, Airborne Mowers. To simplify, we shall assume that it has identical cost curves to those of Rollermowers, but differs in that it has a patent for its particular mower, thereby excluding competitors. In short, Airborne Mowers is a monopolist. Since its output is also the market supply, the number of the mowers which it puts on the market affects the price. Thus if it produces only 20 mowers a week, each will sell at £790; if total output is increased to 90, the price drops to £440.

Airborne Mowers has the same problem as Rollermowers – to decide which output yields maximum profit. But it has an extra complication on the revenue side – as output increases, price falls for the *whole* of the output. The result can be seen in marginal receipts (Table 10.1). These figures are plotted in Figure 10.3.

By inspection we can see that the maximum profit is made when 65 Airborne mowers are produced each week. At this output, MR = MC (both £240), as in perfect competition. But MR is no longer equal to, but is less than price (£565). Total weekly receipts are £36,725 and total costs £19,825 (by interpolation), giving a maximum profit of £16,900.

Alternatively we can use the price and ATC at an output of 65 units to calculate profit. In Figure 6.14, total receipts equal the rectangle *OMCP* (output times price) = 65 × £565; total cost equals the rectangle *OMAD* (output times average

Table 10.1 Costs, revenue and profits of Airborne Mowers (in £)

Output per week (units)	Total	Average total	Costs Marginal	Price per unit	Receipts Total	Receipts Marginal (p. unit)	Profits
0	10,000	–	–	–	–	–	–10,000
			200			840	
10	12,000	1,200		840	8,400		–3,600
			140			740	
20	13,400	670		790	15,800		2,400
			100			640	
30	14,400	480		740	22,200		7,800
			100			540	
40	15,400	385		690	27,600		12,200
			135			440	
50	16,750	335		640	32,000		15,250
			185			340	
60	18,600	310		590	35,400		16,800
65	19,825	305	240	565	36,725	240	16,900
70	21,000	300		540	37,800		16,800
			300			140	
80	24,000	300		490	39,200		15,200
			390			40	
90	27,900	310		440	39,600		11,700
			510			–60	
100	33,000	330		390	39,000		6,000
			660			–160	
110	39,600	360		340	37,400		–2,200
			840			–260	
120	48,000	400		290	34,800		–13,200

cost) = 65 × £305. Thus profit is the difference between the two: the rectangle *DACP* equals 65 × £260, i.e. £16,900.

(d) Policy considerations

Monopoly is an emotive word, and often the immediate reaction is that it should be replaced by competition. But two considerations suggest a more cautious approach may be preferable.

First, we must refer to our earlier distinction between 'spontaneous' and 'deliberate' monopolies. While the 'spontaneous' monopolies may still abuse their fortunate position in order to make high profits, to a large extent they are inevitable, and usually policy should seek to control rather than destroy them. On the other hand, 'deliberate' monopolies, those designed solely to follow restrictive practices detrimental to the consumer should, where possible, be broken up. In practice, however, it is often difficult to draw a distinct line between the two.

Second, we have to examine more carefully the view that the monopolist will always follow policies harmful to the consumer. The argument runs as follows.

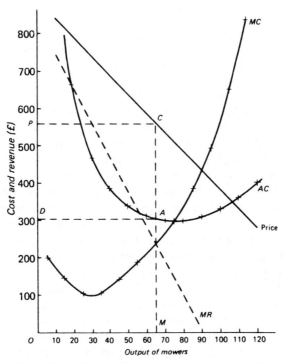

Figure 10.3   The equilibrium output of a monopolist

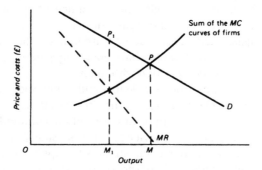

Figure 10.4   Output under perfect competition and monopoly

Where there is perfect competition, output for all firms in the industry will take place where price equals MC, i.e. at *OM* (Figure 10.4). In other words, production is carried to the point, *OM*, where the cost of producing an extra unit, MP, just equals the value which consumers place on that extra unit in the market. Moreover, in the long period, this will be the output where, for all firms, ATC is at a minimum. There are no super-normal profits.

Now suppose a cartel formed from all the individual firms becomes responsible for selling the product. In order to maximise profits the cartel will sell an output where MC = MR, i.e. OM_1 at price M_1P_1. Thus consumers get less of the product and at a higher price than under perfect competition. It means, too, that demand for factors of production in this particular activity is lower than it would be in the absence of monopoly, and so there is a distortion of factor prices – which has its repercussions on more competitive sectors of the economy.

But the above analysis is not infallible. For one thing, it makes certain implicit assumptions; for another, it ignores dynamic considerations.

First, it rests on the assumption that the competitive industry's supply curve will be the same as the MC curve of the monopolist. But this is unlikely to be so. A single firm may be able to achieve economies of scale which are not open to the comparatively small firms which comprise the competitive industry. In addition its investment may be higher since there is now no fear of over-capitalisation of the industry through rival firms carrying out similar investment.

It is probable, therefore, that the monopolist will, at the relevant market output, have lower costs than the firms producing under conditions of perfect competition. Indeed, we can envisage a situation where, even though the monopolist is producing at the maximum profit output, the consumer nevertheless obtains more of the product and at a lower price than under perfect competition. Even so this does not achieve maximum economic efficiency for price is above MC, and super-normal profits are still being made.

Second, our competitive model was purely static in its approach. Profits were maximised on the basis of *given* prices of products and factors. No consideration was *given* to other influences on the growth of firms over time.

But the *development* of firms depends upon innovation and investment in research. Thus we have to ask the question: 'Are firms more likely to innovate and spend on research if, by being granted monopoly powers, they can be assured of the rewards?' In short, are monopolies more conducive to growth than perfect competition? We cannot develop the argument here, but the mere existence of the Patents Acts suggests that there is some truth in it. On the other hand, there have been instances where monopolies have bought up patents in order that they would *not* be developed in competition with them.

Third, price and output may be more stable under monopoly. Where there are many competing producers, as in agriculture, the reactions of each can bring about sharp swings in the total supply and price of the commodity. In contrast, the monopolist can view the market as a whole in assessing likely future demand, probably finding that only marginal adjustments to supply are necessary. Partly for this reason Marketing Boards (now ended) were set up as selling monopolies in certain branches of agriculture, e.g. potatoes, milk.

Finally, in criticising monopoly, we must remember that restriction of output may permit a discriminating monopolist to charge prices which will allow certain markets to be supplied (see p. 147).

10.3 The control of monopoly

(a) Policy difficulties

While monopolies may be 'spontaneous' or 'deliberate', the division does not make the first group 'white' or the second 'black'. In the first place, our analysis has shown that, no matter how the monopoly has arisen, it will restrict output if its aim is to maximise profits. Second, while a monopoly may be 'deliberate', there may still be benefits for reasons given above. All we can say is that some control of monopoly is desirable, but that it must usually be done on an empirical basis. The degree of monopoly power has to be established and the benefits weighed against the possible economic and social disadvantages – restriction of output, a waste of resources in maintaining the monopoly position (e.g. by advertising), a lack of enterprise through the absence of competition, the exertion of political pressure to secure narrow ends (e.g. by trade unions), and a redistribution of wealth from consumers to the monopolist.

As a result, monopolies in the UK are regulated rather than prohibited. Yet any policy is fraught with difficulties. An exact assessment of the public benefits and disadvantages resulting from a monopoly is impossible. Very often, too, the decision as to whether a monopoly is useful or anti-social in character depends on circumstances and therefore varies from one period to another (note the fostering of monopolies in the 1930s). Moreover, if legislation is proposed, the term 'unfair competition' has to be closely defined by lawyers, though, for the purposes of control, it really requires an elastic interpretation based on economic issues. Last, government policy in another field may influence the problem of monopoly. Thus tariff protection, by restricting competition from abroad, enhances the possibility of establishing monopolies in the home market.

(b) Forms of policy

(i) State ownership

When it is important not to destroy the advantages of monopoly, the state may take it over completely; the public then appears to be effectively protected. Freed from the objective of maximising profit, there should be no tendency for the state-owned industries to use their monopoly position to make high profits. Should, however, such profits be made they would eventually be passed on to the public in lower prices, or in reduced taxation.

In practice, however, lower profits may mask inefficiency in operation or the payment of wages to employees above those in comparable occupations elsewhere. Consequently, provision must be made for the prices charged to be examined by an independent body and for efficiency checks to be carried out by independent experts.

(ii) Legislation and administrative machinery to regulate monopolies

This method is usually employed when it is desired to retain monopolies because of their benefits but to leave them under private ownership.

The Monopolies and Restrictive Practices Act 1948 (since amended) set up a Monopolies Commission to investigate monopoly situations. Upon the Commission's report, a ministerial order can declare certain arrangements or practices illegal. Subjects investigated have included: supply of household detergents, breakfast cereals, cross-channel sea-ferries, video games, travellers cheques; and proposed mergers, e.g. GEC and Plessey, Lonrho and the House of Fraser, Capital Radio and Virgin Radio. Alternatively the commission can suggest conditions which would make a monopoly's proposals or practices more acceptable.

(iii) Breaking up or prohibition of the monopoly

Where the monopoly is, on balance, 'against the public interest', policy can take the form of breaking it up or prohibiting it by legislation. Thus the state could reduce the period for which patents are granted or make their renewal more difficult. When the owner of a particular site uses his monopoly power to frustrate a comprehensive city centre development, the site can be compulsorily purchased by the local planning authority.

Alternatively, it could outlaw attempts to eliminate competition, whether by unfair practices, the formation of cartels or restrictive agreements. Total prohibition was the policy at one time followed in the USA.

The Resale Prices Act 1964 made minimum price resale maintenance illegal, except for goods approved by the court. So far only minimum prices for proprietary medicines and books have been authorised, and in practice the Net Book Agreement has been undermined because publishers have found it difficult to enforce.

The Monopolies and Mergers Act 1965 strengthened and extended the legislation on monopolies. A merger or proposed merger can be referred to the Monopolies Commission where it could lead to a monopoly (as with B sky B's bid for Manchester United) or would increase the power of an existing monopoly.

The Fair Trading Act 1973 had the object of 'strengthening the machinery of *promoting competition*'. It created an Office of Fair Trading under a Director-General responsible for discovering probable monopoly situations or uncompetitive practices. It also reduced the criterion for a monopoly situation to a one-quarter (minimum) market share.

These powers were strengthened by the Competition Act 1980 which empowered the Director-General to investigate any business practice which may restrict, distort or prevent competition. If found to be uncompetitive, he may accept an undertaking from the business responsible, or in default refer the practice to the Monopolies and Mergers Commission (now renamed the Competition Commission) to establish whether it operates against the public interest. The President of the Board of Trade can reject the MMC's recommendations, as happened in 1997 when the Bass take-over of fellow brewers Carlsberg-Tetley was blocked since it would have given Bass 35 per cent of the British market.

Agreements and concerted practices with anti-competitive effects or purposes are prohibited outright unless the MMC accepts special circumstances. Thus in 1993 it allowed leading perfume houses to refuse supplies of 'luxury' perfumes to downmarket retailers who were cutting prices.

Single market regulations require British law on monopolies and restrictive trade practices to be compatible with EU law so that UK firms operating in Europe do not have to deal with two fundamentally different forms of legislation. At present the Commission has responsibility for all mergers having a 'Community dimension' where the firms involved have an aggregate turnover of 5bn Euro.

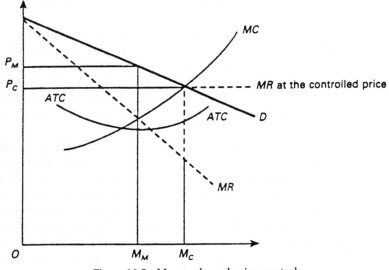

Figure 10.5 Monopoly and price control

(iv) Price control

The object here is to remove the monopolist's power of influencing price. Thus if the government controls the maximum price at OP_C (Figure 10.5) the demand (MR) curve facing the monopolist is perfectly elastic up to that price, and the equilibrium output is OM_C instead of OM_M. Here $P = MC$, but it is only a second-best solution because, although price is lower and output greater, super-normal profit could still be made. This solution should be compared with that where production takes place where costs are decreasing (see below).

(v) Market solutions

The Conservative government of the 1980s, with its preference for market solutions rather than regulation, introduced three new methods for dealing with monopolies, chiefly those monopolies given more independence as a result of privatisation.

(1) Franchising

With respect to independent television programmes, for example, companies have to tender for the right to broadcast programmes, the idea being to foster competition and divert at least a part of the profits to the state. However, some device seems to be required to ensure that quality programmes, for example the existing Channel 4, are not completely ousted by the more profitable low-brow shows.

(2) Contestable markets

The super-normal profits earned by a monopolist firm should attract competitors into the market. But, as we have seen, this may be impossible when fixed costs are so heavy that the penalty of failure is unacceptable. On the other hand if 'sunk costs' (those of specific assets which are of little or no value in other uses) are slight, the risk of having to withdraw should profits disappear is small.

The existence or mere possibility of a 'hit and run' competitor therefore produces a contestable market.

This concept can be used to introduce competition into the natural monopolies. With these decreasing-cost monopolies the initial fixed capital required is so high that would-be entrants could not accept the risk, for in the event of failure they would be left with irrecoverable fixed costs. But suppose those high initial costs can be circumvented. Firms would then be willing to compete because withdrawal would be easier should the venture prove unprofitable.

We can illustrate the method and its results from British Gas (BG). The Oil and Gas (Enterprise) Act 1982 permits independent gas producers to negotiate a contract direct with large consumers and deliver supplies through the BG pipelines system. This the independent supplier would do if BG was making a monopoly profit P_MLRS (Figure 10.6). An independent supplier could now use the pipeline to negotiate a price OP_C which would enable it to break even. In fact when a large American oil company proposed to do this, BG cut its own contract price. Thus the *threat* may be sufficient to avert monopoly pricing, though it should be noted that $P = AC$ (rather than $P = MC$) and so is again only a second-best solution. However it does succeed in a lower price (P_C rather than P_M) and increases output by $M_M M_C$.

This is the best that can be achieved, without government subsidy, in a decreasing MC situation. Of course, a watchdog body would have to ensure that BG's *pipeline* (TransCo) charges to the independent supplier were not excessive, covering only a reasonable rate of return on its investment. Competition by contestable markets can be seen in Mercury's competition with BT and the periodic tendering for regional franchises by TV companies.

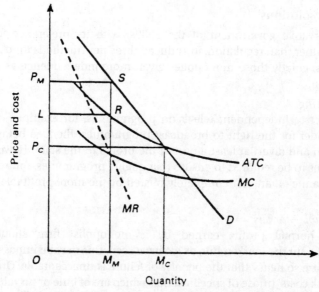

Figure 10.6 Price and output under a contestable market

(3) Price regulation by formula to control profits

To prevent newly privatised monopolies charging a profit-maximising price and yet give them an incentive to be efficient, price increases have been regulated according to a formula which is varied periodically. Usually this incorporates a specific figure, say 2 per cent, by which any price rise must fall behind the rate of inflation as measured by the Retail Price Index. This means that 2 per cent is the productivity increase target, but it provides the supplier with an incentive to do better since any surplus revenue can be retained (see also p. 164).

10.4 Discriminating monopoly

A discriminating monopolist is one who can, and does, sell the *same* product at different prices to different consumers.

Examples of discriminating monopoly are: (a) a doctor who varies fees for the same treatment according to estimates of the wealth of the patients; (b) a car manufacturer who sells cars in export markets at a lower price than on the home market; (c) electricity taken during the night for heat-storage and charged at a lower tariff than that consumed during the day; (d) a small builders' merchant who charges the professional builder less than the 'do-it-yourself' amateur for paint and wallpaper; (e) rail fares, with concessions for senior citizens and students.

(a) The necessary conditions for discriminating monopoly

For discriminating monopoly to be practicable, certain conditions must be fulfilled.

(i) *There must be some imperfection in the market.* Where there are different markets, or where parts of the market are separated by transport costs or time (e.g. off-peak electricity, rail travel), type of customer (e.g. senior citizens), consumers' ignorance or national barriers, sellers can exercise some control over the supply in each market.

(ii) *Elasticities of demand in the markets must be different,* thereby allowing-different prices to be charged by the monopolist.

(iii) *No 'seepage' is possible between markets or different parts of the market.* If an exporter in one country, for instance, sells the good much more cheaply in another country, then either transport costs or physical controls must prevent re-importation to the country of origin.

(b) Can price discrimination be in the interest of consumers?

The term 'discrimination' suggests that consumers are exploited in order to increase the profits of the monopolist. Now price discrimination will enable the monopolist to obtain a higher total revenue (and thus higher profits) than if he merely charged a single price for the whole of the market. But this means he must

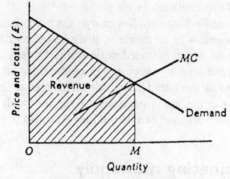

Figure 10.7   Receipts under 'perfect discrimination'

produce a larger output than with a single price. He can do this because, by being able to separate the markets, he does not force down the price in one market by selling extra goods in another market. Indeed, if there were different markets for all units of his product (that is, 'perfect discrimination'), the marginal revenue for each unit of a good would be the price at which it sold. The monopolist's output would then be identical with the perfectly competitive output (Figure 10.7), but super-normal profit would still be made.

Two points of significance to the consumer follow from this.

(i) Price discrimination may make it possible to supply an otherwise unprofitable market

Two possibilities come to mind. If a regional rail company charges all passengers at so much per mile, main line services could be profitable but many local services may not be, and are therefore closed down. Yet local passengers might be willing to pay higher fares to maintain the service.

Or we can consider a doctor whose services are demanded by both wealthy and poor patients. If he opts for a single price, only wealthy people can afford treatment. But with price discrimination between the two markets, poor people can also be treated – and his profits will increase!

(ii) Price discrimination may make it possible to supply a good when no single price would cover total costs

Suppose the demand for the product and the costs of producing are as shown in Figure 10.8. Where a single price is charged, no firm could cover its total costs. But it may be possible for a firm (e.g. a public utility) to charge discriminating prices and thus cover its costs. If the monopolist could discriminate perfectly between every purchaser, he could produce an output up to the point where $\Delta SRC = \Delta PLS$, for $LOMC$ are his total costs and $POMR$ would be his total revenue.

Alternatively, the firm might be able to cover its costs by imposing a fixed standing charge on consumers irrespective of the quantity bought. But, if this is impossible, without price discrimination the firm would either have to close down or have its revenue shortfall covered by a subsidy.

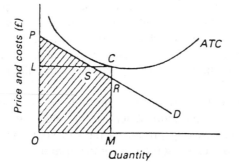

Figure 10.8 The possibility of supply with price discrimination

10.5 Monopolistic competition: imperfect competition with many firms

Perfect competition and monopoly represent two extreme market forms. In the real world, however, there is more likely to be a situation somewhere between the two where many firms or perhaps just a few compete *imperfectly* in the market.

(a) The nature of monopolistic competition

An industry may consist of many firms each making a product which differs only in detail from that of its rivals. Each firm, since its product is not homogeneous with that of other firms, enjoys some monopoly power. On the other hand, because there is no real gap in the chain of substitution, there is competition from other firms. What we really have is a number of small 'monopolists' competing with one another – 'monopolistic competition'. How does this come about?

(b) Conditions giving rise to monopolistic competition

On the demand side, we have a situation which is closely akin to monopoly. Few goods are completely homogeneous. Indeed, nearly every firm tries deliberately to give its product some distinction from those with which it competes. This 'product differentiation', as it is called, takes various forms. Special characteristics of the good are extensively advertised, competitions are run periodically, free gifts are offered, distinctive wrappings are used. Or, quite simply, the brand name is splashed across television screens and street hoardings in the hope that constant repetition will lead consumers to prefer the good. Apart from product differentiation, a seller may depend upon 'goodwill' (arising through habit or social contacts), rather than the actual price charged, to retain customers.

Whichever method is used, product differentiation or goodwill, the result is the same. The producer is not faced with a market demand which is beyond control. If the firm raises its price, some customers will buy competitors' brands. But not all customers will do this. Some will consider other brands inferior, and only a large price rise will induce them to change. Similarly, if the firm lowers its price, it will attract only a limited number of customers from rival producers. In short, the producer of a brand good or a seller possessing goodwill is, like a monopolist, faced with a demand curve which slopes downwards from left to right. Nevertheless, demand tends to be elastic. Although there are not perfect substitutes available, there are fairly good ones – the different brands of rival producers.

On the supply side, because entry to the industry is possible, the situation is similar to perfect competition. Where one producer is seen to be making super-normal profits, existing producers tend to copy the product and new competitors start producing a somewhat similar brand.

(c) The equilibrium of the industry under monopolistic competition

We simplify the analysis by making two important assumptions: (i) individual producers can obtain all their supply of any factor at a given price; (ii) external economies do not affect costs as the number of firms in the group increases.

(i) The short period

In the short period, existing firms cannot increase production by employing additional fixed factors, nor can new firms enter. Each firm, therefore, is a little 'monopolist', having a downward-sloping demand curve for its product and producing where MC equals MR. Because there are many firms, each firm can set its price without having to consider the reactions of competitors. This price will be greater than MR, and super-normal profits are made (Figure 10.9a).

(ii) The long period

In monopolistic competition the full long-period equilibrium position is possible only when both firms and the industry are in equilibrium. Whereas for each firm the condition of equilibrium ($MR = MC$) will apply whatever the output, for the industry we must allow, as with perfect competition, for the entry of new firms and for increased production by existing firms. This is where monopolistic competition differs essentially from monopoly; with the latter, *one* firm is *the* industry.

The increase in supply in the long period will lead to a fall in the price of the good, and the demand curve facing each producer shifts its position downwards to the left, for more producers are now dividing up the total market. At the same time, it is likely that the demand curve will become more elastic, for all products of the group will tend to become more similar to that of the most successful. In other words, each brand becomes a better substitute for other brands.

This will continue until super-normal profits have disappeared with each firm earning only normal profits (Figure 10.9b). However, in practice the full equilibrium position is unlikely to be reached. Differences between firms will persist, and most will be earning small super-normal profits.

Certain points regarding this long-period equilibrium output should be noted:

(i) No super-normal profits are made; as in perfect competition, there is free entry to the industry.

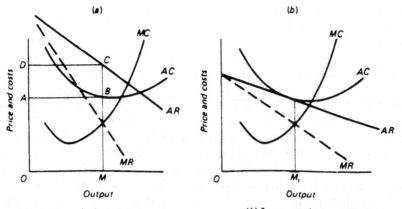

(a) Short-period equilibrium   (b) Long-period equilibrium

Figure 10.9   Monopolistic competition: equilibrium of firms in the short and long periods

(ii) The same conditions of full equilibrium hold as in perfect competition – *MC* = *MR* (equilibrium of the firm), and *AC* = *AR* (equilibrium of the industry).

(iii) Price is greater than *MC* and *MR* – a result of the falling *AR* curve.

(iv) The equilibrium output is less than that under perfect competition. This again is the result of the downward-sloping *AR* curve, which can be tangential to a U-shaped average-cost curve only at an output less than the minimum average cost.

(d) The economic and social effects of monopolistic competition – the 'wastes of competition'

(i) Even in the long period firms operate at less than the optimum size

Under perfect competition, not only are super-normal profits eliminated, but in the long period each firm is producing where *AC* is a minimum – the optimum output. At this output factors of production are combined in the correct proportions and the full advantages of large-scale economies are achieved. What happens under monopolistic competition is that firms operate at less than their optimum size and thus there is inefficiency in the allocation of factors of production.

But we should not assume from the above argument that monopolistic competition is necessarily a 'bad' thing. Not every consumer will want to buy goods which are identical with those bought by other consumers. Different individuals have slightly different tastes. Thus waste in the use of the scarce resources can be regarded as the part of the price that has to be paid for variety of choice.

(ii) Costs are incurred in competitive advertising

Perfect competition assumes perfect knowledge and homogeneous goods. Advertising is therefore unnecessary. If any one firm incurred costs in this way, it would benefit no more than its rivals.

In practice, however, knowledge is not perfect, and most firms marketing a new product have to spend money in bringing its merits to the notice of the public. Such costs are as justifiable as those incurred in the actual production of the good. Indeed, they may even be beneficial in that, by expanding demand, they allow the advantages of large-scale production to be achieved.

But 'informative' advertising forms only a small proportion of modern advertising. The main object is to *persuade*. Firms, having made their product somewhat different, then incur large costs in advertising this difference and in persuading the customer that their brand of good is superior to other brands. Put in economic terms, they aim at decreasing the elasticity of demand for their particular product as well as shifting the demand curve to the right. In reality, there may be little basic difference between brands – but labour and other scarce resources are wasted in trying to convince the public that it is otherwise. The *AC* curve includes this cost of advertising, so raising the final equilibrium price (Figure 10.9b).

In practice it is not always easy to draw the line between informative and persuasive advertising. What is 'one man's meat is another man's poison'; and if you adhere to the principle of allowing people to exercise freedom of choice, then you must accept what follows – that they are open to be persuaded. What consumers lack is knowledge of the good, and they are thus easy victims to the pressures of advertising. Today there is only a private body, the Consumers' Association (publishers of *Which?*), to report on goods to subscribers.

10.6 Oligopoly: imperfect competition with few firms

(a) Pricing where there are few firms

In real life many goods and services are produced by just a few firms, e.g. cigarettes, cars, petrol, tyres, screws, detergents, electric cable, newspapers and lawnmowers. Here we have 'oligopoly', where pricing and output policy conforms to no given principles. Sometimes one large firm is a 'price leader', setting the price which will maximise its profit and taking its share of the market. Smaller firms have to take this price as given and consider themselves as operating in a competitive market.

In other cases, firms may be of fairly equal strength but, since their number is small, no one firm can set a price *without considering the likely reaction of its competitors*. If, for instance, it reduces its price, it cannot guarantee that it will win a greater share of the market since other firms may retaliate and cut their prices.

It is impossible, therefore, to predict the exact behaviour of the oligopolist. Whereas with monopoly and monopolistic competition the relationship of marginal revenue and marginal cost determines price and output, the oligopolistic firm has the added dimension of having to make a guess about the reaction of its competitors to a change in price. There are many different assumptions it can make, and each will give a different solution.

(b) Oligopoly policy in practice

Since in an oligopolistic market situation firms are reluctant to engage in price-cutting, other policies are often pursued in practice.

First, the few firms concerned are able and usually willing to come to a tacit agreement on price in order to achieve joint profit maximisation. Often this takes the form of following the price set by the largest firm. Thus Brooke Bond Oxo appears to give the lead in tea prices. The extent to which such collusion is possible depends on the ability to exclude new firms, for example because production has to be on a large scale from the outset.

Second, non-price competition is prevalent, e.g. through extensive advertising (detergents), discounts, free gift stamps, competitions, temporary special offers (newspapers), low interest rates (cars), better after-sales service, etc.

10.7 Pricing policy in the real world

(a) Difficulties of the MC = MR principle

Following the above brief discussion of oligopoly, we have to admit that in many other cases the strict principle of fixing a price where MC equals MR may not be rigidly adhered to. For one thing the optimum output may be unobtainable because of cash-flow difficulties, the result of the capital market not being perfect. For another, few markets are so perfectly competitive that individual producers have no control over their price and have such an exact knowledge of the shape of their demand curve that MR can be equated with MC at all outputs.

Pricing policy therefore usually follows more pragmatic methods. Sometimes, for example with government contracts, the firm may follow a 'cost-plus' approach, being allowed what is considered to be a fair percentage addition to basic costs to cover overheads and normal profit; or the firm will, by a process of trial and error, seek to charge 'what the traffic will bear', e.g. the 'black-market' ticket seller.

(b) Mark-up pricing

More usually where a producer has some control in fixing a price, pricing is on a 'mark-up' basis. Only the cost of manufacturing is calculated accurately, and to this is added a rather arbitrary percentage for overheads in order to arrive at the final selling price. Thus, in selling a book, the publisher calculates the cost of printing and binding, adds a percentage (say 40 per cent) to cover overheads and normal profit, and fixes a final bookshop price which covers these costs plus the author's royalty and the bookseller's margin based on the retail price.

Indeed, this may be the only practicable method when, as is usual, firms are producing more than one product. A publisher, for instance, could not exist on the sales of one book and, in any case, would want the extra security of publishing different types of books. Furthermore, in order to survive, producers have to pay regard to what is known as 'the product life-cycle', which consists of innovation,

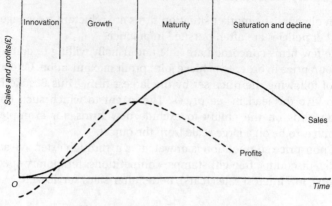

Figure 10.10 The product life-cycle

growth, maturity, saturation and decline (Figure 10.10). In the growth period the product shows increasing profitability, for the firm enjoys almost a monopoly position. With time, competitors enter: sales increase, but only at the expense of rising advertising costs. Thereafter the market becomes oversupplied or competitors produce improved models, and sales decline. Thus the go-ahead firm will always be planning new products so that one replaces another as each passes through its life-cyle.

With a many-product firm the exact share of overheads attributable to any one product would be difficult, if not impossible, to ascertain. The mark-up method sidetracks this difficulty. Furthermore, it allows control by the cost accountant, especially as regards maintaining cash flow and ensuring profitable production. Where pricing is on the $MC = MR$ principle, there is no certainty that total costs are covered.

QUESTIONS

1 For a monopoly to exist, what two conditions must be fulfilled?

2 The following demand schedule faces a monopolist producer of oil. Assume that his marginal costs are nil.
(a) Beyond what output would it not be profitable for him to expand?
(b) What is elasticity of demand at this output?

Price (£)	Oil demanded (tons)
60	250
50	900
40	1,500
30	2,000
20	2,500

3 Give examples of discriminating monopoly from the following:
(a) bus travel
(b) sale of cars abroad as compared with the home market

(c) railway freight charges

(d) telephone calls

4 The Ford Motor Company spends large sums of money on advertising its products. Why does not Farmer Jones spend a similar fraction of his income on advertising his wheat, milk and eggs?

5 How do petrol firms reflect an oligopolistic situation in their pricing policies?

■ ▼ ❙ ❙ The provision of goods and services by the public sector

Objectives

1 To consider reasons for the provision of certain goods and services through a 'public sector'
2 To indicate the difficulties of the public sector in achieving 'economic efficiency'
3 To describe forms of 'privatisation'

11.1 The case for public sector provision

(a) The market's inability to provide 'community goods'

In competitive markets: (a) the individual has to pay a price (the opportunity cost) in order to benefit from the consumption of a good; (b) the more the individual consumes, the less is available for others.

But as noted earlier (p. 6), with some goods these conditions do not hold, and so the government itself has to undertake the provision of such goods.

With *community goods*, e.g. defence, police, street lighting, flood control, there is indivisibility in that there must be a complete supply or none at all. Above all, 'free-riders' cannot be excluded. This '*non-excludability*' means that individuals cannot be charged a price on the basis of use.

(b) State provision of other goods

In practice the government often provides *collective goods*, such as parks, beaches, motorways, bridges and drainage, which, although indivisible differ from community goods in that it is possible be exclude 'free-riders' by levying fees, charges or tolls. One reason for not doing so is that the costs of collection are regarded as being disproportionate to the revenue raised. A more fundamental reason is that with most indivisible goods, the use by one extra person does not impose a sacrifice on others since there is no addition to the cost of provision. This 'non-rivalry' means that, because MC is nil, the maximum benefits can only be enjoyed if no charge is made (MC = MR = O), the full cost being met by the state from taxation.

Merit goods, e.g. education, health care, are provided by the state because it is felt that they would be inadequately consumed (either through lack of income or simply spending preferences) if left entirely to market forces. Undesirable external costs, such as an untrained or physically poor labour force, could result. In subsidising the consumption of such goods, the government redistributes income and so makes a subjective judgement.

Other economic reasons for state participation are: (i) the need to embrace widespread external costs and benefits, e.g. urban renewal, a new airport; (ii) an exceptionally large initial capital requirement, e.g. new town development, nuclear energy, Airbus.

(c) Problems of public provision

Public provision of goods and services gives rise to its own particular problems. These concern:

  (i) reconciling the principles of accountability and economic efficiency;
 (ii) assessing 'needs';
(iii) a pricing policy if charges can be made;
(iv) the pros and cons of possible privatisation.

We shall consider each in turn.

11.2 Accountability v. economic efficiency

Even after it has been decided that the state should provide goods and services, consideration has still to be given to two fundamental principles which pull in opposite directions.

The first, *'public accountability'*, arises because the citizen requires some assurance that powers granted to the state to produce goods and services are not abused by authoritarianism, inefficiency or monopolistic exploitation.

The second principle is *'economic efficiency'*. The difficulty is that, by insisting on strict public accountability, we may so tie the hands of those running the state services that they cannot operate efficiently, e.g. by parliamentary questions on day-to-day operations and restrictive Treasury control of finance.

The *government department* form of organisation achieves a high degree of public accountability through ministerial responsibility, parliamentary questioning and Treasury control of finance. But such accountability can undermine economic efficiency. Thus the *government department* is most appropriate for dealing with community and collective goods which are of national importance and where local differences in the standard of provision would be unacceptable, e.g. defence, trunk roads, health care. Their cost is covered, therefore, by taxation.

Because the strict accountability of the government department form of organisation may conflict with economic efficiency, the *nationalised industries* were organised as *public corporations*. The minister concerned exercised control over their broad policies, but not their day-to-day operations. They were fairly free to choose their own pricing policies but had to submit an annual report to Parliament. Thus some accountability was sacrificed in the interests of economic efficiency.

Where goods are still produced under the auspices of the government, e.g. the coinage, the current practice is where possible to give the enterprise, e.g. the Royal Mint, the status of an executive *agency*, thereby affording management greater freedom to develop its business, e.g. by producing coins for other countries. Nevertheless its commercial performance is still subject to periodic official review.

Quasi-government bodies have usually been formed to operate particular services where only minimum accountability is required, e.g. the National Parks Commission, the Countryside Commission. In practice the degree of accountability varies.

Local authorities carry out functions, delegated by Parliament, chiefly where economies of scale and spill-over effects are relatively weak, e.g. education, police, roads, fire services, refuse collection, local planning control. Such local administration can respond to local needs.

11.3 The problem of assessing 'needs'

(a) Differences between 'demand' and 'needs'

Whereas goods and services are supplied by private-sector firms in response to effective demand, government departments and local authorities provide goods and services according to 'needs', a social rather than an economic concept since it cannot be defined objectively. As a result 'needs' are more difficult to assess than demand.

For example, in the private sector owner-occupied houses are built according to the price which people are able and willing to pay for them. *Demand* will depend upon the price of the house, the prices of other goods and services (particularly near-substitutes), the level of income, the distribution of wealth and all the other factors mentioned in Chapter 2 as influencing the conditions of demand. Supply responds automatically to this demand; the number and type of houses supplied depends ultimately on the equilibrium price determined in the market.

In contrast, in providing housing according to *needs* the public-sector authorities regard housing as a social obligation. Consequently, price signals are either inadequate or non-existent. This increases the difficulties of decision-making. Consider the factors which have to be borne in mind in planning a housing programme based on needs. First, the authorities have to estimate the number of households seeking accommodation according to the sizes of the family units, the ages of their members, their location, their preferences as between houses and high-rise flats, and so on. Moreover, since houses are very durable, some consideration has to be given to future requirements. Second, the authorities have to decide arbitrarily on the standard of an adequate housing unit. Third, they have to get the dwellings built, either through a private contractor or by their own direct-labour building organisations.

(b) Subjective assessment of 'needs'

The task of estimating needs is made more difficult because there is no price system in operation to provide reliable criteria. Thus rents charged by local authorities are less than the open-market rent. This means that demand exceeds supply, and the only indication of needs thrown up by this restricted-price system is the number of households waiting their turn on the housing list.

And, all the time, the authorities must be conscious of dealing with limited resources – more spent on housing may mean less available for the health services. In the last resort, therefore, the standard of goods and services provided on the basis of needs is determined by the political views of the central government and local councils.

11.4 Pricing policy in the public sector

The problem arises as to how goods and services are to be paid for. There are three sources of funds: borrowing, taxation and user-charges.

(a) Borrowing

In principle, long-term *government borrowing* should cover only spending on capital items, e.g. motorways, bridges. In practice, however, the government's yearly expenditure is so vast that what would normally be regarded as capital items are included in current expenditure, e.g. the cost of warships. In any case, from the point of view of control of the economy, it is the *total* spending of the government relative to revenue which is of major significance.

What happens, therefore, is that any excess of public sector expenditure over current income is covered by borrowing – the Public Sector Borrowing Requirement (PSBR). For most of the past ten years the size of the PSBR has proved embarrassing for government economic policy (see p. 281).

(b) Taxation

With *community goods*, no price can be charged, since nobody will pay when private rights to them cannot be granted, e.g. with defence and flood control. Here the cost has to be covered entirely from taxation.

Charges can be levied on *collective goods* (see p. 156). But if their marginal cost is nil, e.g. for crossing bridges, visiting museums, welfare can only be maximised if no charge is levied, with taxation covering the cost.

With *merit* goods in particular, it may be desirable to recognise the uneven distribution of income when considering charges. For instance, charges for essential education would be highly regressive on low-income families with children of school-age. Alternatively, the regressive impact of charges can be modified by price discrimination. Thus low-income families are given housing benefits, while persons over retirement age do not pay prescription charges.

Where demand for a public service is not likely to be too high at zero price, the choice between tax financing and user-charging could reasonably rest on the question, who benefits from the service? Where the community as a whole benefits – e.g. street lighting and by-pass roads – tax-financing is appropriate. In contrast, if certain individuals benefit, the cost is best, and more fairly, covered by individual fees (e.g. public tennis courts and swimming pools).

(c) User-charges

For goods other than community goods, the choice between charges, taxation or a combination of both is governed by technical, economic and political considerations. Thus while motorways could be financed by toll charges, the effect on the traffic flow, especially during rush hours, has led the UK to pay for them from general taxation. However, users contribute heavily through motor-vehicle licences and petrol duties. On the other hand, while public transport could be financed from taxation, economic factors favour charges, for elasticity of demand is such that, at a zero price (financed wholly from taxation), demand would be so high that a misallocation of resources would result. This applies to many othar services, e.g. postal services, National Health prescriptions, dental treatment, sight testing and spectacles.

One other advantage of charges is that they can throw up a valuable guideline for investment. For example, metered water charges reveal demand at the current price and from this some estimate can be made of future demand.

In practice, the choice between charges and taxation is likely to be decided politically, especially where income redistribution figures prominently. But there are economic constraints on charging less than the free market price for an extended demand may impose a heavy burden on taxation generally. The result is that some form of administrative rationing according to need may have to be imposed, e.g. the 'points' system for allocating Council dwellings. More seriously, hidden rationing may prevail through depreciation of the quality of service provided, e.g. state medical services and education. Indeed this could apply to BBC television, where a 'community good' has been converted to a 'collective good' by a legal licence which creates excludability so that the cost falls on TV owners.

(d) Determining user-charges

Even when it has been decided to cover the cost of a service by charges, difficulties may arise where there are relatively very high fixed costs, e.g. as with public transport, electricity, and natural gas, for supply by competing firms would mean that no one firm could be financially viable. In any case, for technical reasons, a monopoly may be necessary. For instance, only one firm can be given the right to acquire land for laying a gas main, while, for public transport, competing firms cannot be allowed to 'skim' the profitable commuter traffic with none providing a service at other times or on other routes.

There is also the difficulty that fixed costs may be so high that total cost can never be covered by a single price. Thus in Figure 10.8 where average total cost and demand are as depicted by curves *ATC* and *PD* respectively, it is impossible to cover total cost at a single price since at all outputs *ATC* will always exceed average revenue.

In practice the problem has been overcome in three ways:

(i) The difference has been covered by a *subsidy*, either directly, e.g. for city transport, or indirectly, through writing off accumulated deficits from time to time, e.g. for coal and railways.

(ii) A *standing charge* is levied irrespective of units consumed, e.g. for electricity. The standing charge goes to meet fixed costs; the price per unit consumed covers variable costs.

(iii) The industry is allowed to exploit its monopoly position by *price discrimination*. This is possible where different customers, having a different elasticity of demand for the product, can be kept separate, each being charged the price he is willing to pay. By 'charging what the traffic will bear', total revenue is increased. Such price discrimination by consumer category is used by railways where, for example, cheap-day trippers, senior citizens and students are charged lower fares than commuters.

The highest degree of charging 'what the traffic will bear' is where the undertaking could discriminate perfectly between every consumer and charge different prices to each (Figure 10.7). While this is impractical, a modified form, 'block pricing', separates additional amounts of the product and charges them at decreasing prices.

Thus in Figure 11.1 total revenue from a single electricity price OP would be $POMR$. But if a consumer is charged OP_1 for the first OM_1 units, OP for the second block of M_1M units, and OP_2 for the third block of MM_2 units, the extra revenue realised is shown by the two shaded areas.

11.5 The nationalised industries and privatisation

(a) The nationalised industries

State provision of community, collective and merit goods is widely accepted, provided that where provision is possible through the market, e.g. health care, education, people are free to prefer this source.

But when the state takes over major industries from the private sector, its reasons for doing so must be justified by results. In other words, is such state interference an improvement on the market's allocation of resources or is it merely the application of a political dogma?

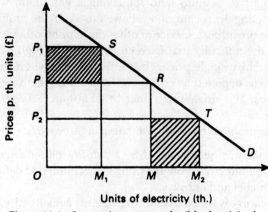

Figure 11.1 Increasing revenue by 'block pricing'

The stark fact is that neither Communism in the USSR nor the 'middle way' socialism of the UK have fulfilled the advantages claimed. The resurgence of the market economy through Mrs Thatcher's privatisation measures beginning in 1983 and the demise of Communism in Eastern Europe from 1990 were the ultimate recognition of the failure of the 'command economy'.

Since at present there seems little likelihood of any resurgence of nationalisation in the UK, we concentrate on the reasons advanced for 'privatisation'.

(b) Nature of privatisation

'Privatisation' implies more than the movement of assets from the public to the private sector. Rather it embraces all the different means by which the disciplines of the free market in the provision of goods and services can be applied to the public sector. Thus this 'pushing back the frontiers of the state' covers:

(i) the transfer of the nationalised industries to private ownership, e.g. British Telecom, British Gas, British Airways, British Airports Authority;

(ii) selling other state assets, either completely (e.g. Britoil, Rolls-Royce, motorway service areas) or partially (e.g. woodlands owned by the Forestry Authority, British Petroleum shares, council housing);

(iii) opening-up state monopolies to outside competition, e.g. relaxing licensing restrictions to allow private bus firms to compete with publicly owned services;

(iv) 'contracting-out' to the private sector services paid for out of public funds, e.g. refuse collection, street cleaning, hospital ancillary services;

(v) charging beneficiaries for publicly provided goods and services, e.g. museums, medical prescriptions, school meals, council housing;

(vi) the private finance initiative, where the private sector is induced to fund and see through projects in which the government has a strong interest (see below).

(c) The success of privatisation

While Mrs Thatcher's first term of office concentrated on reducing the PSBR, privatisation took the form of returning to the private sector firms which had been recently acquried (e.g. British Aerospace and Cable and Wireless) and by encouraging contracting-out of services. But during her second term beginning in 1983 privatisation measures were extended and integrated in line with her private enterprise views and supply-side policies (see pp. 284–6). The advantages claimed for the privatisation policy were that it would:

(i) reduce the burden of providing continual subsidies to cover the operating deficits of many state industries;

(ii) enable the sale proceeds to reduce a worrying PSBR;

(iii) remove detailed political control and permit managers to pursue their own pricing and long-term investment strategies;

(iv) improve efficiency through competition in the market;

(v) provide more resistance to trade unions' inflationary wage demands;

(vi) create a property-owning democracy by wider share ownership.

(d) Problems of privatisation

Difficulty was experienced in fixing a satisfactory price at which an industry's shares were to be offered to the public. If the offer were oversubscribed, the government would be accused of not realising the full potential of public assets; if shares were left with the underwriters, the object of achieving wide ownership would be defeated since eventually they would be bought by the institutions. A different method (British Airports Authority) was to offer a proportion of the shares at a fixed price, and the rest by tender. The device of offering a bonus royalty share for every ten shares held for the first three years was less successful than hoped for, since many small purchasers soon took their profits by selling. In the event, most offer prices undervalued assets, and recognition of this enabled the new Labour government of 1997 to impose windfall taxes on the privatised utilities amounting in all to £5.2 billion.

Steps also had to be taken to provide some form of competition for many of the industries and to introduce devices which would ensure regard was paid to the 'public interest'. The major difficulty is that while privatisation eliminates direct government involvement in decision-making and operating responsibility for particular industries, many, especially the 'natural monopolies' (chiefly public utilities) have retained their monopolist and monopsonist positions. This can result in exploitation of consumers by monopoly pricing and inefficiency through lack of competition.

Consequently, where possible, indirect competition has been fostered. For example, gas still has to compete with coal, oil and electricity, while Mercury has been granted a licence to compete in telecommunications with British Telecom. Similarly, Racal's Vodafone is a major competitor in mobile telephones with British Telecom's Cellnet. The most striking progress has been in the rapid growth of express coach services with reduced fares after competition with the National Bus Company was allowed.

An alternative arrangement has been to grant independence to firms on a franchise basis for a limited period, e.g. regional television companies. Provision is made to prevent mergers and, in reviewing the franchise, consideration can be given to past conduct as regards quality of service and sensitivity to the wishes of the public as well as to the price tendered. The difficulty with this method is that investment may be inhibited by lack of certainty of long-term future operations.

Where some form of competition is difficult to devise, the responsibility for protecting the public interest may rest with a regulatory body. Thus the Office for Telecommunications (OFTEL) acts as a watchdog to ensure fair competition by restraining British Telecom from behaviour to weaken competing firms, e.g. by delaying the installation of other firm's equipment. Furthermore, price rises are limited to 7 per cent *less* than the rate of inflation. This ensures that the consumer receives some benefit of technical improvements, but encourages efficiency in that the company is allowed to retain any additional cost savings. An aggrieved firm can appeal to the Monopolies and Mergers Commission. But in 1997 the Commission supported OFGAS which had imposed on TransCo, British Gas' pipeline business, a 21 per cent one-off price cut for the next year followed by price rises limited to 2.5 per cent *less* than the rate of inflation for each of the next four years.

In spite of these difficulties, however, we must recognise the radical nature and achievement of the Thatcher government. Until 1977 the public sector was growing and this seemed to be generally accepted. What the Thatcher government did was to reopen the debate on the proper role of the state in the economy, and other countries, e.g. France, with mixed economies are privatising their State-run industries. Even Russia, with the breakdown of the communist regime, has followed the same path.

Yet not all government activities can be satisfactorily privatised, e.g. education and medical treatment for the majority of people. For these there must be a continuing process of improving their management and accountability by efficiency scrutinies and by monitoring their progress within the financial limits imposed.

(e) The private finance initiative (PFI)

The return of rail services to the private sector virtually completed the programme of privatisation. But the PFI, formally launched in 1992, emphasised how the strengths of the private sector could be introduced to other activities traditionally regarded as within the province of the State.

The logic of the PFI is as follows. What people really want is services, for example quick transport, custody of prisoners, care of the aged, etc. But to provide these services there has to be investment e.g. roads, railways, prisons, old peoples's homes. Such investment involves assessing the financial risk, obtaining the necessary funds, and constructing and subsequently managing the project. Since these functions, it is held, are performed better by the private sector than by the state, there would be an improvement in efficiency if they were undertaken by the former. The state would then be able to obtain the services it required simply by purchasing or leasing them from the private sector provider.

In practice, the PFI covers three types of project:

(i) *Financially free standing*, in that the contractor covers his costs (including normal profit) from charges on users, e.g. the Channel Tunnel, the Heathrow-Paddington Express rail link. Here the state's contribution to the project is simply that of planning and determining the route, the private sector being responsible for its construction and management.
(ii) *Services leased to the public sector by a private contractor*, e.g. prison places, new government offices.
(iii) *Joint ventures*, where part of the cost is met from public funds to take account of the social benefits (externalities) of the scheme, e.g. less road congestion, urban regeneration. But risk-bearing, construction and subsequent management would still remain with the private sector contractor.

It is considered that involving private participation in the above ways could mean an overall increase in investment in such projects, for it would lie outside any public sector borrowing restraint.

QUESTIONS

    1 Give four reasons why the state has to provide certain goods and services.

    2 'It is in the nature of the public services that demands are literally limitless, because they are not restrained by the price mechanism which forces those making demands to balance them against costs. (*Economic Progress Report*, HM Treasury).

      (a) What is the weakness of not charging for public services?

      (b) How does a market economy indicate the level of demand and appropriate investment?

      (c) What is the difficulty of charging for health services?

      (d) When no charges are made, how in practice does the government control costs?

      (e) Give two examples of this 'administrative rationing'.

Part V

The environment

■ Ṁ 12 Externalities and cost–benefit analysis

Objectives

1 To define externalities
2 To examine possible ways of allowing for externalities in the allocation of resources
3 To outline the technique of cost–benefit analysis (CBA)

12.1 Externalities

(a) Definition

In the pure market economy, resource allocation is the result of the decisions of consumers (households) and producers (firms) who seek to maximize the difference between benefits and incurred costs. We refer to these as *private benefits* and *private costs*.

But one weakness of the market economy is that it may fail to take account of any additional benefits or costs which 'spill over' from the original decisions. A firm may decide to build a new factory on a derelict site in a depressed district. In doing so it confers external benefits – tidying up the site and reducing the cost of unemployment benefit payments. On the other hand, should the factory be built in a residential district, it would incur spill-over costs of heavy vehicle movement, noise, loss of visual beauty, etc.

Externalities (spillovers) are the costs or benefits additional to the private costs or benefits of a transaction and which are not provided for directly in the market price. Thus social costs (benefits) = private costs (benefits) + external costs (benefits).

(b) Externalities and the allocation of resources

The effect of externalities on the optimum allocation of resources can be shown diagrammatically (Figure 12.1). Suppose that a farmer applies nitrates to his field up to the point where the marginal revenue product (in terms of the value of the extra grass which will result) equals the marginal cost, *OC* kilos per hectare will be applied.

However, some of the nitrate may find its way into the water supply, and this increases as the application of nitrate per hectare increases.

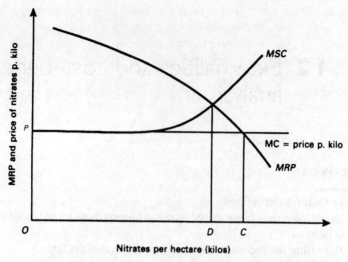

Figure 12.1 The external cost of nitrates applied to land

This external cost has had to be added to the private cost (*MC*) to obtain the true marginal social cost, shown by the curve *MSC*, so that the socially efficient application of nitrates is reduced to *OD* per hectare.

12.2 Possible methods of dealing with externalities

It should not be assumed that the *market economy* completely fails to allow for externalities. Often they are reflected in the market price. Thus shops where traffic congestion is a serious problem will, other things being equal, command lower rents than shops having nearby parking facilities. Similarly, supermarkets, with their own extensive car parks, are partly a response to parking problems in city High Streets.

Or externalities may be provided for by *private negotiation*. Thus, because weed cutting, although necessary, interferes with the fly-fishing on the Hampshire chalk streams, owners have mutually agreed to restrict it to four specified weeks in the season.

Taking this a stage further, a *pressure group* may be formed, e.g. Greenpeace, to oppose what they perceive as an environmental cost of a proposal, or to protect an external benefit, e.g. the Worldwide Fund For Nature.

Nevertheless private arrangements often prove inadequate. Where 'free-riders' cannot be excluded, it may be impossible to organise sufficient collective bargaining strength to negotiate effectively. In any case, costs (or benefits) are often so far-ranging e.g. the detrimental effects of exhaust fumes, that not all the losers (or beneficiaries) can be identified. Usually, therefore, some form of *government action* is necessary.

Because there are a variety of methods by which externalities can be allowed for the government can choose according to the particular case.

First, it may introduce a pricing system to bring externalities into the reckoning. For example, to deal with traffic congestion, parking-meters may be installed.

Second, taxation and subsidies may take this a stage further. Thus the extra tax imposed on leaded petrol reflects its higher pollution effect. On the other hand, external benefits may be allowed for by subsidies, e.g. towards the costs of repairing ancient monuments and listed buildings.

Third, externalities may be covered by physical controls. Most evident are the planning consents required for building.

Fourth, externalities may be internalised by widening the area of control. The National Trust, for instance, harmonises the interest, both of farmers and walkers, in order to secure maximum benefits from its Lake District properties.

Fifth, the government may itself assume responsibility for providing certain goods and services. This is usual when externalities are: (a) so extensive that only government authority can adequately allow for them, e.g. providing a major airport; (b) cumulative, e.g., vaccination against small-pox.

To sum up, externalities are central to many of the problems facing governments today, and especially those concerning the environment. They therefore have to be incorporated into the decision-making process, where possible through the technique of cost–benefit analysis.

12.3 Why cost–benefit analysis (CBA)?

(a) The allocation of resources in the public sector

In the market economy, resources are allocated through the interaction of demand and supply in the market. Prices are the signals which co-ordinate the wishes of consumers with the cost of supplying goods.

But market signals may be either non-existent or defective. This applies particularly to many of the goods supplied by the government, e.g. roads, bridges, airports, parks, amenity land, education, health services, new urban areas and housing. Not only are such goods provided free or at less than cost, but their scale is such that externalities loom large.

Without firm market signals, decisions on the desirability of a project may rest mainly on subjective political views, e.g. subsidisation of city transport.

But allocating resources largely through the ballot box has serious defects in deciding investment in many public projects. First, the one-man, one-vote principle does not weight votes according to the intensity of satisfaction gained or lost. Thus, the simple majority decision could allow two voters marginally in favour of, say, a by-pass to outvote one who would suffer considerably from it. Second, economic efficiency in resource allocation requires that objective criteria should be used as far as possible.

(b) The nature of CBA

CBA is a technique which seeks to bring greater objectivity into decision-making. It does this by identifying all the relevant benefits and costs of a particular scheme and quantifying them in money terms to provide, as it were, a balance sheet upon which the ultimate decision can be made.

For example, the benefits of a new motorway would obviously include the time saved in travel, fuel economies, reduced congestion in towns through which motor traffic formerly passed, fewer road accidents and the pleasure derived by the extra motorists who could now make day trips. Against this, however, would have to be set the cost of constructing the motorway, the additional noise suffered by nearby residents, the congestion on the feeder roads, the toll of animal life and so on.

12.4 Difficulties of CBA

However, in giving a monetary value to such benefits and costs, we run up against both theoretical and practical difficulties.

First, there is likely to be some form of income redistribution. Thus those who suffer from the noise of the traffic on the by-pass, lose; the motorists and lorry drivers who save travelling time, gain. Only if the losers can be fully compensated by the gainers can we be satisfied that there has been no loss of satisfaction. But can we identify all those who are adversely affected by noise, and the extent of the noise on them? If not, full compensation cannot actually be paid.

Second, even if market prices are available, they may not, through indirect taxes, subsidies, imperfect competition or government price control reflect true opportunity costs. It is impossible, therefore, to achieve consistency in making adjustments.

Third, if no charges are made for the use of the by-pass, how do we know the possible value of the benefits received? The number of motorists likely to use the road can be estimated, but how do we value the journey each makes, since some are travelling on business and others on leisure pursuits? Similarly with the reduction in accidents; we can estimate the saving to the hospital service, in police time, etc., but how do we value the physical suffering avoided? And the by-pass may result in fewer deaths: what price do we put on the saving of human life? Similar problems arise in valuing such intangibles as noise, traffic congestion and the toll of animal life. It may be possible to obtain a price by analogy, e.g. the life-span earning-power of people dying in accidents, but no such calculation can be completely satisfactory.

Fourth, when estimating spillover costs and benefits which are not priced in the market, e.g. noise and human life, should the same importance be attached to them as actual market prices when drawing up the balance sheet? Errors in such estimates, especially when 'shadow prices' form a large proportion of the balance sheet, could affect the decision on the viability of a project.

Fifth, there is the problem of deciding the cut-off point as to what externalities should be included and the 'time horizon' when assessing future benefits and costs. A project's viability could rest on these, and interested parties may be tempted to extend the cut-off point or the time-horizon to justify particular preferences.

Finally, in order to compare competing projects, we have to reduce them to present values by discounting future costs and benefits. But there are many different rates of interest to choose from, e.g. the rate at which the government can borrow, the going rate for firms, the current rate determined largely by short-term monetary considerations. If there is less risk in a public project than in a private one, the lower government borrowing rate could be used. Such a lower rate is justified by the fact that the government must consider the needs of future generations. Thus the social time preference rate is lower than the market rate since the latter is influenced by the limited time preferences of individuals.

12.5 An assessment of CBA

The theoretical and practical difficulties outlined above weaken CBA's usefulness as a tool for quantifying externalities in decision-making. But its use is further limited by other considerations.

In particular, CBA cannot be used where political decisions dominate, e.g. the continued development of nuclear weapons.

Nor can CBA be the sole basis for a project which involves irreversible decisions, such as the survival of a species of animal or plant. This is because it is impossible to estimate the current cost of a decision which would deny future generations the opportunity to choose.

To sum up, while CBA provides a rational technique for appraising projects where market information is deficient, it must not make false claims for objectivity by dealing in precise sums. It is simply an aid to decision-making, not a substitute for it. Its main role, therefore, is to present systematically all the information relevant to a decision, indicating the weight which can be placed on the accuracy of the calculations submitted. Drawing up such an agenda ensures that all the relevant issues are fully debated before the ultimate political decision is taken.

QUESTIONS

1 Before houses can be erected on a greenfield site, planning permission is required.
   (a) Why is this?
   (b) What is likely to be the effect on the price of building land?

2 At present the New Forest is the responsibility of nine separate authorities including the Forestry Commission which manages the crown lands and the public forest estate, English Nature supervises Sites of Special Scientific Interest, and the Verderers who manage the grazing and commoning. The Department of the Environment, Transport and the Regions (DETR) has proposed a new statutory body with overall responsibility for the area. What is the reasoning behind this proposal?

3 Do the methods of taxing road transport encourage more use of vehicles and thus increase congestion?

4 The DETR is proposing to build a new route for the A3, which could have the effect of spoiling a Surrey beauty spot, the Devil's Punchbowl, and crossing Hindhead Common, mostly lowland heathland which is disappearing fast.

One difficulty facing the DETR is that one route would take 72 acres of National Trust land. An alternative route would not only require an ugly viaduct, but goes through ancient woodland.

Land of the National Trust is protected from development by the National Trust Act which established it, and it can therefore refuse to surrender the land for the road. As an alternative, it has proposed a route which follows the contours of the present A3, and which it claims would inflict much less environment damage. On the other hand, this route would limit traffic speed to 44 mph, whereas the DETR routes could be up to 75 mph.

The DETR will have to decide which scheme to put before a public enquiry. But it can only take National Trust land *compulsorily* with the approval of Parliament.

(a) Would the proposal to divert the A3 be an appropriate subject for a CBA?

(b) Once the need for a new route had been accepted what would be the main thrust of the CBA?

(c) Suggest five items where there would be some difficulty in apportioning a money value.

(d) What purpose is served by:
    (i) having a National Trust?
    (ii) protecting its land by statute?

(e) Important lowland heaths are 'very vulnerable and fast disappearing in Europe'. How might a CBA allow for this?

(f) What ensures that the objections of opponents to a proposed route are given adequate consideration?

▓ M ▌3 Protecting the environment

Objectives

1 To present the environment as an 'economic problem'
2 To indicate how the government may use pricing policies to protect the environment
3 To explain why government policy will usually have to include regulation especially for conservation, pollution and road traffic problems

13.1 Economic aspects of the environment

(a) The environment as an economic good

The term 'environment 'extends our earlier concept of land (p. 89) to include the sea and the atmosphere. As such it provides a flow of goods and services:

(i) materials (such as soil, minerals and timber) and energy (from fossil fuels, tides and wind);
(ii) space, to produce food, erect buildings, develop communications and provide for sporting activities;
(iii) the 'natural world', a consumer good in that it affords utility directly for walking, holidays, safaris, nature study or just enjoyment of peaceful surroundings;
(iv) a 'sink' for waste products.

In essence, the natural environment is nature's capital, an economic good, 'scarce' yet capable of being put to *competing* alternative uses.

(b) The role of economics

Since economics is concerned with the allocation of scarce resources between alternative uses, we have to ask what contribution it can make towards solving problems of the environment, such as those of conservation, pollution and traffic congestion especially in city centres.

First, it can identify the major economic aspects. With conservation, for instance, it highlights the link between a rising standard of living and the increasing demand of future generations for open spaces and buildings of historical interest. For both conservation and pollution it can define sustainable growth. Second, it can indicate how externalities can be measured by CBA, thereby giving substance to the claims of rival pressure groups and producers' interests. Third, it can suggest appropriate measures, especially those that can operate through the market. Fourth, economics must emphasise, not only the scarcity of the environment, but its indivisibility and the possible irreversibility of decisions. Such resources as tropical rain forests, ancient woodland, fossil fuels, historical buildings and species of flora and fauna can be lost for ever as population increases and man seeks to produce more. And although in what follows the environment is discussed under the headings of 'conservation', 'pollution' and 'traffic', it must be recognised that the problems are interlocking. Woodlands and forests may be conserved because of their richness in trees and flowers or because of their historical uniqueness. Yet their very existence fulfils the further function of absorbing the emissions of CO_2 from cars and power-stations and releasing oxygen. In other words, they are recycling waste and helping to prevent global warming. In contrast, the dumping of waste products, such as nuclear waste, cadmium and sulphurous gases can even threaten man's very existence.

Finally, economics should draw attention to the limitations of economic solutions, especially as regards the cultural and moral aspects. For instance, should the market be left to decide where a plant for processing poisonous substances is located? Local people may be so poor that they require the employment opportunities it can provide, and their economic weakness may force them to accept the accompanying health hazard.

13.2 Conservation

(a) The nature of conservation

With the exception of the special case of protecting an irreplaceable resource conservation is not simply preservation. Instead it seeks *creative continuity* by promoting vitality of use of the environment while ensuring that change is sympathetic to the quality of life for both present and future generations. Thus, in the UK, conservation embraces a wide field – green belts around towns, national parks, public bridle ways and footpaths, animal, fish, butterfly protection, sites of Special Scientific Interest, National Trust property, mineral and oil reserves, museums, buildings of special architectural and historical interest, and so on.

Certain aspects of conservation need emphasising. First, there is an *opportunity cost*. A 'green belt', for instance, keeps land in agriculture at a lower current market value than, say, housing, and also extends the journey to work of those city workers who live beyond it.

Second, externalities loom large. A farmer who rips out a hedge does so because a larger field will cost less to work. Yet there are external costs, e.g. for nature lovers and walkers who prefer the patchwork landscape of small fields.

Third, conservation is concerned with changes over time in both demand and supply. But, because individuals have a restricted time horizon, it often means that decisions cannot be left entirely to market forces – particularly those concerned with estimating demand in the distant future, allowing for externalities, preserving stocks of renewable resources, and the impossibility of reversing wrong decisions.

(b) The conservation of stocks

Using a resource in excess of its capacity to reproduce itself eventually reduces supply to the point where its price rises. This produces a contraction of demand and a search for substitutes. Such market responses help to conserve both renewable stocks, e.g. of trees for timber and non-renewable stocks, e.g. fossil fuels and minerals.

However, some environmental resources, e.g. fish, whales, grouse, are renewable, only if the contraction in demand occurs soon enough to leave a stock which does not fall below the minimum necessary to effect a recovery. Conservation here has to be concerned with limiting what is harvested in order to maintain a stable stock at least at this minimum.

In contrast, some resources are not only non-renewable but, if lost, irreplaceable, e.g. an historic building, ancient woodland, species of animals, birds, insects and flowers on the verge of extinction. Once they disappear, they are lost for ever. This is a special case of conservation since here the over-riding objective is preservation.

In order to illustrate how economic analysis may assist in both forms of conservation, we take two examples – maintaining fish stocks and preserving an historic building.

13.3 Maintaining a renewable stock of fish

(a) The function of private property rights

Overfishing means that over a period catches are so large that they exceed the rate of growth of the stock, which therefore declines in size. This could be a cumulative process resulting in the progressive shrinking of stock below the minimum necessary for recovery.

The basic reason for the failure to conserve the stock is the absence of private property rights over the fishing grounds. As a result, no one fisherman will voluntarily limit his catch, because that simply means that others can catch more. Figure 13.1 illustrates.

We assume:

(i) the price of fish is constant;
(ii) as the size of the catch increases beyond a certain level, the stock of fish declines because the catch exceeds the rate of fish renewal;
(iii) the marginal productivity of effort falls as the stock of fish falls since it becomes increasingly more difficult to catch fish. Thus, even with the

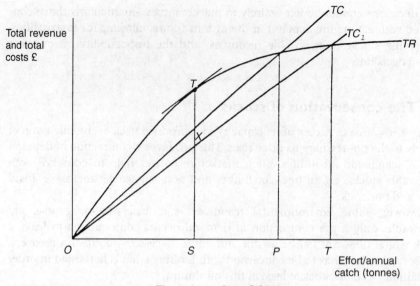

Figure 13.1 Over-fishing

assumed constant price of fish, marginal revenue productivity falls (shown by the declining slope of the total revenue curve, *TR*);
(iv) the marginal cost of effort is constant, giving a total cost curve (*TC*).

If there were individual property rights over the fishing grounds – only with shellfish would this be possible – the owner would fix an annual catch which maximised profit. In Figure 13.1 this would be *OS* where *TR* – *TC* is at a maximum. For the sake of simplicity we will assume that this catch equals the renewal rate of the present stock; it is the sustainable catch. But up to *OP* super-normal profit can still be made. Competition between boats would eliminate this by pushing the catch to *OP*. This represents gross overfishing for the sustainable stock is only *OS*.

It should be noted that larger ships and new techniques will lower costs, e.g. *TC* to TC_1. This will have the effect of increasing the catch size to *OT*, thereby aggravating the problem of maintaining the stock.

(b) Methods of controlling overfishing

On our simplifying assumptions, overfishing occurs between *S* and *P*. To maintain the stock the annual catch has to be restricted to *OS*. Possible ways in which this can be achieved are:

(i) *Vesting fishing rights in a single body* which owns the fishing boats. Thus Iceland took the first step in this direction by confining fishing within 200 miles of its coast to Icelandic vessels. But this only goes a part of the way. Unless the Icelandic government also owns the fishing fleet, there must be some further control over the catch.

(ii) *Imposing such physical controls* as: restricting the number of vessels by license; enlarging the net mesh to ensure only mature fish of a certain size are taken; requiring each boat to stay in harbour for so many days a year.

The difficulty with most physical controls is enforcement. They are also resented by the fishermen since some suffer a loss of livelihood as marginal boats are forced out of the industry.

(iii) *Taxing catches at so much a tonne is administratively easier.* In Figure 13.1 the tax would have to yield *TX*. Such a tax is also flexible in that different rates of tax can be applied to different types of fish according to their relative scarcity.

(iv) *Introducing quotas* for each ship, which in total will allow an aggregate catch of *OS*. Since abnormal profit can be made by those fishing, these quotas could be sold to cover the administrative costs. Once in existence, quotas can be traded on a 'quota market' (see p. 187).

13.4 Preserving an historic building

Where a building of historical importance e.g. an Elizabethan manor house, has outlived its usefulness as a residence, conservation has to take into account the irreversibility of a decision to demolish it. Moreover, while demolition may be the current market solution, it could be based on defective criteria, e.g. in estimating future demand and in choosing the appropriate discount rate for arriving at present values. Consider the following example.

(a) The market solution

The historic building (which we will assume is a house in the centre of town) will be demolished when the site can be put to a more 'profitable' use. This necessitates calculating its present capital value, obtained by totalling the discounted flow of net benefits expected in the future. It is likely that, ignoring inflation, the value of the house will fall over time as it becomes increasingly unsuitable for modern living requirements. This is shown by the curve *PP* (Figure 13.2).

In contrast, the capital value of a new office block (*RR*) will eventually be such that, even allowing for the cost of rebuilding, the cleared site is worth more than the historic house. If left to market forces, therefore, demolition of the historic house occurs in year *D*.

(b) Possible weaknesses of the market solution

On what grounds may *economics* justify interference with this market solution?

First, it is unlikely that the curve *PP* reflects the true opportunity cost of the historic house at any one time. For one thing, certain benefits are likely to have been ignored.

Apart from *external benefits* (such as the pleasure which the view of a historic house gives to passers-by), we should recognise the existence of an 'option

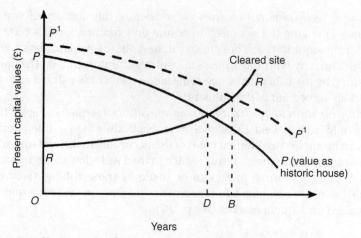

Figure 13.2 Adjustments to the present value of a historic building for different uses

demand'. Where decisions are irreversible (as with the destruction of a historic building), many people would pay something just to postpone such a decision. The difficulty lies in quantifying such 'option demand', but its existence is evident in the fact that many people subscribe voluntarily to the National Trust and the Worldwide Fund for Nature, for example. The rest enjoy the option as 'free riders', but their demand should also be included.

Furthermore, because the rate of social time-preference is lower than that of private time-preference (see p. 173), a present capital value derived from the lower rate of discount appropriate to the social time-preference would be higher than one based on a rate of discount which merely reflected *private* time-preference.

These additional benefits and the lower discount rate would give the historic house a higher capital value curve, P^1P^1, with demolition being postponed until year B.

Second, and even more important, we have to recognise that, when dealing with the future, knowledge is not perfect. Thus a decision to demolish a building may be based on a defective assessment of the future conditions of demand and supply. This is not serious when we are dealing with *flows*, such as the services provided by offices, since new offices can always be built if demand increases in the future. But demolishing a historic building diminishes a stock which cannot be replaced. The situation is illustrated in Figure 13.2.

In period t, the historic building has a low value, OH. On the other hand, an office block would command price OP_1. Over time, however, the value of the historic building increases relatively to that of offices. This is because, with higher incomes and more leisure, people take a greater interest in historic buildings. Increased demand means that in period $t + 2$ the price of the historic building has risen to OH_2. On the other hand, the demand for offices is not likely to increase so quickly, income-elasticity of demand being lower. Moreover, with technological improvements in construction, the supply curve shifts to the right over time. As a result, in period $t + 2$ the price of offices falls to OP_{t+2}.

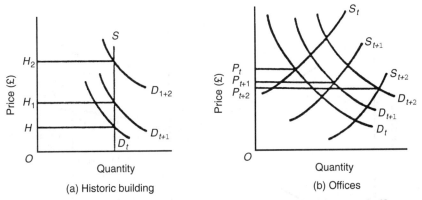

Figure 13.3   Changes in future relative prices of historic buildings and offices

The situation is transferred to Figure 13.4. We can assume that the price of the office block in period *t* gives a cleared site value of *FD*, so that demolition of the historic building and redevelopment of the site as offices has become a viable economic proposition. Eventually, however, the value of the historic building starts to rise, while the rate of increase in the value of the cleared site declines. Indeed, if demolition in year *D* could be prevented, by year *E* the present value of the historic building once again exceeds the value of the cleared site.

(c) Government policy for preserving historic buildings

The above analysis suggests that the government must intervene in the free operation of the price system in order to preserve historic buildings. Its action can take a variety of forms.

First, the building could be brought under public ownership. Such a policy would usually be followed where the cost of excluding free-riders would be prohibitive, e.g. Hadrian's Wall. Equally important, it would allow welfare to be maximised (see p. 159). Finally, public ownership would automatically allow external benefits to be internalised.

Second, the historic building could be left in private ownership but a subsidy given through repair grants or tax concessions on the grounds of the external benefits conferred. Such a subsidy would increase net benefits to the owner and so raise the present value (as shown by the dotted line in Figure 13.4). However, there are difficulties. Many external benefits cannot be quantified while shortage of funds could mean that the subsidy was insufficient to raise the present-use value curve permanently above the cleared-site curve so that demolition is only postponed to year *B*, unless other action is taken.

Third, any building of special architectural or historic interest may be 'listed'. This means that it cannot be altered or demolished without the consent of the local planning authority. While this gives protection against positive acts of demolition, it may not cover destruction by the neglect of the owner. Such neglect occurs because high maintenance costs result in negative net benefits. Even though in such circumstances the local authority can appropriate the building,

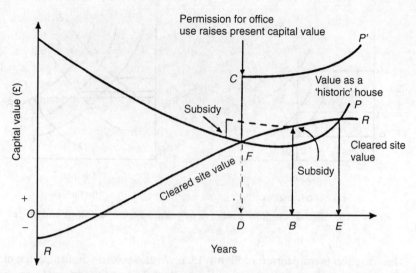

Figure 13.4 Methods of preserving a historic building

there is reluctance to do so since the cost of maintenance now falls on public funds. Thus, in practice, 'listing' in year *D* may be only a 'stop-gap' measure, bridging the years between *D* and *E* (Figure 13.4) until increasing demand raises the value of the historic building above that of the cleared site. More frequently, 'listing' simply imposes a prohibition on demolition until an alternative policy can be formulated.

Fourth, giving permission for the building to be adapted to a more profitable use provides such a policy. Thus stables may be converted into a dwelling, and houses into offices. This has the effect of increasing net benefits and thus raising the present value curve so that it is above the cleared-site curve. This change of use is shown as taking place in year *D* and the new present value product is depicted by the line FCP^1 (Figure 13.4).

In consenting to a change of use of a historic building, the objective of the authorities must be to retain as many of the original features as possible. Thus some flexibility of building regulations is necessary, for example, as regards height of rooms, window space and even fire precautions. As in Figure 13.3a the distinctive character of the converted building may produce increasing rentals over time, e.g. for prestige reasons, so that not only is it preserved but there is no charge on public funds.

13.5 Pollution

(a) Aspects of pollution

Pollution occurs when man introduces waste matter into the environment directly or indirectly causing damage to persons other than himself. While residual waste is created in consumption (e.g. household waste, scrapped consumer durables, litter), it is pollution resulting from production which is more serious (e.g. acid rain, smoke, gases, toxic chemicals, pesticide contaminants, liquid effluents, noise, oil spillages) for it affects the whole of the environment – land, sea and the atmosphere. It is harmful to human health, e.g. through carbon monoxide fumes; to agriculture, e.g. resulting in lower yields or poorer quality; to buildings, e.g. in corrosion of stonework; to amenity, e.g. causing damage to fish, fauna and flora; and to the life of the whole planet through the 'greenhouse' effect produced by carbon dioxide discharged into the atmosphere.

It is the rapid increase over the last century in population and economic growth, with its accompanying industrialisation, that has given rise to pollution. What is new, however, is the recognition of the *problem* of pollution. Paradoxically, while economic growth may cause pollution, growth may be an essential prerequisite of environmental improvement. Economic poverty compels people to accept visual squalor, poor buildings and polluted watercourses. Prosperity enables us to buy a better environment. For example, the EU's excess production of foodstuffs has made it easier to switch to preserving the landscape.

(b) Degradation of the environment: definition of pollution

Everybody can recognise evidence of pollution. The economist, however, must have a precise definition. Present-day concern is with the increasing environmental pollution resulting from both population and economic growth. Production involves unwanted residuals – smoke, poisonous chemicals and gases, noise, household waste, etc. Some, such as carbon dioxide gas, can be transformed by the environment into harmless or even beneficial materials (e.g. oxygen). But this takes time, and *pollution occurs when the flow of residual emissions exceeds the natural environment's capacity to absorb them.* Indeed pollution may even reduce the environment's ability to assimilate waste.

(c) Technology and the control of pollution

While technological developments stimulate growth, it could be that new technology will allow growth, while containing pollution. Such developments could take the form of: (a) substitute products which are more environmentally friendly, e.g. degradable containers; (b) greater efficiency in production to reduce waste; (c) on-site treatment of controlled disposal of waste, e.g. desulphurisation of gases by power stations, catalytic converters on cars; (d) the replacement of coal and oil with 'greener' sources of energy, e.g. natural gas, wind, tide.

But while such technical developments are likely to occur eventually, what is 'sustainable pollution' must be assessed in the context of the current technology employed. It is here that economic analysis can contribute to a solution of the problem by suggesting and examining a range of broad options.

(d) The economist's approach

As we have seen in previous chapters, the economist emphasises *marginal* decisions. While everybody likes clear air, pure water, a peaceful environment, clean pavements, roads free from congestion, etc., pollution abatement incurs costs. Thus the choice is not the simple one between clean air and polluted air, but between various levels of dirty air. In short, we have to apply the marginal principle and accept that level of pollution where the cost of further abatement exceeds the extra benefit which results.

(e) Why does the market economy fail to control pollution?

In most cases pollution represents external costs. The right to peace and quiet, the right to enjoy a landscape unspoiled by electricity pylons, the right to swim from an oil-free beach are not private legal rights which can be easily enforced. Often, therefore, no *private* cost is incurred for infringing those rights. Thus in Figure 13.5 if there is no cost to a chemical manufacturer of discharging effluent into the river, he will produce chemicals up to the point *OC*. But when we take into account the poisoning of fish, the destruction of vegetation which provides a habitat for insects and birds and the overall loss of visual beauty for ramblers, such spillover costs have to be added to private costs to obtain the aggregate social cost. This means that while *OC* is the efficient level of production for the chemical manufacturer, the *socially* efficient level of production is *OD*, because here marginal social cost equals marginal social benefit (assuming marginal private benefit equals marginal social benefit). In other words, if more than *OD* is produced there is a misallocation of resources.

(f) Policy difficulties

While this analysis of the nature of the problem is fairly straightforward, difficulties occur in devising and applying an appropriate policy.

First, although the costs of pollution control can be measured in money terms, the benefits are 'intangibles', having no price-tag since they are not traded in the

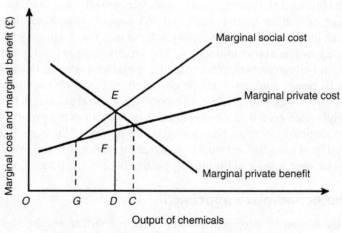

Figure 13.5 Efficient output with external costs

market. Take as an example the chemical factory which discharges effluent into a river. While the value of the fishing rights lost can be measured by market information, the value of the loss suffered by bird-watchers and ramblers has no direct market price. This means that the technique of shadow pricing, with all its weaknesses, has to be employed (see p. 172).

Second, most economic assessments of damage are made after the pollution has occurred. But adjustments in response to such pollution may already have been made. For example, the cabbage yield in a market garden may be 20 per cent below that which could have been expected in a clean-air environment. Yet this loss would understate the damage if, in an environment originally free from smoke, more profitable tomatoes would have been grown. In practice, it is extremely difficult to ascertain and measure this 'adjustment factor'.

Third, since pollution occurs in different forms, circumstances and scale, it is necessary to apply different policies to deal with the problem.

(g) Possible policies

(i) 'Greening' public opinion

Publicity drawing people's attention to the nature of the pollution problem by the government and pressure groups, such as the Green Party and Friends of the Earth, has had a remarkable success in recent years. Households have become waste-recycling conscious and the 'greenhouse' effect has become part of every-day conversation whenever there is a prolonged spell of hot weather.

Firms have responded. Pilkington Glass. for instance, encourage managers to integrate environmental responsibility in all business decision-making, covering such matters as waste and emission reduction, recycling waste and energy saving. Similarly, B&Q, Homebase and MFI have pledged to supply only goods made with timber from sustainable forests, with the sources being monitored.

(ii) Setting up an environmental protection agency

Externalities arise because of non-existent, ill-defined or unenforceable private property rights. To overcome this, it may be possible to create an agency in which these property rights are vested, in effect internalising externalities in order to maximise benefits and minimise costs. For example, the Environment Agency coordinates drainage, water supply, waste disposal and angling interests.

(iii) Market negotiation

If a 'market' in the pollution can be established, the optimum amount of pollution can be arrived at. Suppose a garden owner wishes to burn all his rubbish at the weekend when his neighbours just want to enjoy sitting in their gardens. They could negotiate with the burner to burn at some other time, either by arrangement or at a price. In the latter case, the externality is being 'priced'.

The same principle could apply on the international scale. Brazil could be paid not to clear her equatorial rain forests, and Sweden already assists Poland in reducing acid rain, because the acid rain from Poland damages Sweden.

Usually, however, if the market is to be used to control pollution there must be incentives to avoid pollution by conserving energy or to reduce pollution by the controlled disposal of waste products.

(iv) Direct regulation imposing a maximum level of pollution

Here the government decides what each polluter must do to reduce pollution, and enforces it under penalty of law, e.g. environmental conditions of planning, no discharge of oil waste by ships within so many miles of the coast. Such a policy, however, provides little incentive to instal anti-pollution devices so that the specified standard becomes the target, involves constant inspection, and tends to impose national (sometimes international) standards instead of allowing for different local circumstances. On the other hand, the policy does allow the polluter to find the cheapest means of keeping within the specified maximum.

It should be noted that rigid control is essential where: (a) pollution is a threat to existence, e.g. blue asbestos dust in workshops; and (b) pollution is cumulative and becomes dangerous at a certain level. e.g. cadmium absorption by the soil.

(v) Subsidising the reduction of pollution

Where it is impossible or too costly to identify the polluters (e.g. litter louts) the government itself takes responsibility for pollution control, the cost being covered from the proceeds of taxation. Alternatively, the government may decide that specific compensation is adequate to deal with the particular pollution, especially where this is localised. Thus in clean-air zones, people are given subsidies to instal smokeless fuel appliances. On the other hand, losers may be compensated, e.g. grants to provide double glazing to reduce noise from aircraft. The difficulty is that such public schemes simply mean that polluters are passing on the cost to the taxpayer. Often, therefore, where polluters can be identified, control has to be enforced through individual penalties imposed by the courts, e.g. for dropping litter, polluting watercourses.

Alternatively, the government could seek to reduce pollution by directly subsidising: (a) the development of new techniques to reduce pollution or save energy; (b) the production of cleaner substitutes e.g. a reduced tax on unleaded petrol; or (c) the recycling of waste, e.g. bottles.

(vi) Taxing pollution

A charge or tax according to the level of pollution seeks to ensure that the 'polluter pays'. In terms of Figure 13.5 a tax of EF would induce the factory-owner to limit his production to OD.

Such a policy has the merit of flexibility, and is thus particularly desirable where the benefits can only be ascertained by trial and error or where the aim is to achieve a progressive reduction in pollution since charges can be adjusted accordingly. Moreover, charges have the effect of 'internalising externalities': once the tax is set, the polluter can respond to it as he chooses. Thus a profit-maximising polluter would instal his own pollution control to the point where the marginal cost of doing so was less than the tax saved. Furthermore, the proceeds of a tax can be used to compensate those losing by the residual pollution. Finally, in as much as the charge raises the price of the product, the actual consumer now pays the full opportunity cost of production – a fairer solution than passing on the external costs to society at large.

Even so, a charges policy has its limitations. First, a tax can only be imposed if the individual polluter can be identified. Second, there is the problem of *how* to tax. If it is on units of output, e.g. tonnes of nitrate fertiliser, the larger producer pays more as his pollution is likely to be greater. But this does nothing to encourage a reduction in the pollution *per unit*. If, however, the degree of pollution can be measured, e.g. the quantity of toxic waste being discharged into the river, and taxed accordingly, there would be an incentive to instal an anti-pollution device.

Second, there are distributional implications if the product whose price rises is one which is bought mainly by poor persons, though the proceeds of the tax can be used to compensate.

Third, if a country imposes a tax unilaterally, e.g. on the burning of fossil fuels, it may give an unfair advantage to its foreign competitors.

(vii) Tradeable permits

Suppose in Figure 13.5 that output represents the aggregate of all chemical firms on a given river. The government decides to limit pollution to *GD*. Each firm is given a licence to emit a share of *GD*. If the government wishes to raise revenue (equal, say to *EF*), it can sell or auction the licence. The essence of these pollution permits is that they can be traded on the 'permit' market. Those firms having a high cost of reducing emission will want to buy permits from the efficient firms who sell them for more than it costs them to abate.

This method provides an incentive to those who sell permits to instal equipment which reduces pollution. At the same time, it uses the market to cover much of the regulation required. One difficulty is that as firms become more abatement-efficient, the supply of permits coming on to the market will increase, and their fall in price will allow firms inefficient in pollution control to buy them. Here the government could itself buy on the market and, by confiscating permits, keep up the cost of pollution.

13.6 Road traffic

(a) The benefits and costs of motor transport

In the twentieth century motor transport has increased accessibility for both resources and people through the mobility, flexibility and convenience it affords. It has thus contributed to the improvement of living standards.

Unfortunately as the use of road vehicles has increased, the benefits they afford have been progressively diminished by external costs. In providing a motorway network and by passing cities and towns, inroads are made into the countryside, even on occasions intruding on areas of natural beauty or of special scientific interest.

But it is the concentration of motor traffic in urban areas which presents the major environmental problems. The greater mobility afforded by the car has enabled workers to live some distance from their place of employment and has thus been a major cause of urban sprawl. Moreover, people still have to travel from the suburbs to the city centre for work, shopping and leisure activities. Whereas traffic increases as we approach the centre, road capacity decreases. The resulting concentration of traffic imposes social costs on non-car users by exhaust-fume pollution, noise, the danger of accident, visual blight, inconvenience to pedestrians and loss of time to bus travellers. More than that, the expansion of motor transport has led to the demand for road space exceeding supply so that one road-user imposes on other road-users the extra costs of congestion – higher fuel consumption, reduced speed and time spent in traffic jams. Indeed, the problem is likely to become more acute as income and population increase and the use of cars and commercial vehicles expands.

(b) The urban traffic problem

The major external cost is congestion, for this undermines the chief advantage – accessibility – which motor transport affords. It is necessary, therefore, to analyse the problem and to consider possible ways of dealing with it.

Two salient points should be noted. First, it is basically a peak-hour problem, confined to approximately five hours a day on fewer than 250 working days of the year. Second, it is largely the result of the increased use of the private car for journeys to work. The former tends to restrict the amount of investment which can be profitably undertaken in the transport system. The latter indicates that some effort should be directed towards making the road-user pay the full costs (including external costs) of taking his vehicle on the road.

Bearing these principles in mind, actual policy can follow six main lines:

(i) do nothing;
(ii) invest in the construction of more roads;
(iii) impose physical controls to improve traffic flows;
(iv) restrict parking;
(v) use the price system to allocate existing road space;
(vi) use the existing road system more efficiently through a better distribution of the means of travel as between the car and public transport.

(i) Do nothing

Some people argue that trying to improve movement on the roads is self-defeating: the easier it is to travel, the more people use their cars. As congestion increases, there comes a point where the cost in terms of wasted time and frustration is such that motorists switch to public transport.

But such a policy has snags. First, it provides no *incentive* for motorists to switch to public transport. There should be such an incentive, since those who do switch make travelling easier for those who do not. Second, the high level of congestion envisaged would become a permanent feature, penalising equally the essential car-users and the optional users, those for whom using public transport would impose no severe hardship. Third, the congestion would affect non-car users, such as pedestrians.

(ii) Invest in more roads

The long-term solution is increased investment to improve the urban environment and the circulation of traffic. This could take the form of comprehensive redevelopment of existing city centres and improved town planning, such as siting industry away from city centres.

The main thrust, however, would be to build more roads linking the suburbs and city centre. But by-passes also play a part, in that through traffic is siphoned off.

It is doubtful, however, whether this would be a complete solution.

(i) As it is difficult to impose tolls on short-run roads, they have to be financed from taxation and made freely available to all wishing to use them. But as the amount which can be devoted to public investment in general is limited, roads have to compete with defence, health care, social welfare, the modernisation of public transport, and so on. Yet, without direct pricing of road use, there is no precise indication of what people are prepared to pay for more roads and therefore no firm basis for comparing the rate of return with that of alternative capital projects (though CBA may help). Thus there is no answer to the basic question of whether vast investment in new urban road systems is economically viable, bearing in mind that it is largely to provide only for peak-hour travel between the suburbs and the city centre.

(ii) Investment in roads, as opposed to extending public transport, involves an income redistribution, since public transport is used mainly by poorer persons. The result is that the decision on whether to invest in more roads is eventually a political one and pressure groups in favour may be successful in spite of the very high cost of urban road construction.

(iii) It would take many years for a complete road network to be built. In the meantime, movements in industry and population and transport developments could change needs considerably.

(iv) The demand for road space seems to respond to supply, with better roads generating more motor transport. Demand and supply, therefore, are never in equilibrium. This was recognised in 1994 when the government announced a major curtailment of its road-building programme.

This means that we are always faced with a short-term situation of making the best possible use of existing road-space, as follows.

(iii) Manage traffic flows

Some immediate improvement in traffic flows can be achieved by clearways, reversible lanes, linked traffic signals, bus lanes, miniroundabouts, etc. Such adaptation can often be combined with schemes which improve the environment e.g. designating pedestrian-only areas, constructing culs-de-sac in residential districts or simply restricting the movement of heavy vehicles in residential zones.

In the longer term attempts can be made to spread the flow of rush-hour traffic over a longer period (e.g. by staggering working hours) or to reverse the flow (e.g. by encouraging offices to locate in the suburbs and the building of out-of-town shopping centres). Nevertheless care must be taken to ensure that the commercial heart of the city is not destroyed as a result. This latter consideration has led to government discouragement of further out-of-town shopping developments.

It must be noted, however, that traffic management can only increase the capacity of the road network when the initial *pattern* of movement is sub-optimal. Even then it only provides a short-term relief from congestion since, unless entry is restrained, improving the traffic flow eventually generates additional traffic.

(iv) Restrict parking

Perhaps the greatest advantage of the motor vehicle is the convenience of door-to-door travel. This needs parking facilities. These contribute to accessibility and – by increasing catchment areas – to the prosperity of shopping and business centres. Yet, paradoxically, too many facilities lead to congestion, and so an appropriate balance between parking and movement has to be sought. Indeed the old Greater London Council proposed taxing each private office parking space provided, in order to divert commuters to public transport.

Parkers are of two sorts: the 'long-term' parker (the commuter) and the 'short-term' parker (the shopper and the business visitor). The problem is largely one of removing the 'long-term' parker from the streets, so that there will be sufficient accommodation for 'short-term' parkers to pursue their shopping or business activities. Two approaches are possible: physical control and road pricing. Both involve costs of adequate administration.

Physical controls take various forms, from the restriction of parking to certain days, time, side of street or type of vehicle (such as taxis only) to the complete prohibition of all kinds of waiting, including the loading and unloading of commercial vehicles. Permits may also be issued to give priority to essential users and residents. Furthermore, planning consents for new buildings usually stipulate the minimum number of parking spaces to be provided.

While physical controls are unrelated to ability to pay, they lack the subtlety of the price mechanism's rationing function. Where parking is possible, charges can be imposed to bring demand into line with the limited number of spaces available. In order that street parking should be confined to short-term parkers, it is usually linked with the physical control of limiting the time which can be spent at any one bay.

Kerbside parking has to be supplemented by off-street parking, especially for the long-term commuter. Since the cost of this is high, it is more likely to be provided where meter charges are also high. Local-authority car parks are mostly hardstands and tend to be for short-term parkers only. Multi-storey and underground garages are expensive to build. Since demand drops off at night, they are largely dependent financially on there being sufficient day-time parkers to pay the relatively high charges. If these, however, induce commuters to travel by public transport, there is a net benefit to the community through reduced congestion and less cost of road construction. This would justify any shortfall in revenue being underwritten by the local authority.

The provision of cheaper parking for shoppers and other short-term parkers has also to be considered, especially in the light of current government policy of protecting the vitality of city centres by restricting new out-of-town shopping developments. But without massive local authority subsidy, such parking cannot be provided in the city centre. This suggests that 'park and ride' arrangements will have to be the preferred solution.

(v) Use the price system to allocate scarce road space

The principle of allocating limited parking space by charges can also be applied to moving vehicles by imposing a tax to reduce the use of vehicles and so relieve congestion.

In addition to his running costs, the private motorist allows for the time his journey will take. The greater the traffic flow, the longer this time. There is thus a rising cost curve, *MPC* (Figure 13.6). The demand curve, *D*, also takes account of this time factor: the greater the congestion, the longer the time journey, so that demand falls as the intensity of traffic-flow increases. Thus, left to the private motorists' decisions, the flow of traffic will be *OP*, where private marginal cost equals marginal benefit (price).

But while the private motorist allows for the time-cost of a heavy traffic-flow, the very fact of his taking his car on the road will add to the time-cost of others. Congestion can be defined as occurring when the private use of his car by a motorist 'impedes' the movement of other road-users, that is, at *OC* (Figure 13.6). There is a marginal social cost which, if added to the marginal private cost, gives the curve *MSC*. Applying the principle that output should take place where marginal social benefit equals marginal social cost the economically efficient flow of traffic would be *OS*.

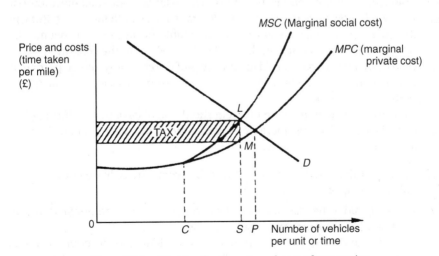

Figure 13.6 Allowing for the external cost of congestion

This could be achieved by imposing a charge equal to *LM*. Ideally such a charge should reflect the time, miles covered on the road, the degree of congestion, the size of car and the location and direction of the journey in relation to the city centre. The difficulty lies in devising a single tax which covers all these requirements and is practical.

Imposing tolls on certain roads discriminates against the poor essential motorist, especially where no suitable alternative route is available. A high motor vehicle licence, by raising fixed costs, simply penalises car ownership rather than congestion costs. A petrol tax reflects only mileage and size of car, and is thus unfair to the country-dweller. Requiring the motorist to buy a permit to enter a congested area does not take account of the degree of congestion or the extent of use within the congested area.

The most appropriate method of charging is to fit each car with a meter which would electronically register 'units' as certain control points were passed. These control points could be located more closely to each other as the city centre was approached, and the number of units could be varied according to the time of day.

Some economists consider that an additional advantage of such road-pricing is that it would establish 'road values' and thus rates of return to guide future road investment. But metering faces difficulties.

(i) Though it is economically valid and technically possible, it is only practical if the cost of installation, the periodic reading of the meter and the payment of charges are accepted by the motorist. The costs of administration and enforcement could be high.

(ii) Since this meter does not catch the parker, there would have to be additional parking charges.

(iii) It raises a distributional problem in that the wealthier motorist would be able to travel on the now uncongested roads, while the poorer *non*-motorist would enjoy better public transport. The relatively-low-income motorist, who would now have to resort to public transport, would lose most. But why should the price mechanism be unacceptable on account of income differences in the road price market and not elsewhere in the economy?

(iv) Unless *MC* pricing is imposed in all sectors of the economy and, in particular, on all modes of transport, an optimal allocation of road use will not be achieved.

(v) It has to be decided how the tax yield should be disposed of. Returning it to motorists would simply increase their income so that they could reclaim the road-use they have given up.

(vi) Pricing policies to improve the split between the private car and public transport

We have to consider the respective merits of the private car and public transport from both the demand and supply sides.

On the demand side, the car affords a convenient door-to-door means of transport and, in comparison with public transport, is comfortable. Even traffic jams can be made tolerable by listening to the radio or cassette player. In contrast, public transport may be irregular and incur the discomfort of standing. Its great merit is speed, especially with rail travel for the long-distance commuter. Moreover, the method of charging for car travel as opposed to public transport favours the former. Much of the car's costs are fixed costs – the initial purchase price, the motor vehicle tax, insurance, and so on. The cost of actually using the car – the variable cost – is the cost of fuel and wear and tear (though motorists are inclined to ignore the latter). Thus the private motorist adopts a marginal-cost basis of pricing.

In contrast, apart from any subsidies given, fares on public transport have to cover both fixed and variable costs; that is, the fare per mile tends to equal *average* total cost. The price system cannot yield an efficient allocation of resources between private and public transport when different principles are adopted as the basis of pricing.

Moreover, since fixed costs, particularly for the railways, are high, public transport tends to operate under conditions of decreasing cost. This means that the principle of marginal-cost pricing cannot be used if total costs are to be covered (Figure 13.7). Instead public transport seeks to cover total costs by price discrimination, charging higher fares to passengers whose demand is least elastic. Such passengers tend to be commuters and business people – and higher fares simply induce them to switch to travelling by car. The alternative is to make good the shortfall by government subsidy.

On the supply side, consideration has to be given to the respective cost patterns of the car and public transport. Figure 13.8 shows that when a relatively small number of passengers have to be coped with, the car has a cost advantage. Since the initial fixed costs to put a car on the road are so small compared with the bus and train, for exposition purposes average cost per passenger can be regarded as constant.

However, as the number of passengers increases, the higher fixed costs of the bus are spread more thinly, so that eventually at *OB* average cost per passenger mile falls below that of the car. Rail transport has to incur even higher fixed costs in maintaining tracks, stations, expensive rolling stock, and so on, and so costs

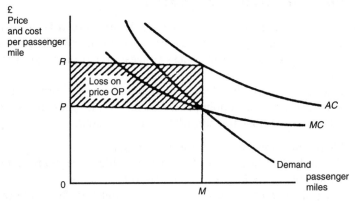

Figure 13.7 The effect of high fixed costs on public transport

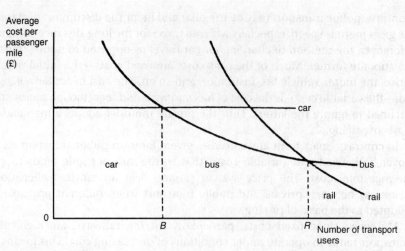

Figure 13.8 Difference in average costs per passenger mile of car, bus and rail transport

per passenger mile are only below those of the bus at a high level of passenger use, *OR*. In addition, development density should be high so that the number travelling from a single station is large. Hence urban rail travel is limited to very large cities.

One further point should be noted: the bus is more flexible in use than the train both in routeing and in dealing with small variations in the number of passengers. In its turn, the car is more flexible than the bus, especially for cross-commuting to employment in suburban offices, and so on.

It must again be emphasised that while the bus and train have a *cost* advantage over the car in dealing with passenger-users above *OB* and *OR* respectively, relative prices for each mode of travel will also depend upon demand. It may be that people's preference for car travel is so high its price would indicate that this mode should prevail even when the number of transport-users is high.

(c) A policy for traffic congestion

The above analysis suggests that on *cost* considerations rush-hour travel is most economically provided by public transport, since this follows the predominantly radial flow to the centre and causes less congestion per passenger carried than the private car.

The logical first step, therefore, would be to tax the private car-user as described earlier. This tax, supplemented by funds from general taxation, could be used to subsidise public transport. The subsidy would:

(i) enable public transport to cover its fixed costs;
(ii) recognise the 'fall-back' or 'option' benefit which everybody enjoys simply from there being available public transport facilities;
(iii) reward public transport users for the external benefits conferred by not increasing road congestion and other environmental costs, and

(iv) redistribute income in favour of the poorer sections of the community who are most dependent on public transport.

In addition, price discrimination could be introduced into the fare structure to allow for differences in the time and direction of travel so that passengers travelling in the direction of the traffic flow during the rush hours pay more.

But there are difficulties. First, the policy is dependent upon the extent to which travellers would respond to the change in relative prices and switch to public transport. People seem wedded to their cars, and public transport is regarded as an inferior good. In other words, there is a low price-elasticity of demand for the private car and a high income-elasticity of demand. Indeed, it can be argued that the decline in the use of public transport is a result more of inconvenience and discomfort (such as draughty bus-stops and overcrowding) than of cost. If this is so, in fairly affluent societies, more convenient and better transport even at *higher* prices would attract more customers than cheaper transport of the traditional type.

Second, the efficiency and equity of public transport subsidies have to be considered. If one aim is to make public transport cheaper for poor persons, then some form of income supplement would be more efficient. Furthermore, a subsidy financed by general taxation is unfair to the person who does not use public transport.

(d) Conclusions

There are many approaches to the traffic problem and considerable controversy as to the most appropriate 'mix' of policies. A system which relies on any *one* mode of transport, or on one single approach, is unlikely to be satisfactory. There is a need for facilities which permit all types of transport: walking, cycling (through the provision of cycle tracks or lanes), car, minibus, bus and rail transport.

The cost of providing new roads to cater for the increasing number of private motorists may be such that some form of congestion tax may have to be imposed. But eventually an integrated city system could be introduced, with some flexibility to allow for individual preferences. The car would be used to get people from places where demand was insufficient to justify the fixed costs of providing public transport. Such people would be taken to collecting points from which they could transfer to public transport, as with 'park and ride.' In the absence of adjustments through the price system, methods of diverting travellers to public transport will have to be effected by physical controls, such as banning cars and goods vehicles from certain areas, extending and enforcing rigorously parking restrictions and creating bus lanes. In the long term, large cities may find that the solution to their traffic problems lies in building new underground railways.

Finally, the traffic problem cannot be solved in isolation from the location of urban activities. In the long run, one of the most effective ways of dealing with it may be to reduce the need for travel by so organising cities that work-places and residences are nearer each other.

13.7 Concluding observations

In suggesting measures to protect the environment, the economist is bound by certain fundamental considerations.

First, it has to be recognised that the market usually fails to allow fully for externalities. Indeed external costs may be increased by the extension of the market. Thus one of the reasons why Britain has lost 50 per cent of her ancient woodland over the last fifty years is that it is no longer profitable to retain them as a source of timber. Their oak and ash cannot compete with the cheaper hardwoods imported from countries who are destroying their own rainforests!

Second, the environment is indivisible, and piecemeal 'micro' solutions may be inadequate for dealing with the delicate balance of the ecological system. For example, it was found that putting lime into lakes to counteract the effect of acid rain did restore the trout. But the lime, by damaging bog and moorland plants, harmed the insects and thus the birds, such as the golden plover, which fed on them. Even more important, adding lime merely distracts attention from the fundamental problem – acid rain.

Third, a 'sustainable earth' requires international agreement to deal with pollution e.g. from 'greenhouse' gases, acid rain and nuclear fallout. Unfortunately national interests intrude, usually for economic reasons, e.g. the USA's low tax on petrol, or Norway's whaling. It really needs a United Nations organisation to be established as an 'environment protection agency'. Since it is the richest nations who have the greatest interest in preserving the environment, they should provide funds which can be used in different ways to compensate the adversely affected poorer countries, e.g. by leasing the Serengeti from Tanzania to ensure that its unique ecosystem is preserved.

QUESTIONS

1 Because stocks of haddock recovered from the low level of 1990, total quota for the UK was increased from 43,000 to 75,000 tonnes. But this still meant that fishing boats would be required to spend half the year tied up in port. Suggest two methods which the government might adopt for a long-term solution.

2 At present the UK government restricts fertiliser application only in designated 'nitrate sensitive areas'.
   (a) Why does it impose such restrictions?
   (b) Why does it not simply impose a selective sales tax on each tonne of nitrate applied?
   (c) What could be the chief merit of such a tax?

3 To combat traffic congestion it has been proposed that cars entering central London should pay a toll of £4 a day.
   (a) What are the main advantages of such a scheme?
   (b) What are the main disadvantages?

4 In pollution cases, externalities occur because those polluting take no, or limited, account of the cost of their action for others. This will generally result in the output of polluting industries being higher than is optimal. In other words, failure

to take account of the cost of use of a scarce resource (the environment) results in market distortions. The market distortions take the form of sub-optimal production techniques and spending patterns. Were potential polluters forced to pay for any external effects, they might choose another production process, using a different mix of labour and capital and economising on their pollution emission. At the same time, if the resultant prices of their products rise, the effect would be to switch consumer demand away from such products.

The cure for market distortion is, therefore, to make the polluters pay the cost of their pollution, measured by the damage caused or by the cost of cleaning up. The most straightforward way of accomplishing this is to impose a tax on polluters, related to the amount of pollution generated for each unit of output.

(Source: *Lloyds Bank Economic Bulletin*, number 129, September 1989)

(a) Define an 'externality'.
(b) If not corrected, how will pollution 'distort the market'?
(c) How is it suggested that the 'polluter pays'?
(d) What is the advantage of taxing over physical control of pollution?
(e) Is it possible to put the tax on the consumer good rather than the actual producer?

Part VI

Money and financial institutions

■ ⌄ 14 Money and financial markets

Objectives

1 To analyse the functions and types of 'money'
2 To distinguish the different financial markets

14.1 Money

(a) What is money?

It is possible to exchange goods by a direct swap. But barter is rare in advanced economies. Where there is a high degree of specialisation, exchanges must take place quickly and smoothly. Hence we have a 'go-between': money.

Anything which is generally acceptable in purchasing goods or settling debts can be said to be money. It need not consist of coins and notes. Oxen, salt, amber, woodpecker scalps and cotton cloth have at times all been used as money. In fact the precise substance, its size and shape, are largely a matter of convenience and custom. But whatever is used, it should be immediately and unquestioningly accepted in exchange for goods and services. Thus the use of the particular good should be backed by custom, and people must feel that it will retain its value by remaining relatively scarce.

Sometimes an attempt is made to confer acceptability by law. In the UK notes have unlimited *legal tender*, in that a creditor *must* accept them in payment of a debt. But a commodity does not have to be legal tender for it to be money.

A commodity will only be accepted as money if people feel confident it will retain its value.

(b) The functions of money

Money, it is usually stated, performs four functions:

(i) It is a *medium of exchange* – the oil, as it were, which allows the machinery of modern buying and selling to run smoothly.
(ii) It is a *measure of value and a unit of account*, making possible the operation of a price system and automatically providing the basis for keeping accounts, calculating profit and loss, costing, etc.

(iii) It is *a standard of deferred payments* – the unit in which, provided its value is stable, loans and future contracts are fixed. Without money there would be no common basis for dealing in debts – the work, for example, of such institutions as insurance companies, building societies, banks, pension funds and discount houses. By providing a standard for repayment, money makes borrowing and lending much easier.

(iv) It is a *store of wealth* – the most convenient way of keeping any income which is surplus to immediate requirements. More than that, because money is also the medium of exchange, wealth stored in this form is completely liquid: it can be converted into other goods immediately and without cost. Indeed, it is this 'liquidity' which is the most distinctive characteristic of money, and it results in money's playing an active rather than a merely neutral part in the operation of the economy.

(c) The supply of money

The supply of money consists of:

(i) Coins and notes

Since these are regarded as the small change of the monetary system, sufficient coins and notes are always provided for the everyday convenience of the community.

(ii) Bank deposits

While purchases of everyday goods – bus-rides, cigarettes, petrol, etc. – are usually paid for in coins and notes, about 90 per cent (in value) of all transactions are effected by cheque or credit card. When a person writes a cheque, the bank is instructed to transfer deposits in his or her account to the person to whom money is owed. Bank deposits therefore act as money. How deposits are 'created' by banks is described in the next chapter.

The acceptance by the government of the view that the money supply is an important influence in the economy has required that it be defined so that it can be measured and monitored as a guide to policy. Two classifications have been adopted.

'Narrow money' refers to money balances which are readily available to finance current spending, that is, for transactions purposes. The chosen monetary target is now M_0 which consists of notes and coin in circulation, plus banks' holding of cash (till money) and their operational balances at the Bank of England.

'Broad money' reflects the overall liquidity in the economy through the private sector's holdings of assets which, while a store of value, can be converted with relative ease and without capital loss into spending on goods and services. Here the chosen target is M_4 which consists of notes and coins in circulation with the public plus all private sector sterling deposits (sight and time) held in UK banks and building societies (see also p. 283).

14.2 The provision of liquid capital

(a) The need for liquid capital

Where expenditure exceeds the receipts of firms or of the government, the deficit has to be bridged by borrowing. Such funds come from the community, which lends savings. Saving represents refraining from spending on consumer goods, thereby setting free resources for the production of capital goods required by firms or for additional expenditure by the government.

(b) Markets for liquid capital

The market is the institution which brings borrowers and lenders together, making funds available to firms and the government at a price – the rate of interest. But, because finance is required by different types of firm and by the government for different purposes and for different periods of time, there is a great variety in the types of loan available and in the institutions providing or arranging such loans. Nevertheless, markets can be classified into two broad groups: (i) the *money markets* (dealing in short-term loans) and (ii) the *capital market* (where medium-and-long-term capital is raised). The clearing banks (the major source of firms' working capital) and the Bank of England (which, by varying the rate of interest, exercises an overall control over the availability of finance) are discussed in Chapter 15.

None of the money markets nor the capital market are formal organisations in that buyers and sellers meet regularly in a particular building to conduct business. Instead they are merely collections of institutions which are connected, in the case of the money markets by dealings in bills of exchange and short-term loans, and in the case of the capital market more loosely – through channelling medium- and long-term finance to those requiring it. Moreover, as we shall see later, within each market there is a high degree of specialisation. The complete structure is shown in simplified form in Figure 14.1.

14.3 Money markets

(a) The functioning of the old discount market

Although what was known as the 'London discount market' was virtually brought to an end in 1997 when the Bank of England modernised its relationship with the money markets (see p. 227), a description of how it operated is helpful to an understanding of the Bank's present technique for implementing its base rate decisions (Chapter 16).

Until the middle of the twentieth century, it was customary in foreign trade for an importer to settle payment through a bill of exchange, which granted him a 3-month period of grace. To accelerate payment, the exporter contacted a

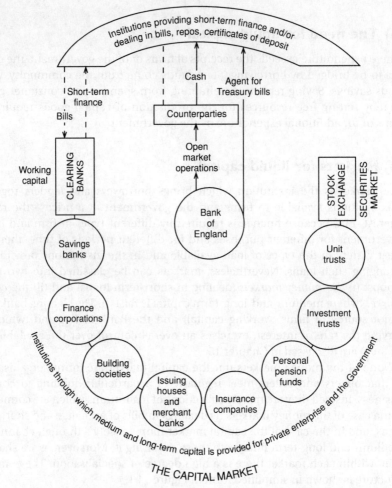

Figure 14.1   The provision of finance in the United Kingdom

succession of specialist dealers. Eventually the Bank of England found it convenient to use this arrangement in implementing monetary policy.

(b) The bill of exchange

Suppose *A* in London was exporting cars worth £100,000 to *B* in New York. When ready to ship the cars, he drew up a bill of exchange, as shown in Figure 14.2. This was sent to *B*, together with proof that the cars were on the ship. *B* accepted the bill by writing 'Accepted' and his signature across the face of the bill. Such acceptance and its receipt by A was necessary before the original *bill of lading*, the documentary title to the cars, was handed over.

Instead of holding *B*'s bill until it matured in 3 months' time, he can obtain immediate cash by selling it.

```
┌─────────────────────────────────────────────────────────────┐
│                                                               │
│  £100,000                                                     │
│                                            A's address        │
│                                                               │
│                                          26 April 1959        │
│                                                               │
│            Three months after date, pay to me or to my        │
│            order One Hundred Thousand Pounds, value           │
│            received.                                          │
│                                                               │
│                                                               │
│                                          (Signed) 'A'         │
│                                                               │
│                                                               │
│   To 'B',                                                     │
│       B's address.                                            │
│                                                               │
└─────────────────────────────────────────────────────────────┘
```

Figure 14.2   A commercial bill of exchange

(i) Discount houses

Probably *A* will choose the latter course. So, after endorsing it, he takes it to one of the *London discount houses*. The exact amount paid for the bill will depend on the length of time to maturity, the prevailing short-term rate of interest and the opinion of the discount house as to B's financial standing. If the bill has three months to run and the prevailing rate of interest on that class of bill is 6 per cent, the discount house will pay about £9,850 for it.

Bills were not usually held by a discount house for the full three months. Instead after about a month, they were sold in 'parcels' to the commercial banks, with so many maturing each day.

(ii) Acceptance houses

As bills were drawn on importers throughout the world, a discount house might have little knowledge of B's financial standing and could thus be reluctant to discount the bill or only do so at a high rate of interest. The difficulty could be overcome by getting a firm of international repute to 'accept' responsibility for payment should *B* default. It is obvious that any firm accepting such a bill must have adequate knowledge of B's creditworthiness in New York. Such knowledge was possessed by merchant banks, such as Lazard and Rothschild, who specialised in financing trade in particular parts of the world. For the service, they charged a small commission of about $\frac{3}{4}$ per cent, which was paid willingly because the rate of discount on a 'bank bill', i.e. one bearing the name of a bank would be lower than that on a 'trade bill' (accepted only by a trader).

The business of accepting has now declined. Originally this was the result of the diminished use of the trade bill in international trade as the commercial banks competed through the cheaper method of the 'reimbursement credit'. With this, *B*, the importer in New York, simply asks his own bank to obtain an acceptance credit in London to make itself responsible for payment. Thus the

London bank has only to satisfy itself as to the financial standing of the New York bank. This simpler procedure, speeded up by electronic communication, means that credits can be granted at very low rates.

The decline in the use of the commercial bill in international trade initially coincided with a large increase in government borrowing through Treasury bills. A *Treasury bill* is really a bill of exchange drawn by the Treasury on itself, usually for a period of three months (ninety-one days). Since Treasury bills are only issued in high denominations, they are primarily for institutional investors.

Financial developments in the 1960s affected both the discount houses and merchant banks. The restrictions on the lending powers of the banks before 1971 led to the development of other means of short-term borrowing, e.g. internal commercial bills, local authority bills, certificates of deposit, etc. Furthermore, the government reduced its dependence on short-term borrowing through Treasury bills. Thus dealings in these short-term instruments became the mainstay of the *discount houses.*

The functions of the *merchant banks* have also changed. The work of accepting is not required for Treasury bills or for most of the new short-term instruments since the standing of the borrower is generally known to be first class. Instead, they arrange and underwrite new issues, advise on the terms of 'takeovers' and mergers, and pay dividends to stockholders as they fall due. They compete in specialist fields, e.g. property development, dealing in securities, domestic banking, and also act as trustees and manage investment portfolios. Other functions have resulted from their overseas trading connections. Thus they have important business in the bullion and foreign exchange markets.

(iii) The commercial banks

The commercial banks fulfilled two main functions in the discount market – providing the discount houses with funds and holding bills to maturity.

The discount houses had themselves insufficient finance to buy all the bills, commercial and Treasury, offered them, so they borrowed money from the commercial banks at a comparatively low rate of interest. Then, by discounting at a slightly higher rate, they made a small profit. The banks were willing to lend at a low rate because the loans were of short duration, often for only a day, and need not be renewed if there were a heavy demand for cash from their ordinary customers. For the discount houses, the trouble involved in the daily renewal of this money at call and the slight risk of its non-renewal were compensated for by the comparatively low rate of interest charged.

The commercial banks can earn a higher rate of interest by themselves holding bills for a part of their currency. However, they could not bid for them directly but bought them from the discount houses when they still had about two months to run.

(iv) The Bank of England

The Bank of England entered the money market as: (1) the agency by which the government issued Treasury bills (see p. 226); and (2) the provider of cash when there was a liquidity deficiency in the market.

Following a financial crisis in 1825 a more controlled market for dealing in bills was established by the Bank of England's licensing certain discount houses to act as intermediaries between the Bank and other financial institutions. In this way the London discount market came into being.

Each day the bill brokers went the round of the clearing banks and reported their cash position to the Bank of England. If the Bank considered there was excessive liquidity, it increased its weekly offering of Treasury bills and sold securities in the market. In as much as the fall in price induced the banks and their customers to buy, the bank's operational cash reserves fell below the safe level.

However, instead of lending directly to the banks, the Bank of England forced them to demand the 'money at call' which they had lent to the discount houses. But these loans had already been used to buy bills, and so the discount houses were forced to ask the Bank of England either to buy their bills or lend against them. The Bank, in its role of 'lender of last resort' agreed – but only at its penal bank rate.

(c) Parallel money markets

As a result of restrictions placed on bank lending, new secondary markets in short-term loans developed to meet the specific requirements of particular borrowers and lenders. The following are the most important of these markets:

(i) Sterling interbank market

This is a market bringing together all banks, including merchant banks, British overseas banks and foreign banks, so that those having considerable funds surplus to their immediate requirements can lend to those having outlets for short-term loans or requiring greater liquidity. It is described as a 'wholesale' market, as opposed to a 'retail' market where funds are collected directly from the public, e.g. by building societies and clearing banks.

The going London Inter-Bank Offered Rate (LIBOR) is the key rate for other short-term loans.

(ii) Local authority market

Local authorities borrow on the open market to bridge the time difference between expenditure and revenue. Brokers place with them short-term funds of banks, industrial and commercial companies, charitable funds, etc., and also deal in longer-term local authority bonds.

Today the market is integrated very closely with the interbank market, as funds from the latter are often deposited with local authorities.

(iii) Negotiable certificates of deposit market

Certificates of deposit enable the banks and building societies to obtain 'wholesale deposits' for periods from three months to five years. They are like bills of exchange but drawn on themselves. Since they are for a longer period than an ordinary time deposit, they facilitate medium-term lending. For the lender they offer a higher rate of interest, while the market in them means that they can be sold whenever cash is required.

(iv) Eurocurrency market

Eurocurrency deposits are simply funds which are deposited with banks outside the country of origin but which continue to be designated in terms of the original currency. The most important Eurocurrency is the dollar. As a result of the USA's continuing adverse balance of payments, branches of European banks have built up dollar balances as customers were paid for exports. These balances are offered to brokers in London (where interest rates have been higher than in New York), and are placed mainly with companies or banks (e.g. Japanese) operating on an international scale to finance foreign investment. While the dollar still dominates the market, other European currencies are now dealt in, chiefly the Deutschemark, the Swiss franc and the Japanese yen.

(v) Eurobond market

Financial transactions are based on market information which, through computers, is assembled rapidly and displayed on screens worldwide. This has meant that dealings in long-term capital – bonds, equities and foreign exchange – now take place globally 24 hours a day. New markets have developed, for example, in bonds raised in different parts of the world (the Eurobond Market), in foreign exchange and in 'futures' and 'options' (derivatives).

(vi) The repo market

Bonds issued by the government are termed 'gilt-edged', referred to as 'gilts'. A 'repo' is a sale and repurchase agreement using gilts as security. For example, 'A' sells gilts to 'B' with a legally binding agreement to repurchase equivalent gilts from B at a pre-determined date and price. In effect this affords 'A' a short-term cash loan with his gilts used as security.

Today it is mainly the repo market in which the Bank of England conducts its daily open market operations (see Chapter 16).

(vii) Other markets

Smaller specialist markets have developed in *finance-house deposits* and *intercompany deposits*. Thus finance houses have obtained funds by issuing bills which are accepted by banks and discount houses. Similarly, in periods of tight credit, firms which are short of finance turn to other companies which temporarily have funds to spare.

14.4 The capital market

Whereas the money markets developed to supply short-term finance to trade and the government, industry obtains most of its 'working' capital from the clearing banks (see Chapter 15). But long-term capital for both the public and private sectors is obtained through the capital market.

As can be seen from Figure 14.4, this consists of, on the one hand, the suppliers of long-term capital and, on the other, those requiring such capital, the two being connected by a number of intermediaries, usually of a specialist nature. Some of

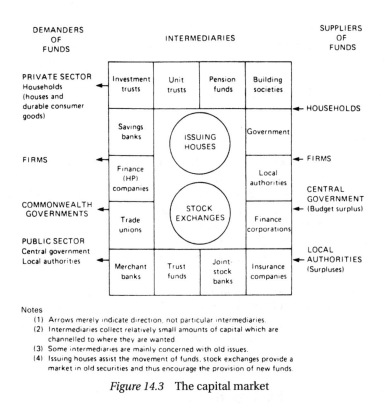

Notes
(1) Arrows merely indicate direction, not particular intermediaries.
(2) Intermediaries collect relatively small amounts of capital which are
channelled to where they are wanted
(3) Some intermediaries are mainly concerned with old issues.
(4) Issuing houses assist the movement of funds, stock exchanges provide a
market in old securities and thus encourage the provision of new funds.

Figure 14.3 The capital market

these intermediaries have already been described; here we look briefly at the others.

(a) Insurance companies

Insurance companies receive premiums for insuring against various risks. Some of these premiums, such as those for insuring ships and property, are held only for relatively short periods – having, apart from the profit made, to be paid out against claims. But with life insurance, endowments and annuities, premiums are usually held for a long time before payments are made. Hence insurance companies have large sums of money to invest in long-term securities. These investments are spread over government and other public stocks, the shares and debentures of companies, property and mortgages. Today 'institutional investors', of which insurance companies are the most important, supply the bulk of savings required for new issues.

(b) Investment trusts

Investors usually try to avoid 'putting all their eggs in one basket' and therefore buy securities in different types of enterprise. However, this requires knowledge of investment possibilities and, above all, sufficient resources. The small investor can overcome these difficulties by buying shares in an investment trust. This invests over a wide range of securities, and after paying management expenses the net yields from these investments are distributed as a dividend on its own shares. Thus investment trusts are not 'trusts' in the legal sense but merely companies formed for the purpose of investment.

(c) Unit trusts

Unit trusts are a development of the investment-trust idea, but they differ in two main respects. First, they are trusts in the legal sense of the term. Trustees are appointed, while the trust deed often limits investments to a specified range of securities. Second, the aggregate holding is split into many 'units' of low nominal value. Thus even a small investment covers a range of securities, though it is possible to concentrate on a particular group, e.g. minerals, financial securities, property, energy, European growth, capital accumulation, high income, etc.

Many unit trusts have schemes linked with insurance, to which savers subscribe on a regular basis. While most of the funds are used to purchase existing securities, trusts do make capital available for new investment, particularly when they take up 'rights' issues of companies whose shares are already held.

(d) The National Savings Bank

The National Savings Bank operates mainly through Post Offices. It is the government's 'retail' means of collecting relatively small deposits from the public by providing savings facilities of different kinds, e.g. a Savings Book, National Savings Certificates, Savings Bonds and Premium Bonds. Although holdings are limited, these sums, when aggregated, make a significant contribution towards covering the PSBR.

(e) The Girobank

The Girobank, now part of the Alliance and Leicester Bank, carries out all essential banking services, mostly for private customers. Its strength is that it operates through the countrywide network of Post Offices. All records are kept at the computerised centre in Bootle, Lancashire.

(f) Foreign banks

Branches of over 400 foreign banks are now located in London. Early on they thrived because they were free of the strict credit controls imposed by the government on the clearing banks. Their more recent expansion reflects the development of the international banking and financial system. While they carry out normal banking functions, their work is heavily concentrated on foreign exchange dealing.

(g) Trust, pension and trade-union funds

All these accumulate income which is re-invested in government securities, shares, property, etc.

(h) Building societies

The main functions of building societies are still the collection of retail deposits from the general public and the granting of long-term loans for the purchase of dwellings for owner-occupation. In recent years they have supplied cheque-books, credit cards and other services to depositors, thereby competing with the banks.

The Building Society Act 1987 allowed them to convert into companies (e.g. Abbey National), own property (mostly residential), grant second mortgages and unsecured loans up to 10 per cent of their total lending and to provide a variety of financial services connected with house purchase, e.g. arrange surveys, insurance. Some, such as the Halifax and Woolwich, have now converted into banks.

(i) Finance corporations

There are a number of consortiums, e.g. the Agricultural Mortgage Corporation, the Export Credits Guarantee Department of the Department of Trade, and the British Screen Finance Consortium which provide finance in their specialist fields.

(j) Finance houses

These were originally independent companies set up to borrow from the public and banks in order to finance hire purchase of both consumer goods and machinery. Today the industry is dominated by the larger commercial banks. For instance, Mercantile Credit is now part of Barclays Bank, and the United Dominion Trust and the Trustee Savings Bank a part of Lloyds TSB.

14.5 Markets in securities: the Stock Exchange

(a) History

By the second half of the seventeenth century there was a recognisable market for dealing in securities. This was gradually formalised and in 1773 the Stock Exchange occupied its first settled premises and from 1803 published its *Official List* of prices. From 1908 its organisation was based on a separation between 'brokers' and 'jobbers'. Brokers acted on behalf of their clients buying from and selling shares to jobbers, the dealers in the shares. This 'single capacity' requirement was designed to protect clients. Whereas brokers worked on a commission basis, jobbers relied on profits from their dealings.

(b) Steps to 'Big Bang'

This cosy arrangement was jolted in the early 1980s by two developments. First, in 1970 government policy put greater emphasis on extending competition throughout the economy, and the Office of Fair Trading frowned upon fixed commissions as a monopolistic practice. Furthermore, the government was keen to maintain and even develop London's invisible earnings capacity (see p. 348). The abolition of fixed commissions in New York in 1979 made dealing costs for British institutions lower there than in London, while the ending of exchange control in the same year meant that British investors were unhampered in investing in foreign securities.

The second development was technological – the introduction of electronic information and communication systems. This meant that changes in security prices could be indicated visually on screens in all centres. Thus the three leading centres, Tokyo, London and New York, became one market in which, because of the time difference, dealings take place throughout the twenty-four hours of the day.

Thus the pressure was on the Stock Exchange to end fixed commission arrangements. The actual change, 'Big Bang', took place on 27 October 1986. But since this would have forced many brokers out of business it was necessary to end the 'single capacity' rule and allow members to act in a dual capacity as agents for both clients and dealers. The main dealers are termed 'market-makers'.

Market-makers negotiate their own commissions for buying and selling shares, and on the larger orders put through by the institutions can offer attractive terms. While private investors can also negotiate terms, the size of their business is not deemed profitable by the market-makers and commission rates remain much as they were before 'Big Bang'. This leaves room for *brokers* to earn a respectable living by acting as the retailer for the private investor, providing a personal contact and offering advice and even research.

(c) Further developments

'Big Bang' proved to be the catalyst for even more far-reaching developments. The government's desire to establish London as an international trading centre necessitated making dealing costs more competitive and so stamp duty on buying shares was reduced to $\frac{1}{2}$ per cent. But to trade in competition with the larger Japanese and American firms UK dealers had to have access to considerably more capital in order to carry stocks of securities. Thus firms had to merge or, more usually, were taken over by larger financial institutions, such as the merchant banks.

In this, however, 'Big Bang' simply gave impetus to the movement which was already taking place of linking related services in one firm. The major clearing banks, for example, are now interested in hire purchase finance, granting mortgages and even acquiring estate agents. The idea has been extended into stock-broking. Market-making, however, has been left to the merchant banks who are less interested in the retail side of finance.

We still refer to the 'Stock Exchange' although dealing is no longer on the 'floor of the House'. Instead there is the Stock Exchange Automated Quotation system (SEAQ) which is the electronic market-place of the London stock market. Information from the sixty-four market-makers on prices and deals made is fed into SEAQ and displayed on screens. This enables the market-maker to quote a selling price and a lower buying price. This 'spread' will be larger when the shares are only dealt in infrequently or where the sale of comparatively few shares can lead to a large fall in price. Unfavourable news, such as a poor monthly balance of payments figure, will cause him to lower prices as a precautionary measure. These new prices would be recorded on the SEAQ screen for the rest of the market.

In 1995 the London Stock Exchange launched the Alternative Investment Market (AIM). While the financial standing of applicant companies is still vetted, the cost of joining is much lower than that of the main market. It is therefore particularly attractive to smaller, and often young and growing, companies who wish to have a quotation for their shares with the aim of raising further capital.

There have also been recent changes in *share trading arrangements*. To eliminate most of the paperwork involved in changes in share ownership, a new computerised system (CREST) has been introduced. Moreover, when shares are bought or sold, settlement must now take place within 5 days.

The government has a strong interest in the integrity of financial markets but opted for allowing the City to regulate itself rather than impose centralised control. The Secretary of State for Trade and Industry appointed a Securities and Investments Board (SIB) which oversees these Self-Regulating Organisations (SROs) and City dealers have to belong to one of these. The Stock Exchange, as a SRO, issues guidelines to members and ensures that these rules are adhered to.

(d) Economic functions

While some short-term speculation does take place on the Stock Exchange, most securities are held on a long-term basis by investment trusts, insurance companies, pension funds, building societies and private individuals.

The truth is that, for the following reasons, an organised market in securities is an indispensable part of the mechanism of a capitalist economy.

(i) It facilitates borrowing by the government and industry

If people are to be encouraged to lend to industry and the government by the purchase of securities, they must be satisfied that they will subsequently be able to sell easily those investments which they no longer wish to hold. Such an assurance is afforded to any holder of a fairly well-known security by the Stock Exchange, for it provides a permanent market bringing together sellers and buyers.

Thus, indirectly, the Stock Exchange encourages savers to lend to the government or to invest in industry. Indeed, if a new issue receives a Stock Exchange quotation, the chances of its success are considerably enhanced.

(ii) Through the market-makers, it helps to even out short-run price fluctuations in securities

By holding stocks of shares, a dealer provides in the short run a buffer against speculation by outsiders. This is because he does not merely 'match' a buyer with a seller but acts like a wholesaler, holding stocks of securities. Since he usually specialises in dealing in certain securities, he obtains an intimate knowledge of them. Thus when the public is pessimistic and selling, he may be more optimistic in his outlook and consider that the drop in price is not likely to continue. He therefore takes these securities on to his book. Similarly, when the public is rushing to buy he will, when he considers the price has reached its zenith, sell from his stocks. The effect in both cases is to even out the fluctuations in price, for, in the first case, he increases his demand as supply increases, and, in the second, he increases supply as demand increases.

(iii) It advertises security prices

The publication of current Stock Exchange prices enables the public to follow the fortunes of their investment and to channel their savings into profitable enterprises.

(iv) It protects the public against malpractices and fraud

With dealers acting in a dual capacity, the previous safeguard of a client that his broker acted solely on his behalf was lost. Under the new arrangements there are two safeguards, the open display of prices on the SEAQ screen and the regulations of the Stock Exchange Council as a SRO. The Council insists on a high standard of professional conduct from its members. Should any authorised member default, the investor is indemnified out of the Securities Association Compensation Fund.

The *Official List* of securities indicates that the Stock Exchange considers shares are reputable. Permission to deal is withdrawn if any doubts arise about the conduct of a company's affairs.

(v) It provides a mechanism for the raising of capital by the issue of securities

While the Stock Exchange is essentially a market for dealing in 'old' securities, the success of a new issue to raise capital is enhanced if a promise can be made of a Stock Exchange quotation for it. More directly, brokers and dealers will actively arrange for certain clients to provide capital for firms wishing to expand (see p. 51).

(vi) It reflects the country's economic prospects

The movement of the market acts as a barometer which points to the economic prospects of the country – whether as 'set fair', or otherwise!

QUESTIONS

1   What is the major attribute which distinguishes money from all other assets?

2   The closing prices (to the nearest £) on undated government stocks on a certain day were:

$2\frac{1}{2}$% Consols 36   4% Consols 57

$3\frac{1}{2}$% War Loan 50   3% Treasury 43

From this information, calculate the long-term rate of interest.

3 Will an investor buy a bond at £1,000 which yields £120 a year if he thinks there is a chance of the pure rate of interest rising to $12\frac{1}{2}$ per cent? State the capital value of the bond if the rate of interest does rise to $12\frac{1}{2}$ per cent.

4 A 91-day bank bill for £1,000 is discounted. Given that the rate of discount is 8 per cent, what price (approximately) will be obtained for it if it is presented: (a) immediately, (b) when it has only one month to run?

5 Why was it important for the Bank of England to act as a 'lender of last resort'?

▮ ▾ **15** Clearing banks

Objectives

1 To show how bank lending through credit creation increases the supply of money
2 To indicate how loans based on credit may be limited by the banks' own financial prudence

15.1 Types of banks in the UK

Banks vary, both in the type of function they perform and in size. They can be classified as:

(a) The central bank

This is the Bank of England, which, on behalf of the government, exercises a general control over the banking system (see Chapter 16).

(b) Clearing banks

These 22 'retail' banks, once dominated by the 'Big Four' (Lloyds TSB, Barclays, Natwest and HSBC (which look over the Midland) now include former building societies, such as the Halifax, Abbey National, Woolwich and Alliance and Leicester. Even so, unlike the systems of other countries, such as the USA, which are composed of a large number of unitary small banks, Britain has only a few large banks, each having a network of branches throughout the country.

This system of branch banking has two main merits. The first is that the larger unit of operation can enjoy the advantages of large-scale production. The second, and more important, is that there is less risk of failure when financial reserves are concentrated in a large bank than where the banking activities for a locality are conducted by a small bank. In short, with a large bank, risks are spread geographically. On the other hand, a branch manager has usually to get loans of any size sanctioned by Head Office. This is in sharp contrast to the manager of the small unit who can grant even large loans on the spot according to his own judgement.

It is mostly with the branches of the clearing banks that people in general come into contact, and so they are often termed 'retail banks'.

(c) Merchant banks (see p. 205)

(d) Foreign and commonwealth banks having branches in the UK (see p. 210)

(e) The National Savings Bank (see p. 210)

The retail banks are the subject of the rest of this chapter. Their importance in the financial system stems from the fact that most of their business is conducted by way of cheques which, through their central clearing arrangements, enables them to economise in cash and so 'create' credit. Since this affects the supply of money we have to explain how they can do this.

15.2 The creation of credit

(a) The cheque system

Banks are companies which exist to make profits for their shareholders. They do this by borrowing money from 'depositors' and relending it at a higher rate of interest to other people. Borrowers are private persons, companies, public corporations, the money market and the government. The more a bank can lend, the greater will be its profits.

People who hold a current account at a bank can settle their debts by cheque. This is a very convenient form of payment. Cheques may be sent safely through the post, can be written for the exact amount, obviate carrying around large sums of money and form a permanent record of payment.

Credit cards possess somewhat similar attributes, and in addition can be used to pay for goods ordered over the phone but usually only up to a stipulated limit.

But the use of cheques and credit cards, is, as we shall see, advantageous to banks. Thus, to advertise their business, to induce customers to pay by cheque rather than by cash, and to encourage people to keep sums of money with them, banks perform many services outside their main business of borrowing and lending money – keeping accounts, making regular payments by direct debit, providing night-safe and cash dispenser facilities, paying bills by credit transfers, purchasing securities, transacting foreign work, storing valuables, acting as executors, granting mortgages, arranging insurance and so on.

(b) The cheque as a substitute for cash

Cheques lead to a reduction in the use of cash. Suppose that I have paid £1,000 into my banking account. Imagine, too, that my builder banks at the same branch and that I owe him £500. I simply write him a cheque for that amount, and he pays this into the bank. To complete the transaction, my account is debited by £500, and his account is credited by that amount. What it is important to observe, however, is that in the settlement of the debt no actual *cash* changes hands. A mere book entry in both accounts has completed the transaction.

Perhaps my builder will, towards the end of the week, withdraw some cash to pay workers' wages. But it is likely that most payments, e.g. for building materials, petrol and lorry servicing, will be by cheque. Similarly, while from the £500 still standing to my account I may withdraw some cash to cover everyday expenses, the probability is that many of my bills, e.g. club subscription, half-yearly rates, hire-purchase instalments on the car, mortgage repayments, will be settled by cheque or by transfer directly from my account. Furthermore, even where cash is withdrawn by one customer, it is often compensated for by cash being paid in by other customers.

With the development of the cheque system, the proportion of cash which is required for transactions has decreased. Let us assume a simple model in which the banks operate free of government control but have discovered that in practice only 10 per cent of their total deposits need be retained in cash to cover all cash withdrawals. In short, only £100 of my original deposit of £1,000 is needed to form an adequate cash reserve.

(c) The creation of credit

It is obvious, therefore, that £900 of my original cash deposit of £1,000 could be lent by the bank to a third party without me or anybody else being the wiser. What is not quite so obvious is that the bank can go much further than this – and does!

Let us assume that there is only one bank and that all lending is in the form of advances (see p. 221). When a person is granted a loan by a bank manager, all that happens is that the borrower's account is credited with the amount of the loan, or, alternatively, he is authorised to overdraw his account up to the stipulated limit. In other words, a deposit is created by the bank in the name of the borrower.

When the loan is spent, the borrower will probably pay by cheque. If this happens, there is no immediate demand for cash. There is no reason, therefore, why the whole of my cash deposit of £1,000 should not act as the safe cash reserve for deposits of a much larger sum created by the bank's lending activities.

But the bank must not overdo this credit creation. To be safe, our model has assumed, cash must always form one-tenth of total deposits. This means that the bank can grant a loan of up to £9,000. Because it is the only bank, there is no need to fear that cheques drawn on it will be paid into another bank and eventually presented for cash. In general, the deposit to cash multiplier equals

$$\frac{1}{\text{the reserve asset ratio}}.$$

The process of credit creation is illustrated in Figure 15.1. *X* pays £1,000 in cash into the bank. This allows the bank to make a loan of £9,000 to *B* who now settles debts to *C* and *D* of £4,000 and £5,000 respectively by sending them cheques. These cheques are paid into the bank. *C* withdraws cash rather heavily, £700; but this is compensated for by *D*, who only withdraws £200 in cash. This leaves £100 cash – enough to cover the average withdrawal which *X* is likely to make. At the

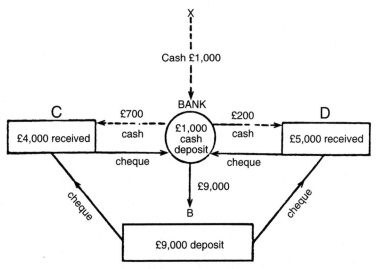

Figure 15.1   How a bank creates credit

same time as these cash withdrawals are being made, other cash is being paid in, thereby maintaining the 10 per cent ratio.

In practice, there are many banks, but for the purpose of credit creation they are virtually one bank, because they are able to eliminate a large demand for cash from each other by their central clearing arrangements. Moreover, banks keep in line with one another as regards their credit creation. Were one bank to adopt, say a 6 per cent cash ratio, it would find that because its customers were making such a large volume of payments to persons who banked elsewhere, it would be continually called upon to settle a debt with the other banks in cash at the end of the day's clearing, so that its cash reserve would fall below the safe level.

(d) The effect of lending on the bank's balance-sheet

Suppose that the receipt of the £1,000 in cash and the loan to *B* are the sole activities of the bank so far. We ignore shareholders' capital. Its balance sheet would then be as follows:

Liabilities	£	Assets	£
Deposits:			
deposit account	1,000	Cash in till	1,000
current account	9,000	Advances	9,000
	10,000		10,000

The advance to *B* is an asset; it is an outstanding debt. On the other hand, *B*'s account has been credited with a deposit of £9,000 – just as though *B* had paid it in. It can be seen, therefore that *every loan creates a deposit*.

B would pay the £1,000 into his current account if he himself had an overdraft. But if he had a sufficient credit balance there, he could pay it into a deposit account where it would earn some interest. Such deposits are referred to as 'time deposits' since technically they are subject to an agreed withdrawal notice (though banks usually waive this subject to loss of interest). The loan to B would be credited to B's current account and, since it is available for immediate spending, is known as a 'sight deposit'.

15.3 Bank lending

(a) Considerations determining a bank's lending policy

In practice, the structure of the bank's assets is more varied than that above. This can be explained as follows.

Creating deposits in order to lend at a profit entails certain risks. In the first place, the loan may not be repaid. Second, and more important, there may be a run on the bank for cash, X (the original depositor) wishing to withdraw the £1,000, or B, C and D requiring between them an abnormally large amount of cash. Any suggestion that the bank could not meet these demands would lead to such a loss of confidence that other depositors would ask for cash, and the bank would have to close its doors.

Hence, although a permanent cash reserve ratio must always be retained, a bank must have a second and third line of defence so that in an emergency it can raise cash easily and quickly. This means, therefore, that it must not lend entirely by means of advances, for these are usually required by the borrower for a minimum of six months and even longer. Some loans must, if possible, be made for a shorter period – even for as little as a day at a time.

On the other hand, the shorter the period of the loan, the lower will be the rate of interest that the bank can charge. Yet it wants profits for its shareholders to be as high as possible.

The bank is therefore limited in its lending policy both quantitatively and qualitatively. Not only must credit be restricted to a multiple of the liquid reserves, but it must afford adequate *security, liquidity* and *profitability*.

As regards *security*, the bank endeavours not to lend if there is any risk of inability to repay. While it usually requires collateral, e.g. an insurance policy, the deeds of a house, or share certificates, this is regarded more as a weapon to strengthen its demand for repayment against an evasive borrower than as a safeguard against default. Collateral therefore really assists liquidity. Nevertheless, lending does involve some risk, especially if economic conditions worsen through recession.

Liquidity and *profitability* pull in opposite directions – the shorter the period of the loan, the greater the bank's liquidity, but the less it will earn by way of interest. The difficulty is resolved by a compromise: (a) loans are divided among different types of borrower and for different periods of time; (b) the different types of loan are kept fairly close to carefully worked out proportions. In short, the bank, for financial prudence, maintains a 'portfolio' of assets.

(b) The distribution of a bank's assets

How in practice a bank reconciles the aim of liquidity and profitability can be seen by studying its sterling assets. This is possible because, apart from its cash, buildings and goodwill, loans represent its sole assets. Just as 'sundry debtors' appears on the asset side of a firm's balance sheet, so debt outstanding to a bank represent assets to it. The position is shown in Figures 15.2 and 15.3.

Cash covers: (a) till money, to meet customers' demand for coin and notes; (b) the operational balance at the Bank of England to cover any liability on the day's clearing; (c) a non-interest-bearing 0.15 per cent of total liabilities which has to be deposited with the Bank of England (see p. 226).

Bills, which are Treasury bills, local authority and trade bills, are obtained chiefly through the money markets (though some may be discounted directly for customers) and are held for the remainder of their currency – usually two months.

Market loans consist mainly of: (a) money at call and short notice borrowed by firms in the money market to discount bills and hold them for a month or so before passing them on to the banks (see p. 206); (b) loans of less than a year to local authorities; (c) certificates of deposit (see p. 207); (d) short-term loans to other monetary authorities.

Investments are medium- and long-term government securities bought on the open market.

Advances, to companies, partnerships and personal borrowers, are the most profitable (1 to 3 per cent above base rate) but also the least liquid of all the bank's assets. The main object of advances is to provide the working capital for industry and commerce. The type of loan preferred is 'self-liquidating' within a period of about six months. A good example is a loan made to a farmer, who borrows to buy seed and fertilisers and to pay wages, and repays the loan when the harvest is

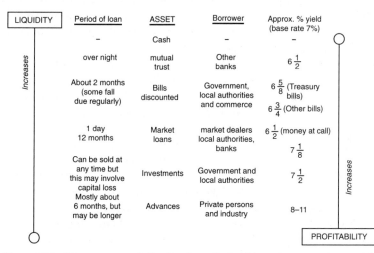

Figure 15.2 The nature and distribution of a bank's main assets, August 1998

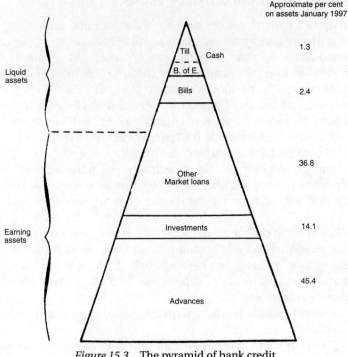

Liquid
assets

Till

B. of E.

Cash

1.3

Bills

2.4

36.8

Other
Market loans

Earning
assets

Investments

14.1

45.4

Advances

Figure 15.3   The pyramid of bank credit
Source: *Annual Abstract of Statistics*

sold. Similarly, a manufacturer may borrow to employ additional labour and raw materials just prior to Christmas in order to increase production. When payment is received for those goods the overdraft can be repaid. Borrowers are often allowed to 'roll over' their overdrafts.

Banks also make a large number of 'personal loans', usually modest sums to cover exceptional items of personal expenditure. Repayments are spread over the term of the loan, though interest is charged at an agreed rate on the full amount of the loan for the whole of the period.

At one time banks refrained from providing long-term capital leaving this to the capital market. In recent years, however, they have competed in financing such long-term projects as commercial buildings and the purchase of farms and owner-occupied houses. These fixed assets are the security required, though the bank's main consideration is whether or not the venture is likely to succeed.

It must be emphasised that, apart from cash and bank buildings, these assets are covered only by credit created by the bank to make a loan or to buy securities. For example, Treasury bills and government securities are paid for by cheques which will increase the accounts of the sellers. If they are new issues, there is an addition to the government account at the Bank of England; if they are old issues, the bank is virtually taking over from somebody a loan already made to the government. In writing these cheques, the bank increases its liabilities, for only book-entry deposits cover them. This 'pyramid of credit', created to buy earning assets and to make loans upon a liquid assets basis, is shown in Figure 15.3.

15.4 Modification of the cash-ratio approach

(a) The importance of liquid assets as a whole

Our explanation of how a bank creates credit has followed traditional lines: credit bears a fixed relationship to the cash reserves. This approach is the easiest to understand and underlines the main principles involved.

However, while the basic principles of credit creation still hold true, some modification is necessary to allow for modern banking practice.

Today, banks are more concerned with their general liquidity position when lending rather than with one item, cash. This tendency of cash to lose significance originally stemmed from the introduction of the Treasury bill, which, through government support, became almost as good as cash. Improved markets for loans e.g. the parallel money markets described in Chapter 25, also increase liquidity and, as a result, such loans can be regarded as 'near money'.

(b) External limitations on the banks' lending policy

Indeed, the monetary authorities (that is, the Bank of England acting as agent for the Treasury) now regard cash simply as the small change of the monetary system, and so they vary it according to the needs of trade.

It follows, therefore, that, if the authorities wish to control the amount of credit which can be created by banks, their attention will have to be directed to the size of the total assets which the banks hold. It is the external limitations on the banks' lending ability which we examine in the following chapter.

15.5 The effects of recent increased competition

The above describes the fundamental credit-creation principle of banking. But the role of the clearing banks in the financial structure of the UK has been revolutionised since 1960 as they have had to respond to increased competition. This has come in five stages:

(i) Overseas banks (now over 400) came to London in the 1960s to share the Eurocurrency market there. In addition to dominating foreign currency lending, they now have some 30 per cent of lending in sterling to British companies and financial institutions.
(ii) The Competition and Credit Control policy of 1971 removed restrictions on lending, thereby ending the clearing banks' 'interest rate' cartel. No longer could they simply rely on recycling personal deposits into loans to business. Now each bank had to compete for personal customers, e.g. by extending banking hours, increasing lending (especially through mortgages) and offering higher interest on deposits.
(iii) The ending of exchange controls in 1979 removed the remaining restrictions on foreign lending institutions.

(iv) The development of information technology has made possible credit cards, point of sales transfers and dealing in securities on an international scale.

(v) When in 1997 three large building societies converted into banks they retained their excellent network of high street offices, thereby enabling them to collect retail deposits at a comparatively low rate of interest and to supplement their basic mortgage business with other banking activities, such as personal loans and arranging insurance. This presented a serious challenge to the 'Big Four' who, following their losses in 1992 on Third World debt and property development financing, had secured excellent profits by reducing their dependence on corporate lending and concentrating on the personal sector where margins were wider, e.g. personal loans, credit cards. Increased competition has meant that bank margins between borrowing and lending rates have been squeezed and many personal customers' services which were previously given free are now charged for. In their turn the banks have had to improve customer relations.

With the growth of financial services and freer competition, the major banks have diversified into other operations, owning finance houses, leasing and factoring companies, merchant banks, securities dealers, insurance companies and venture capital companies.

QUESTIONS

1 Name three advantages of large-scale production enjoyed by the large bank with branches over the small unit bank. What is the large bank's main disadvantage?

2 What are the main advantages of cheques to (a) the customer, (b) the bank?

3 Name four factors which limit the bank's powers to create credit.

4 The 1980s have seen a revolution in British banking, due to the lifting of controls on foreign exchange, credit and money, and the encouragement of competition and innovation.

The essence of the revolution is that banks have given up their traditional function of recycling deposits from persons into loans to business. They now recycle personal deposits back to the personal sector as loans, and recoup as business deposits a large part of their loans to business. The major areas of expansion have been personal mortgage lending, and both lending to and deposits from non-bank financial companies. Home ownership and the City have been two poles of banking growth.

(*Lloyds Bank Economic Bulletin*, no. 119, November 1988)

(a) What factors led to a 'revolution in British banking?

(b) How did increased competition affect the banks' previous approach?

(c) How would it affect the margins between the interest rates at which they borrow and lend?

(d) Name two ways in which the banks responded to this competition.

(e) How did bank customers: (i) lose, (ii) gain from this new environment?

■ Ⅴ **16** The Bank of England

Objectives

1 To describe the Bank of England's functions as a 'central bank'
2 To outline the Bank's technique of securing the desired response to changes in its base rate

16.1 Functions of the Bank of England

For the past 300 years, the Bank of England has followed policies which have placed the needs of the country as a whole before its own financial interests. Nationalisation in 1946 merely formalised its position as a 'central bank' – the institution which conducts monetary policy in accordance with the government's economic objectives.

We need deal only briefly with most of its functions.

(a) It issues notes

The Bank is the sole issuer of currency notes in England and Wales. Although certain Scottish and Northern Ireland banks can issue their own notes, these have to be backed by Bank of England notes. (Coin is issued by the Royal Mint on behalf of the Treasury, and is not the responsibility of the Bank of England).

Today the note issue is backed by government securities.

(b) It is the government's banker

The government has always been the most important customer of the Bank of England. As a result the Bank performs many tasks for the government which spring from the normal banker–customer relationship:

(i) It keeps the central government accounts (the Consolidated Fund and the National Loans Fund) and the accounts of many government departments.
(ii) It gives overnight assistance by means of 'Ways and Means' advances if the account goes 'into the red'.
(iii) It is the agency by which the government issues Treasury bills to cover a short time-lag between expenditure and revenue or for the daily adjustment of liquidity. This is achieved by two methods, 'tap' and 'tender'.

Government departments, the National Savings Bank, the National Insurance Fund and Bank of England Issue Department, and certain other customers, all of which have funds to invest for a short period, can buy bills as required at a fixed price, i.e. 'on tap'. This price is not published.

Money market dealers and other purchasers (such as Commonwealth and foreign banks) can obtain bills by 'tender'. Every Friday, the Treasury, acting through the Bank of England, invites tenders for a specified amount of bills (usually about £100 million), the size depending on the official forecast of the money market position for the period ahead.

At one time the Bank managed the government's long term debt by issuing and selling gilts. This role, however, has now passed to a new Debt Management Office, an executive agency of the Treasury. The Bank's Registrar's Department still maintains a register of gilt holders, records transfers and pays interest as due.

(c) It is the banker's bank

The clearing banks (about 22) keep their accounts at the Bank of England chiefly to settle their daily clearing differences with each other. They are expected to maintain adequate operational balances for this, and not to overdraw.

In addition, all banks and building societies operating in the UK have to keep 0.15 per cent of their sterling deposits on non-interest-bearing deposit with the Bank of England. These provide the main source of income for the Bank to enable it to carry out its functions.

(d) It manages the government's gold and foreign currency reserves

(i) The reserves of foreign currency in the Exchange Equalisation Account can be used to influence the sterling exchange rate (see p. 357). Under the new policy arrangements of 1997 (see p. 227), the Bank may also undertake foreign currency operations in support of its monetary policy objectives.

(ii) It may conduct foreign exchange and bullion business for the government and those central banks which keep accounts and bullion at the Bank.

(e) It has financial responsibilities internationally

(i) The Bank of England maintains close contact with other central banks and monetary authorities and co-operates with them chiefly with the aim of bringing greater stability to international monetary affairs.

(ii) It provides banking services for the central banks of non-sterling countries, e.g. holds and manages their holdings of sterling.

(iii) It participates in the work of certain international financial institutions, such as the Bank for International Settlements, the International Monetary Fund, the International Bank for Reconstruction and Development.

(iv) It ensures that proper representations are made on the impact on the UK of the EU's banking directives and is assisting the UK financial sector in its the technical preparations for Economic and Monetary Union (EMU).

(f) It is responsible for maintaining the stability of the banking system

Until recently the Bank of England had the task of regularly examining the accounts of all British banks to ensure their adequate liquidity and safe exposure to risk. But in 1998 this task was transferred to a new Financial Services Authority (FSA), responsible for supervising the entire financial services industry.

However, the function of ensuring the efficiency and stability of the banking system as a whole remains with the Bank.

But when the Bank acts as a 'lender of last resort' to rescue an institution whose failure could bring down other healthy businesses, public funds are put at risk. It is essential, therefore, that such help is given only on rare occasions, lest it is viewed as a safety-net, thereby encouraging excessive risk-taking by banks.

16.2 Responsibility for operating monetary policy

On 6 May 1997 the Labour government introduced a new framework for monetary policy, which was given legislative force by the Bank of England Act 1998. Under the Act, the Bank's objective is to maintain price stability and, subject to that, to support the economic policy of the government, including its objectives for employment and growth. The Chancellor of the Exchequer defined the price stability objective in terms of an inflation target of 2.5 per cent. The Bank pursues this objective through the interest rate decisions taken by the *Monetary Policy Committee.*

How *Monetary Policy Committee* decides on the apropriate rate of interest is described on pp. 287–8. Here we concentrate on the Bank's *technique* for making its interest-rate decision effective.

Each day the Bank of England estimates the cash available in the banking system. This will be affected by the operational balances the clearing banks aim at holding at the Bank, their cash flow, the net proceeds of maturing Treasury bills and other short-term assets, and the timing of their customers' tax payments.

With this knowledge the Bank can keep the banks on a tight rein. This is possible because the banking system is so competitive that banks are forced to work on slim margins and to be fully lent by keeping their non-earning operational cash balances to a minimum.

Thus daily at 9.45 am and 2.30 pm the Bank enters the repo market and invites its 'counterparties' (see below) to bid for their cash requirements by offering repos and gilts in exchange. A decision of its Monetary Policy Committee (see p. 288) to raise base rate, for example, would be accompanied by the Bank's hardening its terms, with open market operations as described in Chapter 14 in support.

The Bank's preference to operate in the repo market can be explained as follows. The electronic transmission of information changed the London market in securities into a world market. Furthermore, the relatively new repo market outgrew the bill market. In 1997, therefore, the Bank announced two important changes to its operational requirements.

First, the instruments acceptable as collateral for borrowing would not be confined to Treasury bills and eligible local authority and bank bills, but would be extended to include repos and gilts (including bonds issued by certain foreign governments and international agencies).

Second, instead of lending only to the specialist discount houses, the Bank would operate through 'counterparties' selected from active participants in the repo and bill markets, such as banks, building societies and securities firms. No details concerning these counterparties are announced and they can be changed from time to time. But this development does mean that the Bank is now providing liquidity directly to banks, etc. and not indirectly through the discount houses as previously. The discount houses, were given two years to adapt, and when the last one handed in its licence in December 1998, it signified the end of the old discount market.

In its loans through gilt sale and repurchase agreements at the two-week maturity, the Bank gives the market a signal as to what it considers the level of interest rates will be over the next three months. But while the Bank of England can *influence* the very short-term rate, the market may take a different view over longer-term rates where the level of government funding and the future requirements of the institutions, such as pension funds, dominate the market.

QUESTIONS

1 When the Bank of England sells long-term bonds in the market, what is likely to happen to: (a) their price; (b) the rate of interest?

2 How can the Bank of England influence liquidity by its management of the National Debt?

3 Give three reasons why 'funding' may be necessary to reduce bank advances.

4 Name two difficulties in carrying out a funding policy.

Part VII

The government's overall management of the economy

▣ ⋎ 17 Outline of government management policy

Objectives

1 To outline the reasons for government overall control of the economy
2 To show why a macro-economics method of analysis is required
3 To consider government policy with regard to the distribution of income

17.1 The government's macro objectives

(a) The inherent instability of the market economy

In Chapter 9 we drew together the various reasons for government interference in the market economy, classifying them under three broad objectives: (i) allocation of resources, (ii) stabilisation and (iii) growth.

The first objective – improving the allocation of resources – was discussed in Part IV with reference to market failure.

But government economic policy faces the far more difficult problem of keeping resources fully employed so that output remains on the production possibility curve (see p. 129). This arises because the market economy is itself dynamic, producing in the short-term the instability of booms and recessions, and yet in the long-term being capable of generating a growing output capacity.

(b) Major aspects of stabilisation policy

In practice, stability of the economy involves the government taking measures to achieve:

(i) full employment, especially of labour;
(ii) a stable price level;
(iii) a balanced regional development;
(iv) a steady and acceptable rate of growth;
(v) a healthy balance of payments.

As we shall see, because these policies may not be fully compatible, there may have to be some 'trade-off' between them. The late Harold Macmillan, a former prime minister, likened the role of the government to that of a juggler whose task is to keep many balls in the air at the same time. Some balls are going up because they have been given special attention, while others are on their way down. In short, therefore, the government is unlikely to achieve all these policies simultaneously.

17.2 Differences in the method of analysis

(a) Micro-economics

So far we have concentrated mainly on the first problem of the allocation of a given quantity of resources between different uses. By dividing the economy into a number of comparatively small parts, we have been able to study how each part functions – the demand of consumers in a particular market, the behaviour of the firm, the price of the commodity, and so on. Such subjects come within the realm of 'micro-economics'. Thus, if we ask ourselves what forces determine the price of potatoes, the rent of an acre of land in London, the dividend on a particular equity or the wage of a Nottingham bus-driver, we are dealing with micro-economic questions. When dealing with such specific small parts of the whole economy, we are able to exclude any repercussions by assuming 'other things being equal'. Referring back to Figure 1.2, micro-economics is concerned with the centre of the diagram – an examination of a particular market and of the connection between one market and another, e.g. those for pencils and pens.

(b) Macro-economics

In contrast, when considering fluctuations in the level of employment, prices in general, the rate of growth and the balance of payments, we are concerned with the economy as a whole – in terms of Figure 1.2 with the aggregate outer flows of goods and services and of factors of production.

This gives rise to a wider type of question. Is the individual market so important, e.g. cars, computer components, that we cannot ignore the effect which changes in the conditions of demand will have on the economic system as a whole? How do fluctuations in the overall level of employment occur? How can aggregate demand in the economy change? How do firms in general respond to such a change in demand? What brings about changes in the general level of prices? Such questions are the concern of *macro-economics*.

(c) The method of macro-economics

Because micro- and macro-economics differ in the types of subject they study, their methods of analysis also differ. A simple analogy will explain why.

We can investigate the working of a motor-car by examining its different parts in isolation from one another. Thus we look at the wheels, then the gearbox, the engine, the carburettor, the electric fuel-pump, and so on. In this way we can find out how each part of the car works in detail.

Now, while such an examination is very important and useful, it has its limitations. This is because we just spotlight one component and see how it operates, *ignoring the rest of the car*. It will not enable us to predict what will happen if, for instance, we replace a one-litre engine by a two-litre engine. We cannot assume that, 'other things being equal', the larger engine will make the car run faster. There will be certain 'feedbacks' on the other parts of the car which will affect its running efficiency as a whole. Thus the larger engine may be too powerful for the gearbox; the carburettor may be unable to supply sufficient fuel; the suspension may not be capable of withstanding higher speeds; and so on. It is not enough to examine how one part of the car works in isolation; we have also to consider how the various components are interrelated, and the relative importance of each.

The same applies when we study how an economic system works. The micro-approach will only take us so far, for it merely examines how small parts of the economy operate in isolation. Changes which are simultaneously taking place in other parts of the economy and in the level of activity in general are ignored by inserting the phrase 'other things being equal'. So are the repercussions – the feedbacks – which may result from the single change being analysed.

Now this is legitimate enough if we are analysing a comparatively insignificant part of the economy, for example a small industry. Thus if we wish to discover the effects of an increase in the demand for pencils, we are unlikely to make serious errors by assuming 'other things equal', for such a change is unlikely to cause repercussions on the economy as a whole.

But what if we are examining the effects of a considerable increase in the demand for cars? The car industry is a significant part of the whole economy, and so we cannot merely analyse the effects in isolation, stopping at the point where the price of cars rises or the wages of car workers increase. To indicate the full economic results, we shall have to consider (i) possible 'feedbacks' on the demand for cars, and (ii) repercussions on the economy as a whole – which in turn can produce further feedbacks. For one thing, we shall have to know the level of employment in the economy. If this is low, the increased demand for cars may lead to a considerable expansion of activity throughout the economy, leading to a further increase in the demand for cars. On the other hand, if the economy is already running at full employment, the increased demand may merely cause higher prices.

(d) Simplifying by aggregating

Although, when dealing with changes in the economy as a whole, we cannot assume 'other things being equal', we still need to simplify if we are to build up a satisfactory model. This we do by 'aggregating' variables into a few broad groups.

The main aggregates we examine in macro-economics are national income, national output and national expenditure. But we can also deal with sub-aggregates and analyse the factors that determine these. Thus, in analysing national expenditure, we examine consumption spending, investment spending, government spending, export receipts, spending on imports, etc. Similarly, when looking at national income, we consider wages, rent and profits (see Chapter 16). Aggregating in this way enables us to handle all the different variables so that we can bear in mind the effects which a change in any one of them will have on the other groups and upon the level of activity as a whole (see Chapter 20).

(e) The economic system

What we have said so far must not be taken to imply that particular markets and the economy as a whole are mutually exclusive. To return to our analogy of the car, all the parts of a car are 'ticking over' when the car is running. Each bit of the carburettor and gearbox, and the way each is functioning, affect the overall running of the car. And how the car is driven will influence the performance of the individual parts – the engine, the suspension, the wheels, and so on. So it is with the economy. The millions of independent decisions made by individual firms and consumers affect the overall functioning of the economy. For example, each decision of an individual firm regarding alterations to its factory, plant or stocks affects the amount of investment spending which the economy as a whole is undertaking. And the firm's decisions will also be influenced by the price of its product – which in its turn depends upon the demands of individual purchasers.

Both micro- and macro-economics are necessary, therefore, to an understanding of how the economy functions. However, before considering the influences on the level of activity, we look at the determinants of the material standard of living of a country (that is, the current position of the production-possibility curve) and the nature of government economic policy.

17.3 The government and the distribution of income

(a) Redistribution of income: the economist's limitation

In Chapter 1 it was pointed out that a possible defect of the market economy was that it could lead to and even increase an inequitable distribution of wealth and income (p. 7). It was further emphasised that, because satisfaction is personal to the individual, the economist could not approach the problem objectively since it is impossible to give a cardinal measurement to the satisfaction which consumers derive from the goods they buy.

(b) The government's interest in income redistribution

Even so, the economist must recognise that government policy must embrace the redistribution of wealth and income for four main reasons:

(i) Especially in the richer Western economies, people's social conscience will not tolerate 'poverty in the midst of plenty'. Yet private giving through charitable institutions is irregular, unreliable and inadequate in dealing with the relative size of the problem of inequality in a 'caring society'.
(ii) Gross inequality of income is divisive of society and disruptive of economic life, e.g. through strikes for higher pay.

(iii) The distribution of income affects the broad macro variables, e.g. saving and taxation yield, which the government has to take into account in formulating stabilisation policies.

(iv) Especially when its measures fail to prevent high unemployment and rising prices, the government has a moral obligation to compensate the main losers by providing unemployment benefit and 'indexing' social security payments.

(c) How redistribution is implemented

The government may carry out redistribution directly and deliberately through its spending and taxation. But redistribution may also take place as an offshoot of measures designed to achieve other objectives, e.g. raising the tax on petrol to discourage car use. The economist's task is limited to revealing where such redistribution occurs and suggesting the likely economic effects. But the ultimate decision is left to the politician's subjective judgement.

QUESTIONS

1 What is the distinction between micro-economics and macro-economics?

2 How is the difference reflected in the economist's method of 'model-building'?

■ ⋎ **18** Measuring the level of activity: national-income calculations

Objectives

1 To outline the principles of calculating the national income
2 To indicate the uses of national income calculations

18.1 The principle of national income calculations

Fluctuations in the level of activity are monitored by quantitative information on the national income. Although the collection of statistics proceeds continuously, the principal figures are published annually in *The United Kingdom National Accounts* (*The Blue Book*).

The principle of calculating national income is as follows. Income is a flow of goods and services over time: if our income rises, we can enjoy more goods and services. But for goods to be enjoyed they must first be produced. A nation's income over a period, then, is basically the same as its output over a period. Thus, as a first approach, we can say that national income is the total money value of all goods and services produced by a country during the year. The question is how we can measure this money value.

We can tackle the problem by studying the different ways in which we can arrive at the value of a table.

Figure 18.1 shows that the value of the table can be obtained by taking the value of the final product (£100) or by totalling the value added by each firm in the different stages of production. The output of the tree-grower is what he receives for the tree (£30) which, we will assume, cost £20 in wages to produce, leaving £10 profit. The output of the sawmiller is what he receives for the timber (£50) less what he paid for the tree. Again, this output (£20) is made up of wages and profit. And so on. The total of these added values equals the value of the final table. Thus we could obtain the value of the table by adding the *net outputs* of the tree-grower (forestry), the sawmiller and the table-maker (manufacturing) and the retailer (distribution).

Alternatively, instead of putting these individual outputs in industry categories, we could have added then according to the type of factor payment – wages, salaries, rent or profit. This gives us the *income* method of measuring output.

Thus, if we assume (i) no government taxation or spending and (ii) no economic connections with the outside world, we can obtain the national

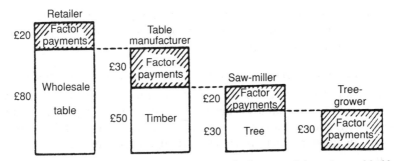

Figure 18.1 The value of the total product equals the sum of the values added by each firm

income either by totalling the value of final output during the year (i.e. the total of the value added to the goods and services by each firm) or by totalling the various factor payments during the year – wages, rent and profit.

There is, however, a third method of calculating the national income. The value of the table in Figure 18.1 is what was spent on it. If the table had sold for only £90, that would have been the value of the final output, with the final factor payment – profit to the retailer – reduced to £10. Thus we can obtain the national income by totalling *expenditure* on final products over the year.

It must be emphasised that the money values of output, income and expenditure are *identical by definition*. They simply *measure* the national income in different ways. This was shown by the fact that factor payments were automatically reduced by £10 when the table sold for £90 instead of £100.

Before we proceed to examine in more detail the actual process of measuring these three identities, it is convenient if we first consider some of the inherent difficulties.

18.2 National income calculations in practice

Complications arise through:

(a) Arbitrary definitions

(i) Production

In calculating the national income, only those goods and services which are paid for are normally included. Because calculations have to be made in money terms, the inclusion of other goods and services would involve imputing a value to them. But where would you draw the line? If you give a value to jobs which a person does for himself – growing vegetables in the garden or cleaning the car – then why not include shaving himself, driving to work, and so on? On the other hand, excluding such jobs distorts national-income figures, for, as an economy becomes more dependent on exchanges, the income figure increases although there has been no addition to real output (see p. 245)!

An *imputed* money value is included for certain payments in kind which are recognised as a regular part of a person's income earnings, e.g. cars provided by a company to directors and employees.

(ii) The value of the services rendered by consumer durable goods

A TV set, dishwasher, car, etc., render services for many years. But where would we stop if we imputed a value to such services? A toothbrush, pots and pans, for example, all render services over their lives. All consumer durable goods are therefore included at their price when bought, subsequent services being ignored.

The one exception is owner-occupied houses. These are given a notional rent to keep them in line with property owned for letting, whose rents are included, either directly or as profits of property companies. This also prevents national income falling as more people become owner–occupiers!

(iii) Government services

Education and health services, although provided by the State, are no different from similar services for which some persons pay. Consequently, they are included in national income at cost. But what of certain other government services? A policeman, for instance, when helping children to cross the road is providing a consumer service. But at night his chief task may be guarding banks and factories, and in doing so he is really furthering the productive process. To avoid double-counting, this part ought to be excluded from output calculations. In practice, however, it would be impossible to differentiate between the two activities, and so all the policeman's services – indeed all government services (including defence) – are included at cost in calculating national output (see p. 245).

(b) Inadequate information

The sources from which data are obtained were not specifically designed for national-income calculations. For instance, the Census of Production and the Census of Distribution are only taken at approximately five-year intervals. As a result many figures are estimates based on samples.

Information, too, may be incomplete. Thus not only do income tax returns fail to cover the small-income groups, but they err on the side of understatement.

But it is 'depreciation' which presents the major problem, for what firms show in their profit and loss accounts is affected by tax regulations. Since there is no accurate assessment of real depreciation, it is now usual to refer to gross national product (GNP) rather than to national income (see Figure 18.3).

(c) The danger of double-counting

Care must be taken to exclude transfer incomes when adding up national income (see p. 240), the contribution to production of intermediary firms when calculating national output (see Table 18.1) and indirect taxes when measuring national expenditure (see p. 242).

Table 18.1   Calculations of Gross National Product of the UK, 1996

INCOME	£m
Income from employment	400,354
Income from self-employment	69,898
Gross trading profits of companies	101,409
Gross trading surplus, public corporations	3,959
Gross trading surplus, general government enterprises	681
Rent	63,850
Imputed charge for consumption of non-trading capital	4,333
Total domestic income	644,484
less stock appreciation	−973
Statistical discrepancy	−595
GROSS DOMESTIC PRODUCT	642,916
Net property income from abroad	9,652
GROSS NATIONAL PRODUCT	652,568

EXPENDITURE	
Consumers' expenditure	473,509
General government final consumption	155,732
Gross domestic fixed capital formation	114,623
Value of physical increase in stocks and works in progress	2,917
Total domestic expenditure	746,781
Export of goods and services	217,147
Total final expenditure	963,928
less imports of goods and services	−222,603
Statistical discrepancy	975
GROSS DOMESTIC PRODUCT (at *market prices*)	742,300
less taxes on expenditure	−108,484
plus subsidies	9,100
GROSS DOMESTIC PRODUCT (at *factor cost*)	642,916
Net property income from abroad	9,652
GROSS NATIONAL PRODUCT	652,568

OUTPUT	
Agriculture, forestry, and fishing	11,790
Mining, quarrying, oil and gas extraction	18,068
Manufacturing	137,006
Electricity, gas and water supply	13,606
Construction	33,746
Distribution, hotels and catering: repairs	93,091
Transport and communication	54,506
Banking, finance, insurance, business services and leasing	164,282
Public administration, national defence and compulsory social security	38,244
Education and health social work	81,876
Other services	24,713
Total	670,479
Adjustment for financial services, etc.	−26,968
Statistical discrepancy (income adjustment)	−595
GROSS DOMESTIC PRODUCT	642,916
Net property income from abroad	9,652
GROSS NATIONAL PRODUCT	652,568

Source: Annual Abstract of Statistics.

A fourth way in which a form of double-counting can occur is through 'stock appreciation'. Inflation increases the value of stocks, but although this adds to firms' profits it represents no increase in real income. Such gains must therefore be deducted from the income figure.

(d) Relationship with other countries

(i) Trade

British people spend on foreign goods, while foreigners buy British goods. In calculating national *expenditure*, therefore, we have to deduct the value of goods and services imported (since they have not been produced by Britain) and add the value of goods and services exported (where income has been earned in Britain).

(ii) International indebtedness

If a father increases his son's pocket-money, it does not increase the family income. Instead it merely achieves a redistribution, the father having less and the son more. But if the boy's aunt makes him a regular allowance, the family income is increased. Similarly, with the nation: while transfer incomes, e.g. retirement pensions and student grants, do not increase national income, payments by foreigners do. These payments arise chiefly as interest on loans and dividends from investments made abroad. In the same way, foreigners receive payments for investments in Britain. Net property income from abroad (receipts less payments) must therefore be added to both domestic expenditure and output.

(e) Government calculations of the national income

We start off by measuring Gross Domestic Product (GDP). The GDP is simply the money value of the final output of all resources located within a country irrespective of whether their owners live there or abroad. Hence in order to obtain Gross National Product (GNP) we have to add the balance of *net* property income from abroad (Figure 18.2).

Figures for GNP are calculated for income, expenditure and output. Because information is incomplete and derived from a variety of sources, results are not identical. Hence from the residuals a 'statistical discrepancy' is calculated.

(i) National income

National income is the total money value of all incomes received by persons and enterprises in the country during the year. Such incomes may be in the form of wages, salaries, rent, or profit.

In practice income figures are obtained mostly from income tax returns, but estimates are necessary for small incomes. Two major adjustments have to be made:

(1) Transfer incomes
Sometimes an income is received although there has been no corresponding contribution to the output of goods and services, e.g. unemployment-insurance

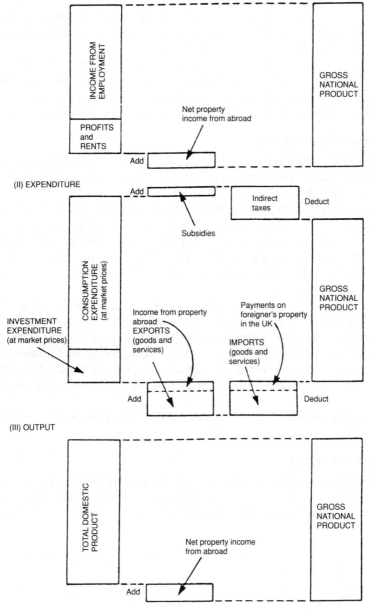

Figure 18.2 Summary of Gross National Product calculations

benefit and interest on the National Debt. Such incomes are really only a redistribution of income within the nation – chiefly from taxpayers to the recipients. Transfer incomes must therefore be deducted from the total. Other forms of transfer income which must be excluded are private money gifts and receipts from the sale of financial assets and of second-hand goods, e.g. a house, furniture, a car.

(2) Income from government activities

Personal incomes and the profits of companies are obtained from tax returns. But since dividends and interest payments are already included in profits, to avoid double-counting they are not shown separately.

Trading activities of public corporations, e.g. the Post Office, the BBC, and of local authorities e.g. housing, transport, may also show surpluses which have to be added in, while an imputed rental value is given to the property owned and occupied by the government and local authorities (non-trading income).

(ii) National expenditure

National expenditure is the total amount spent on final goods and services by households and central and local government and by firms on net additions to capital goods and stocks in the course of the year.

Figures for calculating national expenditure are obtained from a variety of sources. The *Census of Distribution* records the value of shop sales, while the *Census of Production* gives the value of capital goods produced and additions to stocks. But these censuses are not taken every year, and gaps are filled by estimates from data provided by the *National Food Survey*, and the *Family Expenditure Survey*.

Market prices are swollen by indirect taxes on goods and services, e.g. VAT, and reduced by subsidies, e.g. on council housing. What we are trying to measure is the value of the national expenditure which corresponds to the cost of the factors of production (including profits) used in producing the national product. This is known as 'national expenditure at factor cost' and is obtained by deducting indirect taxes from and adding subsidies to national expenditure at market prices.

Adjustments necessary for exports and imports have already been referred to (see p. 240).

(iii) National output

National output is the total of consumer goods and services and investment goods (including additions to stocks) produced by the country during the year. It can be measured by totalling either the value of the *final* goods and services

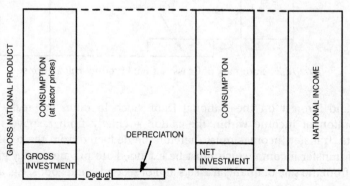

Figure 18.3 Gross National Product and National Income

produced or the *value added* to the goods and services by each firm, including the government.

(f) Gross National Product and National Income

In the course of production, machinery wears out and stocks are used up. This represents depreciation of capital. If we make no allowance for this but simply add in the value of new investment goods produced, we have *gross national product*. But, to be accurate, the calculation of total output should include only net investment – that is, the value of new investment goods and stocks *less depreciation* on existing capital and stocks used up. Because depreciation is difficult to measure, GNP is more generally used. For 1996 we have (in £ million) GNP = 652,568 – depreciation 77,372 = Net National Product = National Income = 575,196.

(g) Summary

GDP at market prices

$$\begin{array}{l} -\text{indirect taxes} \\ \underline{+\text{subsidies}} \\ = \text{GDP at factor cost} \\ \underline{+\text{net property income from abroad}} \\ = \text{GNP} \\ -\text{depreciation} \\ \underline{= \text{NI}} \end{array}$$

(h) Personal disposable income

For some purposes, e.g. as an indication of people's current living standards, a measurement of personal disposable income, that is, what people actually have to spend, is more significant. The necessary adjustments to gross national product to obtain personal disposable income are shown in Figure 18.4, giving a figure of £537,677 mn for 1996.

18.3 Uses of national income statistics

(a) To indicate the overall standard of living

Welfare is not identical with wealth (see p. 9), but wealth bears the closest single relationship to it. Income, the flow of wealth, is therefore the nearest indication of welfare.

Nevertheless, the national income figure cannot be accepted solely at its face value. Thus, although the national income of the UK was £287,816 million in 1986 and £575,196 million 1996, it does not automatically follow that everybody had

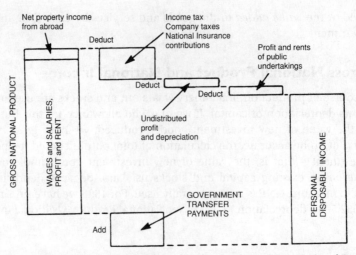

Figure 18.4 Calculating personal disposable income from Gross National Product

doubled their standard of living over that period. The following qualifications have to be made:

(i) Some of the increase may be due to inflation (see Chapter 22), whereas what is relevant is real national income. One way of handling the difficulty is to re-value all money national incomes at 'constant prices' by applying the prices prevailing in a common base year.

(ii) The national income figure must be related to the size of population; thus average income per head is a better indication of well-being.

(iii) A person's standard of living depends upon the quantity of consumer goods and services he enjoys. But the increase in national income may have come about mainly through an increase in the production of producer goods. While these goods enable a higher standard of living to be enjoyed in the future, they do not increase *present* welfare. Thus average personal disposable income might provide a better indication of current living standards, though national income per head is the more satisfactory in the long run.

(iv) The increase in national income may have come about through a surplus of exports over imports. This represents investment overseas, and thus (iii) above applies.

(v) The average-income-per-head figure is merely a statistical average. It does not indicate how any increase in national income is distributed; it may go mostly to a few rich people (as in the oil sheikhdoms), perhaps leaving the others little better off.

(vi) National income figures do not reflect the 'quality' of life. An increase in national income may be the result of longer working hours, inferior working conditions, longer journeys to work, or the presence of more housewives at work (with less comfort in the home). The national income does not value leisure time.

(vii) The quality of goods may have improved without any increase in price, e.g. biros, razors, personal computers.

(viii) All government spending is included at cost in national income calculations, no distinction being made between expenditure on consumer services and expenditure on defence. As a result, if spending on the social services were cut to pay for rearmament, national income would be unchanged!

(ix) The national income figure is swollen when people pay for services which they previously performed themselves. Thus a married woman who returns to teaching but pays a woman to do her housework adds to the national income twice – although the only net addition is her teaching services. Indeed, even an oil spillage can increase national income by the costs of cleaning up, unless these are covered by the polluting shipping company.

(x) Because national income figures are based on private costs and benefits, external costs or benefits do not enter into the calculations. Thus the erection of electricity pylons would be included at cost, no allowance being made for the social cost of spoiling the landscape.

(xi) The increase in national income may have incurred an excessive consumption of irreplaceable resources, e.g. fossil fuels.

(xii) National income figures do not include the 'black' economy (some estimates would add 10 per cent) where services are exchanged for cash in order to evade taxes.

(xiii) National income includes payments for services necessitated by the stress of modern living, e.g. anti-depressant drugs, clinics for alcoholics.

(b) To compare the standards of living of different countries

Comparisons of the national incomes of different countries are often necessary for practical purposes. How much help should be given by the rich countries to the very poor? Which are the very poor countries? What contribution should be made by a country to an international body, such as the United Nations, the Red Cross and NATO? What is the war potential of a country?

But, when used to compare countries' standards of living, national income figures must be subjected to qualifications *additional* to those mentioned above.

(i) Because figures are expressed in different currencies they have to be converted into a common denominator. Using the exchange rate for this purpose is not entirely satisfactory, for the rate is determined by factors other than the internal purchasing powers of currencies, e.g. capital movements. More satisfactory is the use of a conversion rate based on the purchasing power parity for a common basket of goods.

(ii) Different people have different needs. The Englishman has to spend more on heating than the Indian. Obviously, the Englishman is no better off in this respect – though the national income figures, by valuing goods at cost, would indicate that he is.

(iii) The proportion of national income spent by different countries on defence varies. Countries which spend less can enjoy consumer goods instead, but average national income does not indicate the difference.

(iv) Countries vary as regards the length of the average working week, the proportion of women who work, the number of jobs which people do for themselves, the degree to which goods are exchanged against money, the size of the 'black economy' and the accuracy of tax returns. Some allowance must be made for each of these factors.

(v) Differences exist in the distribution of income (see p. 244).

(vi) The availability of educational and medical facilities per head may differ although these affect welfare.

(c) To calculate the rate at which a nation's income is growing

Is the national income growing? Is it growing as fast as it should? Are the incomes of other countries growing faster? Is there sufficient investment to maintain future living standards? The answers to these and similar questions can be found by comparing national income figures, though for the reasons given above some caution must be observed.

(d) To establish relationships which arise between various parts of the economy

If, for example, national income figures revealed a relationship between the level of investment and growth, or between educational expenditure and growth, or between profits and the level of investment, such information would be useful in planning the economy.

The figures might also indicate trends, e.g. the proportion of national income which is taken by the government.

(e) To assist the government in managing the economy

Some central government management is now regarded as essential for achieving full employment, a stable currency and a satisfactory rate of growth. But this requires having figures for the various components of the national income, such as consumption spending, investment, exports and imports. How they can be used will be explained later.

(f) To assist businesses, trade unions, financial journalists, etc. to ascertain economic trends and forecast future movements

(g) To indicate changes in the distribution of income

While, as a scientist, the economist is not concerned with the 'fairness' of the distribution of income, the government is, for taxation and political considerations. National income figures provide the statistical basis when deciding on such matters.

QUESTIONS

1 What do you understand by 'the standard of living'?

2 Name two ways by which a nation could, in the short period, increase its standard of living without increasing its production.

3 You are given the following information for country X:

	1978	1988	1998
National Income (£m)	15,000	20,000	30,000
Investment and defence expenditure (£m)	5,000	5,000	6,000
Population (m)	40	45	50
Average number of hours worked per week	50	45	45
Index of Retail Prices	100	120	140

During which period do you think the standard of living improved the most?

4 Name six differences between the UK and India which make it difficult to compare their national incomes.

5 'The GNP does not allow for the health of our youth, the quality of their education or the joy of their play. It does not include the beauty of our poetry or the strength of our marriages, the intelligence of our public debate or the integrity of our public officials. It measures neither our wit nor our courage, neither our wisdom nor our learning, neither our compassion nor our devotion to country. It measures everything, in short, except that which makes life worth while.'

(John F. Kennedy, US President, 1961–3)

(a) What is the weakness of GNP to which Kennedy is really referring?

(b) Can you suggest other aspects of welfare which should be set off against a rise in the material standard of living as measured by GNP?

◼ ⍐ **19** Unemployment

Objectives

1 To indicate the human aspect of unemployment
2 To examine the different causes of unemployment

19.1 The nature of unemployment

Although today (November 1998) 5.1 per cent of the working population are unemployed, this compares favourably with the situation in pre-war Britain, where in the worst year – 1932 – the national unemployment rate was 22.1 per cent. Unemployment means that labour, machines, land and buildings stand idle; as a result, the standard of living is lower than it need be. But the real curse is the human misery that results. Many people, without work for years, lose hope of ever finding a job; in any case skills deteriorate as the period of unemployment lengthens. Thus unemployment is usually discussed in terms of labour.

Unemployment is said to occur when persons capable of and willing to work are unable to find suitable paid employment. Important points concerning and arising out of this definition, however, need to be stressed:

(i) Unemployment must be involuntary; persons on strike are not reckoned as being unemployed.
(ii) 'Persons capable of work' must exclude the 'unemployable' – those not capable of work through mental or physical disability. On the other hand, unemployables are usually in the pool of unemployed labour seeking jobs and, where labour is scarce, more use will be made of them – provided that minimum wage regulations do not prevent this.
(iii) Full employment does not mean that workers will never be required to switch jobs or occupations. Changes in the conditions of demand and supply are bound to occur, and such changes will be more frequent the more dynamic the economy and the more a country is dependent on international trade.

Thus there will always be some workers unemployed. A full employment policy must identify and deal with the particular cause of the unemployment.

(a) Interpreting unemployment figures

Measuring unemployment involves problems of definition. How, for example, should part-time workers be treated? Is registration at a Jobcentre to be the test for inclusion? In comparing changes in the rate of unemployment over time, has the official definition of unemployment changed? Since 1982 official unemployment figures have counted only those persons actually claiming benefit.

But interpretation of the figures also necessitates subjective judgements as to the extent to which they are over or understated. When employment is buoyant, does the figure conceal 'disguised' unemployment in that firms are reluctant to release redundant workers or because some employees are working at less than their full potential? Is a high rate of job turnover adding to frictional unemployment? Are minimum wage regulations leading to unemployment? Is the rate of unemployment benefit, especially the 'poverty trap', discouraging an active search for work? In comparing unemployment rates over time should not some allowance be made for a changing age structure?

19.2 Causes of unemployment

(a) Frictional

Unless the economy is completely static, there will always be people changing their jobs. Some merely desire a change of employment or a move to a different part of the country. In certain occupations, e.g. unskilled labour in the construction industry, workers are not employed regularly by any one employer; when a particular contract is completed, labour is made redundant. Occasionally, too, workers are discharged when a factory is being reorganised.

Unemployed workers usually register at the local Jobcentre, forming a pool of labour from which employers can fill vacancies. But how large should this pool be? If it is too large, workers remain unemployed for long periods. If it is too small, production is dislocated by bottlenecks in filling vacancies (with employers holding on to labour not currently needed), by job-switching just for the sake of change and, above all, by strikes in support of claims for higher wages.

Frictional unemployment is partly unavoidable, and the grant of unemployment benefit affords the worker some protection against its effects. Moreover, the installation of expensive machinery which must be kept fully employed has quite often had the indirect effect of 'decasualising' labour.

(b) Seasonal

Employment in some industries, e.g. building, fruit-picking and holiday catering, is seasonal in character. The difficulty is that the skills required by different seasonal jobs are not 'substitutable'. To what extent, for example, can hotel workers become shop assistants in the January sales? Seasonal employment is not completely avoidable. But it can be reduced if a small, regular labour force will work overtime during the 'season' and admit, say, students during the busy periods. Moreover, the price system may help. By offering off-season rates, hotels at holiday resorts can attract autumn conferences.

(c) International

Because the UK is so dependent on international trade, she is particularly vulnerable to unemployment brought about by a fall in the demand for her exports. Such a fall may occur because:

(i) The prices of UK goods are too high to be competitive in world markets

If home prices rise, for example because of wage increases, the export market is likely to be hit severely. The demand for exports is usually highly elastic, since substitutes are often available from competing countries. The effect on employment is shown in Figure 19.1. The wage increase moves the supply curve from S to S_1. Because demand is elastic there is a considerable fall in the demand for the good, from OM to OM_1. The industry, and therefore employment, contract.

(ii) Incomes of major importing countries may be reduced by a recession or a deterioration in the terms of trade

If incomes of importing countries fall, their demand for UK goods, especially those having a high income-elasticity of demand, will be likely to decrease. This is what happened in 1998 when the economies of Russia, Japan and other Southeast Asia countries ran into difficulties.

(d) Structural

Structural unemployment, like frictional, results largely from the immobility of labour (see p. 102). Ignorance of opportunities elsewhere or, more likely, obstacles to moving mean that workers do not move to available jobs in other parts of the country. Thus employers in the south of England have found it difficult, because of the higher cost of housing there, to recruit from high unemployment regions.

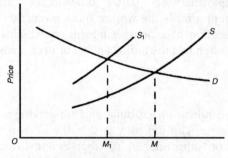

Quantity of export good demanded and supplied

Figure 19.1 The effect on employment of a wage increase in an export industry

More serious, however, is occupational immobility resulting from long-term changes in the conditions of demand and supply in certain industries, especially exporting industries.

On the demand side, there may be a change in any of the factors influencing the conditions of demand. The price of substitutes may fall (Dundee jute products have largely been replaced by plastics), or foreign buyers may switch to competitors' goods (British shipyards have been hit by competition from other countries). On the supply side, new techniques or the exhaustion of mineral deposits may make labour redundant. Automation has reduced ICI's demand for workers at Stockton; exhaustion of the better coal seams has led to the closure of pits in South Wales and mid-Scotland.

Where an industry is highly localised in a particular area, the resulting unemployment may be particularly serious (see Chapter 23).

(e) Cyclical

The term 'cyclical unemployment' refers to the alternate booms and slumps in the level of industrial activity which have occurred over the last hundred years. It was the major cause of the high unemployment of the 1930s, and while we no longer speak of a 'trade cycle', we do still move between boom and recession.

This is the most serious form of unemployment and is the subject-matter of Chapters 20–23.

QUESTIONS

1 Give two reasons why unemployment of labour is more serious than the unemployment of other factors.

2 It is estimated that the direct cost to the Exchequer of an unemployed person is on average about £5,000 a year. Under each of the headings (a) lost revenue, (b) extra government spending, suggest two items contributing to this.

■ ☑ 20 The level of output and aggregate demand: the Keynesian approach to full employment

Objectives

1 To outline Keynes's theory that cyclical unemployment resulted from a deficiency of aggregate demand (AD)
2 To explain how variations in AD can occur
3 To examine the major determinants of investment
4 To indicate how the government can adjust AD

20.1 The link between spending and production

(a) The circular flow of income

We will begin by repeating in simplified form the identity which exists between income and expenditure. Take a simple example. A teacher buys a table from a carpenter. With the money he receives, the carpenter pays the timber merchant for the wood, who in turn pays the man who cut the wood. But where did the teacher obtain the original money to buy the table? Simply from the carpenter, the timber merchant and the tree-feller, who each use part of their receipts to pay fees to the teacher for instructing their children. So with the other goods the teacher buys. Thus there is a circular flow of income – one person's spending becomes another person's income. Spending is therefore necessary for earnings.

The same applies to the economy as a whole; at any one time spending equals income. Suppose, for instance, that all production in the economy is in the hands of a giant firm which owns all the land and raw materials and employs all the labour. The firm's income consists of the receipts from the sale of its product. Since it owns all the raw materials and land, these receipts must equal what it pays out in wages and what it has left in profits. This was the principle upon which we measured national income.

Since spending on goods determines the receipts and thus the profits of firms, it is of vital importance in deciding the level of their output and thus of the aggregate level of activity. To explain more fully, we use Figure 20.1, which shows the *money* flows which correspond to the movement of factors and goods in the

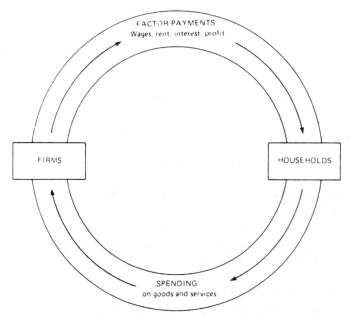

FACTOR PAYMENTS
Wages, rent, interest, profit

FIRMS

HOUSEHOLDS

SPENDING
on goods and services

Figure 20.1   The circular flow of income

outer ring of Figure 1.2 – payments by firms for factors and expenditure of households on goods. The first represents income of households; the second represents receipts of firms.

If spending on goods and services is maintained, factor payments can be maintained; in other words the profitability of production is unchanged and thus firms have no cause to vary output. If, however, for some reason or another, spending should fall, some of the goods produced by firms will not be sold, and stocks will accumulate. On the other hand, if spending on goods and services increases, stocks will be run down. Production has become more profitable and, as a result, output is expanded.

Three important points emerge from our discussion so far:

(i) There is no impetus towards a contraction or expansion of production if spending on goods and services equals spending (including normal profits) by firms on factors of production.
(ii) The level of production, and therefore employment, is closely related to the level of spending.
(iii) There is nothing to guarantee that spending will be sufficient to ensure a level of production where all factors are fully employed.

(b) Definitions and assumptions

Before we show how changes in spending occur, we must make simplifying assumptions.

We define net profit as gross profit less retentions for depreciation. We assume:

(i) All retentions for depreciation are actually spent on replacement investment

Thus, when in future we speak of 'investment' it refers solely to net additions to fixed capital and stocks, i.e. net investment.

(ii) All net profit is distributed to the owners of the risk capital

If we define net profit as being gross profit less retentions for actual spending on depreciation, this means that there is no 'saving' by firms.

(iii) There is no government taxation or spending

(iv) There are no economic connections with the outside world; it is a 'closed' economy

From the above assumptions it follows that: (1) the sum of the factor payments is equal to national income (equals national output) as defined in Chapter 18; and (2) income equals disposable income.

(v) There are no changes in the price level

Thus any changes in the money value of national income reflect changes in real output.

(vi) The level of employment is directly proportionate to the level of output

In practice this may not be strictly true: existing machinery, for example, may be able to produce extra output without additional labour. But until there is full employment, the simplification does allow employment to vary directly with the level of national income.

20.2 Reasons for changes in aggregate demand

(a) Aggregate demand

Our task, therefore, is to discover why changes occur in the national income (hereafter symbolised by Y). Now, as we have just shown, Y depends upon the level of spending, which we shall refer to as aggregate demand (abbreviated to AD). Thus we can find out why Y changes by discovering why AD changes.

(b) Changes in AD

Let us return to our example of the teacher Suppose he earns £20,852 in a given year. Most of it will be spent on consumer goods and services – but not all. Some will probably be put aside for a 'rainy day'. That part of income which is not spent we can say is 'saved'. What happens to it? The money could be hidden under the mattress; in that case it is obviously lost to the circular flow of income. But the teacher is more likely to put it in a bank, where it is safer and earns interest.

Nevertheless, at this point it is still lost to the circular flow. Saving represents a 'leak' from the flow of income.

So far, however, we have looked only at spending on consumer goods. But spending may also be on capital goods. Firms borrow money from their banks (and other institutions) for such purchases. Thus the sum deposited by the teacher stands a good chance of being returned to the circular flow of income by being 'invested', i.e. spent on capital goods or additions to stocks. Investment, therefore, can be regarded as an 'injection'. And, if exactly the amount of money saved by households is spent by firms on investment, the level of AD is maintained (Figure 20.2), and Y is unchanged.

But suppose that the amount saved does not coincide with what firms wish to invest. This can come about either by a change in the amount invested or by a change in the amount spent by consumers.

Let us first assume that households' spending on consumer goods remains constant. If now firms reduce the amount they borrow for investment, AD is smaller. On the other hand, if firms increase their investment, AD will be larger.

Alternatively the amount of income spent on consumer goods may alter. Investment, we will now assume, remains unchanged. Here, if more is spent out of a given income, AD will increase; if less, AD decreases.

What is important to recognise is that in an economy where people are free to dispose of their income as they please, and where firms make their own investment decisions, a difference can easily exist between the amount of income

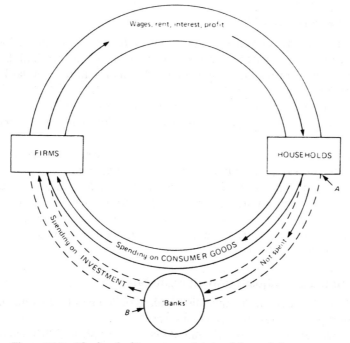

Figure 20.2 The level of income maintained through investment

which people plan to 'save' (i.e. which they do not wish to spend) and the amount which firms wish to invest. This is because, in their spending, households and firms act for different reasons. Two questions have therefore to be asked: (i) What determines spending on consumer goods and therefore saving (at position A)? (ii) What determines investment spending (at position B)?

In our analysis, consumption, that is spending on consumer goods and services, will be given the symbol C; saving, i.e. income not spent on consumption, S; investment, i.e. spending on net additions to capital goods and stocks, I.

20.3 Consumption spending

(a) Consumption and saving by households: 'personal saving'

Income is received as wages or salaries, rent, interest and profits. With it households buy the consumer goods they need. That part of income which is not spent has been defined as 'saving'. Hence $Y = C + S$, $C = Y - S$, and $S = Y - C$.

C and S, therefore, are merely two sides of the same coin. Thus, whenever we consider C or S, we must examine the factors which influence both spending and thrift.

Spending decisions are more important in the short run, for people's first concern is to maintain their standard of living. They are influenced by:

(i) Size of income

A small income leaves no margin for saving. Only when basic needs have been satisfied will a part of income be saved. Indeed, if current income falls below this level, past savings or borrowing may be used to maintain the standard of living accustomed to.

But we can go further. As income increases, the proportion spent tends to decrease; or, as it is often put, there is a *diminishing marginal propensity to consume (c)*.

The above conclusions are illustrated diagrammatically in Figure 20.3, where the curve C shows how consumption changes with income.

Below an income of OD there is 'dis-saving'. At OD all income is consumed. At higher incomes the proportion spent falls and saving occurs. This diminishing marginal propensity to consume is shown by the decreasing slope of the consumption curve: for any given increase in income, the extra amount spent grows successively smaller.

(ii) The timelag in adjusting spending habits

It takes time for a person to adjust his standard of living as his income increases. In the short period, therefore, saving increases.

The above two factors explain the *shape* of the consumption curve – how spending changes as income changes. But we still have to account for the

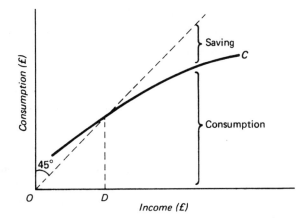

Figure 20.3   The relationship between consumption and income

position of the curve – what determines the proportion of any given income which is spent. This amount can vary (that is, the position of the *C* curve may change) as a result of:

(iii) Changes in disposable income

We have assumed that firms have distributed all net profits and that there are no government taxation or transfers. In practice both profit distribution and government taxation will affect the size of income available for spending. Increasing direct taxation, for instance, would, by reducing disposable income, lower the *C* curve.

(iv) The size of wealth owned by an individual

(v) The invention of new consumer goods

In recent years family cars, TV, video recorders, hi-fi equipment, camcorders, central heating and dishwaters have all induced spending.

(vi) Hire-purchase and other credit facilities

Easier hire-purchase or bank credit terms encourage spending.

(vii) An anticipated fall in the value of money

If people considered that the prices of goods were likely to rise, they would bring forward their spending rather than save for the future.

(viii) Inflation

Uncertainty regarding possible government measures to reduce inflation may lead to increased saving. Furthermore, inflation reduces the real value of money assets. People may be induced to save more to restore the real value of their assets, as happened, for example, in 1990–2.

(ix) The age-distribution of the population

Since most saving is done by people over thirty-five years of age, an ageing population will tend to reduce the propensity to consume of the community as a whole.

In the long period, people have some concern for their future standard of living, and *thrift* exercises a greater influence on the disposal of income.

The main *factors determining thrift* are:

(i) Size of income

As already shown, saving increases as income increases and at an increasing rate.

(ii) The life cycle

(iii) Psychological attitudes

Some communities are by nature more thrifty than others, providing against sickness, unemployment and old age. On the other hand, ostentation – the desire to 'keep up with the Joneses' – may motivate a high rate of spending.

(iv) Social environment

Apart from influencing the general attitude to saving, environment can be a major factor in other ways. Such institutions as savings banks, building societies, insurance companies and unit trusts encourage regular saving.

Political conditions, too, influence saving habits. Countries continually threatened by war or revolution do not provide the stable background necessary to encourage thrift.

(v) Government policy

The government can influence people's attitude to saving in a variety of ways. In the UK it tries to stimulate personal saving through the rate of interest offered, income-tax concessions (e.g. on National Savings Bank interest) and special devices (e.g. Personal Equity Plans, Premium Bonds). On the other hand, a comprehensive state social-insurance and pension scheme may reduce the incentive to save.

At one time it was thought that people could only be induced to postpone consumption, i.e. to save, by offering interest as compensation. This view, however, is now largely rejected, chiefly because much saving is contractual, e.g. pension and mortgage payments. The dominant factor is the *ability* to save, i.e. the level of income.

Under our simplifying assumptions that all net profits are distributed and that there is no government taxation or spending, all saving is done by households. But saving can be achieved through retentions by firms and the government. In order to consider these, we will temporarily relax assumptions (ii) and (iii), page 254.

(b) Business saving

Saving by businesses (which in volume remains fairly stable) is achieved by not distributing all the profits made in a year. Some profits are usually retained, either to be 'ploughed back' for the expansion of the business, or to be held as liquid reserves in order to meet tax liabilities or maintain dividends when profits fluctuate. The chief factors affecting this type of saving are:

(i) Profits

Transfers to reserves are dependent upon and stimulated by the level of current profits. In practice, therefore, business saving is determined principally by the level of AD.

(ii) Subjective factors

Profits are likely to be retained when directors are expansion-minded or financially prudent.

(iii) Government policy

An increased tax on *distributed* profits would tend to increase company saving.

(c) Government saving

Government saving covers the saving of the public sector – the central government, public corporations and local authorities – when their combined revenue exceeds expenditure. In practice, this net public sector saving is dominated by the central government's budget, the other two together contributing only about 5 per cent of saving.

In recent years, central government expenditure has been so high that there has been a *Public Sector Net Cash Requirement* (PSNCR), which has to be covered by borrowing (see p. 283).

(d) Conclusion

In the private sector, spending (and therefore saving) depend upon (i) the level of Y, i.e. the size of AD, and (ii) other factors influencing the amount spent out of income. Since in comparison with changes in AD these other factors are fairly stable, the main influence on short-term changes in consumption spending is the size of AD itself!

We have therefore to look elsewhere for the reason why AD changes. It is to be found in the comparative instability of the other form of spending – investment.

20.4 Investment spending

(a) What do we mean by 'investment'?

Investment, for purposes of national-income calculations, is spending over a given period on the production of capital goods (houses, factories, machinery, etc.) or on net additions to stocks (raw materials, consumer goods in shops, etc.).

It is important to distinguish between this definition of *real* investment and *asset* investment – putting money in a bank or buying securities. In national-income analysis, investment takes place only when there is an actual net addition to capital goods or stocks.

Investment takes place in both the private and public sectors (Table 20.1).

(b) Investment in the private sector

A firm will only spend on investment if it thinks that it will eventually prove profitable. There are, therefore, two main considerations to bear in mind: (i) the expected yield from the investment; and (ii) its cost.

The *yield* on the investment will depend largely on the demand for the consumer good the firm produces (see p. 116). In *estimating* such demand, the firm is most likely to commence from a position regarding which it does have some definite knowledge, i.e. the present demand for those goods. If that demand is buoyant and has remained so for a fairly long period, the firm will probably view the future optimistically. On the other hand, if present demand is low and has shown itself resistant to attempts to increase it, the future, to say the least, will appear somewhat gloomy. But since the current demand for goods, i.e. the level of consumption, depends chiefly on the level of income, we can say that, the higher AD is, the greater investment is likely to be.

Technical developments, like the internal-combustion engine, atomic energy, automation, computer technology and North Sea gas and oil, give an added impetus to investment.

Furthermore, the effect of government policy has to be considered. Changes in policy add to uncertainty. Is corporation tax likely to be increased? Will inflation compel the government to carry out restrictive policies? In contrast the government may stimulate private investment by subsidies or generous tax allowances, and revive optimism by increasing its own investment.

This brings us to the *cost* of investment – the rate of interest. A low rate tends to stimulate investment. If the rate rises, marginal projects cease to be profitable, and so the level of investment falls (see p. 116).

However, whether the rate of interest has a *major* influence on investment is doubtful. For one thing, investment decisions, especially for large firms, are the result of long-term planning. Any alteration of plans just because of a change in

Table 20.1   Investment in the UK 1997: Gross Fixed Capital Formation, £mn

Private Sector	
Private (mostly dwellings)	30,154
Business	91,356
	121,510
Public Sector	
Central and local government	10,489
National Health Service Trusts, Agencies, etc.	1,711
	12,200
Total UK. fixed investment	133,710

Source: UK Economic Accounts, 1998.

the rate of interest might throw the whole programme out of phase. For another, firms allow a considerable safety margin when deciding on investment, probably expecting to recover its cost within five years. This margin is thus sufficient to absorb a relatively small rise in the rate of interest. Even the holding of stocks may not be affected by the rate of interest. Convenience is more likely to decide the minimum held. In any case the rate of interest may be only a small part of the cost of holding stocks – warehousing, etc., being relatively far more important. Above all, compared with firms' expectations, the rate of interest is of secondary importance. Thus, especially when it comes to reviving investment, a fall in the rate of interest may have its main impact through the psychological improvement in expectations.

(c) Investment in the public sector

Capital expenditure is incurred by the central government, local authorities and National Heath Service Trusts, the post office, etc.

Much of central-government investment is fairly stable, depending chiefly on policy commitments. To a large extent, too, this is also true of the NHS Trusts.

Local-authority investment tends, however, to react to changes in the rate of interest. This is especially true of spending on new dwellings. If, after applying government grants, the cost of borrowing is not covered by the rents charged, local taxes have to be raised with adverse political consequences.

The real importance of public investment is that it is subject to direct government control. Thus, should private investment be deficient, the government can increase its spending on its own capital projects.

(d) Summary

Employment depends upon the level of AD – the total amount of money spent on the goods produced. AD fluctuates according to the relationship between intended saving and investment.

(i) AD expands if:
    (1) investment increases but saving remains unchanged;
    (2) saving decreases but investment remains unchanged.
(ii) AD contracts if:
    (1) investment decreases but saving remains unchanged;
    (2) saving increases but investment remains unchanged.

In practice investment is more liable to frequent change than is saving. Whereas firms' expectations are highly sensitive to new conditions, people's spending habits are fairly stable. Fluctuations in the level of AD, and therefore of income, are thus mainly the result of changes in the level of investment.

There is another important way in which saving differs from investment in the process of income creation. Whereas an increase in investment will, other things being equal, automatically produce an increase in saving through an expansion of income, an addition to saving need not lead to an increase in investment. Instead income merely contracts until what is saved from it equals investment.

20.5 The effect on the level of income of changes in investment

(a) The 'multiplier'

Given no change in saving, an increase in investment spending will raise the level of income by more than the increase in investment. Firms producing capital goods will take on additional workers. A part of these workers' earnings will be spent, providing additional income for shopkeepers and others, who in turn will spend a part of their extra income. There is thus a 'multiplier' effect. How the process works in real life can be illustrated from Nevil Shute's *Ruined City*. The shipyard in the town obtained an order for three tankers. 'A shop, long closed, reopened to sell meat pies . . . A man who gleaned a sack of holly in the country lanes disposed of it within an hour . . . A hot roast chestnut barrow came upon the streets, and did good trade.'

The multiplier is defined as the

$$\frac{\text{increase in income}}{\text{increase in investment}}$$

Its size depends upon the fraction of additional income which is spent, that is, the marginal propensity to consume. Suppose investment increases by £100 million a year, and that households spend half of any additional income. Producers of capital goods can now pay an extra £100 million on wages, rent, interest and profit. Households receiving this extra income spend £50 million with shopkeepers who, in turn, spend £25 million. The sum of these additional incomes will eventually total £200 million. The multiplier equals 2.

To generalise, the multiplier equals

$$\frac{1}{1 - \text{the marginal propensity to consume}}$$

If, in the above example, the marginal propensity to consume had been $\frac{3}{4}$ instead of $\frac{1}{2}$, income would have increased by £400 million, giving a multiplier of 4. Since the marginal propensity to consume + the marginal propensity to save = 1, we can write the multiplier as equalling $1/s$, where s equals the marginal propensity to save.

Although the above assumes that the marginal propensity to consume is constant at all levels of income, even if the propensity to consume diminishes as income increases, the principle of the multiplier is the same. The only difference is that the calculations are more complicated because, for each period increment, we have to apply a smaller multiplier as income increases.

(b) Diagrammatic representation

Figure 20.4 presents the essentials of the determination of the level of income. It is assumed that investment is autonomous, that is, its level is independent of the level of income (as shown by the horizontal line *I*). Saving varies with income.

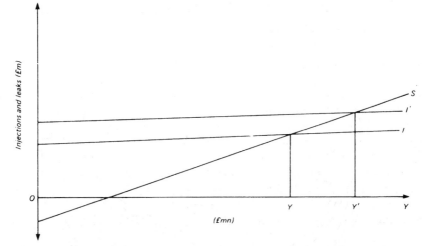

Figure 20.4 The effect on income of an increase in the level of investment

Initially saving is negative – households maintain spending at a low level of income by drawing on accumulated savings or by borrowing. When income increases and dis-saving becomes unnecessary, only $\frac{2}{3}$ of additional income is spent, $\frac{1}{3}$ being saved as shown by the line S having a constant slope of $\frac{1}{3}$.

The equilibrium level of income is Y, where $S = I$. At any income less than this, AD will expand because I is greater than S; and vice versa.

If now investment increases to I', there will be a new equilibrium level of income, Y'. Diagrammatically, the multiplier equals YY'/II', i.e. 3. Similarly, income would decrease if the level of investment fell below I.

20.6 Leaks and injections in general

In the above discussion, saving has been the only leak from the flow of aggregate demand. Similarly investment has represented the sole injection. However, the relaxation of the assumptions that there is no government and a closed economy introduces the consideration of other leaks and injections.

Direct taxation takes income from households, leaving them with less available spending power. Indirect taxes siphon off a part of consumer spending to the government, thereby reducing firms' receipts. Thus taxation is a leak from the circular flow of income. On the other hand, it can be put back by government spending – an injection.

Finally we have to consider the effect of imports and exports. When British households spend on foreign goods and services, there is a leak of AD from the circular flow, since this spending is received by foreign firms. On the other hand, spending by foreigners on British goods and services is received by British firms, and therefore represents an injection (Figure 20.5).

These other leaks – taxation and imports – and injections – government

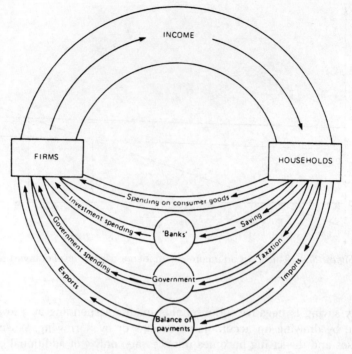

Figure 20.5 Total leaks and injections

spending and exports – affect AD and Y in the same way as do, respectively, S and I.

20.7 Aggregate demand and full employment policy

The above is an outline of Lord Keynes's theory of how the level of employment is determined (*The General Theory of Employment, Interest and Money*, 1936).

Employment depends upon the level of national income (Y). If the level of AD is too low, the economy will be in equilibrium where Y is below the full-employment level of Y_{fe} (Figure 20.6). Thus, Keynes considered, the government's task is to estimate that level of AD which will produce full employment, and then arrange that AD is increased to this level.

The policies which the government can follow to adjust AD can be classified as fiscal or monetary.

(a) Fiscal policy

AD can be adjusted by changes in taxation and government expenditure.

Certain of these changes operate automatically to adjust AD in the appropriate direction without direct government action. Such an *automatic stabiliser* is

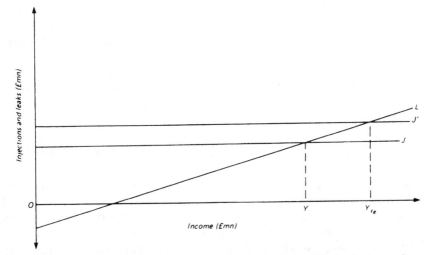

Figure 20.6 Achieving a full-employment aggregate demand by budgetary policy

taxation. As incomes increase, so does the yield from taxation especially if taxation is progressive, e.g. income tax, or, like VAT, is applied on an *ad valorem* basis to expensive goods having a high income elasticity of demand. One important point must be made: if the stabilising effects of taxation are to work, the government must not increase its own expenditure as tax receipts rise, and vice versa.

Government spending on unemployment benefits and agricultural price support also has stabilising effects for, as unemployment increases, so do benefit payments, while there are likely to be increased subsidies to maintain farmers' incomes.

Alternatively, government measures may be *discretionary* in that it can influence private consumption and investment by simply changing the *type* of taxes levied. Thus a switch from indirect taxation would tend to increase consumption, for it would mean greater spending power for poorer people (those having a high propensity to consume). Similarly, reduced taxes on companies would tend to increase investment through improved profitability.

But altering the structure of taxation simply to effect short-term adjustments in AD is too cumbersome a weapon. The government, therefore, relies mainly on *budgetary policy* to adjust AD by altering the relationship between its own revenue and expenditure.

As we have seen, taxation represents an appropriation by the government of a part of private incomes, and will be retained in the circular flow of income only in so far as it is spent by the government. Hence AD will be increased if taxation is less than government spending, and vice versa. If previously the budget was balanced, there would now be a budget deficit, and vice versa. In Figure 20.6, current *Y* is *OY*, less than the full-employment *OY*$_{fe}$. It is therefore necessary to increase total injections from *J* to *J*', e.g. by increased government spending or additional private consumption.

Thus the budget was to be regarded not simply as the means of raising revenue to cover estimated government expenditure, but as a weapon for adjusting private spending to the output which available resources could produce given the requirements of the public sector.

It is important to note, however, that while changes in government spending increase AD directly, the ability to do so is limited. Much government spending, however, is more or less contractual (e.g. social welfare benefits, interest on the National Debt), while public projects, such as motorways, schools and hospitals cannot be put on ice until there is a deficiency in *AD*. Long-term government policy, not short-term marginal adjustments according to the level of activity, must decide priorities for such projects.

This means that in practice it is taxation which has to take the strain of adjustment. Yet even this presents difficulties: (i) The convention of annual budgets tends to dictate the timing of adjustments. (ii) Reducing taxes may, because of the administration necessary, take time to be effective; for example, new PAYE tax tables have to be distributed. (iii) Taxation has other objectives, e.g. redistributing income. (iv) Measures can conflict. If, because of disincentive effects of high income tax, an increase in tax revenue has to be achieved by raising indirect taxes, these are not only regressive but can instigate wage-cost inflation (see p. 271). (v) Overall budgetary policy cannot direct demand into those districts and industries where unemployment is highest and has to be supplemented by a regional policy (see Chapter 23). Finally, the deficit may be so large and persistent that the size of the PSBR creates problems elsewhere (see p. 283). As a result, monetary policy becomes indispensable.

(b) Monetary policy

Monetary policy now operates through the cost of money, the rate of interest, influencing the amount demanded.

Using the rate of interest to adjust *AD* depends on the fact that both households and firms depend upon borrowing for much of their expenditure. Furthermore it can be applied quickly and to a fine degree and, if implemented early, can provide advance warning of the authorities' intentions. Indeed the psychological effects of changes are probably as important as any direct effect on investment spending.

But there are weaknesses. Only when the rate of interest is high is it likely to affect long-term investment programmes. Nor does it discriminate in its operation, e.g. as between firms which export a high proportion of their output and those which do not; projects of high social value (e.g. slum clearance) and those of less certain merit (e.g. gaming casinos); and between industries the demand for whose products is particularly dependent on borrowed funds (e.g. housing construction, property development, consumer durable goods) and those having a strong cash flow (e.g. advertising). Most serious of all is that interest policy cannot be operated in isolation from the general level of world rates (see p. 344) and, in fact, could not be decided independently if the UK joined the Economic and Monetary Union (EMU) of the EU(see p. 373).

(c) Conclusion

Keynes's main contribution to full employment theory was his highlighting of the need to maintain an adequate level of AD.

But he failed to link AD with changes in the price level. Chapters 21 and 22 outline the refinements to his theory made necessary by this and other weaknesses which became increasingly apparent from the 1960s onwards:

QUESTIONS

1. Give three examples of contractual saving by individuals.

2. Suggest three ways in which the government could reduce spending (consumption) by individuals.

3. Give two reasons why businesses save.

4. Suggest four ways in which the government could raise the level of investment.

5. The following figures (in £ m) relate to an economy in which there is no government expenditure or taxation: investment = 10; exports = 10; consumption expenditure = $\frac{9}{10}$ income at all income; imports = $\frac{1}{9}$ consumers' expenditure at all levels of income.
   (a) What is the level of national income in equilibrium?
   (b) What is the level of imports?
   (c) Is the balance of payments in equilibrium?
   (d) What will be the new equilibrium level of national income if investment expenditure increases to 15, exports remaining unchanged?
   (e) What will be the effect of this increase in investment on the balance of payments?

6. Give three reasons why only the government is in a position to maintain an adequate AD.

■ ☑ **21** The relationship of the price level and the level of employment

Objectives

1 To explain the shape of the Aggregate Supply (AS) curve
2 To show how the level of employment and the price level are related through the interaction of the AS and AD curves
3 To indicate the main tenets of 'monetarism'
4 To develop a model which incorporates 'expectations' regarding the future rate of inflation

21.1 The development of 'full employment' theory

While the presentation of the Keynesian theory in the previous chapter has, for the sake of clarity, shown the full-employment level of income as a single point, in practice there can be no single precise AD target. Instead AD has to be related to changes in the price level. This involves paying more attention to the supply side.

Our task is to build a model which (1) shows how aggregate demand (AD) and aggregate supply (AS) change with respect to the price level, and (2) brings AD and AS together to determine both the level of activity and the corresponding price level, and (3) explains the inflationary process.

21.2 AD and AS curves

(a) The AD curve

As we have seen (Chapter 19), AD consists of consumption, investment and government spending, together with exports less imports – in symbol form: $C + I + G + (X - M)$. In this new analytical approach, however, increases or decreases in AD have to be shown by *shifts* of the curve.

Nevertheless we still have to explain the *shape* of the curve, that is, how AD is related to the price level. To simplify we will concentrate on C and I.

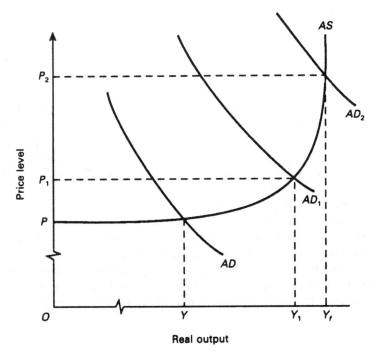

Figure 21.1 The relationship of output and the price level to AD and AS

The AD curve slopes downwards from left to right (Figure 21.1) showing that, as the price level falls, AD expands. In other words, the lower the price level, the greater will be the total real output demanded in the economy.

The reasons for this are:

(i) *Consumers feel wealthier* since balances held in cash will buy more (the 'real balance effect'). As a result spending is likely to increase.
(ii) *The rate of interest falls.* A fall in prices means that less money is required for everyday spending. With no change in the money supply, more money is left for buying, not only goods, but also financial assets such as government bonds. The resulting rise in bond prices represents a fall in the rate of interest (see chap. 14, qu. 2).
(iii) *The balance of payments (X – M) improves* as home-produced goods become more competitive, increasing exports and decreasing imported substitutes.

The opposite applies for a rise in the price level.

(b) The AS curve

The AS curve shows the relationship between the price level and the real output of the economy. It is, however, a short-run supply curve in the sense that productive capacity is fixed: output can be increased only by increasing inputs of the variable factors, chiefly labour.

In general, high prices enable firms to extend output. But for analytical purposes, we have to distinguish between three broadly different situations.

(i) At a low level of output, supply can be increased at a constant cost. Firms have surplus capacity and equally efficient labour, basic materials, components, etc. can be obtained at existing prices. Thus the AS curve is perfectly elastic up to output OY with the price level at P (Figure 21.1).

(ii) As output increases beyond OY, fixed capital has to be used more intensively and diminishing returns set in. In addition 'bottlenecks' appear through skilled labour shortages, longer delivery dates for components, etc. Above all, trade unions are in a stronger position and negotiate wage increases. Thus firms' costs rise and the AS curve turns upwards.

(iii) The AS curve slopes upwards at an increasing rate the nearer output approaches OY_f, the maximum potential output which is attainable with given limited resources and current technology. The vertical portion is thus the equivalent of the long period AS curve. It can be shifted to the right only by factors which make for long-term growth (see Chapter 24). Given this absolutely inelastic AS curve, any attempt to expand output by increasing AD will be impossible and simply finds its outlet in steeply rising prices.

(c) AD and AS combined

Equilibrium occurs at the intersection of the AD and AS curves because at this point the output which households and firms are willing to spend on C and I equals the output which firms will supply. Thus in Figure 21.1 when aggregate demand is AD_1, real national output is OY_1 per year (still less than full employment) and the price level is P_1. Full employment can only be achieved by increasing aggregate demand to AD_2, when the price level will rise to P_2.

21.3 A first step towards an explanation of inflation

Prices rise when there is excess purchasing power for goods available at current prices. But what brings about the excess purchasing power? Early explanations of the persistent rise in prices reflect the above model and were often divided into *demand-pull* and *cost-push*.

(a) Demand-pull

When an increase in AD causes output to expand above OY (Figure 21.1), prices start to rise. Thereafter, if AD continues to increase, the price rise accelerates. Indeed should AD increase after the full employment output (OY_f) has been reached, we have true inflation, the extra AD finding its outlet entirely in higher prices.

(b) Cost-push

The price rise can start on the supply side through a rise in import prices. More usually, however, it follows from demand pull as labour seeks compensating wage increases. Indeed wage demands may exceed the current rate of inflation even though there has been no corresponding increase in productivity. Employers tend to concede these wage demands, and raise prices accordingly. Such price rises can be absorbed by the higher earnings. Here, therefore, prices have been pushed up by an initial increase in costs.

(c) Policy implications

The foregoing simple explanation of the direct relationship between output and rising prices seemed to be supported in 1958 by Professor A.W. Phillips whose research indicated a strong negative relationship between the annual *rate of inflation* and the annual *rate of unemployment* in the UK over the past century (Figure 21.2).

The policy conclusion was that a reduction in the rate of inflation could be 'traded off' by reducing AD though this could lead to higher unemployment.

(d) The failure of the above model to explain 'stagflation'

Unitil the mid-1960s the Phillips curve relationship held, but then both unemployment and inflation increased together, a situation described as 'stagflation'.

The weakness of the above analysis is that it suffers from being too static. As a result it sees inflation as being a *condition* whereas it is really a *process*.

First, unlike the demand and supply curves which we studied in Chapter 2, the

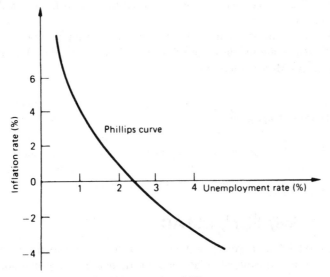

Figure 21.2   The Phillips curve

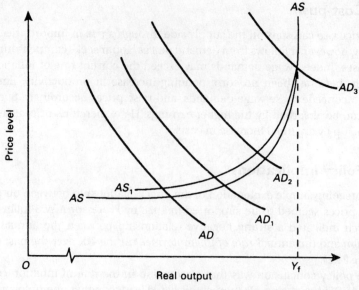

Figure 21.3   The inflationary process

AD and AS curves are not independent of each other. Thus in Figure 21.3 an increase in AD to AD_1 produces a rise in the price level. As a result, increased wage rates are negotiated, so that the AS curve moves to AS_1. But since this also means an increase in money spending power, aggregate demand moves from AD_1 to AD_2 at a higher price level. This, by generating further wage catching up, produces an inflationary spiral.

Second, wage demands may eventually be geared to an *expected* higher rate of inflation. The rate of the inflationary spiral now gathers momentum. Thus the remedy is not a simple piece of surgery to remove excess fat, but rather a fight against a cancerous growth.

The experience of 'stagflation' showed that an alternative theory of inflation embodying expectations was required. This has been built up by the 'monetarists' led by Professor Milton Friedman.

21.4 Monetarism

The monetarist theory of inflation emphasises: (a) the *direct impact* of the money supply on AD; (b) *expectations* as the cause of the inflationary spiral; and (c) *the natural rate of unemployment*. We will explain each in turn.

(a) The money supply and AD

It was observed that there was a positive correlation between increases in the money supply and the rate of inflation. But is there a causal connection? Does an increase in the money supply *directly* increase AD?

Keynes considered that the supply of money does not enter directly into spending decisions. In the short run these depend on the level of income; over time they will be affected by long-term factors, such as contractual commitments to regular saving. Any increase in the supply of money simply increases liquidity in the economy, and the rate of interest – the price paid for liquidity – therefore falls. AD will expand only indirectly, through a lower rate of interest leading to more investment spending.

In contrast, Milton Friedman holds that an increase in the supply of money can lead *directly* to additional spending and thus *cause* inflation. He argues that people maintain a fraction of their nominal income in cash balances. An increase in the money supply results in their having larger cash balances than they require, and so run them down by spending. Such spending increases AD and money incomes until cash balances are equal to their former fraction. Nor does this surplus cash have to be spent on 'bonds', Keynes' omnibus term for non-money assets. Wealth can be held in many forms: cash which yields liquidity, 'bonds' which yield interest and possible capital appreciation, and, the Monetarists emphasise, *consumer goods* which yield utility. People distribute their spending according to their marginal preferences for these different forms of yield (which in turn can be influenced by their expected rate of inflation).

Thus any increase in the money supply is, after a little while, likely to lead to some increase in the demand for consumer goods, resulting in a rise in their prices.

(b) Inflation expectations

Once inflation expectations enter into wage negotiations, the monetarists argue that increasing AD will not achieve a *long-term* decrease in the rate of unemployment but simply result in higher inflation. In short there is no trade-off between inflation and unemployment. We return to the Phillips curve.

In Figure 21.4 we assume that the rate of inflation is 4 per cent and the rate of unemployment is 5 per cent. This position at D is stable because wage-bargainers have expected 4 per cent to be the inflation rate.

The government now decides that it wants to reduce the unemployment rate to 4 per cent and accordingly increases AD. Prices rise to 6 per cent inflation at F, but money wage rates do not rise since workers expect only a 4 per cent rise in inflation. Thus firms, enjoying increased profitability, increase output so that initially unemployment falls to 4 per cent on curve P_4.

But this is only a short-term position depending on the fact that workers tend to concentrate on nominal money wages, which have not fallen, rather than on real wages, which have – the 'money illusion'. Eventually, however, they realise that real wages have fallen and in their next wage negotiations they obtain a 6 per cent rise in money wages (based on the previous year's inflation rate) to cover what they expect to be the rate of inflation. The recovery in real wage-rates increases costs, so that firms reduce output and unemployment reverts to 5 per cent. The Phillips curve has moved outwards to P_6 and there is a new equilibrium at E.

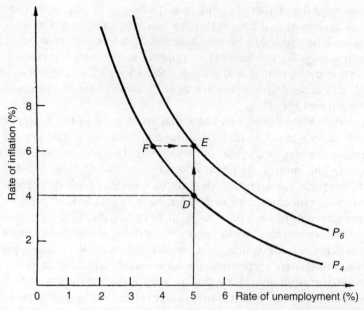

Figure 21.4 The effect of inflation-expectations on the rate of unemployment

(c) The 'natural rate of unemployment'

In the above example, *D* and *E* represent two long-term equilibrium positions. Thus the long-run Phillips curve is a vertical straight line at 5 per cent. The monetarists would term this 5 per cent the 'natural rate of unemployment' – the rate to which unemployment will eventually revert *given the current real wage-rate, imperfections in the labour market, immobility costs, etc.* If the expected rate is less than the actual rate, an increase in AD can lead to lower unemployment; if it is more, the current rate of unemployment can only be sustained by a higher rate of inflation. There will be long-run equilibrium when the expected rate of inflation has been *adapted* to take account of and equals the actual rate.

(d) 'Rational expectations'

Some economists dispute whether even in the short-term employment can be increased by simply increasing AD.

Wage-bargainers learn by experience and have available information by which they *predict* and allow for the future rate of inflation. Thus any increase in the money supply evokes the correct estimate of the rate of inflation which will result, and this is embodied immediately in the new wage-rate. This assertion of '*rational expectations*' in place of a mere *adaptation* to an inflation rate based on the previous year's inflation rate means that there is now no short-run curve, only a long-run one because the rate of inflation goes directly to *E* (Figure 21.4). There is thus no room for reducing unemployment by increasing AD.

We now proceed to examine why the control of inflation should be prominent in government economic policy and how the foregoing theory developments have influenced, and been applied by, the government.

QUESTIONS

1 Why in practice must the government's full employment target be flexible?

2 What is the basic difference between Fig. 20.4 and Fig. 21.1?

3 Given that $AD = C + I + G + (X - M)$, why should AD expand as the price level falls?

4 Give three reasons why the AS curve should start to rise as full employment is approached.

5 What proved to be the main weakness of the Phillips curve?

6 How does Friedman's view of the demand for money differ from that of Keynes?

7 How does this difference of view affect the impact of the money supply on the level of prices?

8 Give two reasons why an increase in the money supply could directly increase C.

9 (a) Define the 'natural rate of unemployment'.
   (b) How does the 'natural rate' arise?
   (c) What is its implication regarding government inflation policy?

10 How do 'adaptive expectations' differ from 'rational expectations'?

11 Use the figure below to explain how the spiral of inflation occurs.

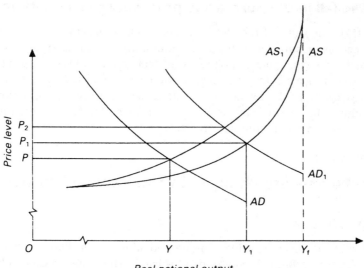

Real national output

■ ☑ **22** Government policy to control inflation

Objectives

1 To describe the method of constructing the Retail Prices Index (RPI)
2 To consider the RPI's weaknesses as a means of measuring changes in the rate of inflation over time
3 To underline the necessity of controlling inflation
4 To indicate the inherent weaknesses in Keynes's macro theory
5 To outline the development over time of government policy for controlling inflation
6 To examine the pros and cons of giving an independent Bank of England the responsibility for base rate policy

22.1 Introduction

(a) The fall in the purchasing power of the £ over time

Since 1520, the value of the UK £ has been falling, usually gradually over the earlier centuries, but after 1900 almost continuously (Table 22.1).

What is significant, however, is the rate of decline, after 1900 halving in the next 20 years, halving again in the 13 years between 1960 and 1973, and again in the next 5 years to 1978. The rate of inflation has now become so serious that containing it has become in the UK (as with most developed economies) the dominant government economic objective.

22.2 Measuring changes in the value of money

(a) Difficulties

In theory, a change in the value of money would refer to a change in the level of prices in general. But different kinds of prices – wholesale prices, retail prices, capital goods prices, security prices, import prices, etc. – change differently. If we tried to measure changes in all prices, therefore, our task would be stupendous. But more than that, it would lack practical significance. Suppose, for instance, that security prices rose considerably, other prices remaining unchanged. But a

	Table 22.1 The £'s falling purchasing power 1526–1996

Year	Money (£) required to purchase the goods bought by £1 in 1996
1520	382.25
1600	109.21
1700	66.48
1790	47.78
1900	49.32
1940	23.17
1960	12.33
1973	6.45
1978	3.06
1987	1.50
1996	1.00

Source: Bank of England.

rise in such a general level of prices would be of little interest to persons owning no securities.

When measuring changes in the value of money, therefore, it is usual to concentrate on changes in the prices of those goods which are of most general significance – the goods bought by the majority of people, for it is upon the prices of these that the cost of living really depends. But again, since different people spend their income differently, the value of money could be different for each.

(b) Method

Since we are mainly interested in the extent to which the value of money has altered between one date and another, it can be measured as a relative change by means of an *index number*. The steps are as follows:

(i) A base year is selected. This is now referred to as the 'reference date'.
(ii) In order to ensure that the same goods are valued over the period under consideration, a 'basket' of goods, based on the current spending habits and income of the 'typical' family is chosen.
(iii) The basket is valued at reference date prices, and expressed as 100.
(iv) The same basket is revalued at current prices.
(v) The cost of the current basket is then expressed as a percentage of the base year. Thus if the cost of living had risen by 5 per cent, the index for the current year would be 105.

In practice, the percentage price relatives of the selected goods are calculated, and are then 'weighted' according to the relative expenditure on the commodity at the reference date. Suppose, for instance, that there are only two commodities, bread and meat, upon which income is spent. The index between two years is calculated as follows. The price in year II is expressed as a percentage of the price in year I. This is multiplied by the appropriate weight to give a 'weighted price relative'. These weighted price relatives are then totalled and divided by the total of the weights to give the new index number.

	YEAR I				YEAR II		
					Price relatives		
	Price	*Units bought*	*Expenditure*	*Weight*	*Price*	*Year II as % of Year I*	*Weighted price relative*
Bread	30p	5	150p	10	45p	150	1,500
Meat	150p	11	1,650p	110	180p	120	13,200
				120			14,700

divide by total weights 120

= 122.5

Index
Year I (base)   100
Year II   122.5

(c) Weaknesses of the Retail Prices Index

The method outlined above of calculating changes in the value of money has obvious snags:

(i) The basket and the weighting are merely an arbitrary average. Different income groups have widely different baskets, and even within the same group the amount spent on each good varies. Thus a change in the Retail Prices Index does not affect all people equally.

(ii) The basket becomes more unreal the further we move from the reference date (at present 13 January 1987 = 100). For instance, an increase in income gives a different pattern of expenditure, new goods are produced and the quality of goods changes, and spending is varied according to relative price changes. The Retail Prices Index tries to overcome this defect by revising the weights each January on the basis of the *Family Expenditure Survey* for the previous year.

(iii) Technical difficulties may arise both in choosing the reference date and in collecting information. For instance, the reference date may coincide with abnormally high prices, while the development of discount stores may upset standardised methods of collecting prices.

Thus a Retail Prices Index is merely an indication of changes in the cost of living. But if we bear its limitations in mind, it is the most useful measurement we have of changes in the value of money. It therefore provides the yardstick for calculating changes in real earnings and for 'inflation-proofing' public sector pay and pensions.

22.3 Why control inflation?

Inflation can be defined as a sustained rise in money prices generally. Today the control of inflation is given priority in government policy. To appreciate why, we have to look at the effects of rising prices or – what is the same thing – a fall in the value of money.

(a) Possible benefits

At one time a gently rising price level was not viewed with too much concern. It improved the climate for investment and so helped to maintain AD. Moreover, it tended to reduce the real burden of servicing the national debt: while interest is fixed in money terms, receipts from taxation increase as national money income rises.

The snag, however, is that, once started, the rise in prices can prove difficult to contain, producing undesirable results both internal and external.

(b) Internal disadvantages

(i) Real income and wealth are re-distributed arbitrarily. Not only does inflation reduce the standard of living of those dependent on fixed incomes, e.g. pensions not 'inflation-proofed', but it benefits debtors and penalises lenders. Not only does this undermine the stability upon which all lending and borrowing depends, but re-distribution may conflict with the government's own policy on this.

(ii) Interest rates rise, both because people require a higher reward for lending money which is falling in value and also because the government is forced to take disinflationary measures. Not only may this discourage investment but it can have social consequences, e.g. in meeting monthly mortgage payments.

(iii) Saving is discouraged because postponing consumption simply means that goods cost more later.

(iv) The allocation of resources is distorted. Thus institutions, such as insurance companies, invest funds in assets having a strong inflation hedge. As a result the capital value of such assets rises, encouraging developers, for instance, to build office blocks rather than houses for letting.

(v) Efficiency is reduced because:
  (1) a buoyant sellers' market blunts competition as higher selling prices allow even inefficient firms to survive;
  (2) uncertainty is increased, thereby discouraging long-term investment and undermining sustainable long-term economic growth;
  (3) market signals are less clear since some inflation-hedge may be included e.g. in contracts, and relative price changes tend to pass undetected within the general rise in prices;
  (4) it strengthens the possibility of disruption of production until demands for wage increases are agreed;
  (5) financial services spring up to advise on protecting savings from losses through inflation.

(vi) Inflation generates industrial and social unrest since there is competition for higher incomes. Thus, because of rising prices, trade unions ask for annual wage rises. Often demands exceed the rate of inflation, anticipating future rises or seeking a larger share of the national cake to improve their members' real standard of living. Those with the most 'muscle' gain at the expense of weaker groups.

(vii) Additional administrative costs are incurred in off-setting go-slow and work to rule disruptions, allowing for inflation in negotiating contracts and wage rates, revising price lists and labels, etc.

(viii) The rate of inflation tends to increase, largely because high wage settlements in anticipation of higher future prices help to bring about the very rise which people fear.

(c) External effects

Inflation can create balance-of-payments difficulties for a country, like Britain, which is dependent on international trade.

(i) Exports tend to decline because they are relatively dearer in foreign markets. Exporting firms may therefore have to lay off workers.

(ii) Imports tend to increase because foreign goods are relatively cheaper on the British market.

(iii) Higher money incomes in the UK increase the demand for imports and tend to decrease exports because the buoyant home market makes it less vital for manufacturers to seek outlets abroad for their goods.

(iv) An outward movement of capital may take place if price rises continue since foreign traders and financiers lose confidence in the pound sterling maintaining its current rate of exchange.

While the above effects are uncomfortable, it is possible to live with a moderate rise in prices. The snag is that where rising prices are thought likely to continue, people bring forward their spending, thereby producing the very price rise feared – an example of 'self-justified expectations'. So the process, stimulated by further wage demands, gathers momentum, the *rate* of inflation increasing. Thus the longer the government postpones action, the more difficult it becomes to reverse the upward trend.

We now describe how anti-inflation policy has developed in the light of experience over the last 40 years.

22.4 Post-war demand management in the UK

(a) The concentration of policy on AD

Keynes's theory dominated economic policy during the 1950s and 1960s. Successive UK governments maintained an AD which until 1974 (apart from 1971–2) kept unemployment below 3 per cent. Whenever expansion of AD led to balance-of-payments difficulties, the government imposed temporary 'stop' policies, such as raising the rate of interest to halt the outflow of short-term capital.

But 'fine-tuning' the economy to maintain a high level of demand produced a state of 'overfull' employment, with vacancies consistently exceeding unemployed workers. The outcome was inflation, balance-of-payments difficulties, shortages of skilled workers, high labour turnover, firms holding on to surplus workers in case they should be required in the future ('disguised' unemployment), underinvestment in new equipment, a failure by industry to adopt new techniques or to switch to the production of high-technology products, and an unsatisfactory rate of growth (see Chapter 24).

As a result Keynes's views came under increasing scrutiny.

(b) Weaknesses of the Keynesian approach

It must be remembered that Keynes was writing his *General Theory* against the background of the high cyclical unemployment of the 1930s. For him, therefore, unemployment was the major problem. In reality, though, the many objectives of government stabilisation policy are interrelated and cannot be dropped into different boxes with separate measures for each.

First, too little attention was given to how supply responds to increases in AD as full employment is approached. The Keynesian analysis assumes a stable price level. This is justifiable at higher rates of unemployment. Firms have spare capacity and can increase output at constant costs. Increased AD is therefore covered by increased output and the price level remains stable. But eventually, as output increases, firms experience rising costs owing to more intensive use of existing capacity. As a result prices rise (see p. 271).

Keynes recognised that this rise in prices would occur: the remedy was to remove the inflationary pressure by reducing AD. But this ignores the dynamic forces which come into play once prices start to rise, chiefly the role of trade union inflationary expectations in the wage-bargaining process (see Chapter 21).

Second, Keynes's theory of the price level denied that increases in the money supply could increase AD directly (see p. 273).

Third, Keynes underplayed the side effects of a large PSBR which high government spending could give rise to. He recognised that government deficit-spending would increase the National Debt, but since loans could be 'rolled over' as they matured, only interest had to be currently paid. What Keynes did not foresee was the big increase in government borrowing necessary to pay for the welfare state. Servicing a large PSBR creates difficulties for both monetary and fiscal policy (see p. 283).

Fourth, a high level of AD, together with rising prices, may result in a serious balance of payments deficit.

Of the above, the increasing rate of inflation was recognised as the major problem.

(c) The limited role of monetary policy prior to 1979

Until 1971 policy for influencing AD concentrated on varying taxation, supplemented by government regulation of hire-purchase terms. But as Friedman's

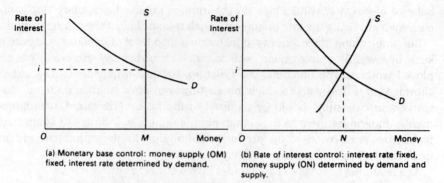

(a) Monetary base control: money supply (OM) fixed, interest rate determined by demand.

(b) Rate of interest control: interest rate fixed, money supply (ON) determined by demand and supply.

Figure 22.1　Monetary control alternatives

view, that the supply of money (through bank credit) affected spending directly, gained acceptance, so fiscal policy gave way to monetary policy.

Alternative ways of controlling the supply of money are: (i) controlling the supply of credit quantitively – that is, restraining lending by financial institutions (Figure 22.1a); (ii) restricting the demand for credit through its price – the rate of interest (Figure 22.1b).

Between 1971 and 1979 the emphasis was on controlling credit quantitatively, the main purpose being to avoid raising interest rates, at least in the short term. The banks' ability to lend was restricted chiefly by squeezing their liquid assets, but also by direct controls. In practice, however, borrowers overcame the banks' rationing of loans by moving to institutions not subject to government controls, such as merchant banks, finance houses and foreign banks. Finally, in 1979 when foreign exchange controls were abolished, the policy of limiting bank credit became inoperable since funds could now be obtained from overseas sources, for example, through the Eurocurrency market.

22.5　The implementation of 'monetarism' by the Thatcher Government

The Conservative government which came to power in 1979 made the control of inflation its principal economic objective. Policy followed four lines: (a) implementing monetarist views on the money supply; (b) reducing the PSBR; (c) reconciling the trade unions to monetarist measures; (d) giving more attention to the supply side.

(a) Monetarist policy

The rate of interest replaced quantitative controls as the means by which increases in the money supply could be checked.

Initially an attempt was made to measure the money supply in order to provide a target for interest rate policy. But M_3 (broadly M_0 + the sterling deposits of banks) proved to be an unsatisfactory measure in that it failed to respond as expected to changes in the rate of interest – largely because credit for spending could be obtained outside the banks from other sources, e.g. building societies, finance houses and foreign banks.

As a result, in 1987, M_0 (notes and coin + banks' holding of cash and operational balances at the Bank of England) was substituted, not as a target, but simply as an indicator of changes in the money supply. Actual monetary restraint was based on shadowing the £/DM exchange rate. This was formalised in October 1990 when the UK joined the ERM committed to maintaining £1 = 2.95 DM (See p. 370).

(b) The PSBR (from 1988, the Public Sector Net Cash Requirement – PSNCR)

Reducing the PSBR was necessary because it creates monetary problems through the borrowing necessary to cover it.

If the government borrows by selling Treasury bills, the cheapest method, it runs into difficulties. The major holders of Treasury bills are the commercial banks, who buy them because an increased offering forces up the yield. Such purchases, however, directly add to the banks' liquid assets, allowing them to increase their deposits. In other words, short-term bank borrowing involves an inflationary increase in the money supply.

As a result, the government has to rely on long-term borrowing, that is 'funding' by selling medium- and long-term bonds in the market to the *non-bank* sector, the institutions and private purchasers. Since such sources of funds rely mainly on current saving, this method is not inflationary. The difficulty, however, is that extra bonds can only be disposed of at a lower price – that is, by a rise in the long-term rate of interest. This has the overall effect of discouraging private investment, 'crowded out' by the increased government spending, thereby retarding growth. Nor is this all. Interest payments on this borrowing add to the PSBR. Furthermore, inasmuch as higher interest rates attract funds from abroad, the money supply is increased.

It is important to note the real significance of this. Whereas budgetary policy was the main weapon of Keynesian demand management, it is now merely a support to monetary policy, enabling liquidity to be controlled at a lower rate of interest than would otherwise be necessary.

By exercising a stricter control over government spending, the Thatcher government succeeded in reducing the PSBR. It was also helped by the 'privatisation' proceeds of selling government assets in the nationalised industries. Above all, since much of the PSBR is cyclical, as the economy expanded taxation yields increased and employment-related payments fell. During 1987–9 the government achieved an annual surplus of revenue over expenditure.

(c) Reconciling trade unions to monetarist policy

It is possible to identify three strands in the way the government sought to change trade union policy on inflation.

(i) The implication of 'rational expectations' – that trade unions incorporated an increasing rate of inflation in their yearly wage demands – was that government policy had to be directed to convincing them that the trend of the future rate would be downwards.

The announcement of strict monetary and fiscal targets was the first step. Here success largely depended on how far trade unions could be convinced of the government's resolve to adhere to such targets.

(ii) The rate of interest was to be the weapon for achieving monetary targets. The government now stood aloof from wage negotiations, leaving employers to negotiate terms with the unions. Any inflationary wage increases would no longer be financed by an increase in the money supply. Instead firms' profits would fall, and unemployment follow.

In the public sector where output is not related to profits, the situation was somewhat different. Here the government stipulated limits on wage increases – a virtual wages policy! In doing so it indicated a norm for private sector settlements.

(iii) Prior to the Thatcher government, wages policy varied between 'voluntary restraint' and a 'wage freeze' accompanied by restrictions on price rises. Both broke down through trade union resistance.

Initially, therefore, some militant unions clashed with the government. However, with the collapse in March 1985 of the year-long National Union of Mineworkers' strike, the battle was won, and Parliament proceeded to limit the ability of trade unions to strike and to regulate members.

(d) Supply-side measures

The introduction of the hypothesis of a 'natural rate of unemployment' suggests that, since expanding AD is ineffective in reducing unemployment, less emphasis should be placed on demand and more attention given to supply. Reducing the costs of production would mean that a greater output could be supplied at any given price level.

The strategy is illustrated in simplified form in Figure 22.1, which concentrates on the rising portion of the short-run aggregate supply curve.

If, for example, the curve can be shifted from AS to AS_1, aggregate demand can be increased from AD to AD_1 so that output expands from OM to OM_1 with no rise in the price level.

Policy to achieve this embraces a variety of incentives usually included under the umbrella term 'supply-side economics'. It integrates longer-term micro measures within the overall macro policy. These seek to achieve greater market freedom and efficiency, a reduction in costs, and incentives to increase effort, reward enterprise and encourage investment.

(a) Market freedom may be enhanced by:
   (i) freeing them from government controls (e.g. incomes policy, minimum wage regulations, pricing policies of the nationalised industries);
   (ii) promoting competition (e.g. in real property conveyancing, and financial services);

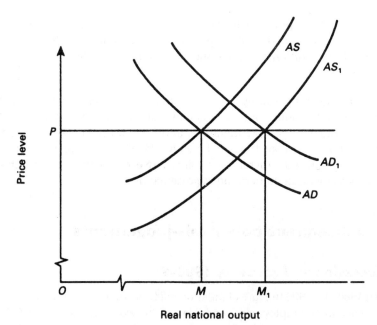

Figure 22.2 Supply-side policy

(iii) restricting the power of trade unions (e.g. through precipitate and sympathetic strike action, unofficial strikes, closed shop enforcement);
(iv) the privatisation programme;
(v) introducing competition in the natural monopolies by new devices;
(vi) removing institutional barriers in the capital market (e.g. exchange control, the Stock Exchange);
(vii) using the rate of interest (the price of liquid capital) as the main weapon for adjusting aggregate demand.

(b) Costs reduction include:
(i) lowering national insurance contributions (an *ad valorem* tax on employing labour);
(ii) improving the supply and quality of labour, e.g. by developing training schemes, encouraging flexible working hours to attract part-time workers, improving mobility, granting subsidies to firms to locate in the Assisted Areas;
(iii) providing advisory services (e.g. on the EU's Single Market).

(c) Incentives cover:
(i) a reduction in the marginal rate of income tax on effort, etc. even though it may reduce total tax revenue;
(ii) a lower corporation tax to encourage investment and the taking of entrepreneurial risks;
(iii) special help for new firms to obtain the initial capital, e.g. 'start-up' schemes, the encouragement of 'venture capital' institutions;

(iv) profit-related pay (which gives employees a direct stake in the success of the company and enables pay to respond more readily to changing market conditions), share option schemes and wider share ownership generally.

The importance of supply-side economics has been realised by both Conservative and Labour governments and many of the above measures have been incorporated in, or now influence, anti-inflation policy. But it has to be recognised that they take time to be fully effective and are unlikely to be sufficient. They are not, therefore, an alternative to obtaining from labour a workable agreement on moderating wage demands.

22.6 Subsequent policy mis-judgements

(a) Recession and recovery 1980–9

Between 1980 and 1986 the rate of inflation fell from 18.0 per cent to 3.4 per cent. But the cost in unemployment was heavy. The world recession 1980–2 was prolonged in the UK by a high base rate, still 13.5 per cent in 1986. Over this period unemployment rose, in round figures, from 2 million (5 per cent of all workers) to just over 3 million (11 per cent). Indeed some economists consider that it was unemployment rather than monetary control which brought down the rate of inflation.

From 1986 the rate of interest was gradually reduced and the UK economy expanded rapidly until 1989.

(b) A return to recession and recovery

The turning-point can be traced back to the Chancellor of the Exchequer's apprehensive response to the crash in the world's stock markets in October 1987. An easier monetary and fiscal policy proved a blunder. Imprudent bank lending financed a property boom, with a rapid rise in house prices and an increase in the inflation rate to nearly 8 per cent in 1989. Consequently the rate of interest was increased, rising to 15 per cent in October 1989.

The high cost of borrowing led to a *cumulative recession* through reduced investment, a slump in the demand for houses, a rise in the personal saving ratio, the failure of businesses (particularly of over-geared property companies), bank write-offs of losses and the recession becoming worldwide.

In addition, by joining the ERM in 1990, the UK had to retain a relatively high rate of interest to support an overvalued £1 = 2.95 DM exchange rate. While the rate of inflation fell rapidly, the rate of interest could be reduced only gradually since Germany retained a relatively high rate to control her own inflationary pressure resulting from reunification. By 1993 unemployment had increased to 2.9 million and the PSBR to £45.4 billion (8 per cent of GDP).

The beginning of recovery can be dated to 16 September 1992, when speculation against sterling forced the government to leave the ERM. The fixed exchange rate was replaced by a floating £. This permitted a reduction in the rate of interest to stimulate the economy, so that by November 1992 base rate had fallen to 7 per cent. In addition, by holding the annual growth of M_0 to under 4 per cent and *monitoring* changes in M_4 within a range of 4 and 8 per cent, the aim was to keep the rate of inflation to between 1 and 4 per cent, with a long-term aim of 2 per cent.

Eventually anti-inflation policy concentrated on adjustments to the short-term rate of interest according to *prospective* inflationary trends. The Chancellor of the Exchequer had monthly meetings with the Governor of the Bank of England. But the final decision was his, and twice the Governor's recommendation to raise base rate was overruled. Thus while this procedure achieved a rate of inflation around 2.5 per cent, it was always open to the suspicion of being influenced by political considerations.

(c) The Bank of England is given sole operational responsibility for delivering the Chancellor's target rate of inflation

In May 1997 the Chancellor of the Exchequer of the new Labour government replaced these ad hoc, person-to-person discussions with a set of clear rules covering, first, the respective responsibilities of the Chancellor and the Bank of England, and, second, the procedures to be followed.

(i) The *Chancellor of the Exchequer* fixes a target for the Retail Price Index, excluding mortgage payments (RPIX); (ii) the *Bank of England* is given sole operational responsibility for delivering this target by using its base rate technique to influence short-term interest rates (see p. 227).

The procedure for implementing these separate responsibilities also follows a prescribed sequence. Thus in June 1997 the Chancellor set a RPIX target of 2.5 per cent which will be confirmed in each subsequent Budget. (In fact, the Treasury view is that it will remain the same throughout the current Parliament).

To fulfil its responsibility of achieving and maintaining this 2.5 per cent target, the Bank set up a new *Monetary Policy Committee* (MPC) whose composition and procedure again follow a carefully-devised pattern. The MPC has nine members: five, (including the Governor) drawn from the Bank; four, who are economic and financial experts in their own different fields, appointed by the Chancellor.

The MPC convenes officially on the Wednesday following the first Monday in each month. But for the whole of the previous Friday it has been briefed by the Bank's professional staff on the latest information relevant to its forthcoming meeting. The data covers a wide range of topics, especially recent changes in: the money supply, the PSBR, average earnings, wage settlements, house and asset prices, import and export flows and prices, the sterling exchange rate, investment and consumer spending.

At its prescribed Wednesday meeting, the MPC discusses possible alternative interpretations of the data presented. The ultimate objective of its deliberations is to identify the issues of current importance and to arrive at an assessment of their likely impact on the future price level.

The Committee then adjourns for the night, thereby providing time for members to reflect individually before the Committee re-assembles on the Thursday morning. There could then be further discussion.

Eventually, however, members have to make up their own minds on whether base rate should be changed and, if so, by how much. Each member has one vote, and the MPC's decision is on a majority basis, with the Governor having the casting vote should the other eight members be split equally.

The actual base rate decision is announced at noon the same day (Thursday).

Minutes of the two-day meeting, together with a summary of the information presented, are published six weeks later. They record, not only how each individual voted, but the views of any dissenting members. Additionally, the Bank publishes a quarterly Inflation Report accounting for past monetary policy and assessing the future economic position. It is hoped that such transparency of the decision-making process will enable the public to understand what the Bank is trying to do and, by influencing expectations, reduce the cost (through a lower interest rate) of maintaining low inflation.

The measure of the Bank's success will be how close it comes to achieving an average 2.5 per cent RPIX over time. The government has made it a requirement that, should the target be missed by 1 per cent or more in either direction, the MPC must write an open letter to the Chancellor, explaining why, how it is being dealt with, and the expected period for bringing it back on course.

Over its first two years, the MPC's decision-making has consistently achieved the 2.5 per cent target. This is an encouraging debut especially when it is remembered that there could well be a time-lag between today's base rate decision and its impact on the future RPIX.

(d) Reflections on the government's reliance on monetary policy

It should be noted that this new independence of the Bank of England puts the whole onus of controlling inflation on monetary policy and restricts government use of fiscal policy for demand management. Suppose, for instance, that the budget unexpectedly cut taxes in order to reduce unemployment. Other things being equal, if the Bank of England considers that this could lead to higher future inflation, it would now have to respond by raising interest rates.

Nevertheless, using the rate of interest as the *sole* weapon for controlling inflation has certain weaknesses. First it does not discriminate in its operation (see p. 283). Second, in comparison with fiscal measures as a means of dampening consumer spending, it is less direct in its impact. Third, its operation may clash with other government objectives. A high rate of interest discourages investment and thus impinges on growth. It also attracts foreign short-term capital, resulting in the appreciation of sterling (see Chapter 23). While this lowers the price of imports, it raises the price of British exports which could therefore be uncompetitive in world markets. In the face of falling demand and reduced profits, exporting firms lay off workers so that both industrialists and trade unions exert pressure on the Bank to lower base rate.

QUESTIONS

1 Name the three essentials of an index number.

2 Assume that: (a) Year I is the base year; (b) The basket consists of only two commodities. What is the price index for Year II?

	Year I		Year II
	Price (per lb.)	Quantity bought per week (lb.)	Price (per lb.)
Potatoes	10p	8	6p
Meat	80p	4	120p

3 (a) Distinguish between the 'headline' and 'underlying' rates of inflation.
  (b) What is the weakness of the 'headline' rate as a measure of inflation?

4 What is meant by saying that an asset has 'an inflation hedge'?

5 Name two assets which:
  (a) are likely to have an inflation hedge;
  (b) have no inflation hedge.

6 With respect to the government's main economic objectives, what difficulties arose when only AD expansion was used to confine the unemployment rate to 3 per cent?

7 Suggest four weaknesses of the Keynesian model.

8 Why was it difficult to 'target' the money supply?

9 How did the September 1992 devaluation of sterling produce:
  (a) a consumer-led recovery?
  (b) an export-led recovery?

10 Give: (a) three advantages, and (b) three disadvantages of monetary policy as a means of easing inflationary pressure.

▪ ☑ **23** Balanced regional development

Objectives

1 To show how the 'regional problem' arises and its resulting difficulties
2 To describe government policy to regenerate the 'Assisted Areas'
3 To indicate the likelihood of increased EU involvement in the regional problem

23.1 The nature of the problem

(a) Causes of regional depression

In broad terms, a regional problem can arise because:

(i) The particular region may be endowed with poor natural resources

An example is the Highlands of Scotland. More generally, with the growth of national income, an agricultural region which does not attract expanding industries – e.g. Cornwall and Devon – cannot provide its population with living standards comparable with those of the rest of the country.

(ii) The resources of the region may not be fully developed, usually through lack of capital

This applies particularly to the less developed countries. Here the more immediate solution is for capital to be provided on favourable terms by richer regions.

In the long term an improvement in the imbalance may depend mainly on the exploitation of the area's resources becoming economically viable. For example, prosperity came to Aberdeen and the Shetlands only when the rise in the price of oil and the development of modern technology made extraction of North Sea oil an economic proposition. Alternatively, rising incomes in other regions may allow tourism to be developed, e.g. North Wales, the Lake District.

(iii) A region's basic industry is either stagnant or in decline

Such a region is usually characterised by: a rising rate of unemployment; a level of income which is falling relatively to other regions; a low activity rate, particularly of female workers; a high rate of outward migration; and an

Table 23.1	Percentage rate of unemployment by Government Office Region, October 1998
United Kingdom	4.6
Region:	
North East	7.3
North West	4.2
Merseyside	9
Yorkshire and Humber	5.6
East Midlands	4.1
West Midlands	4.7
South West	3.4
Eastern	3.3
London	5.3
South East	2.6
Wales	5.4
Scotland	5.5
N. Ireland	7.2

Source: Office for National Statistics.

inadequate infrastructure. It is thus this type of regional imbalance which creates the problem for *national* governments; indeed the depressed regions are normally identified by their unemployment rates (Table 23.1).

(b) Weaknesses of correction through the market economy

Theoretically the market should move workers who become unemployed to other jobs. The fall in the demand for a good, and the consequent unemployment, should result in a relative wage fall. On the other hand, where demand is buoyant wages should rise. Such changes in relative wages should move: (a) workers from low-wage to high-wage industries, and (b) industries from high-wage to low-wage areas.

The attraction of this model is that the correction of an imbalance can be brought about by the market. Yet in suggesting that a government regional policy is largely superfluous, it has serious weaknesses:

(i) Factor markets adjust much less perfectly than the theory implies. Labour is immobile (see p. 102), while factor prices especially wage rates, tend to be resistant to any downward movement. Moreover, national wage-bargaining weakens the response to the price signals of regional imbalance.

(ii) The assumption of constant returns to scale which is implicit in the theory may not hold. Manufacturing in particular is characterised by increasing returns to scale over the relevant output range so that high-wage regions may also generate high returns to capital. Thus firms, like labour, may migrate to the prosperous high-wage regions. Indeed, as communications improve, these regions may gain with the progressive opening of trade at the expense of the decaying region. Thus the south-east region of England has benefited from its close connections with the EU.

Should movement be entirely outwards, the model has additional weaknesses:

(iii) It ignores the external costs to society of (a) the loss of social capital and the disintegration of communities in the depressed regions, and (b) the congestion and inflationary pressures generated in the expanding areas (see below).

(iv) Those workers who do move from the depressed regions are mainly the better educated, most highly skilled and more enterprising young adults. As such they are often the leaders of the community. The result is that the region becomes still further depressed *and* thus unattractive to new industries.

(v) The model ignores the fact that migration from the depressed regions leads to a loss of income there. The multiplier effect of reduced consumer spending and investment serves to depress the area still further.

(c) Consequences of regional depression

The existence of prolonged depression in certain regions has adverse consequences which can be summarised as follows:

(i) An underutilisation of resources through unemployment

Not only does regional unemployment result in lost output for the community as a whole, but it can also have serious social and psychological effects on the workers concerned. Moreover, significant differences in people's income between regions has equity implications.

(ii) A loss of social capital as towns and cities decay

Where the nation's population is static or falling, outward migration from depressed areas involves social costs in that schools, churches, etc. fall into decay while certain public services have to be operated below capacity. In contrast new roads and public buildings, such as hospitals, have to be provided in the expanding areas.

(iii) External social costs

Migration from decaying regions often results in a loss of welfare through the break-up of communities and the destruction of the 'social character' of an area.

Similarly, there may be external costs of excessive urbanisation (e.g. traffic congestion, noise, pollution and intensive housing) through migration to a prosperous region.

(iv) Differences in unemployment between regions make it more difficult to manage the economy

Prosperous regions tend to become 'overheated' through the pressure of demand. This is reflected in higher wage-rates and labour shortages. Higher wage-rates tend to be transmitted even to the depressed regions through national wage agreements, the insistence on traditional wage differentials, etc. But anti-inflationary measures, both monetary and fiscal, add to the unemployment problem of the depressed regions.

(v) Economic integration between nations may be undermined by the political opposition of depressed regions' pressure groups

The rationale of economic integration between nations, e.g. the EU, is to secure greater comparative advantages by the removal of trade barriers and increased factor mobility. However, it may exacerbate the problem of regional imbalance because certain industries, particularly in areas on the periphery, such as Northern Ireland and Scotland, find it more difficult to compete. Political pressure groups in such areas, therefore, may react by opposing integration.

(d) Broad outlines of regional policy

The objectives of regional policy have widened in the light of experience. In brief, it now seeks to:

(i) reduce the relatively high level of unemployment in certain regions;
(ii) achieve a better balance between the population and the environment;
(iii) preserve regional cultures and identities;
(iv) relieve inflation by reducing the pressure of demand in the expanding regions;
(v) counter possible adverse regional effects of greater international economic integration and of more open economies.

It has to be recognised, however, that these objectives are not always compatible with national economic policy. For instance, diverting firms from their optimum location to a depressed area may hamper growth, while it may be necessary to stimulate exports of goods and services produced in the more prosperous regions in order to improve the national balance of payments.

Where an area is depressed, the government can give first aid by placing its contracts there e.g. for defence equipment, and awarding it priority for public-works programmes – schools, new roads, hospitals, the physical regeneration of urban areas, etc. Subsidies may also be granted to secure contracts, for example, to build ships.

In the long term, however, the government must take measures that will, on the one hand, encourage the outward movement of workers, and on the other induce firms to move in to employ those workers who find it difficult to move and also to halt further degeneration of the region. The first is usually referred to as 'workers to the work', the second as 'work to the workers'.

23.2 Workers to the work

Taking workers to the work is basically a micro approach to overcome market frictions, chiefly the immobility and imperfect knowledge of labour. In pursuing this policy, however, the government must bear in mind the following:

(i) Unemployment arising through immobility is far more difficult to cure when cyclical unemployment also exists, for an unemployed person has little incentive to move if there is unemployment even in the relatively prosperous areas.

(ii) Other government interference in the economy may add to the problem of immobility. Thus high rates of income tax whittle away monetary inducements to move and unemployment benefit may reduce the incentive to seek a job elsewhere. Similarly, rent control and residential qualifications for local authority housing priorities lead to difficulties in finding accommodation.

(iii) Even owner-occupiers in depressed regions may be restricted in mobility by the much higher cost of housing in the prosperous areas.

(iv) Many changes of both occupation and area take place in a series of ripples. Thus an agricultural labourer may move to road construction to take the place of the labourer who transfers to the building industry.

The government's first task must be to improve occupational mobility. Entry into certain occupations should be made less difficult, e.g. by giving information on opportunities in other industries and occupations and by persuading trade unions to relax their apprenticeship rules. More important, people must be trained in the new skills required by expanding industries, e.g. through local Training and Enterprise Councils.

Improving the geographical mobility of workers to the more prosperous regions operates chiefly under the government's Employment Transfer Scheme. This consists of granting financial aid towards moving costs, providing information on prospects in other parts of the country and giving free fares to a place of work away from the home town.

23.3 Work to the workers

Although a 'workers-to-the-work' policy has a role to play in correcting regional imbalance, it suffers from: (i) an exclusive concern with unemployment to the neglect of other consequences of regional imbalance; (ii) a failure to recognise the macro effects of the outward movement of workers.

(a) Pros and cons of 'work-to-the-workers'

Thus taking work to the workers is now regarded as the policy most likely to effect a long-term solution to the problem for it reduces regional differences in income and the rate of growth as well as in unemployment. By helping the more immobile workers, such as older people and married women, it stimulates the activity rate. It also avoids forcing workers to leave areas to which they are attached, relieves the growing congestion in south-east England, and prevents the loss of social capital resulting from the depopulation of depressed areas. Above all, it works in harmony with Keynesian macro theory. The 'multiplier' operates for regional economies in much the same way as it does for the national economy. Moving unemployed workers and their families reduces spending in the area (e.g. because unemployment benefits are no longer being drawn) and this gives rise to a negative multiplier. In contrast, moving firms into the area generates spending power and produces a positive multiplier, variously calculated at between 1.25 and 1.50.

On the other hand, a policy of locating firms in depressed areas may involve them in higher costs. Their desire to establish plant in the South East is to secure location advantages, such as a supply of skilled workers, easier and less costly communications, contact with complementary firms and nearness to EU markets.

(b) Regional assistance

The government, therefore, has to offer financial grants to induce firms to establish or expand in Assisted Areas (Figure 23.1). These were revised in August 1993 to take account of new regions with structural weaknesses where unemployment problems were significant because of major closures (for example, Mansfield – coalmines), or even in the south of England through the contraction of defence or holiday demand (for example, Portland, Thanet, Isle of Wight).

However, since Assisted Area status confers eligibility of aid from the EU, as part of EU policy of reducing the level of aid to industry and to prepare for the entry of new states, present members have been requested to submit proposals for revised Assisted Areas which will come into effect on 1 January 2000. It is likely that Britain's improved unemployment rate and per capita GDP will lead to a reduction in her Assisted Areas and thus in the grants at present available to 34 per cent of the working population.

In the Assisted Areas *Regional Selective Assistance* is given on a discretionary basis, mainly through *Project Grants* based on the capital cost and the number of jobs created. The budget of over £100 million is under the control of the Department of Trade and Industry's *Invest in Britain Bureau* (IBB) which has had an outstanding success in inducing US, Japanese and South Korean firms to establish overseas centres in Britain, often in the depressed regions.

In the dispersal of industry the government has set an example. Thus the Department of Health and Social Security is based in Newcastle, and the Driving and Vehicle Licensing Centre in Swansea, while much of the work of departments (e.g. Defence, Inland Revenue) has been re-located to the Assisted Areas.

(c) Regional regeneration

Until 1980 the concentration on interregional differences tended to divert attention away from the problems existing within regions. The failure to replace the declining traditional industries with commerce or new industry left a picture of physical dereliction and decay. Moreover, because workers did not have the necessary skills or could not afford to emigrate to the greenfield sites of the new industries, some areas often suffer a high rate of unemployment.

It was recognised, however, that regeneration was not simply tidying up derelict land. It has to rebuild communities by providing them with jobs and decent living conditions, chiefly by attracting investment from the private sector. As a result urban regeneration had to be co-ordinated with regional industrial

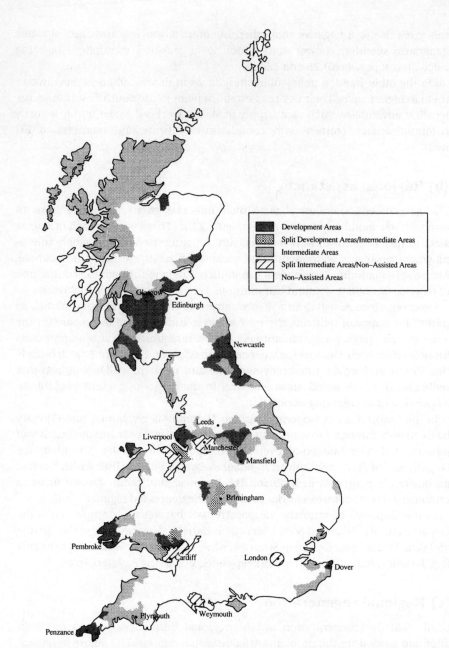

■	Development Areas
▒	Split Development Areas/Intermediate Areas
▨	Intermediate Areas
▨	Split Intermediate Areas/Non–Assisted Areas
□	Non–Assisted Areas

Figure 23.1   Assisted Areas, GB: as defined by the Department of Trade and Industry at
1 August 1993

policy. In fact funds were switched from regional assistance to the urban
regeneration programme, though it must be recognised that much of the urban
degeneration was in the Assisted Areas. With the object of regenerating these run-
down areas the government introduced a variety of Schemes – Enterprise Zones,
Urban Development Corporations, City Grants, City challenge – which were

amended in the light of experience or the need to reduce the financial commitment.

These administrative and spending initiatives have now been replaced by English Partnerships, a single Regional Budget and Regional Development Agencies, all responsible to the Department of the Environment, Transport and the Regions (DETR).

English Partnerships (EP) a *national* government agency, has powers to acquire land and decide on planning in a designated area. Furthermore, unlike the previous City Grant where the Treasury required a stipulated rate of public to private funding, EP can itself decide on how it uses its investment fund, amounting in 1997–8 to £300 million. This means that EP can shoulder risk, providing even 100 per cent of the initial funds as a pump-priming exercise to draw in developers. It was thus able, for instance, to use its investment fund to put together a co-ordinated package which induced Samsung to locate a manufacturing base at Stockton-on-Tees in the North-east region. Its original fund can be augmented by any profits it makes on its initiative and by EU funding where spending occurs in an Assisted Area.

The Single Regional Budget (SRB) was set up to achieve overall control of spending on urban regeneration by providing a global sum to cover all the spending of the operating bodies. Its aim is to fund flexible and locally responsive forms of regeneration administered by the Regional Development Agencies.

Much of this funding is competed for on a 'challenge' basis, grants for regeneration schemes and even neighbourhood projects being awarded on an assessment of their relative merit.

For England, nine Regional Development Agencies (RDA) have been set up to decide on local regeneration priorities, promote inward investment, help small businesses and co-ordinate regional economic development. Apart from the North-west Region which now includes Merseyside, these have the same boundaries as the Government Office Regions, with which they will work closely.

Scotland, Wales and Northern Ireland have their own agencies for similar functions, as will the new Greater London Authority in 2000.

23.4 Regional policy in the context of the EU

A healthy integrated EU – at both economic and political levels – is possible only if progress is made towards reducing disparities in economic opportunity between regions within the Community. Indeed, while the foregoing reasons for regional policy are all relevant at the Community level, additional considerations apply:

(i) Physical controls are more difficult to operate in the EU context. Not only are they at variance with the objective of greater mobility within the EU, but firms have the option of relocating in a prosperous region of another member state.

(ii) The depressed peripheral regions of Scotland, Northern Ireland, Southern Italy, etc., are more distant from the expanding centre of the Community –

south-east England through to north-east France and Germany – than they are from the centres of their own countries. This EU 'centre' forms a concentrated market to which industries are likely to be increasingly attracted, thereby adding to its dominance.

(iii) The EU embraces regions exhibiting wider economic disparities than in any one member state. Moreover, regional problems are more heterogeneous – for example, whereas the UK depressed regions are mainly industrial, Italy has many depressed agricultural areas.

These additional considerations mean that the formulation of an effective EU regional policy is a difficult task. Not only must it respond quickly as new regional problems arise, but it has to be linked with, and be complementary to, the individual nation's regional policy. Indeed EU policy should also co-ordinate the regional policies of member states, for example a physical control in one country must not be undermined by a firm being able to locate in another country.

It follows, therefore, that regional policy must be handled to a substantial degree at the EU level and be wide-ranging in the measures employed so that one reinforces the others. Above all, to achieve greater equity, it must envisage substantial transfers of income through incentive funds which are additional to and not a substitute for those provided by the member states.

The emphasis of the EU's three Structural Funds is now on regional development programmes rather than on individual projects, and the EU Commission can insist that grants are actually spent in the specified region. These funds are as follows:

(i) The *European Regional Development Fund* (ERDF) funds the development and structural adjustment of less-developed regions (such as Spain, Italy, Portugal and Greece) and declining industrial regions (for example, within the UK, Spain and France). The UK's depressed regions are major beneficiaries of the ERDF.

(ii) The *European Social Fund* (ESF) provides funds to organisations running vocational training and job-creation schemes.

(iii) The *European Agricultural Guidance and Guarantee Fund* (EAGGF) supports farming in less-favoured or environmentally sensitive areas, and the modernisation of infrastructures.

Loans are available on favourable terms from the European Investment Bank (EIB) and the European Coal and Steel Community (ECSC).

QUESTIONS

1   Give four advantages which a 'work-to-the-workers' policy has over a 'workers-to-the-work' policy.

2   A Regional Development Agency is seeking to attract firms to an Assisted Area. What should be the nature of (a) the demand, (b) the supply, of the product made?

3   A firm based in a 'boom' area is considering relocating to an Assisted Area and seeks your advice. What would this be if you were: (a) a private consultant, (b) a government official concerned with the location of industry?

▣ Ⅴ **24** Growth

Objectives

1 To examine the meaning, measurement and possibility of long-term secular growth
2 To indicate the means of achieving growth
3 To explain how the government can promote growth

24.1 The nature of growth

(a) The meaning of 'growth'

When there are unemployed resources, the economy's *actual* output is below its *potential* output; in terms of Figure 24.1 the economy is producing inside the production possibility curve, say at point *A*. Here output can be increased, even in the relatively short term, by measures which absorb unemployed resources.

But, by itself, full employment of an economy's resources does not necessarily mean that the economy will grow. Growth is essentially a long-run phenomenon – the *potential* full-employment output of the economy is increasing over time. Whereas full employment simply means that the economy is producing on a point on the production possibility curve I, growth means that, over time, the curve is pushed outwards to II and III. Even with full employment of resources, advanced economies can achieve an *annual* growth rate of 3 per cent.

Increases in the productive capacity in the economy over time are usually measured by calculating the rate of change of real gross national product per head of the population (see p. 244). However, when people talk about 'growth' they are thinking chiefly of the difference it makes to the standard of living rather than to output itself. Allowances have to be made, therefore, for the defects of GNP as an indication of the standard of living (see pp. 244–5). Also, when measuring long-term *secular* growth by the change in real GNP per head between different years, we must recognise that unemployment rates from which measurement starts may differ.

(b) Advantages of growth

Economic growth is the major factor for achieving improvements in the standard of living – more consumer goods, a shorter working week, and so on. While such

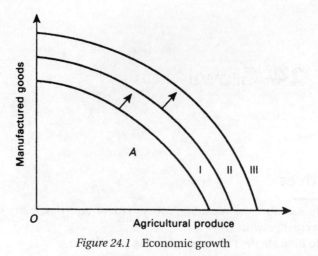

Figure 24.1 Economic growth

improvements occur almost imperceptibly from year to year, small differences in the *annual rate* of growth produce large differences in the *speed* of growth. For instance, a rate of growth of 2.5 per cent per annum will double real GNP in 28 years, whereas a 3 per cent rate doubles GNP in only 24 years.

In addition, growth makes it easier for the government to achieve its economic policy objectives. Revenue from taxation increases, allowing government services, e.g. health care, to be expanded without raising the *rates* of tax. Income can also be redistributed in favour of the poorer members of society while still allowing the standard of living of the better-off to show some improvement.

However, economic growth does have its costs (see p. 302).

24.2 Achieving growth

(a) Factors producing growth

There are five basic causes of growth:

(i) A rise in the productivity of existing factors

In the short run, productivity may be raised by improvements in organisation, which secure, for example, more division of labour and economies of large-scale production, or a more intensive use of capital equipment (e.g. the adoption of shift-working). Physical improvements for the labour force, e.g. better food and working conditions, may also increase productivity.

In the longer run, more significant increases can come with education and the acquisition of skills through training. These really represent, however, an increase in the capital invested in labour.

It is also important to draw attention to the differences in personal incentives provided by the market economy and the command economy. Compare, for instance, the growth rates of Hong Kong and Poland over the last forty years.

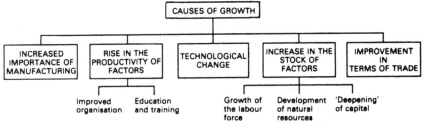

Figure 24.2   Factors leading to growth

(ii) An increase in the available stock of factors of production

(1) A rise in the labour input
The size of the labour input can increase relative to the total population through either an increase in the number of hours worked per worker, or an increase in the ratio of the working population to the total population. The first is hardly likely to be a cause of growth in normal conditions, for as living standards improve the tendency is to demand more leisure. The second, however, may come about if the percentage of the population in the working age group increases or if attitudes to work change (see p. 98).

(2) Development of natural resources
North Sea natural gas and oil, for instance, have allowed Britain to obtain her fuel supplies from fewer factors of production, enabling resources to be transferred to other output and thus promoting growth.

(3) Additional capital equipment
Here we must distinguish between 'widening' and 'deepening' capital. Widening capital – adding similar capital equipment – is necessary if the labor force increases, in order to maintain the existing capital–labour ratio and thus output per head. Suppose 10 men, digging a long ditch, have 5 spades between them. If the labour force is increased to 20 men the capital–labour ratio falls from 1:2 to 1:4 unless 'widening' takes place – that is, unless another 5 spades are provided to maintain the existing ratio. 'Widening' does not increase productivity; it simply prevents diminishing returns to labour setting in.
   'Deepening' capital occurs when the capital–labour ratio is increased. If, for example, when there were 10 spades to 20 men, the men were given a further 10 spades, the capital–labour ratio would be raised to 1:1.

(iii) Technological change

All we have done in our example so far has been to increase the stock of a given kind of capital equipment, spades. Over time, however, productivity can be raised more significantly by innovation and technological improvements. Thus the twenty men and their spades may be replaced by a single trench-digger and its driver. Because this does the job more quickly and efficiently the remaining nineteen men are released for other kinds of work.
   In practice, all three causes are usually operating at the same time to increase

productivity. Thus, as the labour force or natural resources are expanded, new capital is required, and this allows for the introduction of new techniques.

The speed with which new capital and improvements are introduced also depends upon the price of capital equipment relative to the wages of the labour for which it can be substituted. Over the last fifty years, wages have tended to rise relative to the cost of capital equipment. The effect has been to increase the rate of technological change in such industries as agriculture, cargo handling, transport, shipbuilding and mining.

Other factors affecting growth are:

(iv) Fundamental changes in the composition of the national output

As a country's standard of living improves so spending switches from agricultural to manufactured goods and then towards services. Since the opportunities for employing more capital and technical improvement are greatest in manufacturing, the growth rate increases as countries industrialise but then slows down as the relative demand for personal and government services increases.

(v) A sustained improvement in the terms of trade (see p. 332)

(b) Constraints upon growth

In practice the UK has not succeeded in sustaining a 3 per cent annual growth rate. Thus from 1960 to 1996 it has averaged only 2.3 per cent. Why is this?

First, when employment was buoyant, consumer demand left fewer resources available for investment.

Second, inflation has proved inimical to investment (see p. 279). Government disinflationary measures undermine the confidence of entrepreneurs.

Third, at times growth has been incompatible with other government objectives. For instance, 'stop' policies have been necessary because, as the economy expands, increasing imports can produce balance-of-payments difficulties (see p. 280).

Fourth, growth entails costs additional to the reduced current consumption necessary to accumulate capital. Growth usually requires change, and the more rapid the growth, the greater the change. Changes in the structure of the economy are, as we have seen, bound to lead to some unemployment, and if growth is to be achieved people must be willing to change jobs quite radically, three or four times in their working lives. This will entail retraining and probably moving around the country.

Fifth, growth is not achieved without environmental costs – pollution, noise, loss of natural beauty, destruction of wildlife habitat. And, as material wealth grows, people are inclined to question its full costs, preferring some slowing down in the growth rate.

Finally, and on the same theme, Britain's growth has been taken in forms not appearing in GNP calculations (see p. 245). Increasing welfare may mean preferring a quiet life and more leisure to the 'rat-race' and stress of accumulating material goods.

24.3 The government and growth

(a) Difficulties in framing policy

In framing policy for a satisfactory rate of growth, the government faces difficulties.

(i) How is growth to be measured? We have already drawn attention to the ambiguities of GNP figures as a measure of improved living standards. Is growth to take the form of more leisure, less spending on defence, a litter-free environment, the preservation of town and rural beauty, safer and more comfortable travel?

(ii) Of all the factors producing growth, which plays the greatest part – education of the population, training of labour, additional capital equipment, technological advance? There is no real means of measuring.

(iii) Growth does not proceed at a *steady* rate but rather by unavoidable take-offs and slow-downs around an upward trend, and firms are generally able to cope, e.g. by adjusting their stock levels. However, if these fluctuations are too wide, uncertainty can deter investment.

(b) Government policy

Since there is no single satisfactory theory of growth, government action seeks to promote the factors essential to growth.

Growth results mainly from capital investment. But accumulating capital involves foregoing present consumption – saving. Thus a first requirement for the government is to ensure that its policies, especially as regards taxation, will provide the real saving required.

Second, additions to capital take place in both the public and private sectors. The government itself is largely responsible for investment in the public sector – the infrastructure (such as roads, hospitals, schools), education, and the training of the labour force.

On the other hand, the scale of the government's priorities must not 'crowd out' desirable private sector investment. Decisions here are based on expected profitability. Private investment can be increased, therefore, by providing a stable economic background free from 'stop-go' policies so that fixed capital formation, research and development (R & D) are not inhibited.

While we must not ignore micro supply-side measures, the major spurts in growth have come through breakthroughs in technology by research and its application. Most of these, e.g. aircraft, computers, antibiotics and other drugs, plant-breeding, animal selection, pesticides, etc. are the result of long-term R & D. While about a half of R & D is carried out in the private sector, the other half, particularly as regards defence, is largely through government-sponsored research bodies. Britain's civil R & D has tended to lag behind other countries, but with the ending of the Cold War some transfer from defence is likely.

Finally, the government has to encourage the application of the fruits of R & D so that innovation and inventions are transformed into new marketable products.

QUESTIONS

1 What changes in the disposal of income in the UK are likely to occur with economic growth?

2 Give two examples of technological change which have had a major impact on the rate of economic growth.

3 Give an example of a country where a change in the terms of trade has affected the rate of economic growth.

4 Name two 'costs' which could result from economic growth.

■ ▼ **25** Public finance

Objectives

1 To show how government spending and taxation affects the redistribution of income
2 To outline the broad distribution of government spending and of the sources of financing it
3 To consider the 'structure' of taxation
4 To indicate the economic merits and disadvantage of the major direct and indirect taxes
5 To analyse how the burden of a selective indirect tax is distributed between the buyer and seller

25.1 The distribution of income

Public finance is concerned with government spending and revenue, the difference between them (the PSBR), and their magnitudes relative to GDP.

The government is interested in the distribution of income and wealth between its people for reasons of fairness, social harmony and its effect on the macro variables, e.g. saving. And, although the welfare effects of redistribution cannot be measured objectively, the nature of government expenditure and how revenue is raised do effect a redistribution of income.

Thus a survey of UK households in 1995–6 (*Social Trends* 1998) showed that while on average the bottom one-fifth started off with an original yearly income of £2,430, cash benefits less direct taxes and rates gave them a disposable income of £6,210. Indirect taxes took £1,930 of this, but benefits in kind (e.g. education, national health services, housing and travel subsidies) produced a final income of £8,230.

In contrast the top one-fifth had an original income of £41,260 and, after making the same adjustments, had a disposable income of £31,980 and a final income of £29,200.

Thus, although considerable inequality of incomes still persists, government policies do serve to reduce the disparity.

25.2 Government revenue and expenditure

Figure 25.1 shows the main items of government revenue and expenditure.

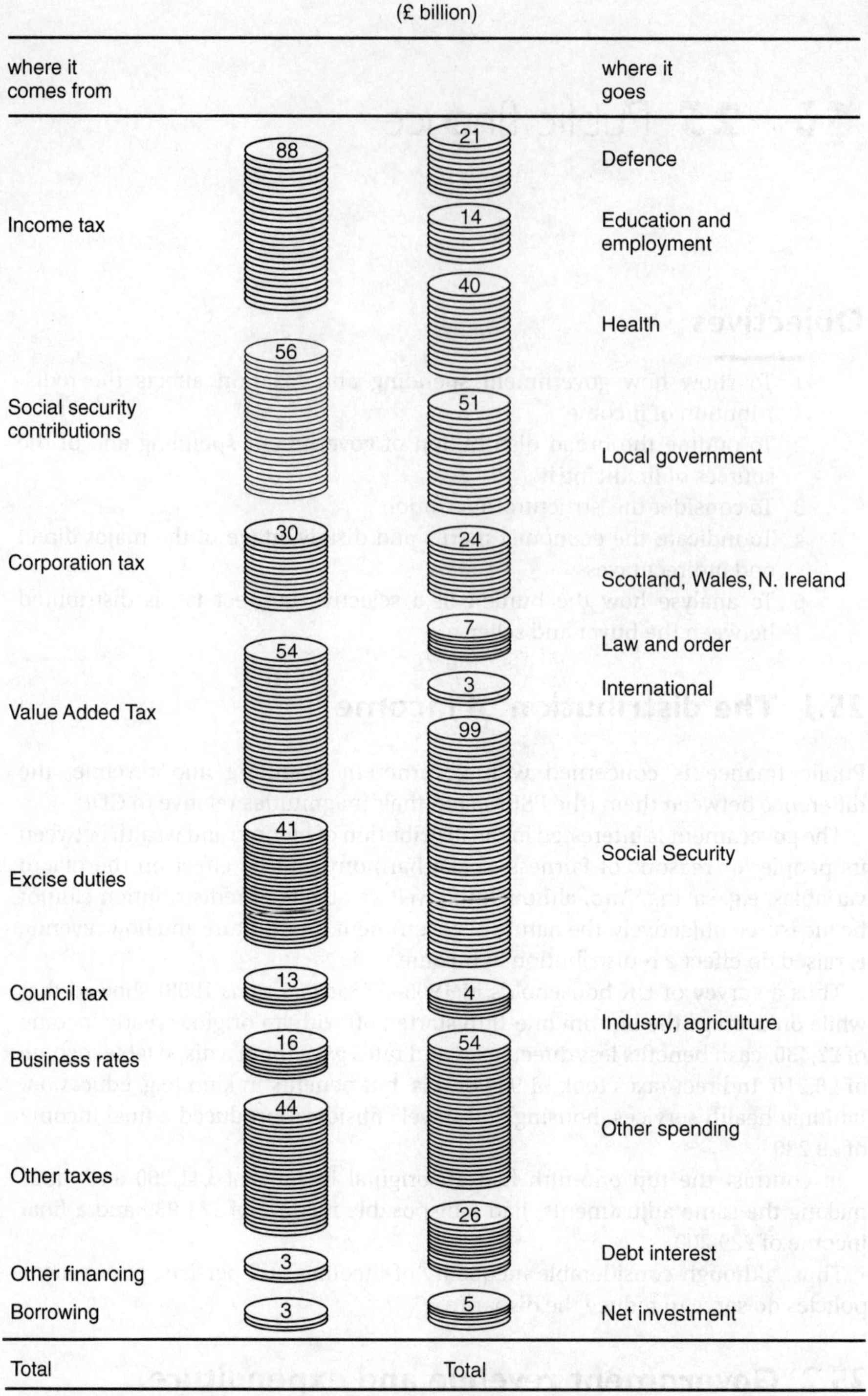

(£ billion)

where it comes from		where it goes

Income tax	88	
		21 — Defence
		14 — Education and employment
		40 — Health
Social security contributions	56	
		51 — Local government
Corporation tax	30	
		24 — Scotland, Wales, N. Ireland
Value Added Tax	54	
		7 — Law and order
		3 — International
		99 — Social Security
Excise duties	41	
Council tax	13	
		4 — Industry, agriculture
Business rates	16	
		54 — Other spending
Other taxes	44	
		26 — Debt interest
Other financing	3	
Borrowing	3	5 — Net investment

Total   Total

Source: Adapted from the Budget Red Book, 1999.

Figure 25.1 Public Money 1999–2000 – where it comes from and where it goes

(a) The distribution of government expenditure

Government spending can be classified under the following headings:

(i) *Defence*, where spending has fallen since the ending of the Cold War in 1989.
(ii) *Internal security* – the police, law enforcement and fire brigades.
(iii) *Social responsibilities* – education, and protection against the hazards of sickness, unemployment and old age.
(iv) *Economic policy*, covering subsidies to agriculture and industry, help for Assisted Areas, worker training and the provision of capital for urban regeneration.
(v) *Miscellaneous*, including expenditure on diplomatic services, grants to local authorities, overseas aid and – the largest single item – interest on the National Debt.

Today government expenditure takes 38 per cent of gross domestic product – a remarkable increase since 1910, when the figure was only about 10 per cent. The government is now spending on a much wider range of activities. It should be noted, however, that, many items, e.g. pensions, National Debt interest and grants to local authorities, are unavoidable since they are basically contractual.

(b) Controlling general government expenditure

It may seem that the government has merely to estimate its expenditure and impose taxes to cover it. But because goods and services in the economy are limited, the government has to cut its coat according to its cloth, asking such questions as: What can be afforded for the Arts Council? How much can be given to local authorities? Can nursery education be introduced? Can National Insurance contributions be reduced? The economic problem confronts private persons and the government alike. The method of dealing with it is as follows.

General government expenditure covers spending by both the central government and local government. But to explain the present principle of control, attention will be focused on the central government's expenditure.

Over the economic cycle, revenue and expenditure should be balanced. Where expenditure exceeds revenue there is a PSBR which, if it exceeds 3 per cent of GNP makes it more difficult to sustain growth since it puts upward pressure on the rate of interest (see p. 281). Furthermore, in adding to the National Debt it increases the government's current interest payments.

The problem is that each spending government department regularly presses for more funds. In the past the overall level of public expenditure has tended to emerge from compromises between the Chief Secretary to the Treasury and the departments, an approach which tended to give weight to what expenditure was desirable rather than what was affordable.

Without extra taxation, an increase in government spending should not in the long term exceed what growth in the economy can provide by way of the additional revenue resulting from higher incomes, profits and consumer spending. Recognising this economic problem of scarcity, the government now determines a global figure for total expenditure for three years ahead on a rolling basis, keeping aggregate departments' allocations within this. In practice most adjustments are relatively marginal and ultimately rest on political considerations.

(c) How government expenditure is financed

In the same way that firms have to pay for both variable and fixed factors, the government has to spend not only on single-use goods and services but also on goods which render services over long periods. The first, which involve regular yearly spending, should be paid for out of regular yearly income. But capital spending, on such items as roads, loans for urban regeneration and university building, is more fairly financed by borrowing, for the repayment of the capital then partly falls on future beneficiaries.

Regular yearly income comes from two main sources: (i) miscellaneous receipts, chiefly interest on loans, rents and charges (such as medical pre-scriptions); and (ii) taxation.

The difference between expenditure and revenue has to be covered by borrowing – the PSBR. Yearly borrowing increases the National Debt, the capital sum of accumulated borrowing.

Government borrowing takes the form of:

(i) Short-term loans from the sale of Treasury bills.
(ii) Medium- and long-term loans are obtained by selling stock having a minimum currency of five years. Some, such as $3\frac{1}{2}$ per cent War Loan, are undated.
(iii) *'Non-market' borrowing*, through National Savings Certificates, Premium Savings Bonds, etc. and the National Savings Bank.

Since 1980 additional capital funds have been obtained by the 'privatisation' sales of publicly owned assets (see p. 163).

25.3 The modern approach to taxation

(a) The attributes of a good tax system

In his *Wealth of Nations* Adam Smith was able to confine his principles of taxation to four simple canons. Stated briefly, these were: persons should pay according to their ability; the tax should be certain and clear to everybody concerned; the convenience of the contributor should be studied as regards payment; the cost of collection should be small relative to yield.

While today the main purpose of any tax is usually to raise money, the additional uses of taxation have rendered Adam Smith's maxims inadequate. Indeed objectives other than revenue may take priority. Nevertheless, it is helpful to list the general attributes which a Chancellor of the Exchequer would wish his system of taxation to possess. As far as possible, taxes should be:

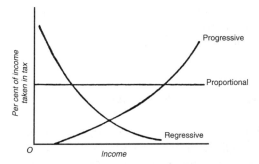

Figure 25.2   The difference between regressive, proportional and progressive taxes

(i) Productive of a worthwhile revenue which the Chancellor can estimate fairly accurately.

(ii) Certain to the taxpayer and difficult to evade.

(iii) Convenient to the taxpayer as regards the time and manner of payment.

(iv) Equitable in the sense that:
   (a) 'the heaviest burden is borne by the broadest back';
   (b) impartial between one person and another.

(v) Adjustable to changes in policy.

(vi) Automatic in stabilising the economy. Thus while, in order to achieve full employment or a stable price level, the Chancellor can adjust taxes to influence consumer spending, it is helpful if they respond automatically in the desired direction (see p. 314).

(vii) Harmless to effort and initiative.

(viii) Consistent with other aspects of government policy. While the tax structure should not change frequently, individual taxes must be constantly reviewed to promote current government policy. To encourage effort, should income from work be taxed at a lower rate than investment income? Will an indirect tax, by raising the cost of living, increase wage-push inflation?

(ix) Minimal in their effect on the optimum allocation of resources.

(x) Equitable in their distribution of the tax burden. Taxes can be classified according to the proportion of a person's income which is deducted:
   (a) A *regressive* tax takes a higher proportion of the poorer person's income than of the richer. Indirect taxes, for instance, which are a fixed sum irrespective of income (e.g. television licences), are regressive.
   (b) A *proportional* tax takes a given proportion of one's income. Thus between £4,301 and £27,100 of taxable income, income tax is proportional, 23 per cent being taken from every pound of taxable income.
   (c) A *progressive* tax takes a higher proportion of income as income increases (Figure 25.2). Thus income tax, which has a higher rates above certain limits (see below), is progressive.

Justification for taxing the rich higher than the poor rests on the assumption that the law of diminishing utility applies to additional income, so that an extra £50 affords less pleasure to the rich person than to the poor person. Thus taking from the rich involves less hardship than taking from the poor. Generally this can be accepted as true, but we can never be sure, simply because there is no absolute measure of personal satisfaction.

25.4 The structure of taxation

Because the objectives of taxation are now so varied and may even be incompatible, no single tax is completely perfect. Consequently, there must be a structure of taxation, combining different taxes which can be varied according to changes in emphasis on different objectives.

The following classification is based on their methods of payment.

(a) Direct taxes

With these taxes the person makes payment direct to the revenue authorities – the Department of Inland Revenue or the local authority. Usually each individual's tax liability is assessed separately.

(i) Income tax

'Taxable income', which is subject to a 10 per cent rate on the first £1,500, a basic 23 per cent up to £28,000 (2000), and 40 per cent above, is arrived at after deductions for a personal allowance, marital status, etc.

(ii) Corporation tax

All profits, whether distributed or not, are taxed at the same rate of 30 per cent (20 per cent for small companies). 10 per cent income tax is imputed to shareholders and deducted when the dividend is paid. For the shareholder it counts as a 'tax credit', but is no longer refundable if income tax is not paid because of low income.

(iii) Capital gains tax

A tax is now levied at income tax rates on any capital gain when an asset is disposed of. Owner-occupied houses, cars, National Savings Certificates and goods and chattels worth no more than £6,000 are excluded, and losses may be offset against gains.

Where the net gain does not exceed £7,100 (1999) in any year, no tax is payable.

(iv) Inheritance tax

Inheritance tax applies to lifetime gifts as well as to legacies, though the former generally bear only half the latter's rate of tax. The starting point is £231,001 (1999) and the rate of duty is 40 per cent. Gifts made more than seven years before death are exempt from tax.

(v) Other taxes

These consist of stamp duties (payable on financial contracts), motor vehicle duties and a Petroleum Revenue Tax.

The Council Tax and Uniform Business Rate levied on business premises can also be regarded as direct taxes.

This also applies to National Insurance contributions – a pay-roll tax of 12.2 per cent on employers, with employees and the self-employed paying a slightly lower rate.

Direct taxes yield nearly two-thirds of total revenue. Their great merit is that, being progressive and assessed according to the individual's circumstances, they ensure that the heaviest burdens are placed on the broadest backs. Their progressive character also gives additional weight to their role as built-in stabilisers.

Their main disadvantage is that when the rate of tax is high there may be disincentive effects. As a result indirect taxes also have to be levied.

(b) Indirect taxes

Indirect taxes on goods and services are so called because the revenue authority (the Department of Customs and Excise) collects them from the seller, who, as far as possible, passes the burden on to the consumer by including the duty in the final selling price of the good (see p. 317). They may be *specific* (i.e. consisting of a fixed sum irrespective of the value of the good) or *ad valorem* (i.e. consisting of a given percentage of the value of the good).

Indirect taxes may be divided into:

(i) Customs duties levied at EU rates on goods imported from outside the EU.

(ii) Excise duties on home-produced goods and services, e.g. beer, whisky, petrol, cigarettes and gambling.

(iii) Value Added Tax (VAT): an *ad valorem* tax, levied on most goods and services at each stage of production at a basic rate. Using Figure 18.1 as an example, a VAT at $17\frac{1}{2}$ per cent paid by the consumer on the table in the shop would be £17.50 making a total purchase price of £117.50. The VAT, however, would have been paid at each stage of production: tree-grower £5.25; saw-miller £3.50 table manufacturer £5.25; retailer £3.50. In practice each producer would pay to the Customs and Excise the full $17\frac{1}{2}$ per cent tax of the goods as invoiced by him *less* the VAT paid by his suppliers of materials, etc., as shown on their invoices. Thus the retailer would pay the Customs and Excise £3.50, i.e. £17.50 minus the VAT of £14 charged to him.

Some goods, e.g. food (except meals out), childrens' clothing, houses, books, newspapers, public transport fares, medicines on prescription, etc. are zero rated. This means that the final seller charges no VAT *and* can reclaim any VAT invoiced by intermediary producers. Other goods, e.g. rents and medical services, are 'exempt'. Here no VAT is charged by the final seller, but any VAT paid by an intermediary, e.g. for building repairs, cannot be reclaimed.

The main merit of VAT is that it is broad based, the yield increasing almost proportionately to consumer spending. Moreover, since VAT covers most forms of spending, it does not distort consumer choice as much as a highly selective tax (p. 316).

25.5 The advantages and disadvantages of direct taxes

We can use our survey of the attributes of a good tax to analyse the merits and demerits of the different types of tax. As regards direct taxes, the main reference will be to the income tax, but most of the arguments will apply to the other direct taxes.

As Figure 25.2 shows, direct taxes account for approximately 61 per cent of the total tax revenue, with income tax providing 25 per cent. Taxes on capital account for only 1 per cent.

(a) Advantages

(i) A high and elastic yield

In the UK, a 1p increase in the income tax yields approximately £2 billion. In comparison with yield, costs of collection are low. Indeed, through the PAYE system, the government makes use of employers as collectors.

On account of its high yield, changes in the income tax are very effective in varying households' spending power.

(ii) Certainty

Income tax payers usually know how much tax they will be expected to pay out of a given income and when they must pay it. Moreover, it is difficult to evade payment. Workers draw their wages less PAYE deductions, while dividends and interest are received less the standard rate of income tax.

Similarly, on the government's side, the Chancellor can rely on the yield from income tax. However, with inheritance tax, the yield may fluctuate.

(iii) Convenience

Weekly PAYE tax deductions enable the tax burden to be spread over the year. Companies and self-employed persons, such as doctors, surveyors, authors, and entertainers, receive a lump-sum demand which is paid in two half-yearly instalments.

Inheritance tax is a form of wealth tax but is convenient in that the owner is able to enjoy his property throughout his life.

(iv) Automatically stabilises the economy

Both income tax and corporation tax have an automatic effect in stabilising the economy (see p. 314).

(v) Equity

In the case of income tax, equality of sacrifice is achieved in two ways:

(i) an allowance is given for being married and for other responsibilities, e.g. a dependent aged relative;

(ii) the tax rate increases from 10 per cent to 23 per cent above £1,500 and 40 per cent above £28,000 taxable income (1999).

(vi) Redistributes income and wealth more equally

By being progressive and giving allowances for special needs, income tax brings about greater equality in incomes. Inheritance tax works similarly as regards wealth.

(b) Disadvantages

The simplest and fairest method of increasing revenue is to raise the rate of income tax. But here there is a major obstacle. When the rate is already high, the disadvantages of direct taxes are magnified.

(i) High rates act as a disincentive to effort

When income tax is around 40 per cent, people may prefer to take their income in the form of leisure (which is not taxed) rather than in money (which is taxed).

The extent to which this occurs, however, is uncertain. If a person has fixed money commitments, e.g. mortgage repayments and insurance premiums, he may have to work *harder* when his income is reduced. Furthermore, if we assume that a high rate of income tax is a disincentive to effort, we infer that people always look upon work as distasteful, and leisure as a pleasurable alternative. For many, this may be true but even in the high-income brackets there are some who find their work enjoyable. Last, we have to remember that most people are not free to vary their hours of work except as regards overtime. The normal working week is often an agreement on a national basis between trade unions and employers.

The disincentive effect, through reduced effort, is more likely to occur when there is a jump in the rate of tax at a given income level, that is, when the marginal rate of tax exceeds the average rate.

The disincentive effect may be reflected in other ways. People on social security may be reluctant to seek employment since taxed wages may leave them little better off, while highly skilled workers may emigrate to a lower tax country – the 'brain drain'.

(ii) High direct taxes stifle enterprise

A higher money reward is usually necessary to induce a person to devote time to training or to incur the cost of moving a home to secure promotion. It follows, therefore, that where the wage differential between skilled and unskilled labour is eroded by income tax, incentives are proportionately reduced. Similarly, firms are only prepared to accept risks if the rewards are commensurate.

(iii) High rates of tax do not encourage efficiency

Companies have 30 per cent of profits taken in taxation. Thus the penalty of inefficiency is not borne entirely by the firm. Because income is smaller, less tax is paid and so a part of the cost falls on the government.

(iv) High rates of direct taxation encourage tax avoidance

Although income tax may not directly reduce effort, it is likely that people will seek to reduce their tax liability by employing accountants to advise on how tax may be legally avoided.

Illegal tax evasion becomes more worthwhile, too, when the tax is high.

(v) High direct taxes may prevent the optimum allocation of resources

Direct taxes may affect the supply of factors, particularly capital, to industry. It may be that high taxation discourages saving; it certainly reduces the power to save. This is not serious for large companies, but the major source of capital for the small private company or sole proprietor is the owner's personal savings out of income. Normally firms which are making the largest profits will be the more likely to want to expand. Thus income tax and corporation tax deprive small, risky, but often progressive companies of much needed capital.

Not only that, but high direct taxes may repel foreign capital. Since a company has to bear corporation tax on profits, the amount available for distribution to shareholders is therefore less. Consequently, people may prefer to invest in companies operating in countries where there is a higher return on capital – the result, not of superior efficiency, but simply of lower taxes.

25.6 The advantages and disadvantages of indirect taxes

(a) Advantages

(i) Revenue yield helps to avoid high direct taxes

The revenue need of the government is now so great that, without indirect taxes, such a high rate would have to borne by direct taxes that it could impact on effort and initiative.

In any case, some people feel that some indirect taxes, which affect everybody, are desirable in that they foster a responsible attitude to government spending.

(ii) Certain and immediate yield

Especially when the Chancellor concentrates tax changes on goods with a fairly inelastic demand, the revenue yield can be calculated fairly accurately. Indirect taxes are cheap to collect and difficult to evade.

Where the Chancellor requires immediate revenue, indirect taxes have a special advantage for any increase produces extra revenue with little time-lag.

(iii) Convenient to the taxpayer

Buyers are able to spread their payments as and when purchases are actually made. Indeed, if the tax does not change frequently, buyers soon regard the combined price and tax at which the good is sold as the usual price, thereby reducing the resentment which taxation normally incites.

(iv) Unharmful to effort and initiative

While direct taxes are linked to earning, indirect taxes fall on spending. With indirect taxes, therefore, there is little disincentive to effort. It may even be that higher prices will cause people to work harder in order to maintain their customary standard of living.

On the other hand, certain 'incentive goods' – cars, camcorders, dish washers, etc. – must not be taxed so heavily that they are priced beyond the reach of persons who would otherwise work overtime in order to buy them.

(v) They may automatically stabilise the economy

In as much as goods having a high income elasticity of demand (chiefly home-produced and imported luxuries) are taxed the most heavily, the yield from indirect taxes increases as incomes rise. This helps to stabilise the economy in an inflationary situation (see p. 308).

Today, the Chancellor of the Exchequer is able to reinforce this automatic mechanism by the 'regulator'. He can alter an indirect tax either way by 25 per cent of the existing rate.

(vi) They are adjustable to specific objectives of policy

Selective taxes can be changed according to the particular needs of government policy. The following are examples:

  (i) *To build up infant or vital defence industries*, protection from competitive foreign products may be afforded by an import duty. The British motor car, aircraft, paper, and chemicals industries have been built up in this way (see p. 338).

  (ii) The effects of *changes in the conditions of demand or supply on the long-term structure of an industry* may be mitigated by favourable tax concessions or by the imposition of duties on competing imports, e.g. cotton goods.

  (iii) The government may encourage the *use of certain goods* by VAT concessions, e.g. books are zero-rated.

  (iv) *Political links may be strengthened* by duties which give favourable treatment to particular countries, e.g. fellow-members of the EU.

  (v) Citizens' health may be safeguarded by taxing certain goods, e.g. spirits, cigarettes.

  (vi) The *terms of trade may be improved* by taxing certain imports (see p. 337).

  (vii) The *balance of payments may be strengthened* by import duties on foreign goods (p. 338).

(b) Disadvantages

(i) Regressive

In so far as they buy the same goods, poor persons pay exactly the same tax as the rich. More than that, purchases are made out of income left after income tax has been paid. Thus not only are indirect taxes regressive, but they undo some of the redistributive effects of direct taxation.

To some extent, the regressive nature of indirect taxes can be offset by: (a) imposing *ad valorem taxes* instead of *specific taxes*; (b) exempting from VAT such items as food, housing and children's clothing.

(ii) Not completely impartial in their application

Although indirect taxes fulfil the requirement that all persons in the same position should pay the same tax, the concentration of taxes on a few goods – chiefly tobacco, alcoholic drink, and motoring – does penalise severely certain forms of spending. Thus a person who obtains his pleasure from walking, reading, cycling, and eating receives many benefits from state expenditure, benefits which are largely paid for by his smoking, drinking, and car-driving neighbour!

(iii) Possibly harmful to industry

Where taxes are subject to frequent variation, they may dislocate industry. This will be more marked the higher the elasticity of demand for the product (see p. 318).

(iv) Rigidity

Protective duties and subsidies (a 'negative tax') may originally be designed to give special assistance to an industry. But the Chancellor often finds his hands tied when he wishes to reduce this form of help. Industries such as agriculture, which have come to rely on protection or subsidies, strenuously resist any such move.

(v) May have inflationary influences

Indirect taxes, by increasing the price of goods, raise the Retail Prices Index. This leads to a demand for wage increases.

(vi) Prevent resources from being allocated in the best possible way

The imposition of an indirect tax on a *particular* good has the effect of resources not being perfectly allocated according to the real preferences of consumers. In the long period, *under perfect competition*, the cost of producing the good is just equal to people's valuation of it. Moreover, consumers have allocated their outlay so that marginal utility relative to the price of the good is equal in all cases. A tax on one good destroys this equilibrium, for the price of the good rises (unless supply is absolutely inelastic). This results in a redistribution of consumers' expenditure and thus of the factors of production. In addition, there will be some dislocation of the industry concerned (see p. 318).

(vii) Result in greater loss to the consumer than an income tax which raises an equivalent amount

Unlike an income tax, indirect taxes change the relative prices of goods so that consumers have to rearrange their pattern of expenditure. This substitution involves a loss of satisfaction in addition to that resulting from the reduction in income.

25.7 The incidence of taxation

(a) What do we mean by the 'incidence' of a tax?

So far we have considered only the *formal* incidence of a tax – how the tax is distributed between the various taxpayers. Thus direct taxes, we saw, are progressive, falling heaviest on the higher income groups. Indirect taxes, on the other hand, are regressive as regards consumers, though the direct incidence falls on producers or distributors who actually pay the tax to the Customs and Excise.

But the economist is chiefly concerned with the *effective* incidence – how the real burden of a tax is distributed after its full effects have worked through the economy.

In the case of *direct* taxes, we have seen that, with some qualifications, both income tax and corporation tax adversely affect effort, enterprise and risk-bearing, economy in expenditure, and saving (312).

An increase in income tax can be passed on only by those workers who can secure some addition to their wages by way of compensation. For this to happen, they must be in a strong bargaining position. Certain conditions must be fulfilled (see p. 106), the chief one being that the demand for the good they produce is fairly inelastic. The increase in the price of the good which results from the higher wages will be borne mainly by consumers – which really means workers in other groups who are not in such a strong bargaining position.

Similarly, in the short period, when supply is fairly inelastic, an increase in a tax on profits will be borne chiefly by producers (see p. 122). But in the long period, when entrepreneurs can transfer from the riskier enterprises (which the tax hits hardest), there will be changes in the relative supply of goods, and consumers of those goods will, according to their elasticity of demand, have to bear a greater part of the tax.

A tax which falls on monopoly profits, however, cannot be passed on. There has been no change in the demand or supply curves, and the monopolist is already producing where his profits are a maximum. Hence if he has to pay, say, a 20 per cent tax, his equilibrium position will be unchanged; four-fifths of maximum profits are still better than four-fifths of anything less.

With *indirect taxes*, the effective incidence can be analysed more precisely. An indirect tax may be *general* or *selective*. A sales tax levied across the board on all goods and services at a standard rate would be a *general* indirect tax. VAT comes closest to such a tax. The important point is that *relative* prices remain unchanged and the consumer cannot switch to a substitute which is relatively cheaper because it bears no tax. If the government wishes to reallocate resources, therefore, it must do so by using the proceeds of the tax to subsidise certain industries, or by imposing additional excise duties on goods whose consumption it would like to curtail, e.g. tobacco.

Any tax which is levied at a higher rate on certain goods is termed *selective*, e.g. tobacco, alcohol, cars, petrol. When a tax is selective, the following questions become important: what is the effect of imposing a selective tax on the size of the particular industry? How will the burden of such a tax be ultimately distributed between the producer and consumer?

We begin by explaining how the imposition of a tax can be shown diagrammatically.

(b) Diagrammatic presentation of a tax

Theoretically, the effect of a tax can be analysed on either the demand or the supply side. No matter which is chosen, the same new equilibrium position for price and output will result. Later we shall prefer one method to the other according to the particular problem being analysed.

Consider the following demand and supply schedules for commodity *X*.

Price of *X* (pence)	Demand (units)	Supply (units)
12	60	150
11	70	130
10	80	110
9	90	90
8	100	70

The equilibrium price is 9p. Now suppose a tax of 3p is charged on the producer for each unit of *X* he puts on the market. This means that whereas before the tax he supplied 70,000 units at a price of 8p, he will now only supply this quantity at 11p (because 3p would go in tax). Similarly, 90,000 units will only be supplied at a price of 12p instead of 9p. Thus the effect of the 3p tax can be shown by the shift in the supply curve from *S* to S_1 (Figure 25.3). This gives a new equilibrium price of 11p, the buyer paying 2p more and the producer receiving 1p less, the quantity traded falling from 90,000 units to 70,000 units.

The result is the same if the 3p tax is levied on purchasers. Before the tax, 100,000 units were demanded at a price of 8p. If purchasers now have to pay a 3p tax, this is equivalent to a price of 11p including tax, and so they will demand only 70,000 units. Similarly, for a price of 9p they will demand only 60,000 units instead of 90,000. Thus the 3p tax imposed on buyers can be shown by the move in the demand curve from *D* to D_1 (Figure 25.4). This gives a new equilibrium price of 11p (8p at which the market is cleared, plus 3p tax), and the quantity traded falls from 90,000 to 70,000.

(c) The effect of an indirect tax on the size of an industry

The greater the elasticities of demand and supply, the greater will be the effect of a tax in reducing production. We can show this diagrammatically.

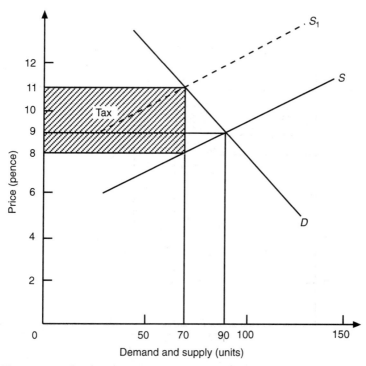

Figure 25.3   The diagrammatic representation of a tax on the supply side

(i) Elasticity of demand

Before the tax is imposed, total output is *OM* (Figure 25.5). The effect of the tax is to raise the supply curve from *S* to S_1. Two demand curves are shown, D_a being less elastic than D_b at price *OP*. The effect of the tax is to reduce output to OM_1 where demand is D_a, and to OM_2 where it is D_b. In the latter case consumers switch to buying substitutes.

(ii) Elasticity of supply

Before the tax is imposed, total output is *OM* (Figure 25.6). The effect of the tax is to lower the demand curve from *D* to D_1. Two supply curves are shown, S_a being less elastic than S_b at price *OP*. The effect of the tax is to reduce output to OM_1 where supply is S_a, and to OM_2 where it is S_b. In the latter case producers can turn to producing alternative goods.

The proposition under this heading has important practical applications.

(i) The government may use a subsidy (which can be illustrated by moving the supply curve to the right – p. 323) to increase the production, and thus employment, of an industry. The effect will be more pronounced where demand and supply are elastic.

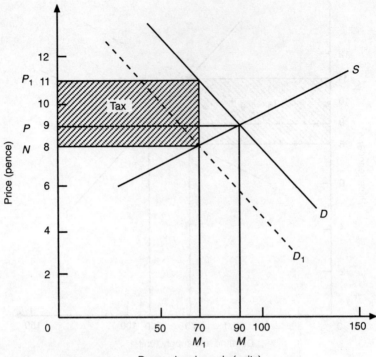

Figure 25.4 The diagrammatic representation of a tax on the demand side

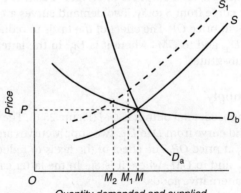

Figure 25.5 The relationship of elasticity of demand and production when a tax is imposed on a good

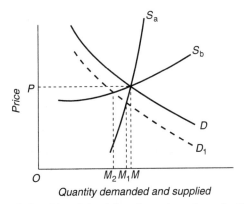

Figure 25.6 The relationship of elasticity of supply and production when a tax is imposed on a good

(ii) Because the effect of a tax is to reduce production, even a temporary tax may be harmful to an industry. This is particularly so where home demand is elastic and production takes place under decreasing costs. Thus a higher selective tax on cars would not only reduce home demand, but, by doing so, lose economies of scale, thereby putting up prices to both home and foreign markets. Even when the tax is subsequently withdrawn, foreign markets may not be regained, for sales organisation, servicing arrangements and goodwill might all have suffered permanent harm.

(d) The distribution of the burden of a selective tax between consumers and producers

When a good is subject to a selective tax, it does not mean that its price will rise by the full amount of the tax. Thus in Figure 25.4 the tax is 3p, but the price of X rises by only 2p. The proposition is that the amount of the tax falling on consumers as compared with that falling on producers is directly proportional to the elasticity of supply as compared with the elasticity of demand. That is:

$$\frac{\text{Consumer's share of tax}}{\text{Producers' share of tax}} = \frac{\text{Elasticity of supply}}{\text{Elasticity of demand}}$$

That this proposition is likely to be true can be seen from the following argument. When a tax is imposed, the reaction of the producer is to try to push the burden of the tax on to the consumer, while similarly the consumer tries to push it on to the producer. Who wins? Simply the one whose bargaining position is stronger. This will depend upon the ability to switch to producing substitutes if the price falls as compared with the ability to switch to buying substitutes if the price rises. Now the possibility of substitution largely determines elasticities of supply and demand. Thus the relative burden of the tax paid by producers and consumers depends upon relative elasticities of supply and demand.

The proposition can be proved geometrically. As a result of the tax, price rises from OP to OP_1, and the quantity demanded and supplied falls from OM to OM_1 (Figure 25.4).

$$\text{Elasticity of supply at } OP = \frac{M_1M/OM}{NP/OP}$$

$$\text{Elasticity of demand at } OP = \frac{M_1M/OM}{PP_1/OP}$$

$$\therefore \quad \frac{\text{Elasticity of supply}}{\text{Elasticity of demand}} = \frac{M_1M}{OM} \times \frac{OP}{NP} \times \frac{OM}{M_1M} \times \frac{PP_1}{OP}$$

$$= \frac{PP_1}{NP}$$

$$\frac{\text{Increase in price (burden of the tax) to the consumer}}{\text{Decrease in price (burden of the tax) to the producer}}$$

This proposition has a number of practical applications:

(i) A tax on a good having an inelastic demand, e.g. cigarettes, falls mainly on the consumer.

(ii) Where supply is inelastic compared with demand, the tax falls mainly on the producer. Thus the imposition of VAT on the construction of new office blocks will have to be borne initially by the current land-owner.

(iii) Because in the long period supply tends to be more elastic than in the short period, so, as time passes, consumers will bear a greater share of the tax.

(iv) Where supply is inelastic even in the long period, a tax will take longer to pass on to the consumer. Thus if there are any unoccupied offices, an increase in the Uniform Business Rate will have to be borne mainly by the owners of the property.

(v) An increase in price as a result of a tax will vary according to the relationship of elasticity of supply to elasticity of demand. The greater the elasticity of supply relative to the elasticity of demand, the greater will be the price rise.

(e) The distribution of the benefit of a subsidy

The grant of a subsidy ('negative tax') can be analysed similarly by moving the demand or supply curve to the right, e.g. S to S_s (Figure 25.7).

Price falls from OP to OP_1, and the quantity traded increases from OM to OM_1. As previously, it can be proved that the benefit of the subsidy to consumers as compared with that of producers is directly proportional to the elasticity of supply to the elasticity of demand. That is:

$$\frac{\text{Consumers' share of subsidy (fall in price paid)}}{\text{Producers' share of subsidy (increase in the price received)}}$$

$$= \frac{\text{Elasticity of supply}}{\text{Elasticity of demand}}$$

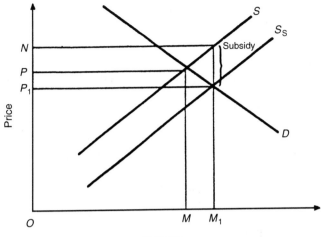

Figure 25.7 The diagrammatic representation of a subsidy

QUESTIONS

1 What do you understand by a 'structure of taxation'? Why is it necessary?

2 To what extent is VAT progressive in its incidence?

3 What is the meaning of the saying 'An old tax is no tax'? What implications has it for taxation policy?

4 Why may a tax on capital be of no help in checking inflation?

5 The following represents the demand and supply schedules for toffee-apples:

Quantity (000s)

Price (pence)	Demanded	supplied
8	50	110
7	70	100
6	90	90
5	110	80
4	130	70
3	150	60

(a) What is the equilibrium price?

(b) What will be the price if a selective tax of 3p is put on each toffee-apple?

(c) How is the burden of the tax shared between the child and the toffee-apple producer?

(d) Which curve is the more elastic at the original equilibrium price?

(e) What is now the equilibrium output?

(f) What is the total yield of the tax?

(g) Suppose that, on the original schedules, the government gave producers a subsidy of 3p on each toffee-apple. What will now be the price?

(h) What is the new equilibrium output?

(i) What is the total cost of the subsidy?

Part VIII

International trade

⊠ 26 The nature of international trade

Objectives

1 To examine how countries' differences in comparative costs and in demand can give rise to international trade
2 To explain the 'terms of trade'
3 To outline the UK's pattern of trade with other countries
4 To consider the case for protecting a home industry from foreign competition

26.1 How international trade arises

International trade arises simply because countries differ in their demand for goods and in their ability to produce them.

On the demand side, a country may be able to produce a particular good but not in the quantity it requires. The USA, for instance, is a net importer of oil. On the other hand, Kuwait does not require all the oil she can produce. Without international trade most of her deposits would remain untapped.

On the supply side, resources are not evenly distributed throughout the world. One country may have an abundance of land; another may have skilled labour. Capital, oil, mineral deposits, cheap unskilled labour and a tropical climate are other factors possessed by different countries in varying amounts.

Nor can these factors be transferred easily from one country to another. Climate, land and mineral deposits are obviously specific. Labour is far more immobile internationally than within its own national boundaries. Capital, too, moves less easily; exchange controls, political risks and simply ignorance of possibilities may prevent investors from moving funds abroad.

Because factors are difficult to shift, the alternative – moving goods made by those factors – is adopted. What happens is that countries specialise in producing those goods in which they have the greatest comparative advantage, exchanging them for the goods of other countries.

26.2 The advantages of international trade

(i) It enables countries to obtain the benefits of specialisation

Specialisation by countries improves their standard of living.

(1) It is obvious that without international trade many countries would have to

go without certain products. Britain, for instance, has no gold or aluminium, and Sweden no oil.

(2) More important, many goods can be enjoyed which if produced at home would be available only to the very wealthy, for instance bananas, spices, oranges and peaches in Britain. But this benefit can be applied generally to all imports. The 'law of comparative costs' shows that, provided countries differ in the relative costs of producing certain goods, they can probably gain by specialisation and trade. We can explain as follows.

Assume:

(i) assume constant unit costs (in terms here of opportunity costs);
(ii) no barriers to trade;
(iii) no transport or trading costs;
(iv) two countries, A and B, producing just two commodities, wheat and cars. Each has the same amount of capital and the same number of labourers, but A has a good climate and fertile soil compared with B. B's workers, on the other hand, are far more skilful;
(v) all factors are fully employed.

When both countries divide their factors equally between the production of wheat and cars, they can produce as follows:

Country	Wheat (*units*)	Cars (*units*)
A	500	100
B	100	500
Total production	600	600

But if A specialises in producing wheat and B in cars, total production would be 1,000 wheat and 1,000 cars. There is thus a net gain of 400 wheat and 400 cars to be shared between them (see p. 331).

Here the gains are obvious, because A has an *absolute* advantage in producing wheat and B in producing cars. But suppose A also has skilled labour and capital, and is better at producing both wheat and cars, as follows:

Country	Wheat (*units*)	Car (*units*)
A	500	300
B	400	100
Total production (no specialisation)	900	400

Are there still gains to be achieved by specialisation?

Provided the rate at which cars can be exchanged for wheat lies within certain limits (see p. 330), the answer is 'yes'. The reason for this is that A's superiority in producing cars is far more marked than her superiority in producing wheat. In the production of the former she is three times as efficient, but with the latter only one-and-a-quarter times. *Comparative*, rather than absolute, advantage is what is really important. The result is that if A specialises in producing cars, leaving B to produce wheat, total production will be 800 wheat and 600 cars.

Suppose now that world conditions of demand and supply are such that 2 wheat exchange for 1 car: that is, the price of cars is exactly twice that of wheat. A now exchanges 200 cars for 400 wheat, giving her a total of 400 wheat and 400 cars, and B 400 wheat and 200 cars.

It can be seen, therefore, that through specialisation B is 100 cars better off. But has specialisation improved A's position? She now has 400 cars but only 400 wheat, a gain of 100 cars but a loss of 100 wheat. But by her own production she would have had to go without $166\frac{2}{3}$ wheat in order to obtain the extra 100 cars. Thus we can conclude that she too is better off.

The above arguments can be put in terms of opportunity costs. If there is no specialisation, A has to give up 3 cars in order to produce 5 units of wheat. On the international market, however, the terms of exchange are such that 3 cars can obtain 6 units of wheat. It will obviously pay A, therefore, to specialise in producing cars and to obtain her wheat by exchange. Similarly with B. For 4 units of wheat she can, by her own efforts, obtain only 1 car. On the world market she gets 2 cars. It will thus pay her to specialise in producing wheat and to obtain her cars by exchange.

The above explanation must be amplified to allow for:

(1) Demand
The law of comparative costs merely shows how two countries can specialise to advantage when their opportunity costs differ. But until we know the demand for goods we cannot say definitely whether specialisation will take place or, if it does, to what extent. Thus, although a country may be favourably placed to produce certain goods, a large home demand and thus a relatively high price may mean that it is a net importer of that good (as the USA is of oil).

(2) Transport and trading costs
These reduce possible gains and therefore make for less specialisation. Indeed, it is conceivable that transport costs could so offset A's superiority in making cars that B found it better to produce her own.

(3) Changes in the conditions of supply
Few production advantages are permanent. Climate and, to a large extent, mineral deposits persist, but new techniques can make factors more productive. Thus India now exports cotton goods to Britain!

(4) Interference by nations with the free movement of goods – by customs duties, etc.
(see pp. 336–9)

(5) The possibility of diminishing returns setting in as the production of a good increases
The theory as stated assumes that, at all stages of production, wheat can always be produced instead of cars by both A and B at a constant ratio. Thus at any output, A can have 5 wheat instead of 3 cars and B 4 wheat instead of 1 car. But it is likely that as B increases her output of wheat, diminishing returns set in, for inferior land and labour have to be used. Thus instead of getting 4 additional wheat for 1 car, she receives only 3, and later only 2, and so on. The same applies, too, as the production of cars is increased by A. Eventually, therefore, it pays to specialise no longer, A can obtain her wheat cheaper by producing herself than by buying it on the world market, and the same applies to B as regards cars. Diminishing returns, and thus increasing costs, usually mean in practice that

there is only partial specialisation – up to the point where opportunity costs are less than those offered by the terms of trade, that is, the quantity of imports obtained for a given quantity of exports. Thereafter it is better for a country to produce the good itself.

(ii) By expanding the market, international trade enables the benefits of large-scale production to be obtained

Many products, e.g. computers, pharmaceuticals, aircraft and cars, are produced under conditions of decreasing cost. Here the home market is too small to exploit fully the advantages of large-scale production. This applies particularly to small countries such as Switzerland. In such cases international trade lowers costs per unit of output.

(iii) International trade increases competition and thereby promotes efficiency in production

As we have seen, any restriction of the market makes it easier for one seller to gain control. In contrast, international trade increases competition. A government must always consider the risk of a monopoly developing when it gives protection to the home industry by tariffs, etc.

(iv) International trade promotes beneficial political links between countries

Examples of this are the EU, and the Commonwealth where trade is still an important link.

26.3 What determines the rate at which goods are traded internationally?

(a) The possible range of the exchange rate

In our example, A specialises in producing cars and B in producing wheat. Since by her own efforts, A could have 5 wheat for 3 cars, she will not specialise in cars if, by exchange, she receives less wheat than this. Similarly, B will not specialise in producing wheat if she has to give up more than 4 wheat for 1 car.

Thus for specialisation to be beneficial to both A and B the rate at which wheat exchanges for cars must lie somewhere between $\frac{5}{3}$ and of 4. But how is the actual rate of exchange (which we assumed to be 2 wheat for 1 car) determined?

The answer is quite simple. When we say that 2 wheat exchange for 1 car, we are really comparing relative values: the price of cars is twice that of wheat. Their relative prices will be fixed in the market, like all other prices, by demand and supply.

(b) The 'terms of trade'

For both A and B, the rate at which wheat exchanges for cars represents their *terms of trade*. Should more wheat have to be given for a car, then the terms of trade have improved for *A*, but worsened for *B*. On the other hand, if less wheat has to be given for a car, the terms of trade have improved for *B* but worsened for *A*.

The terms of trade, therefore, expresses the rate at which a country exchanges its exports for imports. Where goods are traded internationally, this rate is fixed by: (i) real forces: the world conditions of demand and supply; and (ii) monetary influences: the currency exchange rate.

Real forces, through changes in demand or supply, can bring about long-term changes in the terms of trade. Thus, in our example, if there is a large increase in *A*'s demand for wheat, the price of wheat will move nearer to the higher limit of $\frac{5}{3}$: 1. Likewise, if there is a decrease in *A*'s demand for wheat, the price will move nearer to the lower limit of 4 : 1. Or, if on the supply side, *A* can produce 1,000 cars instead of 600, she would probably be willing to supply more cars in exchange for a given quantity of wheat, and so the price of cars falls, the terms of trade moving in favour of *B*.

Thus changes in the terms of trade can originate on both the demand and supply sides. Examples in the real world are:

(i) A large increase in the world *demand* for oil through industrial development would, with no corresponding increase in production, improve the UK's terms of trade.
(ii) Technical improvements, e.g. the extraction of North Sea oil, may so increase *supply* that, through a price fall, the terms of trade improve for oil importers. On the other hand, political unrest or war (e.g. Kuwait) or restriction of production (e.g. by OPEC) may raise the price of oil and so improve the terms of trade for major oil producers.

How *currency* exchange rates are determined is explained in Chapter 27. Predominantly they reflect the relative demand for exports and imports. Thus the improvement in the sterling exchange rate in 1980 was a reflection of Britain's becoming self-sufficient in oil, and even a net exporter.

But the currency exchange rate is also influenced by short-term capital movements. Some of the 1996–8 improvement in the sterling exchange rate resulted from the movement of short-term capital to London because foreigners took advantage of higher interest rates, necessary to control possible inflation.

Thus a country's terms of trade can alter even though there have been no real changes in demand and supply simply because the relative prices of its exports and imports have responded to the appreciation or depreciation of its currency on the foreign exchange market.

(c) Measurement of the terms of trade

The terms of trade express the relationship between the price of imports and the price of exports. In practice, however, our interest is centred on this relationship not so much at any one time but rather as it changes over a period of time. We therefore measure relative changes in the terms of trade from one period to another (Table 26.1).

Because countries import and export many goods, and the prices of different

Table 26.1   The terms of trade of the UK, 1988–96 (base year 1990)

Year	Export unit-value index (1)	Import unit–value index (2)	Terms of trade (1)/(2)
1988	92.4	93.7	98.6
1989	96.5	97.7	98.8
1990	100.0	100.0	100.0
1991	101.4	101.2	100.2
1992	103.5	102.1	101.4
1993	116.2	112.3	103.5
1994	118.6	116.1	102.2
1995	126.4	127.7	99.0
1996	128.4	128.3	100.1

Source: Annual Abstract of Statistics.

goods move in different ways and by varying amounts, we have to measure changes in the price of imports and exports as a whole by index numbers. And, it must be remembered, these are subject to defects (p. 276).

In practice, therefore the terms of trade are measured as follows:

$$\frac{\text{Index showing average price of exports}}{\text{Index showing average price of imports}} \times \frac{100}{1}$$

When a country's exports become cheaper relative to her imports, she will have to give more goods in exchange for a given quantity of imports. It is then said that the terms of trade have 'worsened', 'moved against her', or 'become less favourable'. If the opposite occurs, the terms of trade are said to have 'improved', 'moved in her favour', or 'become more favourable'. Table 26.1 shows that the terms of trade for the UK improved steadily between 1988 and 1993 but thereafter deteriorated slightly.

(d) Results of changes in the terms of trade

The direct effects of an improvement in a country's terms of trade are beneficial. First, she obtains more imports for a given quantity of exports. Second, her balance of payments may be improved. Suppose, for instance, that Britain's imports and exports are equal in value. Now assume that the price of imports in sterling falls, but that the price of Britain's exports in sterling remains unchanged. If Britain's demand for imports is inelastic, the direct effect will be to improve her balance of payments, for less will be spent in sterling on imports. Similarly, if the demand for her exports were inelastic and their price in sterling rose, Britain's balance of payments would improve.

But the indirect results may make an improvement in the terms of trade, especially for a developed country, seem less desirable.

First, countries whose terms of trade have worsened may not be able to afford to buy the exports of the countries whose terms of trade have improved. For example, suppose that the price of wheat falls from £110 to £100 a tonne, but that 'A' a major wheat exporting country, finds that demand increases only from 900,000 tonnes to 950,000 tonnes. Total expenditure on wheat falls, therefore, from £99 m to £95 m. But this expenditure equals approximately the income of her farmers who are exporting the bulk of their crop. As a result of the fall in income, their demand for the manufactured goods of 'B', the wheat-importing country, would drop.

Second, the fall in income will also mean that less is spent on home-produced goods, thereby reducing profits. To the extent that firms of these countries are owned by British shareholders, lower dividend payments reduce the UK's invisible earnings.

Third, a fall in the incomes of less developed countries may mean that the loss must be made good by increased aid.

Fourth, the economies of countries which are dependent on foreign trade may be subjected to frequent adjustments if there are swings in the terms of trade. If, for instance, the price of gold fluctuates, incomes will be greater in South Africa when the price of gold is high, and smaller when the price of gold is low, because demand is inelastic. This has far-reaching effects on a policy aimed at stabilising income and employment.

26.4 The pattern of the UK's overseas trade

(a) Trade with other countries

From our study of the reasons for international trade we can deduce the likely pattern of the UK's trade. Since, in the first place, trade arises because resources are unequally distributed, we have to ask: (i) What are the factors of production of which the UK can be said to have relatively plentiful supply? (ii) What are the factors in which she is deficient?

In answer to (i), we can point to her oil and natural gas reserves, her skilled workers, factories and machinery. In addition she has a high proportion of very skilled and highly educated administrators, engineers and technicians, researchers, and commercial and financial experts. All such persons can render services to other countries.

As regards (ii), the UK lacks land; plentiful supplies of very cheap, unskilled labour; certain minerals (such as nickel, zinc, aluminium and copper); certain chemicals (such as sulphur and nitrates); and the climate which is necessary, in terms of both warmth and rainfall, for the production of many foodstuffs (such as cane sugar, vegetable oils and tropical fruit), beverages (such as tea, coffee and cocoa) and raw materials (such as cotton, rubber and tobacco).

(b) The commodities of the UK's international trade

The relative supply of the UK's resources suggests that she will mostly export manufactured goods and also render services to other countries.

	Imports		Exports	
	£m	%	£m	%
Food, beverages and tobacco	17,540	9.5	11,389	6.8
Crude materials	6,306	3.4	2,621	1.5
Fuels (oil, coal, gas electricity)	7,060	3.8	11,030	6.6
Chemicals	18,540	10.0	22,360	13.3
Manufactured goods	132,540	71.9	118,505	70.5
Miscellaneous (postal packages; animal and vegetable oils; commodities not classified elsewhere)	2,319	1.3	2,136	1.3
	184,305	100	168,041	100

Table 26.2 The UK's imports and exports 1996 (by value)

Source: Annual Abstract of Statistics.

Similarly she will import food, tropical products, together with raw materials, minerals and chemicals in which she is deficient.

Table 26.2 requires some clarification. Food is forming a decreasing proportion of UK imports, partly because increased home production now supplies two-thirds of her requirements, and partly because spending on food takes a smaller percentage of an increasing income.

What may appear more remarkable, however, is the preponderance of trade in manufactured goods as regards both exports (82 per cent) and imports (78 per cent). Indeed such trade is increasing in importance. The main reason is that specialisation is no longer confined to either manufacturing or to agriculture. Now, even within manufacturing, different countries concentrate on producing particular goods or even components. Thus, in cars the Mercedes appeals to certain people in the UK, while the Rolls Royce and Jaguar may be wanted in Germany. Such specialisation can give rise to considerable trade between countries which have reached the same stage of industrial development (see also Figure 26.1).

A further reason is that one-third of manufactured goods consists of semi-manufactures because basic material producers are now adding value by processing themselves e.g. in chemicals, textiles, iron and steel, and non-ferrous metals. Indeed since 1983 the UK has been net importer in value of manufactured goods.

(c) The countries with which the UK trades

Again an analysis of the UK's resources compared with those of other countries suggests that she will import goods from countries having relatively much agricultural land, enjoying a tropical or semi-tropical climate or possessing the minerals and chemicals which she herself lacks. Where these countries need the UK's manufactured goods, as in the case of Norway, imports from them can be paid for directly by the export of such goods as timber. But where the country, like

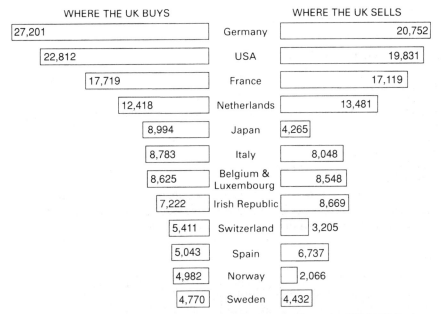

WHERE THE UK BUYS		WHERE THE UK SELLS
27,201	Germany	20,752
22,812	USA	19,831
17,719	France	17,119
12,418	Netherlands	13,481
8,994	Japan	4,265
8,783	Italy	8,048
8,625	Belgium & Luxembourg	8,548
7,222	Irish Republic	8,669
5,411	Switzerland	3,205
5,043	Spain	6,737
4,982	Norway	2,066
4,770	Sweden	4,432

Figure 26.1   The principal exporters to and importers from the UK, 1996 (£m)

Table 26.3   Pecentage distribution of the UK's trade between the EU and the rest of the world,1982 and 1996

	Imports %		Exports %	
	1982	1996	1982	1996
EU	44.3	54.4	41.6	57.3
Rest of the world	55.7	45.6	58.4	42.7
Total	100	100	100	100

Source: Annual Abstract of Statistics.

the USA, does not require manufactured goods, imports have to be paid for indirectly. This is achieved through triangular or multilateral trade. Thus Malaysia exports tin to the USA, but the latter sends comparatively little to them directly in exchange. Instead she exports such goods as cotton, tobacco and machinery to the UK, which in return settles the USA's bill from Malaysia by sending Malaysia manufactured goods.

(d) The UK's trade with the EU

The UK's trade with members of the EU compared with that of the rest of the world is increasing (Table 26.3). In fact, of the UK's twelve main trading countries, nine are EU members (Figure 26.1).

26.5 Free trade and protection

(a) Controlling international trade

Our earlier analysis suggests that trade should be as free as possible, for only then can maximum specialisation according to the law of comparative advantage take place. In practice, however, all countries follow policies which, to varying degrees, prevent goods from moving freely in response to differences in relative prices. Methods vary.

(i) Customs duties

Customs duties, e.g. the common external tariffs of the EU, are both revenue-raising and protective. They become protective when the imported good bears a higher rate of tax than the similar home-produced good.

(ii) Subsidies

While countries which subscribe to the General Agreement on Tariffs and Trade (GATT) cannot follow a policy of 'dumping' exports by giving direct subsidies, the volume and pattern of international trade may be influenced indirectly by other means, e.g. government assistance to the shipbuilding industry. Less obviously, welfare benefits, e.g. child benefits and income supplements which keep down labour costs, may give one country a price advantage over another.

(iii) Quotas

If demand is inelastic, the increase in price resulting from a customs duty will have little effect on the quantity imported. Thus, to restrict imports of a good to a definite quantity, quotas must be imposed.

Compared with duties, quotas have two main disadvantages: (1) As a result of the artificial shortage of supply, the price may be increased by the foreign supplier or by the importer. Hence unless the government also introduces price control, they gain at the expense of consumers (2) Since quotas are usually based on a firm's past imports, the efficient firm finds it difficult to expand.

To avoid having formal quotas imposed, 'voluntary export restraints' may be agreed (e.g. on the import of Japanese cars to the UK).

(iv) Currency control

A tighter check on the amount spent on imported goods can be achieved if quotas are fixed in terms of foreign currency. This necessitates some form of exchange control (see p. 353). All earnings of foreign currency or claims to foreign currency have to be handed over to the government and goods can be imported only under licence. Thus the government, not the free market, decides the priorities for imports.

(v) Physical controls

A complete ban – an embargo – may be placed on the import or export of certain goods. Thus narcotics cannot be imported, while the export of certain high technology goods and works of art require a licence. Similarly, imposing strict technical standards for certain goods (e.g. milk) and regulating the importation of live animals (e.g. cattle, dogs and parrots) make trade more difficult.

(vi) Devices which divert trade

These include: 'Buy British' campaigns, Queen's Awards for Exporting, bilateral arrangements making import purchases dependent on the exporter buying goods of equal value from the importer, quarantine and health regulations and voluntary export restraints.

(b) Reasons for government control of international trade

In general, trade is controlled because governments think and act nationally rather than internationally. Although people as a whole lose when trade is restricted, those of a particular country may gain.

Many reasons are put forward to justify control. Occasionally they have some logical justification; more usually they stem from a narrow interest seeking to gain advantages. We can examine the arguments, therefore, under three main headings: (i) those based on strategic, political, social, and moral grounds; (ii) those having some economic basis; (iii) those depending on shallow economic thinking.

(i) Non-economic arguments

(1) *To encourage the production of a good of strategic importance.* Where a nation is dependent on another for a good of strategic importance, there is a danger of its supply being cut off in the event of war. Thus one argument for subsidising shipbuilding and aircraft production in the UK is to ensure the survival of plant and skilled labour.

(2) *To foster closer political ties.* As a member of the EU, Britain must impose a common external tariff as part of a movement towards political as well as economic unity.

(3) *To support political objectives.* Trade can be a weapon of foreign policy, e.g. the USA will not trade with Cuba because it disapproves of its communist policies.

(4) *To promote social policies.* Although in the past Britain has subsidised her agriculture mainly for strategic reasons, today the purposes are basically social – to avoid depression in rural districts.

(ii) Economic arguments having some justification

(1) *To raise revenue.*

(2) *To improve the terms of trade.* The incidence of a tax is shared between producer and consumer according to the relative elasticities of supply and demand (see p. 321). A government, therefore, can levy a tax on an imported good to improve the terms of trade if demand for the good is more elastic than the supply, for the increase in price is borne mainly by the producer, while the government has the proceeds of the tax. In practice this requires that: (i) the producing country has no alternative markets to which supplies can be easily

diverted; (ii) her factors of production have few alternative uses; (iii) the demand for the exports of the country imposing the tariff must be unaffected by the loss of income suffered by countries who now find their sales abroad reduced.

(3) *To protect an 'infant industry'.* It may be possible to establish an industry in a country if, during its infancy, it is given protection from well-established competitors which are already producing on a large scale. Britain's car industry, for instance, benefited from such protection.

In practice, industries tend to rely on this protection, so that tariffs are never withdrawn; for example, American duties on manufactured goods imposed in the eighteenth century still persist today. Moreover, industries are often encouraged which without protection would have no chance of survival. This leads to maldistribution of a country's resources.

(4) *To enable an industry to decline gradually.* Fundamental changes in demand for a good may severely hit an industry. Such, for instance, was the fate of the British cotton industry in 1975. Restrictions on imports can cushion the shock, but in practice many industries do not make use of the breathing space to restructure.

(5) *To correct a temporary balance-of-payments disequilibrium.* A temporary drain on gold and foreign currency reserves may be halted by controlling imports. But if the depletion of the reserves is due to fundamental and lasting causes, other measures should be used (see Chapter 28).

(6) *To prevent 'dumping'.* Goods may be sold abroad at a lower price than on the home market. This may be possible because: (i) producers are given export subsidies; (ii) discriminating monopoly is possible (see p. 147); or (iii) it enables the producer to obtain the advantages of decreasing costs. People in the importing country benefit directly from the lower prices. If, however, the exporter is trying to obtain a monopoly position which he can exploit once home producers have been driven out, there is a case for protecting the home market.

(iii) Economic arguments having little validity

(1) *To retaliate against tariffs of another country.* The threat of a retaliatory tariff may be used to influence another country to change its restrictive policy. Thus in 1999 the USA imposed levies on certain EU exports because of preferences afforded by the EU to Windward Islands' bananas. Such measures are usually ineffective, for countries often retaliate by imposing still higher duties, with everybody losing.

(2) *To maintain home employment in a period of depression.* Countries may place restrictions on imports to promote employment in the manufacture of home-produced goods. The difficulty is that other countries retaliate, thereby leading to an all-round contraction in world trade. GATT was set up to prevent this from happening (see p. 339).

(3) *To protect home industries from 'unfair' foreign competition.* The demand that British workers must be protected from competition by cheap, 'sweated' foreign labour usually comes from the industry facing competition. The argument, however, has little economic justification. First, it runs counter to the principle that a country should specialise where it has the greatest advantage. That advantage may be cheap labour. Second, low wages do not necessarily

denote low labour costs. Wages may be low because labour is inefficient through low productivity. What is really significant is the wage-cost per unit of output. Thus the USA can export manufactured goods to the UK even though her labour is the most highly paid in the world. The threatened industry can compete by improving productivity to reduce wage-cost per unit. Third, a tax on the goods of a poor country merely makes the country poorer and its labour cheaper. The way to raise wages (and the price of the good produced) is to increase demand in foreign markets. Indeed, if imports from poor countries are restricted, other help has to be given. They prefer 'trade to aid'. Fourth, protection, by reducing the income of the poorer countries, means that they have less to spend on Britain's exports. Fifth, the policy may lead to retaliation or aggressive competition elsewhere, thereby making it more difficult for the protecting country to sell abroad. One reason why Japan captured many of Britain's foreign markets for cotton goods was that her sales to Britain were restricted by protective barriers. Last, restrictions on competitive imports may allow home firms to raise their prices. If wage increases result, exports of goods generally could fall through higher prices.

(c) Conclusions

While restriction of trade tends to lower living standards, there may be benefits – economic, political and social. Thus protection may be given to an industry because home workers cannot adjust quickly to other occupations or industries. Usually, however, such economic gains are doubtful. Others cannot be measured, and it has to be left to politicians to decide where the balance of advantage lies. It must, however, always be remembered that protection creates vested interests opposed to subsequent removal.

(d) The General Agreement on Tariffs and Trade (GATT) and the World Trade Organisation (WTO)

The General Agreement on Tariffs and Trade, established in 1947, has three major objectives: (i) to reduce existing trade barriers; (ii) to eliminate discrimination in international trade; and (iii) to prevent the establishment of further trade barriers by getting nations to agree to consult one another rather than take unilateral action. It operates as follows.

Member nations meet together periodically to try to agree on a round of tariff reductions. Here the 'most-favoured-nation' principle applies. This means that if one country grants a tariff concession to another it must apply automatically to all the other participating countries. Thus if the EU agrees to reduce tariffs on American automatic vending machines by 5 per cent in exchange for a 5 per cent reduction in the American tariff on EU man-made fibres, then both concessions must be extended to every other member of GATT. This principle of non-discrimination also means that bilateral agreements and retaliatory tariffs against another country are out of harmony with GATT.

Today (1999) there are over 120 member nations, accounting between them for over nine-tenths of world trade. Through the organisation, a progressive reduction in existing tariffs has been achieved, and the principle has been established that problems of international trade should be settled by cooperative discussion rather than by independent unilateral action. But difficulties have arisen.

(i) The principle of reciprocity means that low-tariff countries have to begin from an inferior bargaining position, and the concessions they can make are thus limited. Such countries may, therefore, prefer a low-tariff regional arrangement, such as the EU.

(ii) In certain circumstances, the 'most-favoured-nation' principle may deter a country from making a tariff reduction to another country for the simple reason that it has to be applied to all.

(iii) The Articles of the Agreement have had to be relaxed to allow for special circumstances – balance-of-payments difficulties, protection of agriculture, the establishment of 'infant' industries in less-developed countries, and the discriminatory character of the EU.

(iv) While the GATT has been successful in dealing with tariffs and many physical barriers, it has been by-passed by the new forms of protection – voluntary export restraints, orderly marketing arrangements, subsidies for special groups of exports, and trading requirements as conditions for overseas investment.

(e) The Uruguay Round

The trade liberalisation procedure is through 'rounds' which bring together contracting parties. The Uruguay Round, the eighth, covered a period of hard bargaining between 1986 and 1994. The main points agreed were:

(i) Progressive tariff reductions of about 40 per cent to be made over a period of 10 years on 95 per cent of goods traded, with agreement not to raise them again.

(ii) Agriculture was included for the first time with a 36 per cent reduction in tariffs and a cut in subsidies.

(iii) Arrangements were made for opening up markets to firms supplying services. This should be of particular benefit to the UK.

(iv) Multilateral rules governing trade-related intellectual property rights (patents, copyrights, trade marks and design rights) were established.

In 1995 a World Trade Organisation (WTO) was set up as a permanent institution to monitor the observance of the extensive agreements covered. It is estimated that by 2005 these will have provided benefits to world trade amounting to some £330 billion and a 2 per cent increase in the UK's GDP. The WTO has now taken over GATT's responsibility for initiating progressive tariff reductions.

QUESTIONS

1 Suggest eight important differences between international trade and trade within a country.

2 Suggest five reasons why labour is less mobile internationally than within its own boundaries.

3 Given the following production figures, and assuming (a) constant rates of production possibility, (b) two small cars exchange for one large car; (c) each country has divided given factors equally between large and small cars, show how specialisation would benefit both the UK and the USA.

	Large cars	Small cars
UK	100	1,000
USA	700	1,200

4 What special advantage applies to tariff cuts secured under the World Trade Organisation (WTO)?

■ ✓ **27** Foreign currency exchange rates

Objectives

1 To show how currency exchange rates between countries are determined in an international market
2 To indicate the main factors determining the demand for/supply of foreign currency

27.1 The determination of exchange rates

(a) Differences in currencies

Normally the exchange of goods internationally is arranged by private traders who, according to relative prices, decide whether it is profitable to export and import goods.

But each country usually has its own currency – the UK (£ sterling), the USA (dollars), Germany (Deutschemarks), France (francs), and so on. This difference is important for two reasons: (a) a rate has to be established at which one currency will exchange for another; (b) sufficient foreign currency has to be obtained to pay for imports. The first will be considered forthwith, the second in the chapter which follows; but neither is independent of the other.

The exchange rate is the amount of foreign currency which can be exchanged for a unit of the domestic currency. But what determines that today £1 sterling obtains approximately 1.60 American dollars, 3.03 German marks, 10.18 French francs, and so on?

(b) The foreign exchange market

The simple answer is that fundamentally the price of the pound sterling, like other prices. is determined by the forces of demand and supply. In this case the market is the 'foreign-exchange market'. It meets in no one place, but consists of all the institutions and persons – banks of all kinds, dealers, and brokers – who are buying and selling foreign currencies. Furthermore, it is a 24-hour-a-day world market with dealers being in constant contact with one another by telecommunications.

Prices of the different currencies are brought into line by *arbitrage operations.*

Assume for simplicity that £1 = $2 and $1 = 2 marks. Then £1 must equal 4 marks. But suppose in London 5 marks can be obtained for the pound. A dealer would buy marks for pounds in London, sell them for dollars in New York, and exchange the dollars for pounds, making 25p profit on the deal. This would not last for long because the world market in foreign exchange is so perfect that the increased demand for marks in London would soon bring the price there into line with the world price.

(c) The nature of demand and supply

Suppose the current rate is £1 = $1.60 (Figure 27.1). Now assume that there is a large increase in the value of UK imports from the USA with no corresponding increase in the UK's dollar export earnings. The dollar thus appreciates in value to 1.58.

It can be seen that an increased demand for dollars by people in Britain is one and the same thing as an increase in the supply of sterling being offered for dollars. An increased demand for dollars may be counteracted by an increased demand for sterling (that is, an increased supply of dollars) by Americans. For instance Americans would want sterling to: (i) pay for the import of goods from Britain; (ii) pay for 'invisibles', e.g. a tour of Britain, government spending on diplomatic staff in Britain; (iii) move capital into Britain

27.2 What are the main underlying influences on the demand for and supply of foreign currency?

So far we have merely indicated the items for which foreign currency will be demanded or supplied. But what are the economic forces which determine how large each of these items will be?

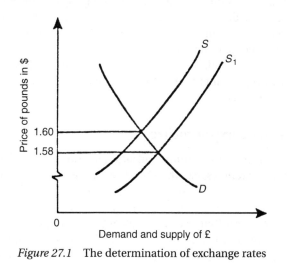

Figure 27.1   The determination of exchange rates

(a) Relative prices

The chief factor affecting trade, both visible and invisible, is the price of home-produced goods as compared with the price of similar goods abroad. If, for example, American prices are high, Americans will wish to import cheaper British goods, whereas the British will prefer home-produced goods to American. The increased demand for sterling will so raise the value of the pound sterling that eventually the prices of British goods are in line with those of the 'high-cost' American producer.

(b) The rate of interest

Short-term capital moves from one country to another as changes take place in the rate of interest being offered by each. The government can therefore vary interest rates to attract or repel foreign capital as it sees fit.

(c) Speculation on the future movements of the exchange rate

Inflation in a country will be interpreted by foreign holders of its currency as being likely to lead eventually to a fall in the external value of the currency. Selling of the currency follows, thereby helping to bring about the fulfilment of those expectations!

(d) Relative money incomes

When a country's money income expands, its demand for imports increases. Potential exports also tend to be diverted to the home market.

(e) Long-term investment prospects

Americans can invest in the UK either by buying government bonds or equities of UK companies, or directly by building factories in the UK. The chief factor influencing such investment decisions is how the prospective yield compares with that which could be obtained elsewhere.

Political risks, e.g. of default on loans, or possible changes in government policy, e.g. of a swingeing increase in corporation tax, have also to be assessed by those investing overseas.

(f) Government expenditure

Military expenditure and economic aid abroad now provide large sources of supply of certain currencies, e.g. the American dollar and the pound sterling, to foreigners.

We conclude, therefore, that exchange rates are not dependent on any single factor, Furthermore, as we shall see (p. 370), while a government may operate to maintain its own preferred short-term rate, eventually the market rate will prevail. The only safe generalisation is that the value of a currency depends upon all the forces which give rise to the purchase or sale of that currency in the foreign-exchange market.

QUESTIONS

1 Suppose that the exchange rates between sterling, dollars and francs are temporarily: £1 = $2; $2 = 11 francs; £1 = 12 francs. A man has £1,000 in sterling
   (a) Can he increase his sterling assets by 'playing the market'?
   (b) What are arbitrage operations?
   (c) Do arbitrage operations only take place in the foreign exchange market?

2 The demand for and supply of sterling in the foreign exchange market on a certain day are as follows:

Price of sterling in US dollars	1.44	1.46	1.48	1.50	1.52	1.54	1.56	1.58
£m demanded per day	30	25	21	18	15	13	11	10
£m supplied per day	9	12	15	18	22	26	32	38

   (a) What will be the equilibrium exchange rate?
   (b) Suppose that the UK's monthly trade returns are published on the following day, and show a disturbing increase in the visible deficit. Demand for sterling decreases by £6m at *all* prices. Other things being equal, what will be the effect on the exchange rate in a free market?
   (c) Suppose it is desired to keep the £ sterling within the limits of $1.48–1.52. What action will the authorities take if:
       (i) the rate is approaching the upper limit?
       (ii) the rate is approaching the lower limit?
   (d) What are the effects of the high-pegged rate?
   (e) Explain the term 'an overvalued pound'.
   (f) What happened as a result of sterling joining the ERM at an overvalued £1 = 2.95 DM?

■ ⊻ **28** Balance-of-payments stability

Objectives

1 To show how foreign currency is earned by both visible trade and invisible trade (mostly services)
2 To describe the Balance of Payments accounts
3 To show how 'balance' is achieved through the relationship between the current balance and capital asset movements
4 To analyse policies for maintaining a satisfactory long-term balance of payments

28.1 The nature of imports and exports

(a) Paying for imports

We can approach the question of how imports are paid for by considering the purchases made by a housewife, Mrs Jones. Each week she buys a variety of goods. However, there are at least seven sources from which she could obtain the money to pay for them.

The most usual is her husband's weekly earnings, and Mrs Jones pays the shopkeeper as she collects her goods. But what Mrs Jones is really doing is exchanging the goods which Mr Jones has specialised in producing for the other goods needed. Thus, if Mr Jones is a tailor, the money from the suits he sells buys Mrs Jones the goods she needs. In addition, money is often earned by performing a service. Thus Mrs Jones herself may earn wages by working for the shopkeeper. Also interest on savings may provide some current income. Provided that all the weekly expenses are met out of this combined weekly income, we should say that the Jones family was 'paying its way'.

It might happen, however, that Mrs Jones's expenditure was not covered by the current weekly income. This might occur, for instance, because she bought a costly good, such as a dish-washer. In such circumstances, she would have to raise the money from other sources. First, she could draw on her savings. Second, she could sell household goods, such as the piano or the TV set, for which she had a less urgent need. Third, she might be able to borrow the money from a friend or, what amounts to the same thing, ask the shopkeeper to forgo being paid for the time being. Finally, if she were extremely fortunate, she might be able to obtain a gift of money, say from a doting father. Such methods of payment would be fairly satisfactory for a good which is in use over a long period, provided that her savings were gradually replenished, or the assets sold were replaced by others of equal value, or the loan was repaid during the lifetime of the good. Otherwise Mrs Jones would not be paying her way. If over-spending continued, her savings would eventually run out, her home would be sold up, and she would be unable to obtain any more loans or credit from the shopkeeper.

Broadly speaking, a nation trading with other nations is in exactly the same position. The same alternatives are open to it in paying for imports. The main source is receipts from current exports. Figure 28.1 shows how exports earn foreign currency. Importing and exporting are arranged by firms, and payments are arranged through banks, who exchange the currency of one country for the currency of another *provided that they have the necessary reserves of that currency*. Such reserves are earned by customers who export to foreign countries.

Let us assume that £1 sterling exchanges for $1.60 and that there are no currency restrictions. Suppose a British merchant, *X*, wishes to import cotton from *A* in the USA to the value of £100,000. The American exporter requires payment in dollars, for all his payments, e.g. his workers' wages, have to be made in dollars. Hence the importer goes to his bank, pays in £100,000 and arranges a 'documentary credit'. The bank contacts its branch in New York, authorising it to make the equivalent dollar payment to *A* on production of the necessary documents, e.g. the bill of lading (see p. 204). (Most banks have branches in foreign capitals; if not, they engage local banks to act for them). But how is it that the branch has dollars available to honour the draft?

We can see the answer if we imagine that another British firm, *Y*, has sold £100,000 worth of sports car to an importer, *B*, in the USA. This firm wants payment in £ sterling. Hence the American importer of the car pays $160,000 into his bank in the USA, and the same procedure follows. It is obvious that the two transactions – buying cotton from the USA and selling sports cars to the USA –

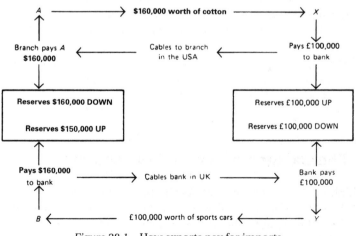

Figure 28.1   How exports pay for imports

balance each other. The British bank has had to pay out dollars, the American bank sterling. The British bank has receive sterling, the American bank dollars. If the two get together, their requirements match. (In practice it is more likely that they would meet their needs through the foreign-exchange market.) The dollars to pay for the cotton are obtained by selling the sports cars, and vice versa. In short, exports pay for imports.

(b) 'Exports' in the wider sense

In this connection the term 'exports' needs qualification. In the same way that Mrs Jones received payment for her services to the shopkeeper, so a nation may receive payment not only for goods but also for services rendered to other countries. Goods exported are termed 'visible exports' because they can be seen and recorded as they cross frontiers. But services performed for people of other countries cannot be seen and recorded; they are therefore called 'invisible exports'. Nevertheless, since services involve payments by persons from abroad, they are exports.

The main sources of invisible earnings and payments are:

(i) *Government expenditure abroad*, e.g. on overseas garrisons, diplomatic services, overseas aid.
(ii) *Shipping services*, e.g. an American cruising in the *Queen Elizabeth II* or shipping exports in a British merchantman.
(iii) *Civil aviation*, e.g. a German flying British Airways.
(iv) *Travel*, e.g. sterling required by an American tourist for spending on a visit to London.
(v) *Financial services*, e.g. earnings of the City of London.
(vi) *Other services*, e.g. royalties earned on books and records, income from the transactions of overseas oil companies which ship direct from wells and refineries abroad to other countries.
(vii) *Interest, profits and dividends from overseas investments.*
(viii) *Government transfers*, e.g. net contribution to the EU.
(ix) *Private transfers*, e.g. remittances to relatives abroad.

Payments for any of the above transactions involve changing into another country's currency. Thus they represent 'imports' to the paying country and 'exports' to the receiving country.

28.2 The balance-of-payments accounts

Most countries give an account each year of their monetary transactions with the rest of the world. The accounts presented are known as 'the balance of payments'. The balance of payments for the UK for the year ended 31 December 1996 is given in Table 28.1

Table 28.1 The balance of payments of the UK, 1996 (£m)

CURRENT ACCOUNT	
Visible trade	
Exports (fob)	+166,340
Imports (fob)	−178,938
Visible balance	−12,598
Invisibles (net)	
Government	−2,377
Sea transport	−505
Civil aviation	−725
Travel	−3,895
Financial and other services	+14,644
Investment income	+9,652
Government and private transfers	−4,631
Invisible balance	+12,163
CURRENT BALANCE	−435
FINANCIAL ACCOUNT	
Transactions in external assests and liabilities:	
Investment abroad (net)	−40,792
Borrowing abroad (net)	+36,628
Official reserves, addition to	+1,966
TOTAL	−2,198
Balancing item	+2,633
CAPITAL BALANCE	+435

Source: Annual Abstract of Statistics.

(a) The current account

The current account shows, on the one hand, the foreign currency which has been *spent* on *imported goods* and *invisibles* in the course of the year, and, on the other, the foreign currency which has been *earned* by *exporting goods* and *invisibles*.

That part of the current account which shows the payments for just the goods exported and imported is known as the *visible balance* (formerly the *balance of trade*). Where the value of goods exported exceeds the value of goods imported, we say that there is a favourable visible balance. If the opposite occurs, the visible balance is 'unfavourable'. Too much, however, must not be read into the terms 'favourable' and 'unfavourable'. In the first place, we have to know the reasons for the unfavourable balance. It may be brought about, for instance, by an increased demand for raw materials and components as a country moves out of a recession. These will later be exported as manufactured goods. Or a less developed country may receive more aid, enabling her to import capital goods. Whereas the value of these is shown as 'imports', 'aid' will appear in the Financial Account. Secondly, a favourable or unfavourable visible balance can be reversed when the invisibles are taken into account.

When we add to the visible balance, payments and income on the invisible items, we have what is known as the *current balance*.

There is no special reason why earnings from goods and invisibles exported between 1 January ad 31 December in any one year should equal expenditure on the goods and invisibles imported during that period. In fact, it would be an extraordinary coincidence if they did so. How often does what you earn during the week tally *exactly* with what you spend?

The current account is therefore likely to show a difference between earnings and expenditure. When the *value* of goods and invisibles exported exceeds the *value* of goods and invisibles imported, we say that there is a surplus current balance; when the reverse occurs, we say that there is a deficit current balance. The importance of the current balance is that it shows how far a country is paying its way.

However, the current account is only part of the statement covering a nation's overseas financial transactions. Capital flows must also be scrutinised. As we shall see, a current deficit need cause no alarm if it is covered by borrowing which will be put to a productive use. On the other hand, a current surplus may be insufficient to offset a heavy drain on the reserves through the outward movement of short- and long-term capital. The balance-of-payments statement must be examined as a whole.

(b) The financial account

The *financial account* sets out the currency flow generated by current account balances and capital movements.

If the current-account transactions were a country's only dealings with the world, the balance-of-payments accounts would be quite simple. A surplus of £100 million, for example, would add that amount to the reserves or allow the country to invest that amount overseas or to pay off short-term borrowings from the International Monetary Fund (IMF) or other foreign creditors. A deficit of £100 million would reduce the reserves by that amount or have to be financed by disinvestment or short-term borrowing abroad.

But *capital* flows also affect a country's ability to build up reserves or to pay off debts. Thus investment by private persons resident in the UK in factories or plant overseas (whether directly or by the purchase of shares), or a loan by the British government to a less-developed country, leads to an outflow of capital and the spending of foreign currency (negative sign in the accounts). Similarly, investment in the UK by persons overseas, or borrowing abroad by the British government, local authorities, or companies, leads to an inflow of foreign capital and the receipt of foreign currency (+ sign).

Whereas the current account covers *income* earning and spending in the course of the year, 'transactions in external assets and liabilities' show the movement of *capital* in and out of the country. This capital may be short- or long-term.

Short-term capital movements arise from the transfer of liquid funds to and from Britain. Because London is a world financial market centre, foreigners hold bank balances or short-term bills there. These short-term funds can move quickly from country to country to take advantage of higher interest rates or to guard against an exchange rate depreciation. They are thus often referred to as 'hot money'.

Long-term capital investment by British residents in factories or plant over-seas (whether directly or by the purchase of shares), or a loan by the British government (e.g. to a less developed country or an international institution) leads to an outflow of capital. Similarly, investment in the UK by persons overseas or borrowing from abroad by the British government, local authorities, or companies leads to an inflow of foreign capital.

Any movement of capital out of Britain gives rise to a demand for foreign currency; a movement into Britain from abroad leads to the receipt of foreign currency.

No distinction is made between short- and long-term investment in presenting the overall balance of payments. In fact much of Britain's overseas investment is financed by short-term capital borrowed from foreigners, e.g. from the pool of Eurocurrency deposited in London. To the extent that this occurs, there is no net outflow of foreign currency. Britain's overseas investment which is undertaken in order to make a profit is, in fact, like private business ventures. And, just as the shopkeeper borrows from the bank to cover the holding of stocks before Christmas, so the UK borrows to finance investment overseas in factories, plantations, oil wells, nickel-mines, etc.

Thus the UK's balance-of-payments accounts concentrate on what is really significant to Britain – the extent to which currency flows as a whole influence the £ sterling exchange rate and her reserves of gold and foreign currencies.

The balancing item arises as follows. When all recorded capital transactions are added to the current balance, the total never adds up exactly to the amount of foreign currency the country has in fact gained or lost, which is known precisely to the Bank of England. Government spending overseas, for instance, is easier to record exactly than the foreign spending of people taking holidays abroad. Exports, too, may go abroad in December, but payments for them come in the following February.

A 'balancing item' is therefore added to make up the difference between the total value of the transactions recorded and the precise accounts kept by the Bank of England. If the balancing item is '+', it means that more foreign currency has actually come in than the estimates of transactions have indicated. When there is a '−' balancing item, the opposite is the case.

(c) An examination of the UK's balance of payments, 1996

The above explanation can be illustrated by examining the UK's Balance of Payments for 1996. Imports exceeded exports; there was a visible balance deficit of £12,598 million. On invisibles, the UK had a favourable balance of £12,163 million. The overall deficit on the Current Balance was thus £435 million.

In addition to the current account deficit of £435 million, net investment of £40,792 million abroad by Britain had to be covered. This was achieved by net borrowing of £36,628 million, drawing £1,966 million from reserves, and a balancing item of £2,633 million.

28.3 The correction of a balance-of-payments disequilibrium

(a) When do corrective measures become necessary?

Taken as a whole, the balance of payments must always balance. Foreign currency necessary for making payments abroad must have come from somewhere. If a current account deficit is not covered by private borrowing from overseas, there is an outward currency flow which has to come from the gold and foreign currency reserves or official borrowing.

In the short period, a balance-of-payments deficit may not be serious. It could easily happen that just prior to 31 December, imports of raw materials were running at a high rate. Later, when the goods manufactured from these raw materials are sold abroad, the reserves will be replenished. Reserves of gold and foreign currencies are held for this very purpose – to provide a 'cushion' when current earnings and private borrowing are temporarily insufficient to cover payments abroad.

Alternatively, a less developed country may run an adverse current balance for a number of years. The deficit is covered by borrowing, both private and official. Loans are used to buy capital equipment to produce export goods the sale of which, it is estimated, will cover the interest due and the eventual repayment of the loan.

But the situation is different when year after year a country is running a current balance deficit and there is little likelihood of being able to reverse the trend. This disequilibrium is then said to be of a 'fundamental nature'. If not corrected, foreign creditors will refuse to lend for they doubt whether the spendthrift will ever be in a position to repay. Action has, therefore, to be taken to remedy the situation.

(b) A broad analysis of the problem

A first-aid measure is for the authorities to raise the short-term rate of interest in order to reverse the outward flow of short-term capital. Furthermore, reserves could be strengthened by borrowing from other central banks and the IMF (see p. 358). This would help to restore confidence in the currency.

Eventually, however, exports must be increased in value and/or imports decreased in value. Two basic policies can be followed: (1) reducing expenditure on imports by deflation; (2) switching expenditure, so that foreigners spend more on British exports and Britons spend less on imports in favour of home-produced goods. Both policies can be followed simultaneously (though with a different emphasis on each), but to clarify the issues it is better to consider them separately.

28.4 Reducing expenditure on imports: deflation

A government may adopt specific measures to promote exports, e.g. the British government guaranteeing payment through the Export Credits Guarantee Department. But these take time and in any case are only marginal in effect. The main thrust has to be directed to reducing spending on imports through physical controls and/or the deflation of home income.

(a) Physical controls

Physical controls may be exercised by import duties, quotas and exchange control.

Import duties and quotas may be levied to increase the price of imports. But if demand is inelastic, imports will not be greatly discouraged nor expenditure on them in terms of foreign currency greatly decreased. Sometimes, therefore, an import quota in terms of volume is imposed. As a result, however, the advantages of free trade are reduced, while the efficiency of home industry may be impaired by its protection from foreign competition. Moreover, other exporting countries may retaliate.

Exchange control may be introduced to:

(i) limit the amount of foreign currency spent on imports;
(ii) discriminate against those countries whose currencies are 'hard' (that is, cannot easily be earned by exporting to them), and to favour those countries whose currencies are 'soft' (because they buy exports from the country concerned);
(iii) distinguish between essential and non-essential imports;
(iv) control the export of capital.

Exchange control is essential when a country's currency is overvalued – that is, its declared exchange rate is higher than it would be if it were determined by demand and supply on the foreign-exchange market. What this really means is that foreign currencies are valued below the market price – and so they have to be rationed.

Nevertheless, exchange control suffers from many of the disadvantages associated with rationing. Inefficient home firms are protected from foreign competition. Regulations are evaded and 'black markets' in the currencies occur. Many administrators are needed who could be more productively employed elsewhere. Moreover, it can lead to uncertainty in international trade. Countries may find their regular markets closed, while firms cannot plan ahead because of uncertainty as to whether they will be allowed to purchase their raw materials from a hard-currency area. Furthermore, the confidence of foreigners is impaired if any attempt is made to prohibit the movement of their funds out of a country. Finally, when people are prevented from buying in hard-currency countries, it often means that they are forced to purchase dearer or inferior goods elsewhere.

(b) Deflation of home income

Since imports increase as income expands, one way in which the value of imports can be brought into line with that of exports is by reducing income. Figure 28.2 explains.

To simplify we assume an economy with no government spending or taxation, injections consisting of autonomous investment and exports, while leaks of saving and imports are related to income. At the current level of income, Y, there

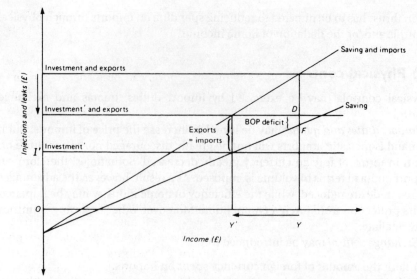

Figure 28.2 Achieving balance-of-payments equilibrium by deflation

is a current balance-of-payments deficit, *DF*. Assuming exports are maintained, this deficit can be elimated by bringing down the level of investment to *I'*, reducing income to *Y'*.

Such a deflationary policy would also tend to put a brake on any rise in home prices. More important, it allows adjustment to take place without altering currency-exchange rates (see below). This has the advantage that it facilitates international trade by removing the uncertainty associated with fluctuating exchange rates when negotiating long-term contracts or making loans.

But there are serious disadvantages. Unless home prices are flexible downwards, a deflationary policy only succeeds at the expense of creating unemployment. Moreover the impact on expenditure on imports is less where these have a low income-elasticity of demand, e.g. essential raw materials and components. Finally a reduction of imports to Britain represents a loss of exports by other countries. Deflationary effects on their economies may result in a reduction in their demand for imports, thereby reducing British exports. In short, deflation is a 'beggar-my-neighbour' policy where the benefit is uncertain even to the deflating country.

28.5 Expenditure-switching by exchange rate depreciation

The merits of a fixed exchange rate is that it facilitates international trade and investment and imposes a discipline on countries to control inflation in order to hold the rate. Its big disadvantage is that a country cannot follow an independent internal monetary policy to avoid unemployment (see p. 374).

An alternative policy is to alter the relative prices of imports and home-produced goods so that foreigners spend more on British exports and British people less on imports, as follows.

Prices of internationally traded goods are composed of (i) the home producer's price and (ii) the exchange rate. Thus British exports can be made more competitive by lowering the rate at which the £ sterling exchanges for foreign currencies. Because fewer units of foreign currency have now to be given up to obtain a pound sterling, foreigners can buy British exports more cheaply. If their elasticity of demand is greater than 1, more revenue will be earned from exports (provided, of course, that supply by British firms can respond to the extra demand). Similarly, imports to Britain now cost more, encouraging people to switch to the relatively cheaper home-produced goods.

Such corrective exchange-rate variations occur automatically through the forces of demand and supply in a freely operating foreign-exchange market. Thus, if country A's exports to B are greater in value than her imports, the demand for A's currency will increase, for importers in B will be wanting it to pay for those imports. Consequently the exchange rate will move in favour of A. Similarly, if A's imports are greater in value than her exports, the exchange rate will move against her.

Where countries maintain an agreed rate of exchange between their currencies (e.g. as in the ERM, p. 374), depreciation takes the form of *devaluation*, a once-for-all reduction in the value of a country's currency by definite government decision as opposed to a continuous fall on the foreign exchange market. But is depreciation/devaluation infallible?

Let us suppose that the UK trades only with the USA and that she has a persistent balance-of-payments deficit. The value of the pound falls from $1.65 to $1.50. Whether such depreciation is successful in reducing the deficit will depend upon the answers to the following questions.

(a) What is the elasticity of demand for exports and imports?

The effect of the depreciation will be to make British exports cheaper in terms of dollars to the American buyer and imports from America dearer in terms of pounds to the British buyer.

A British good formerly selling in the USA for $1.65 need now cost only $1.50. This fall in price should lead to more British goods being demanded, and if elasticity of demand is greater than unity, more dollars will be earned.

Similarly, an American good worth $1.65 formerly cost the British buyer £1. After the depreciation, the price will rise to £1.10. But will this mean that we have to spend more *dollars* on our imports? The answer is 'no'. (Suppose that you are on a camping holiday in the USA and that the pound is devalued. Will your bread, camp site, etc. change in price?) The worst possible situation is when demand for imports is absolutely inelastic; then the same quantity of imports will be demanded and the same amount of dollars spent on them. Otherwise there will be some contraction of demand (because the price in terms of pounds has risen) and then expenditure in dollars will fall.

The two elasticities of demand for exports and imports must be considered together. Even if the demand for imports is absolutely inelastic (so that the same amount of foreign currency is spent on them), the balance of payments will not deteriorate provided that there is a gain of foreign currency from an increased demand for exports.

What in the real world are these elasticities likely to be for the UK? Demand for imports is likely to be fairly inelastic, consisting, for instance, of raw-materials and essential components. Indeed, if her exports expand, demand for these will increase. Offsetting this is a likely fall in British demand for luxuries and foreign travel on account of the greater cost, home-produced goods and holidays now being more competitive.

On the other hand, the demand for British exports as a whole is probably elastic. Not only could she undersell exporting competitors, e.g. in aero engines or electrical equipment, but the lower export price resulting from the depreciation would convert what were formerly 'potential exports' into real exports. Moreover, such items as tourism are likely to have a highly elastic demand. But it must be remembered that the price of exported goods will not fall by the entire amount of the depreciation. Their home price will rise when they are made from imported raw materials or components.

(b) What is the elasticity of supply of exports?

It is on the supply side that the greatest obstacles to a successful depreciation are likely to be encountered. The fall in the price of exports will probably lead to an expansion of demand, but this will provide no lasting cost advantage if exports cannot be increased without the home price rising. Here the reaction of labour to the effects of depreciation is crucial. The increase in the cost of imports raises the cost of living. There is thus a strong temptation to demand wage increases which could soon wipe out Britain's cost advantage and further depreciation would occur.

It should be noted, however, that where demand for British exports is inelastic, then inelasticity of supply may not be detrimental. The exporter can maintain his price *in terms of foreign currency* to foreign importers, and British earnings of foreign currency may not fall.

(c) What is the elasticity of supply of imports?

If foreigners are dependent on the British market, and supply is inelastic, then they may be willing to reduce their prices. This may reduce Britain's expenditure of foreign currency, although in volume imports are almost as great.

(d) What is the nature of British and American investments with each other?

Suppose British investments in the USA are mostly in the form of shares in companies there. Profits will be earned in dollars and so there will be no loss of foreign currency after depreciation.

On the other hand, if American investments in the UK are in stock with interest fixed in sterling, the USA will lose by depreciation of the pound for she gets fewer dollars than formerly in invisible earnings.

(e) Will countries fear further depreciation?

Depreciation reduces the value of sterling securities held by foreigners, including the sterling balances held in London. In the first place, this may destroy confidence in sterling, undermining London's position as a banking centre. Business is transferred elsewhere, and invisible earnings are lost. Second, unless positive measures are taken to correct the underlying inflation, foreigners will fear further depreciation and so hasten to remove their capital from London, bringing about what they fear.

The above arguments suggest that, for a country like Britain, depreciation provides no escape from dealing with inflation. It may entail a serious deterioration in the terms of trade, a large amount of additional exports having to be given to achieve a small gain in the balance of payments. Indeed, where demand for both imports and exports is highly inelastic or where supply is inelastic, depreciation may cause the balance of payments to deteriorate still further. In this case, a country has to resort to physical controls to reduce imports.

28.6 Managed flexibility

While the system of floating exchange rates avoids deflation of incomes and thus increased unemployment at home, it has disadvantages. Apart from the fact that it introduces uncertainty into international trade, the prices of imported food-stuffs and raw materials are raised for the depreciating country, thereby adding to the cost of living and leading to claims for wage increases.

Thus the UK has, in the past, adopted different arrangements aimed at stabilising the £ sterling exchange rate – adhering to a 'gold standard', setting up the Exchange Equalisation Account, agreeing to a system of 'managed flexibility' according with International Monetary Fund rules and, more recently, by joining the EC's Exchange Rate Mechanism (ERM).

But in each case deflationary pressures have led to a reversion to the floating of the £ sterling on the foreign exchange market (see also p. 370).

(a) The exchange equalisation account

When Britain left the gold standard in 1931 for a policy of flexible exchange rates, to reduce fluctuations in the exchange rate brought about by speculative short-term capital movements, the government set up the Exchange Equalisation Account.

The Account operates by the simple application of the laws of price. It has a stock of gold and foreign currencies (mostly borrowed against Treasury bills), and this stock is either replenished or offered on the market according to whether short-term capital is moving into or out of London. For instance, a movement of capital into London from the USA would increase the demand for the £ sterling and drive up its price; the Account can prevent this rise by offering pounds in exchange for dollars (see Figure 27.1). On the other hand, if there were a movement of capital out of London, the Account would offer dollars in exchange for pounds, thereby reducing its stock of dollars and increasing its holding of pounds.

The knowledge that such an Account exists to even out exchange fluctuations has done much to prevent speculation in the value of the pound. Provided it has adequate reserves of foreign currency, the Account can allow that value to appreciate or depreciate, and this it continues to do although the UK has no declared rate with the ERM.

(b) The International Monetary Fund (IMF)

In an attempt to stabilise the exchange value of countries' currencies, the Bretton Woods Conference of 1944 established the International Monetary Fund (IMF) and the International Bank for Reconstruction and Development (IBRD, the 'World Bank'). Whereas the IMF makes short-term funds available to help countries in economic difficulties, the World Bank provides long-term finance for reconstruction and development – the building of roads, irrigation schemes, power stations, etc. – especially in the less developed countries.

A system of 'managed flexibility' was operated through the IMF. Each member country agreed to maintain free convertibility of its currency at an agreed rate and contribute its quota of currency to a pool held by the IMF. From these reserves, the IMF could make foreign currency available to a country running a short-term balance of payments deficit. Should this balance-of-payments disequilibrium prove to be 'fundamental', devaluation of the country's currency was possible under agreed rules.

This is basically the mechanism that operated for members of the ERM prior to the inauguration of a single currency on 1 January 1999.

The Bretton Woods agreement worked tolerably well for twenty-five years, but eventually ceased to operate as intended because the pressure of exchange adjustment fell almost entirely on debtor nations (who were forced to devalue) rather than on creditor nations (who could have eased part of the burden by revaluing).

Today, with most countries allowing their currencies to float, the IMF's function of providing finance from its reserves to support a declared exchange rate, has declined. Furthermore, for the major nations, such bridging finance can be obtained through the private capital markets which, by being international, can marry any excess or deficiency of funds. For the poorer nations, the IMF's approval of their schemes assists in their obtaining the necessary capital.

On the other hand, the increasing interdependence of the world economy has enhanced the importance of the fund's role of co-ordinating economic policies worldwide and, in the face of wide spread economic difficulties, can act as a 'lender of last resort' and marshall funds with the aim of staving off depression worldwide. Thus in 1998 such assistance was given to Russia, Indonesia, Malaysia and Thailand who were facing serious financial difficulties.

QUESTIONS

1 What do we mean by a 'foreign currency payment' to the UK?

2 What are the two main senses in which the balance of payments always balances?

3 From the following information, (a) compile a balance of payments; (b) give the visible balance (the balance of trade); (c) calculate the deficit or surplus on current account; (d) give net loss/addition to the official reserves.

Summary of financial transaction of country X with
the rest of the world, 1999
(£ million)

Exports	1529
Imports	1813
Invisible receipts	772
Invisible payments	158
Loans to foreign governments	96
Investment overseas	131
Investment by foreigners in X	146
Addition to short-term balances	97
Aid given abroad	40

4 How is inflation likely to affect a country's balance-of-payments (a) current account (b) capital account (c) exchange rate?

5 Give three reasons why home prices are slow to fall when a country deflates its income.

6 What is the main disadvantage of maintaining:
   (a) a system of rigid fixed exchange rates?
   (b) internal price stability, with freely fluctuating exchange rates?
   (c) managed flexibility by international agreement under the IMF?

7 State six conditions which would be likely to make exchange depreciation work.

8 Give two reasons why a rise in the value of a country's exports is likely to lead to a rise in the value of her imports.

9 What is the difference between the following terms:
   (a) depreciation; (b) appreciation; (c) devaluation; (d) revaluation?

■ Ṁ **29** The European Union

Objectives

1. To outline the stages of the development of the EU through the European Economic Co-operation (EEC), the Common Market, the European Community, the Single Market and full Economic and Monetary Union (EMU)
2. To consider the advantages to the UK of membership of the EU and the possible difficulties arising
3. To analyse the UK's position regarding acceptance of the full conditions of EMU

29.1 Background to the European Union (EU)

(a) Supranational organisations

The two world wars convinced statesmen in Western European countries that some form of political unity was desirable, and in 1949 the Council of Europe was created – the basis, it was hoped, of a European parliament. But organisations with definite functions – the Organisation for European Economic Co-operation (founded in 1948), the North Atlantic Treaty Organisation (1949) and the Western European Union (1954) proved more fruitful than did the Council of Europe with its broad aims.

Although these organisations involved co-operation, they were merely voluntary associations, not federal bodies exercising supranational powers in the interests of members as a whole. The first supranational organisation, the European Coal and Steel Community (ECSC) was formed in 1951 to control the whole of the iron, steel and coal resources of the six member countries – France, West Germany, Italy, Holland, Belgium and Luxembourg. The old divisions created by inward-looking national interests were thus broken down.

The success of the ECSC led to the setting up in 1957 of the Atomic Energy Community (EURATOM), a similar organisation for the peaceful use of atomic energy, and the European Economic Community (EEC), an organisation to develop a 'common market' between the six member countries. All three communities have now been brought within the European Union (EU).

(b) Present membership and proposed expansion

When first offered membership of the EEC, Britain refused to join. Instead, with six other nations, she joined the looser European Free Trade Area (EFTA).

But contrary to Britain's expectations, the EEC grew in strength, while her trade with EEC countries increased at a faster rate than that with EFTA, since her goods were more complementary to their economies. Accordingly the UK joined the EEC in 1973. The other members are now: France, Germany, Italy, Belgium, the Netherlands, Luxembourg, Denmark, the Irish Republic, Greece, Spain, Portugal, Austria, Finland, and Sweden.

It is proposed to accept Poland, Hungary, the Czech Republic, the Slovak Republic, Slovenia and Cyprus as members in about five years' time.

29.2 The institutions of the EU

The essential point to grasp is that the 1957 Treaty of Rome set up a 'Community' with its own form of government and institutions.

There are four main institutions:

(a) The Commission

This is the most important organ of the EU. Its twenty members (two from the UK) serve for four years. Once chosen, however, the members of the Commission act as an independent body in the interests of the Community as a whole, and not as representatives of their national governments. Each commissioner is responsible for a separate area of policy.

The Commission is responsible for formulating policy proposals and legislation, promoting the Community interest, trying to reconcile national viewpoints, implementing Council decisions, and supervising the day-to-day running of community policies. As the guardian of the Treaty, it can also initiate action against member states which do not comply with EU rules.

(b) The Council of Ministers

Each member country sends a cabinet minister (usually according to the subject under discussion) to the Council of Ministers. This is the supreme decision-making body, the Community's 'cabinet'. Its task is to harmonise the Commission's draft Community policies with the wishes of member governments. The Commission's representative in the Council is present by right, but only to discuss, not to vote. Proposals and compromise plans are exchanged between the Council and the Commission. If the Council becomes deadlocked, the Commission reconsiders the proposal in order to accommodate the views of the opposing countries. Over time, 'specialist' Councils have evolved dealing with particular areas of policy, e.g. agriculture, finance, industry, environment.

By the Single European Act of 1987 most single market measures are subject to majority voting with each member's vote weighted roughly according to its population. However, unanimity is still needed for the politically sensitive areas of taxation and the free movement of people. The UK has retained its right to exercise border controls on people entering.

Council meetings are chaired by the member state holding the *Presidency*, which rotates every six months. This carries with it the management of EU business, often as broker in promoting agreement.

The outgoing President also hosts the *European Council*, a summit of heads of government which meets twice a year and sets the agenda for the incoming Presidency. The major problems confronting them are reviewed in an informal and pragmatic way. The object is to suggest loosely defined strategies so that each member can take into account the impact of its own policies on the others.

(c) The European Parliament

This consists of representatives directly elected separately by each country, but they sit according to party affiliation, not nationality. The Assembly debates Community policies and examines the Community's budget. It can dismiss the Commission by a two-thirds majority.

Its powers were strengthened by the 'co-operation procedure' provided for by the Single Market Act 1987. On most single market proposals, Parliament gives a first opinion on a Commission proposal, and then gives a second opinion after the Council has reached a decision in principle.

Community legislation, therefore, results from a complex and often lengthy process of consultation and negotiation between the institutions.

(d) The court of justice

This consists of judges appointed by member countries, for a six-year term. Its task is to rule on the interpretation of the Rome Treaty and to adjudicate on complaints, whether from member states, private enterprises or the institutions themselves. Its rulings are binding on member countries, community institutions, and individuals, and have primacy over national law.

(e) Special institutions

Apart from the four main institutions above, there are also special institutions to deal with particular policies, e.g. the Economic and Social Committee, the European Investment Bank.

29.3 The establishment of a common market

The overriding aim of the EU is to integrate the policies, both economic and, as far as possible, political, of its members. Priority was given to economic integration, to be achieved in progressive stages through a customs union, a single common market, and eventually full monetary integration.

(a) A customs union

We have to distinguish between free-trade area and a customs union. The former simply removes tariff barriers between member countries but allows individual members to impose their own rates of duty against outsiders. A customs union goes further. While it too has internal free trade, it also imposes common external tariffs.

The EU has a customs union, since this is essential for an integrated common market. Otherwise goods would enter the market through low-duty countries and be resold in those imposing higher rates.

(b) Harmonisation measures

The common market of the EU, however, had to go further than a customs union for it envisages goods and factors of production moving freely within the EC through the operation of the price system; only in this way can the full benefits of the larger market be realised.

But member countries had already developed their own individual taxes, welfare benefits, monopoly policies, methods of removing balance-of-payments imbalances, full employment policies and so on. Such differences could distort the working of the price system because they would give some members advantages over others. For example, suppose Britain taxed refrigerators but not binoculars. This would weight the possibilities of trade against Italy (which has a comparative advantage in producing refrigerators) and in favour of Germany (which has a comparative advantage in producing high-grade binoculars).

Alternatively, the comparative advantage of some countries may lie in the expertise of the professional services they can provide. Usually this means that such services have to be taken to where the customer is (e.g. know-how regarding property development). There must therefore be mobility of labour within the market, e.g. for property developers.

Policy was therefore directed towards the gradual introduction of 'harmonisation' measures in order to achieve as far as possible a 'level playing-field' in trade competition between member states. These included:

(i) *A Common External Tariff* (CET) by which members impose tariffs on imports from non-member countries at the same rates.

(ii) *A common agricultural policy* (CAP) – see below.

(iii) *Removal of barriers to trade and the movement of persons and capital between countries.*

(iv) *Uniform rules on competition* to cover price-fixing, sharing of markets and patent rights.

(v) *A common transport policy* as regards freight rates, licences, taxation and working conditions.

(vi) *Harmonisation of tax systems*, particularly indirect taxes.

(vii) *Exchange rate stability* through the Exchange Rate Mechanism (ERM) to prevent one member obtaining a competitive advantage over others by depreciating its currency (see p. 369).

(viii) *A common regional policy*, with the EU helping regions of high unemployment, especially where this partly stems from agreed EU policies, such as the contraction of steel-producing capacity.

(ix) A *social policy* to secure some uniformity of employment and working conditions as embodied in the 'Social Chapter' and assistance towards retraining.

29.4 The Single Market 1993

The Treaty of Rome 1957 which set up the European Economic Community envisaged a single unified market in which goods of member states could be freely exchanged, but which was protected from imports of other countries by common tariffs.

(a) Frictions affecting the free movement of goods and services

Even after tariffs between members had been scrapped, other frictions to the free movement of goods and services still remained. These included:

(i) frontier delays, e.g. in checking documents, collecting excise duties;

(ii) transport control, e.g. licences, national safety rules, lorry weights;

(iii) differences in national product standards and in national trade mark and patent laws;

(iv) restrictions on public purchasing;

(v) control over capital movements and restrictions on financial services offered across national frontiers by banks, insurance companies, etc;

(vi) differences in recognised professional and technical qualifications;

(vii) state subsidies to industry and agriculture;

(viii) different rates of VAT, corporation tax, and of depreciation and other tax allowances; and

(ix) the necessity of changing currencies.

(b) The elimination of non-tariff barriers

It was recognised that the removal of such barriers would take time, but that in order to keep the momentum going there would have to be a set date. Thus the Single European Act 1993 (a) required all countries to complete or be in the process of completing the necessary harmonisation measures, and (b) introduced qualified majority voting on most single market legislation so that progress would not be delayed by a few dissenting members.

Many of these non-tariff barriers were overcome by harmonisation of national requirements, e.g. as regards transport safety rules, product standards, acceptable professional standards. For example, a new trading form, the Single Administrative Document, replaced about 100 different documents for the export, import and transit of goods over EU frontiers. Alternatively, the

Commission can persuade states to remove national restrictions, e.g. on public purchasing and capital movements.

As far as possible the Commission has sought to eliminate controls by deregulation generally rather than by dealing with each control individually. For instance, if one state imposed an excise duty on a good which was higher than that of another state the market would automatically transfer trade in that good from the dearer country to the cheaper, so that no regulation on duties would be necessary. Nevertheless it can make regulations specific to the practices of an individual state.

29.5 Advantages for the UK of belonging to the EU

Several advantages can accrue to countries by forming a single common market.

First, it increases the possibility of specialisation. The EU provides a market of 340 million people, larger than that of the USA. This allows economies of scale to be achieved, especially as regards sophisticated products requiring high initial research expenditure, e.g. computers, drugs, nuclear reactors, supersonic aircraft and modern weapons. Such economies enable EU firms to compete more effectively in world markets.

Second, keener competition in the larger market can result in greater efficiency. Within the EU there are no trade barriers which in effect protect inefficient firms. Free trade means that goods and services can compete freely in all parts of the market and that factors of production can move to their most efficient uses, not merely within but also between countries. As a result, in value, 57 per cent of the UK's exports go to the EU and 56 per cent of her imports come from there. On the other hand, it must be recognised that protective duties may reduce competition from outside the market.

Third, a faster rate of growth should be achieved as a result of increased economies of scale and competition enjoyed by the EU countries. But it is also possible that the EU generates growth by increasing the *prospects* of growth.

Fourth, there could be significant political benefits. As already explained, the ultimate objective of the original advocates of European co-operation was some form of political union. A Western Europe which could speak with one voice would carry weight when dealing with other major powers, particularly the USA. Moreover, the integration of defence forces and strategy would give its members far greater security. Such benefits, it is held, more than compensate for any loss of political sovereignty (see p. 374).

Fifth, because she is a member of the EU and has a stable political background, the UK can attract investment from countries outside (particularly the USA and Japan) who are anxious to obtain the advantages of having a production base within the EU.

Sixth, the dynamic growth of the EU enables assistance to be given to its poorer regions and to the less developed countries of the world. Already the UK has been a major beneficiary from the Regional Development Fund, the Social Fund and the Agricultural Guidance and Guarantee Fund.

29.6 Problems facing the UK as a member of the EU

While Britain's membership of the EU can secure important benefits and allow her to influence its future development, it does pose special problems.

(a) The CET could lead to the diversion of trade towards less efficient EC suppliers

The duties imposed by the customs union may allow firms within the common market to compete in price with more efficient firms outside.

Suppose, for instance, that the same machine can be produced by both the USA and Germany but, because the American firm is more efficient, its machine is 10 per cent cheaper than the German. In these circumstances, Britain would, other things being equal, import from the USA. As a member of EU, however, Britain would have to discriminate against the American machine by the appropriate CET, say 20 per cent. This would make the German machine cheaper, and so trade would be diverted to the less efficient producer.

(b) The CAP is a drain on the Community funds

Before joining the EU Britain imported food at the lowest world price that could be found. In so far as the UK farmer could not make an adequate living by selling at free market prices, British policy consisted of granting *deficiency payments* (financed out of taxation) sufficient to raise the price received by the farmer to a level set out in an Annual Review. The consumer paid a low price of food and the world had free access to the UK market. The taxpayer paid for farmer support.

But because the Community could not function satisfactorily if the cost of food to consumers differed appreciably in various parts of it, there has to be some equalisation of prices. Yet if this occurred through competition between producing countries it could destroy many small farmers, particularly in France and Germany. Furthermore, because demand for agricultural products tends to be price-inelastic, even in the short run changes in the conditions of supply, e.g. through a good harvest, can have a far-reaching effect on farmers' incomes. Even in the long run farmers face relative falling prices for foodstuffs since demand is income-inelastic while supply conditions improve over time through technical innovation.

The CAP supports farmers' incomes by: (a) an intervention price; (b) granting direct production subsidies, e.g. on ewes held and land 'set-aside'; and (c) restricting imports by protective duties at the Community's external frontier.

Three prices are fixed for each product:

(i) a *target price*, which, it is estimated, will give farmers an adequate return in a normal year;
(ii) the *intervention price*, at which produce of a specified standard will be bought by the various agencies to prevent the price falling more than 8 per

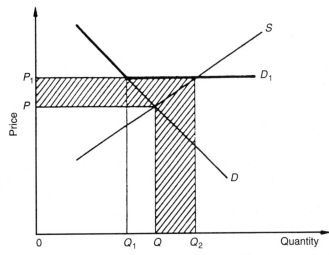

Figure 29.1   The effect on supply of a guaranteed 'intervention' price

cent below the target price. Thus a farmer can choose between selling his
corn on the market or 'putting it into intervention'.

(iii) a *threshold price*, which is the price set for calculating duties on imports
when the world price is 10 per cent below the target price.

In practice, giving farmers a guaranteed price above the market clearing price
for all they can produce simply encourages overproduction, and stocks
accumulate which far exceed those necessary to draw on in the event of a poor
harvest (see p. 23). Thus in Figure 29.1, the market-clearing price would be OP.
However, if the guaranteed intervention price is OP_1, the demand curve becomes
horizontal, D_1, at this price. At price P_1, consumers take OQ_1 but farmers supply
OQ_2. There is thus an excess supply of Q_1Q_2 which is bought for storage by the
authorities of a cost of $P_1 \times Q_1Q_2$. The increase in farmer's incomes is shown by
the shaded area.

To the extent that these stores are actually drawn on when harvests are poor,
costs are recouped. In practice, however, improved techniques have so increased
supply that it has regularly exceeded demand. Thus surpluses have accumulated,
e.g. butter, beef and corn mountains and milk and wine lakes.

Not only does the system represent an inefficient use of resources, but it is
inequitable in that it gives more support to the larger farmer.

(c) 'Dumping' surplus produce on world markets injures the less-developed countries and antagonises the USA, Australia, etc.

Apart from the economic inefficiency resulting from subsidies and storage costs,
the normal pattern of world trade in agricultural products is distorted. Not only
have many world producers lost important markets in Europe, but EU surpluses

are dumped on world markets. This depresses the price received by all exporting countries, including even the less-developed.

The USA, supported by Canada, Australia and New Zealand, linked EU agricultural protection with the Uruguay Round of GATT, making the reduction of tariffs on manufactured goods conditional on an EU reduction in price support for her agricultural produce. While this is in harmony with the British view (see below), it is difficult where the farming lobby is politically important.

A considerable reduction in milk output was achieved by the introduction of production quotas in 1984. As regards cereals, progressive reductions in the real prices received by farmers did not reduce overproduction. Hence in 1993 compulsory 'set aside' was introduced to take 15 per cent (since reduced) of the land under cereals out of production. In addition, intervention prices for cereals were cut by a third, with farmers given income compensation, reducing over three years. Subsidies on other agricultural activities are also being reduced.

(d) There is insufficient control over the EU budget

A Community budget is necessary to meet the costs of administration and policies requiring expenditure, e.g. CAP and regional assistance. There are four main sources – agricultural levies on imported produce, import duties on non-Community goods, a VAT rate up to 1.4 per cent, and payments related to each member's GNP (1.2 per cent).

Today, over 70 per cent of the budget is spent on agricultural support, and this is likely to increase when Eastern European countries become members. Unless spending on agricultural support is tightened up, therefore, the unpopular policy of increasing the budget revenue will have to be followed, placing a greater relative burden on countries depending on industry (e.g. Germany, the UK) rather than on agriculture (e.g. France, Ireland, Greece).

The UK argues that her net contribution to the EU exceeds that of richer members. This arises because, instead of buying her agricultural imports at world prices, she has to impose a levy if they come from non-EU countries. But this levy goes to the EU budget and not the UK's, with the result that the UK is a net contributor to EU funds.

Her policy, therefore, has been to: (i) negotiate a rebate and seek higher payments from the Regional Fund; (ii) reform the CAP; and (iii) resist moves to increase the budget revenue until extravagance and fraud have been eliminated.

(e) The capital structure of British firms increases their exposure to take-over

Tougher competition within the single market will benefit large-scale, low-cost producers at the expense of smaller higher-cost producers, some of whom could be taken over or go out of business. Even the larger British firms, with their greater reliance for expansion on equity finance obtained through the capital market, are now more vulnerable to take-over or merger.

(f) Too many decisions which ought to come within the competence of national governments are taken by EU bureaucrats

One of the UK's apprehensions over the extension of bureacratic control is indicated by her emphasis on adhering to the principle of *subsidiarity*, which simply asserts that the functions of government should be devolved to the lowest competent level. The UK considers that this principle means that things should be done at the EU level only if they cannot be done at the national level. For instance with regard to the environment, dealing with greenhouse warming would be a EU function, but protecting national parks would be a national function.

In contrast to the UK's stance, the Commission would prefer a 'common interest' test of subsidiarity, the object being to widen the scope of its authority rather than limit it to the lowest common denominator. For the UK, this interpretation simply reflects her view that the Brussels bureaucrats wish to use their powers to abrogate to themselves rights and functions which can be performed efficiently by the nation state.

The meeting of the European Council in Edinburgh, in 1992 moved towards the British view by laying down a three-stage test which new and existing legislation would have to pass. First, does the EC have the power to act? If it does, is it impossible to achieve the desired objectives at national level? If so, what is the minimum legislation necessary?

(g) Membership of the Exchange Rate Mechanism (ERM) can prove too rigid a policy for a country in serious recession (see below)

29.7 The Exchange Rate Mechanism (ERM)

(a) Background to the UK's ERM membership

In the past, UK inflation has resulted in balance-of-payments difficulties, temporarily corrected by devaluation of the £. But there was little *resolve* to hold on to the necessary corrective measures, and 'stop–go' policies simply meant that potential rate of growth was not achieved. Furthermore, inflation means that on world capital markets, lenders require a higher sterling rate of interest to cover a possible capital loss through devaluation of the £. This higher rate imposes an extra burden on British exporters as they compete in a free EU market.

During the early 1980s, the weapon used to combat inflation was strict control of the money supply (see p. 282). When this proved deficient, the £ simply 'shadowed' the DM, using the foreign currency reserves and the rate of interest to maintain its exchange value. But it was not until October 1990 that the UK accepted the discipline of the stricter ERM.

(b) Membership conditions and mechanism of the ERM

The ERM has three main elements:

(i) *Members have to maintain their agreed exchange rates.* Each member has a declared *central exchange rate* against other members' currencies which it has to keep within $2\frac{1}{4}$ per cent above or below (the 'narrow' band) or in the case of the UK and Spain, 6 per cent (the 'wide' band). Thus, for the UK, the rate was £1 = DM 2.95.

(ii) *The European Currency Unit* (ECU) is the unit in which currency rates are expressed. It is calculated from a 'basket' of Community currencies, weighted roughly according to each country's relative economic strength.

   The central banks of member states have an equal obligation of symmetrical adjustment at the margins of the band; that is, to act not only by buying when a currency is weak, but by selling it when strong. The idea behind the ECU was that, as the DM had the heaviest weight, pressure would be exerted on Germany to follow an easier monetary policy as the DM approached its upper limit. In practice this did not happen since Germany gave priority to holding her rate of interest in order to control her own inflation resulting from reunification with E. Germany.

(iii) *Short Term Financing* is available to support a currency under pressure.

(c) The case for UK membership of ERM

Given this mechanism of the ERM, we now have to ask how membership might have assisted the UK in reducing the rate of inflation. Here we must re-emphasise a point made earlier with regard to cost-inflation – bringing it down depends largely on establishing confidence that it will be achieved. In essence, success breeds success.

Such confidence is enhanced by ERM membership because there is: (i) a *commitment* to hold the exchange rate; (ii) mutual support from other members if an exchange rate comes under pressure. Should these prove inadequate, the rate of interest could be raised to deal with speculative capital movements.

The UK's task was to demonstrate her resolve to reduce inflation by taking all measures necessary to hold the agreed exchange rate. This meant retaining a high interest rate of 10 per cent, thereby prolonging recession. It was hoped that this short-term cost would achieve the long-term benefits of price-stability.

(d) The UK suspends membership of the ERM

The £1–DM 2.95 exchange rate held until 16 September 1992, when the foreign exchange speculators, after forcing a devaluation of the Italian lira, turned on sterling. The magnitude of the selling surprised the government especially as, unlike Italy, the UK had foreign currency reserves of some £24 billion. The accepted counter measures – raising base rate 10 to 15 per cent, spending £15 billion from the reserves, and support of between £5 billion and £10 billion from the Bundesbank and the Bank of France – proved ineffective. Consequently the

UK suspended her membership of the ERM and allowed the £ to find its own parities on the foreign exchange market (around 2.45 DM, January 1992).

29.8 Economic and Monetary Union (EMU): the single currency

(a) The advantages of a single currency

An exchange rate union which goes no further than agreed irrevocably-locked exchange rates of the member countries would cover the basic harmonisation requirement of the single market. But it has three weaknesses:

(i) a member could renege on the arrangement, realigning its exchange rate unilaterally;
(ii) a risk premium to cover such a possible devaluation would mean having a higher rate of interest set by the EU central bank; and
(iii) costs would still be incurred in exchanging currencies.

A single currency eliminates all three weaknesses. It removes any uncertainty as to possible exchange rate realignment, thereby encouraging trade and investment. More important, it eliminates the costs of currency exchange for firms engaged in intra-EU trade and for individuals travelling within the EU, e.g. tourists.

Moreover, by being managed by an independent European Central Bank (ECB), committed to a low rate of inflation, it would prevent monetary policy being slanted by a state-controlled central bank for electoral advantage. The resulting lower 'uncertainty premium' should produce a ECB rate of interest which would be lower than that required by an individual state to achieve the same low level of inflation.

It is possible, too, that the new currency, the Euro, could be widely used as a reserve currency. If so it should reduce still further exchange risks with outside currencies, and even generate income of the ECB from its Euro holdings.

Finally, a single currency and a common ECB responsible for overall monetary policy would help to unify the single market, especially as cross-border transactions would no longer be distorted by currency uncertainties. Indeed, pricing all goods in Euros should, by making price differences transparent, promote competition within the single market.

(b) The Treaty of Maastricht 1991

In 1989, Jacques Delors, then President of the Commission, presented a report which considered that a genuine single market was only possible if there were Economic and Monetary Union (EMU) involving a single currency. His plan for achieving this was agreed at Maastricht.

To ensure that the adoption of the single currency did not put an unacceptable strain on the economies of participating states, certain convergency criteria were laid down which had to be achieved as a condition of joining the single currency. These criteria are as follows:

(i) *Exchange rate stability*, with exchange rates maintained within the narrow band for the previous two years. This would provide an indication of the once-for-all rate at which a country's currency would be valued in terms of the Euro.

(ii) *Price stability*, with the index of consumer price inflation in the previous year to be no more than 1.5 per cent above that of the average of the best three performing member states.

(iii) *Sustainability of government financial stability*, with government annual net borrowing to be below 3 per cent of GDP.

(iv) *Convergence durability*, with the average nominal long-term government bond rate to be no more than 2 per cent above the average of the three best performing members.

It was considered that failure to meet these conditions could lead to excessive adjustment costs for a country once it was within the single currency (e.g. unemployment resulting from enforced deflation), and could embarrass even the EMU itself. Qualifying countries would be decided upon in 1998.

(c) The present (1999) situation

By May 1998 most EU members had still not satisfied all four criteria. However, by a 'flexible' interpretation, 11 countries were able to proceed. Only Greece failed; the UK, Denmark and Sweden declined, partly for political reasons and partly because they felt that they were not yet economically ready.

The single currency began on 1 January 1999, with a 3-year transitional period as follows:

1 January 1999–

(i) exchange rates of member countries' currencies locked irrevocably with the Euro;

(ii) responsibility for the formulation and implementation of monetary policy passed to the ECB, which also decides on exchange rates with outside currencies, manages the reserves and intervenes in the market. It is the sole issuing authority of the single currency.

(iii) ECB monetary and foreign exchange operations conducted in Euros

1 January 2002 – Euro notes and coins issued with legal tender and become the medium of exchange rather than simply a unit of account. These will circulate alongside national currencies in participating member countries but will be sub-denominations of the euro.

1 July 2002 – national currencies no longer legal tender in participating member countries.

(d) Possible difficulties of EMU membership

First, there are the heavy initial costs of its introduction. Businesses have to alter all their money machines (e.g. cash dispensers, tills, vending machines). In addition, computer programmes have to be recalculated to cover the change from the old currency to the euro.

Individuals, too, would have to adapt to the euro once the transitional period was over. Wages, salaries, state benefits, mortgages, monetary assets, etc., would all have to be expressed in euros. Since this would be less easy for older persons, there is here a 'psychological' cost.

Second, and more serious, is the inherent danger that without considerable assistance from the EU's Structure, Social and Regional Funds, certain regions, especially those on the periphery, could be left facing long-term poverty. Indeed such distributions may run counter to the single market objective of securing the advantages of specialisation through the mobility of labour and capital. Instead, inflexible wage-rates and labour immobility could result in unemployment and poverty persisting in certain regions simply because subsidies reduce the need to accept lower wage rates or to move to the more prosperous regions.

Third, there could be asymmetry in the stage of trade cycle reached by different member countries. Yet the ECB's single short-term rate of interest applies to all. Thus while the Irish economy in 1998 was growing at 10 per cent per annum so that her 6.75 per cent interest rate was appropriate to control inflation, the German economy was sluggish and so a 3.5 per cent interest rate existed.

(e) The UK's response to EMU

The UK co-operated fully in implementing the arrangements for establishing the single market and in doing so recognised that some diminution of sovereignty and majority voting had to be conceded. But the proposal to go ahead with a single currency and full monetary union has been marked by a distinct lack of enthusiasm, often bordering on hostility. Her main reservations are explained as follows.

(i) The speed of transition

The Maastricht Treaty envisaged a 4-year transitional period prior to 1 January 1999 to enable members to achieve exchange rate stability and converge on a low inflation rate, financial and fiscal stability.

The UK felt that this period, truncated by the 1 January 1999 deadline, was too short and that she in particular was still not ready to rejoin the ERM while a comparatively high rate of interest was required to hold the rate of inflation to around 2 per cent.

For the majority of countries, however, the alternative of postponing the timetable was unacceptable on the grounds that the momentum towards EMU would be lost and possibly never regained. Yet many of the eleven who went ahead did not fully meet the criteria, while for a few, such as Germany and France, the run-up costs in terms of unemployment were heavy – thus lending substance to the UK's view.

(ii) Asymmetric sensitivity of countries to ECB interest-rate changes

The impact of a change in the ECB's single short-term rate of interest may differ from one member country to another. Examples as regards the UK will illustrate.

A higher proportion of the UK's borrowing is at floating (short-term) rates compared with Germany's fixed (long-term) borrowing. Thus the UK would be more sensitive than Germany to a change in the ECB's rate.

Additionally trade cycles of countries may differ. Thus in 1999 the UK's economy was on the downturn and a reduction in base rate was appropriate. In contrast Ireland's economy was still booming but facing inflationary pressures so that a higher rate was needed.

These considerations imply that a single interest rate imposed on all EU countries may not always be appropriate for some countries, such as the UK, could bear a disproportionately large share of the burden of adjustment resulting from a rise in the ECB's rate.

(iii) The inability to use exchange rate depreciation as a means of cushioning country-specific economic shocks

While the reverberations of economic shocks are usually felt by most countries, on occasions a shock may be more specific to a particular country. For the UK this might be the case if there were a considerable fall in the price of oil or if a major trading partner, such as the USA, ran into serious recession.

With a single currency, however, where no one member country can alone depreciate, realignment would have to come about by the deflation of prices, including wages, and only after a prolonged period of unemployment. Such a policy has in the past proved unacceptable. The 1992 experience of the UK trying to maintain a fixed ERM exchange rate against heavy speculation illustrates the point. Raising her rate of interest to support sterling merely added to her on-going recession and unemployment.

(iv) The extent and nature of the sovereignty conceded

Provided the agreed exchange rates were maintained by countries, the retention of separate national currencies would have the advantage of leaving considerable freedom of manoeuvre for national governments, for example as regards supervision of financial markets.

With a single currency all such freedoms virtually vanish. Every element of money creation would be controlled as to timing, form and amount by the ECB. The central banks of members countries, such as the Bank of England, would retain only an advisory role through membership of the ESCB. Yet they would still be responsible for implementing the ECB's policy decisions. It also means that European banking systems and financial markets would have to be made more uniform.

Furthermore, in practice monetary control would extend to fiscal policy as follows. If a PSBR is covered from the banking sector, there is an increase in the money supply so that binding rules may be required to limit the size of a country's PSBR, and 3 per cent of GDP has been provisionally agreed. In short, what this means is that national governments would have to accept that macroeconomic control would be largely surrendered to bureaucratic institutions subject to little scrutiny and control by national parliaments.

Such control of monetary and fiscal policy by the ECB, together with the extension of majority voting on harmonisation measures, is a serious loss of political control in that there is no real accountability to parliament. For the UK it has important constitutional implications because it goes directly to the heart of parliamentary sovereignty which rests on the ultimate control by the House of Commons of the public purse. It is for this reason that the loudest critics oppose the single currency and even see in the EMU a major step in the direction of a more federal Europe.

QUESTIONS

1 How does the theory of comparative costs support the UK's membership of the Single Market?

2 How could the theory of comparative costs be used to oppose the UK's membership of the Single Market?

3 For many industries, fixed capital costs form a high proportion of total costs within the relevant range of output.
   (a) Give three examples of such industries.
   (b) How does a large Single Market help such industries?

4 What is the difference between a free-trade area and a customs union?

5 Until 1970 the traditional method of helping British farmers was through 'deficiency payments' to cover the amount by which prices obtained in the market fell short of agreed 'guaranteed prices'. How does the CAP policy for farmers differ from this?

6 What is the importance to the UK of the EU's Regional Fund?

7 What are the advantages of EMU (including the single currency) for EU members?

8 How could the UK lose: (a) economic sovereignty, (b) parliamentary sovereignty under EMU?

Chapter 1

1. Time. This is by no means a trivial question; the time element is continually entering into economic decisions. Thus people are often prepared to pay extra to have *A now*, instead of in the future. It follows that '*A* in the future' is really a different economic good from '*A* now'.

2. (a) A *normative statement* is a subjective opinion because it cannot be tested by facts. *Equity* implies fairness, in this case, in the distribution of wealth.
   (b) Economics can examine:
      (i) whether taxation is the best means of achieving equity;
      (ii) what kind of tax would be most effective;
      (iii) what effect the tax would have on other economic variables, e.g. investment.

Chapter 2

1. Prices throughout the market become known more quickly, e.g. by telephone and information technology, and hence price differences tend to be eliminated more quickly.

2. (a) Stocks fall. (b) Producers' order books lengthen. (c) Queues form. (d) Extended delivery delays.

3. Because tickets are sold by the All-England Tennis Club below the price they would fetch on the open market they are allocated to the general public by ballot with each successful applicant being restricted to two tickets. Some tickets are bought by or are re-sold to 'spivs', and the limited supply is sold at a high 'market clearing' price.

4. (a) (i) Decrease demand for road transport by raising its cost, e.g. increasing price of diesel oil and petrol, heavier duties on vehicles, stricter safety regulations;
   (b) (i) Charge more for resident roadside parking;
      (ii) Give a Council tax rebate when a house has a garage.

Chapter 3

1. 'Take care of the pence, and the pounds will take care of themselves.'

2. (a) (i) $\dfrac{q_1 q}{Oq} \div \dfrac{p_1 p}{Op}$ (ii) $\dfrac{q_1 q}{Oq_1} \div \dfrac{p_1 p}{Op_1}$

   (b) Elastic, because as price falls (rises), total outlay increases (decreases). From the diagram, $p_1 pBA$ is smaller than $q_1 qCB$.

3. Assuming that outlay on agricultural products roughly represents farmers' incomes, then a fall in price (the result, for instance, of a good harvest) would lead to an overall drop in income.

4. (a) Commuters have to travel before 8:40 a.m., that is, during the peak period, and so have a relatively inelastic demand curve. In contrast, other travellers are more price sensitive since they can travel by slower buses and outside the peak periods. Yet, if their demand is price elastic, they can provide a useful addition to revenue.

   (b) (i) A difference in elasticity of demand between the two types of traveller.

   (ii) Separation by time.

Chapter 4

1. He takes the risk that the book will not sell after going to the cost of having it printed, etc. The author who writes a book in return for a percentage of the selling price on each copy sold is a part-entrepreneur, for his labour could be wasted.

2. (i) d; (ii) b; (iii) a; (iv) c.

3. Agriculture, retailing, professional services, personal services.

4. (a) Stocks a variety of books according to likely demand.
   (b) Situates his shop within reach of the consumer.
   (c) Orders books, and may allow customer to have a monthly account.
   (d) Advises publishers of readers' comments on style, price, etc.

5. It is convenient for customers (including dealers) to have all similar shops together in order to be able to compare products and prices; it also establishes a reputation for the locality, thereby inducing further custom. Other examples: jewellers, art galleries, fashion clothing.

Chapter 5

1. (a) Yes; the tax will shift the MC curve upwards, and MC = MR at a smaller output.
   (b) No; this tax is in the form of a fixed cost.

2. (a) Factors of production are not equally available to all firms.
   (b) Entrepreneurs differ in ability and efficiency.

(c) As industry expands, higher rewards must be paid to attract factors of production.

(d) Economy is dynamic, not static, so that some firms are doing better than others.

Chapter 6

1. (i) Physical productivity; (ii) price of product.
2. (a) 20, 140, 380, 260, 150, 130, 120, 100, 80.
   (b) 6.

Chapter 7

1. Chiefly the immobility of labour – for all the reasons given in the text.
2. *Demand* for skilled workers higher, because of higher MRP – they make a more vital contribution to production.
   Supply smaller – cost of training, inherent skill required, etc.
3. (a) Leads to disputes when the Retail Prices Index is falling
   (b) Leads to the wages spiral – wage-push inflation.
4. (a) Where there is monopsony, wage rate will be less than value of marginal product;
   (b) It cannot be applied to the problem of general unemployment;
   (c) Where there is unemployment, a rise in the MRP may lead to increased employment rather than a rise in money wages;
   (d) Where one employer bargains with a strong trade union, there is no determinate position for the wage rate. The wage rate actually agreed upon will lie *somewhere between* the maximum the employer is prepared to offer and the minimum the union is willing to accept.

Chapter 8

1. No; circumstances may change before *future* yields are obtained. For example, Robinson Crusoe may discover a shallow pool where fish trap themselves, or the peasant farmer may suffer a complete crop failure through the weather.
2. Elizabeth Hurley, Terry Wogan, Paul Gascoigne, Posh Spice, Cliff Richard.
3. It will not reduce output or supply of that factor. Difficulty in distinguishing how much of the reward is rent and how much is transfer price.
4. (a) Negative.
   (b) His independence and way of life.
5. (a) Will demand be equal to expectations?
   (b) What kind of weather will prevail in the summer?

(c) Will competitors bring out a rival drink?

(d) Will an improved method of manufacturing be found?

(e) Will the government increase tax on soft drinks?

(f) Will incomes generally decrease?

6. (a) Penalises uncertainty-bearing, particularly ordinary shareholders.

(b) Hits those who bear high risks the hardest, but does not compensate for losses.

(c) Destroys the differential required to accept the high risks connected with innovation. It thus discourages enterprise.

(d) Where profit is earned on patents, a reduction of the return may discourage invention.

(e) Reduces profits available for ploughing back to expand the industry.

(f) Inefficiency not fully penalised (some is borne by the Board of Inland Revenue through reduced tax liability).

Chapter 9

1. *Technical efficiency* refers to maximising output from limited resources. *Economic efficiency* relates demand to supply so that limited resources produce that assortment of goods which yields maximum satisfaction.

2. There may be spillover benefits and costs.

3. (a) It should attempt to ensure that full employment ensures production on the curve.

(b) It should note that a satisfactory growth rate will move the curve outward from the origin.

4. The distribution of income.

5. (a) Since a tax to raise the price of cigarettes is only likely to achieve a small reduction in the demand for cigarettes, the government could try to move the demand curve to the left by: (i) forbidding or curbing promotional advertising; (ii) forbidding smoking in public places; (iii) advertise the harmful effect of smoking on health.

(b) Yes, because there are external costs of: (i) discomfort, etc. to nearby non-smokers; (ii) National Health Service treatment for lung cancer and heart trouble.

Chapter 10

1. (a) The firm is the sole supplier of a good.

(b) It can exclude competitors.

2. (a) 2,000 tons.

(b) Approximately unity.

3. (a) Half-price fare for children.

(b) Sold at a lower price.

(c) Expensive goods charged at a higher rate than coal irrespective of bulk.

(d) Cheaper evening calls and business users pay a higher standing charge than private subscribers.

4. Farmer Jones cannot differentiate his wheat from Farmer Smith's. Hence, if he advertised, he would merely reduce his profits – and sales, too, because Smith would also benefit.

5. Prices tend to be identical, though this tacit arrangement is broken from time to time. Some competition by gifts, lucky draws, etc.

Chapter 11

1. (a) *Community goods* are indivisible, e.g. defence, motorway lighting, and free-riders cannot be excluded (non-excludable).

(b) *Collective goods* are similarly indivisible, but charging would mean they are not fully used because marginal cost is nil (non-rivalry), e.g. bridges, and so the state provides from taxation.

(c) *Merit goods*, where external costs arise from inadequate consumption, e.g. vaccination, hospital treatment, largely through inadequate income.

(d) Project needs to embrace widespread externalities, e.g. urban renewal, or requires exceptionally large initial cost, e.g. new town development.

2. (a) Demand is not related to the costs of provision.

(b) Demand is related to the price people are willing to pay.

(c) Unless everybody can afford private health insurance, poor people would be denied expensive operations, surgical appliances, etc.

(d) Supply restricted by limited funds.

(e) (i) Waiting for non-urgent hospital treatment.

(ii) Lower standards in the provision of school books, etc.

Chapter 12

1. (a) It prevents 'ribbon' development.

(b) It is likely to increase the price of land, as supply is limited to that having planning permission.

2. The existing authorities could have diverse objective priorities, which may confer external costs on each other. The new body could 'internalise' externalities.

3. Two main taxes:

(i) Vehicle licence – car £155 per annum is a fixed cost.

(ii) Petrol at 70p a litre is a variable cost.

If vehicle licences were abolished and revenue recouped by increasing the petrol tax, it would raise the cost of running a car on the road and could therefore reduce its use with beneficial effect on congestion. (A further beneficial effect would be to encourage the production of low-fuel consumption cars.) But there are difficulties in such an approach, especially as regards equity for those dependent on car travel, e.g. country dwellers.

4. (a) Yes.
   (b) To compare the net benefits of the three alternative routes.
   (c) (i) The beauty of the Devil's Punchbowl;
       (ii) lowland heaths;
       (iii) an ugly viaduct;
       (iv) time lost by the reduced speed from 75mph to 44mph;
       (v) possible accident reduction through the lower speed;
       (vi) cost of delay and parliamentary time in overcoming the National Trust's objection;
       (vii) with all the above there would be difficulty in establishing a 'cut-off' point of losers.
   (d) (i) It ensures the national heritage is secured for the distant future;
       (ii) it gives 'teeth' to its functions, ensuring that its objections receive adequate consideration before being overruled.
   (e) Applying a low social time preference rate of discount.
   (f) There has to be a public enquiry at which they can put forward their views.

Chapter 13

1. (a) Introduce a system of tradeable permits.
   (b) Subsidise the decommissioning of ships surplus to long-term requirements.

2. (a) To protect water supply from an excessive nitrate content.
   (b) The water of some areas does not have excessive nitrates.
   (c) It is easy to collect and the revenue raised could support conservation measures. On the other hand, it has been estimated that a 50% tax will reduce the use of nitrate by only 10%.

3. (a) (i) The 'congester pays'.
       (ii) The toll could be adjusted to achieve the flow of traffic desired.
       (iii) Revenue raised could be used to subsidise bus services and commuter trains.
   (b) (i) Administrative costs and difficulties.
       (ii) The tax is regressive as regards the essential motorist or one who cannot charge the toll against expenses.

4. (a) A private action affecting a third party and which is not allowed for.
   (b) (i) Full production costs are not allowed for.
       (ii) Consumers obtain the good at a lower price than if the full cost of resources used were paid.
   (c) Impose a tax.
   (d) Taxation provides an incentive to a firm to invest in pollution-reducing technology, whereas regulation simply imposes a fixed norm.
   (e) Yes. A tax could be levied according to clearly marked 'bands' on the consumer good. Resulting lower sales would mean that the producer

would take measures to move into a lower taxation band, e.g. lead-free petrol.

Chapter 14

1. Perfect liquidity – it can be spent on anything immediately and without question.
2. 7 per cent.
3. No. £960.
4. (a) £980; (b) £993.
5. Without such help, Discount Houses could not repay 'call money'. This would have undermined the financial system.

Chapter 15

1. (a) Central administration through computer achieves economies of scale; (b) staff can be trained for highly specialised tasks, e.g. trustee work; (c) risks spread geographically. Decisions have to be referred to Head Office when loans exceed a given size.
2. (a) Can be sent safely through the post; can be written for any amount; obviate taking around large sums of money; form a record of payment; act as receipts.
   (b) Permit credit creation where cheques are widely used.
3. (a) Cash held; (b) demand for advances; (c) the policy of the other banks through the clearing association; (d) The Bank of England's monetary policy.
4. (a) (i) Lifting controls on foreign exchange, credit and money.
       (ii) Encouragement of competition and innovation.
   (b) Previously their markets for deposits loans were uncompetitive as regards price (the rate of interest) by 'established convention'.
   (c) They would have to observe the competitive rate for deposits from lenders and for borrowers.
   (d) (i) Competed with building societies for retail deposits and mortgage lending, and with merchant banks, etc. for other business (e.g. property development).
       (ii) Used its customer base for extending other business, e.g. insurance and pension advice, Stock Market dealing and, for a short time, even estate agency.
       (iii) Charged customers for services previously performed free, e.g. safe custody, keeping accounts, stopping cheques, exceeding overdraft limit.
   (e) (i) Ancillary services charged for; (ii) interest paid on different deposit accounts.

Chapter 16

1. (a) fall; (b) rise.
2. By 'funding' the debt, i.e. borrowing by selling long-term bonds rather than Treasury bills.
3. (a) Cash is now made available by the Bank of England in whatever quantity is required for transactions, and not to control liquidity.
   (b) Joint-stock banks create credit largely on the basis of the demand and their liquidity.
   (c) Government may find it difficult to decrease its overall borrowing.
4. (a) Adds to cost of government borrowing.
   (b) Raises the long-term rate of interest.

Chapter 17

1. *Micro-economics* is concerned with the relationship between demand, supply and price in *particular* markets.
   Macro-economics considers the level at which resources are being employed in *the economy as a whole*.
2. *Micro-economics* simplifies analysis by assuming other things being equal.
   Macro-economics allows for feedbacks between variables by dealing in 'aggregates'.

Chapter 18

1. The consumer goods and services enjoyed per head of the population over a given period, allowing for the amount of leisure.
2. (a) Reduced investment. (b) Running down capital. (c) Paying for imports by foreign loans.
3. 1988–98; national income increased by £5,000 m. in 1978–88, and by £10,000 m. in 1988–98. But £1,000 extra on investment and defence expenditure will tend to reduce extra consumption to £9,000. In real terms, period 1988–98 had a smaller percentage rise in prices, but this was partly offset by the fact that average weekly hours did not fall (as they did in 1978–88). 1988–98 also had a smaller percentage increase in population.
4. (a) Different currencies.
   (b) Different tastes and needs.
   (c) Larger proportion engaged in subsistence agriculture in India.
   (d) Differences in hours worked.
   (e) Fewer goods exchanged against money in India.
   (f) Tax coverage less complete in India, thereby giving less reliable statistics.

5. (a) GNP covers only measurable wealth, not welfare.
   (b) Increase in crime and homelessness; loss of environmental beauty, e.g. meadow land, ancient woodland, hedges.

Chapter 19

1. (a) Skill deteriorates. (b) Psychological effect of not being able to work.

2. (a) Fall in income tax, national insurance contributions and VAT receipts.
   (b) Increased unemployment benefits, rent and council tax rebates, and other social welfare benefits.

Chapter 20

1. (a) Pension provision. (b) Insurance. (c) Mortgage payments.

2. (a) Increase taxation. (b) Raise interest rate to reward saving. (c) Harden hire-purchase terms. (d) Stabilise value of money.

3. (a) For future investment; (b) for liquid reserves, usually to safeguard future dividend rate.

4. (a) Increase tax allowance on investment.
   (b) Lower the rate of interest.
   (c) Subsidise investment, e.g. in depressed regions.
   (d) Increase its own investment.

5. (a) $Y = C + I + X - M$

$$= \frac{9}{10}Y + 10 + 10 - \frac{1}{9}C$$

$$= \frac{9}{10}Y + 10 + 10 - \frac{1}{10}Y$$

$$\frac{2}{10}Y = 20$$

   (b) 10.
   (c) Yes.
   (d) 125.
   (e) Imports increase to 12.5, thus producing a balance-of-payments deficit of 2.5.

6. The government can:
   (a) Plan and collect statistics.
   (b) Adjust its own spending.
   (c) Eliminate uncertainty by its own commitment.

Chapter 21

1. Other objectives, e.g. the price level, balance of payments, cannot be relaxed any further.

2. In Figure 20.4, AD is related solely to the level of output/income. In 21.1 a given AD is related to the price level through the introduction of the AS curve.

3. (a) C increases the higher real value of cash balances.
   (b) C and I increase as the rate of interest falls (lower transactions demand for money).
   (c) $(X - M)$ improved.

4. (a) Diminishing returns.
   (b) Bottlenecks.
   (c) Accelerating wage increases.

5. Wage demands are adjusted to an expected future higher rate of inflation.

6. Whereas Keynes considered that the demand for money adjusted to an increase in its supply by being held in 'idle' balances (speculative motive), Friedman considers people have a fairly stable demand for money balances so that any increase tends to be spent on goods and services.

7. With Keynes the impact of an increase in the supply of money is on the bond market, and any effect on prices generally is indirect through the resulting fall in the rate of interest, which increases aggregate demand. With Friedman the impact is more direct, the extra money finding its way on to the goods and services market.

8. (a) People spend cash balances surplus to their requirements.
   (b) Expectations of higher future prices reduce saving.

9. (a) The rate to which unemployment will tend given the current real wage rate.
   (b) The real wage rate is higher than that which would clear the labour market when the rest of the economy is in equilibrium. This is because trade unions have obtained a wage increase which exceeds the current rate of inflation.
   (c) (i) It must convince wage bargainers that the future rate of inflation will not increase – and prove this in practice.
       (ii) More emphasis must be placed on supply-side measures.

10. 'Adaptive expectations' are based on past experience; 'rational expectations' are based on all relevant information – past experience, current statistics, an assessment of the effects of actual or proposed government measures – so that wage adjustments are immediate.

11. AD is the initial position of aggregate demand, and equilibrium output is Y and the price level P. AD is now increased to AD_1 and the price level rises to P_1. Trade unions win a compensatory wage increase, thereby moving the AS curve to AS_1 and the price level to P_2. This could increase AD (depending on any resulting unemployment), and so the process continues.

    Expectations of a future higher rate of inflation explain why the rate of inflation gathers momentum.

Chapter 22

1. (a) Base year. (b) Basket. (c) Weights.
2. 132.
3. (a) The headline rate includes mortgage payments.
   (b) It varies with changes in the current rate of interest.
4. The yield from the asset is likely to rise in money terms with inflation.
5. (a) Real property e.g. shops; ordinary shares; antiques.
   (b) Fixed interest bonds; building society deposits. But: to some extent a higher rate of return compensates.
6. (a) The rate of inflation eventually gathered momentum.
   (b) High AD led to an uncomfortable balance of payments deficit as spending on imports increased.
7. (a) Neglected the rising AS and its effect on the price level with the approach to full employment.
   (b) Did not recognise the direct impact of increased money supply on AD.
   (c) Underplayed the consequences of a large PSBR.
   (d) Ignored Balanced-of-Payments difficulties when income buoyant.
   (e) Theory of rate of interest glossed over influences other than 'speculation' in its determination.
8. Because of the difficulty of defining 'money'. For the purposes of controlling inflation, money is any asset which contains an element of immediate spending power or induces the owner to pare down money balances because it can be quickly turned into cash. Thus what is 'money' rests on a spectrum of assets which have some liquidity according to the *personal view of the owner*.
9. (a) By enabling a reduction in the rate of interest, consumer demand could be stimulated through lower mortgage repayments and a restoration of confidence in recovery as investment increased.
   (b) Devaluation made UK exports more price competitive.
10. (a) (i) *C* and *I* respond to interest changes.
        (ii) Can be applied quickly.
        (iii) Boosted by psychological impact.
    (b) (i) May need a high rate of interest to reduce *C* and *I*.
        (ii) Non-discriminatory.
        (iii) An inflow of short-term capital if rate rises above general world rates.

Chapter 23

1. (a) Avoids forcing workers to leave areas to which they are attached.
   (b) Stimulates the activity rate by helping immobile older workers and married women.
   (c) Relieves congestion and inflationary pressure in South-east England.

(d) Prevents loss of social capital through depopulation.

(e) Reduces the adverse multiplier effect resulting from falling expenditure in the depressed area.

2. (a) High income elasticity of demand to ensure increasing demand as income grows, e.g. washing-machines.

   (b) (i) High labour content, e.g. cars.

      (ii) Light raw materials which are not lost in course of production, e.g. electrical and electronics equipment.

      (iii) Flow method of production, where semi-skilled labour can be used, e.g. cars.

3. Firm will seek most advantageous location in terms of 'profit'.

   It will therefore have to compare:

      (i) Transport costs of obtaining materials.

      (ii) Transport costs of distributing products, or contacting customers.

      (iii) Advantages of being associated with similar firms or suppliers.

      (iv) Rent costs and suitability of site.

      (v) Wage costs and availability of type of labour required.

      (vi) Amenities of district, physical and cultural, particularly from viewpoint of attracting and holding key managers.

   (a) A *private consultant* would prepare detailed figures as far as possible, orientated with regard to profit. But he would also mention other aspects, e.g. employee contentment regarding the new area.

   (b) The *government official* would be concerned with attracting growth firms to a depressed area. In dealing with the firm, he would have to cover the same points as the private consultant, but he could stress certain aspects based on his experience of other firms in the Development Area, e.g. drawing attention to the special amenities of the area, the availability of labour, the lack of traffic congestion etc.

   The official would have three advantages over the private consultant. (1) The government would in fact be 'internalising externalities', and so the official could show how the area's advantages for the firm could grow, e.g. as it attracted similar and ancillary firms, improvement in the infrastructure as prosperity returned, and so forth. (2) He could speak for the government's long-term plans, again convincing the firm that it would be moving to a prosperous region, where labour supply could be guaranteed through retraining schemes, and where communications would be improved. (3) He could estimate 'feedbacks' through the 'multiplier' on the particular region and other regions.

Chapter 24

1. (a) Redistribution of consumption towards goods having a high income elasticity of demand.

   (b) Proportion of income saved likely to increase.

2. The internal combustion engine, air transport, microelectronics, computers, information technology.

3. The fall in the world price of oil in 1998 resulted in Saudi Arabia's terms of trade deteriorating.

4. (a) Greater pollution, noise and congestion.
   (b) Destruction of aesthetic beauty.

Chapter 25

1. A taxation system is built up of a variety of taxes because each has different attributes and defects.

2. VAT is not paid on food and rent, upon which poorer people spend a larger proportion of their income. VAT on domestic fuel has a regressive element.

3. People get used to a tax. Tax should not be frequently tampered with.

4. Unless people are dis-saving by spending out of capital, it will merely fall on *past* saving instead of enforcing *present* saving out of income.

5. (a) 6p. (b) 7p. (c) 1p child, 2p producer. (d) Demand. (e) 70,000. (f) £2,100. (g) 5p. (h) 110,000; (i) £3,300.

Chapter 26

1. (a) Longer distances usually involved.
   (b) Immobility of labour.
   (c) Immobility of capital.
   (d) Currencies have to be changed.
   (e) Subject to government control.
   (f) Involves crossing frontiers.
   (g) Internal trade more certain.
   (h) Account has to be taken of differences in languages, customs, tastes, weights and measures, etc.
   (i) Transport costs and difficulties.

2. (a) Language difficulties.
   (b) Different customs.
   (c) Cost of travelling greater.
   (d) Government policies restricting immigration.
   (e) Trade union barriers.

3. Total production with specialisation: 2,000 small cars, 1,400 large cars possessed by UK and USA respectively.

   USA exchanges 700 large cars for 1,400 small cars; therefore, gains 200 small cars by specialisation.

   UK has 600 small cars left and 700 by exchange. She therefore has 1,300 cars instead of 1,100, and 600 of these are large cars (instead of only 100 previously).

4. They are worldwide and multilateral in their operation.

Chapter 27

1. (a) Yes. If the man changes his sterling to francs, he obtains 12,000 f. If he changes the francs to dollars, he obtains $2,182. If he changes these to sterling, he obtains £1,091. (Ignoring any commission charges, etc.)
    (b) In a highly competitive market, arbitrage operations eliminate any price differences which may temporarily emerge; e.g. in (a) above, the dollar–franc rate is out of line with the other two rates.
    (c) Arbitrage operations occur in any organised market where there is a homogeneous commodity, e.g. rubber, foreign exchange, etc.

2. (a) £1 = $1.50.
    (b) The rate falls to £1 = $1.48.
    (c) (i) Sell pounds.
       (ii) Buy pounds.
    (d) To keep the rate at $1.52, when the free market would be $1.50, the authorities must continually buy pounds off the market. This would eventually exhaust the reserves, and lead to the abandonment of the pegged rate, unless other measures are taken, e.g. exchange control.
    (e) An overvalued pound means that the exchange rate does not reflect accurately the cost-price structure of the UK relative to other countries.
    (f) Speculation against sterling led to UK's withdrawal from the ERM in September 1992.

Chapter 28

1. Any non-sterling payment from outside the UK to a recipient requiring sterling.

2. (a) Current account has deficit or surplus added to balance each side.
    (b) Overall the balance-of-payments balances because any difference on current account earning and spending is balanced by capital, including changes in the official reserves.

3. (a)

Balance of payments, country X (£ million)

Current Account

Debit	£	Credit	£
Imports	1,813	Exports	1,529
Invisibles	158	Invisibles	772
Surplus	330		
	£2,301		£2,301

	£		£
Long-term loans	96	Short-term borrowing . .	97
Investment	131	Investment	146
Aid	40		
Addition to reserves . .	306		
	£2,544		£2,544

(b) £284 m deficit. (c) Surplus 330. (d) Addition 306.

4. (a) Worsen; as exports lose competitiveness and imports gain competitiveness over home-produced goods.
   (b) Short-term capital moves out as inflation can lead to depreciation/devaluation of currency.
   (c) Depreciates.

5. (a) Trade unions resist a reduction in money wage-rates.
   (b) Many costs are contractual, e.g. rents.
   (c) Monopoly and restrictive practices can maintain prices.

6. (a) Unemployment resulting from reduction of home income.
   (b) Reduces volume of international trade.
   (c) Depends upon every country acting in full co-operation regarding devaluation, maintaining full employment, etc.

7. (a) Elastic demand for imports and exports.
   (b) No competitive devaluation in retaliation.
   (c) Elastic supply of exports.
   (d) Inelastic supply of imports.
   (e) British investments abroad mostly in equities; foreign investments in UK fixed-interest stock paid in sterling.
   (f) Not regarded abroad as likely to be followed by further depreciation.

8. (a) Demand for raw materials to be manufactured into exports likely to increase.
   (b) Higher home income leads to greater demand for imported goods.

9. (a) and (b) are terms applying to the fall and rise, respectively, of the price of something in a free market, e.g. if the demand for pounds decreases, the value of the pound will tend to depreciate. (c) and (d) refer exclusively to foreign exchange; they refer to the deliberate lowering or raising of the exchange rate officially declared by the government.

Chapter 29

1. By eliminating customs duties between member countries, it allows trade to flow more freely according to comparative cost advantages.

2. It imposes duties against outside countries, thereby hampering trade flows.

3. (a) Aircraft, computers, motor vehicles, patent drugs.

(b) A larger market would enable overheads to be spread on higher output, thus reducing average cost per unit.

4. While a free-trade area simply removes tariff barriers between member countries leaving each country to impose such duties as it wishes against outsiders, a customs union has common external tariffs.

5. High prices for agricultural produce are maintained on the home market by imposing duties on cheaper imports from abroad.

6. Allocations can be made from the Fund to help Britain's Assisted Areas. Britain has been a major recipient.

7. A single currency would:
   (a) eliminate possible exchange rate depreciation by a country;
   (b) eliminate the costs of exchanging currencies;
   (c) through the European Central Bank (ECB), provide stability of the ECU vis-à-vis other currencies;
   (d) bring identity to the single market.

8. (a) UK would be unable to follow an independent economic policy to suit her own domestic conditions.
   (b) Directions from the ECB would cover fiscal (taxation) policy as well as monetary.

Index

ACAS (Advisory, Conciliation and Arbitration Service)   105
acceptance houses   205–6
accountability   157–8
AD   *see* aggregate demand
ad valorem taxes   265, 310, 311, 316
advances   219–20, 221–2
advertising   7–8, 15, 151–2
Advisory, Conciliation and Arbitration Service (ACAS)   105
aggregate demand (AD)
  changes (reasons for)   254–6, 259
  consumption spending   256–9, 273
  demand management   280–2, 288
  full employment policy   264–7, 268
  investment spending   259–61, 262–3
  leaks and injections   263–4
  money supply and   272–3
  spending and production   252–4
aggregate demand curve   268–9, 270, 272
aggregate supply curve   269–70, 272
aggregating variables   233–4
Agricultural Guidance and Guarantee Fund, European (EAGGF)   298, 365, 368
Agricultural Wages Board   105
agriculture   48, 132, 142, 337
  CAP   363, 366–7
  deficiency payments   366
  dumping   367–8
  output   114, 368
  price support   265
  production quotas   368
Alternative Investment Market (AIM)   47, 51, 213
arbitrage   342–3
arbitration (dispute settlement)   105
asset investment   259
assets (of banks)   220–3
Assisted Areas   50, 59, 295, 296, 297
Atomic Energy Authority (EURATOM)   360

balance of payments   269, 315, 332
  accounts   348–51
  correction   352–8
  deficit   281, 352
  difficulties   280, 281
  disequilibrium   338, 352
  exports   348
  imports   346–8
balance of trade   349
balancing item (balance of payments)   351
bank bills   205

bank deposits   202
Bank for International Settlements   226
Bank of England   206–7, 216, 225–8, 287
  Act, 1998   227
  EMU and   374
  responsibilities and procedure   287–8
banks
  assets   220–3
  central   *see* Bank of England
  clearing   212, 216, 217–24, 226
  commercial   206
  foreign   210
  Girobank   210
  loans   219–22
  merchant   51, 205, 206, 212
  overseas   223
  retail   216, 217–24
  security   220
  see also building societies; European Central Bank; European Investment Bank; International Bank for Reconstruction and Development; National Savings Bank; World Bank
'bidding-up' prices   5
Big Bang   212
bills
  bank   205
  of exchange   203–7
  of lading   204
  of trade   205, 221
  see also Treasury Bills
black economy   245, 246
black markets   153, 353
block pricing   161
Blue Book (The United Kingdom National Accounts)   236
bonds   113–14, 283
borrowing   50, 203, 213
  see also credit; loans; Public Sector Borrowing Requirement
Bretton Woods agreement   358
Britain
  banking   287–8
  ERM membership   369–71
  EU membership   365–9
  international trade   16
  labour force   95–6
  mixed economy   9
  pattern of overseas trade   333–5
  trade with EU   365
  unemployment   95
British Aerospace   163

British Airports Authority   162, 163
British Airways   162
British American Tobacco   55
British Gas   146, 162, 164
British Telecom   146, 162, 163, 164
'broad money'   202
brokers   211, 212
budgetary policy   265–6, 283, 287
building societies   211, 216, 224
Building Society Act (1987)   211
business saving   258–9
Business Start-up Scheme   48
buyers   76–8

Cable and Wireless   163
CAP (Common Agricultural Policy)   363, 366
capital
  accumulation of   114–15
  consumer's   113
  definition   113–14
  depreciation   115
  equipment   121–2, 131, 301, 302
  as factor of production   89, 113, 114
  fixed   48–9
  flow   350–1
  investment   *see* investment
  liquid   48–9, 113, 115–16, 203
  long-term   49–50, 208, 222, 351
  maintained intact   115
  national   113–14
  raising   44–51
  short-term   350–1
  social   114
  titles   113–14
  venture   50, 51
  working   48
  see also interest rates; money; profit
capital gains tax   47, 310
capital markets   203, 208–11
car ownership   65
cash   217–18, 221, 223
  see also coins and notes
cash-and-carry warehouses   65, 66
cash-ratio approach   223
cash-reserve ratio   220
CBA (cost–benefit analysis)   171–3
Census of Distribution   238, 242
Census of Production   238, 242
central bank   *see* Bank of England
centrally directed economy   *see* command economy
certificates of deposit   207, 221
CET   *see* Common External Tariff
Chancellor of the Exchequer   287–8
cheque system   217–18
City Challenge   296
City Grants   296, 297
clearing banks   212, 216, 217–24, 226
Coal and Steel Community, European (ECSC)   298, 360
coins and notes   202, 225
  see also cash

collateral   220, 228
collective bargaining   104–11
collective goods   7, 156, 157, 159, 160
command economy   5, 162
  decision-making   7
  defects   8
  merits   7–8
commercial banks   206
commercial bills of exchange   203–7
commercial economies   54–5
'commercial rent'   116–17
Commission (EU)   361
commodities   14–15
  futures markets   16–17
  prices   29
Common Agricultural Policy (CAP)   363, 366
Common External Tariff (CET)   363, 364, 366
common market (EU objective)   362–4
Communism   162
community goods   5–6, 7, 156, 157, 159, 160
comparative cost   328–9
competition   6, 7, 65
  EU and   365
  imperfect   93, 110–11, 136–7, 149–52, 152–3
  indirect   163
  monopolistic   137–8, 149–52
  non-price   153
  perfect   *see* perfect competition
  promoting   144, 330
  'unfair'   143, 338–9
Competition Act (1980)   144
Competition Commission   144
Competition and Credit Control   223
conciliation (dispute settlement)   105
conservation
  nature of   176–7
  preservation   179–82
  of stocks   177–9
Conservative government   163, 164, 165, 282–6
Consolidated Fund   225
consumer choice   5, 6
consumer goods   89, 238, 257, 273, 314
consumers   37–8
  co-operative societies   47–8
  distribution of goods to   60–6
  equilibrium   32–5
  shopping trends   65
Consumers' Association   152
consumption
  postponing   114–15
  spending   256–9, 273
co-operative societies   47–8
Co-operative Wholesale Society   47, 48
copyrights   138
corporation tax   45, 50, 57, 265, 310, 312, 314
corruption   8, 368

cost of living   276–8
cost–benefit analysis (CBA)   171–3
cost-push inflation   271
costs
    advertising   152
    comparative   328–9
    explicit   71
    external   6, 169–70, 179
    fixed   72–3, 80
    implicit   71–2
    labour   110
    marginal   73, 78–9
    of monopolists   139–40, 142
    output and   73–6
    perfect competition   142
    production   71–6
    reduction   285
    schedules   74–6
    'sunk'   145
    variable   72–3
    see also opportunity costs; supply
        (costs and profitability); transport
        costs
Council of Europe   360
Council of Ministers (EU)   361–2, 369
Council Tax   311
counterparties   228
Countryside Commission   158
credit   257, 282
    bank   222
    creation of   218–19
    reimbursement   205–6
credit cards   217, 224
CREST (share trading system)   213
cross-elasticity of demand   38–9
currency
    differences   342
    foreign currency reserves   226, 342
    notes   202, 225
    see also cash; exchange rates (currency)
current account (balance of payments)
    349–50
current balance (balance of payments)
    349–50
Customs and Excise, Department of   45,
    311
customs duties   311, 336
customs union (EU objective)   363
cyclical unemployment   251

debentures   50, 51
debt
    government   114, 241, 266, 281
    international   240
Debt Management Office   226
deflation   352–4
Delors, Jacques   371
demand
    conditions of   18–20, 24–5, 251
    cross-elasticity of   38–9
    curve   35, 91, 92

elasticity of   35–8, 85, 110, 318–22,
    355–6
    income-elasticity   38
    joint   29
    labour   90–1, 93, 107
    marginal-utility theory   32–5
    needs and   158–9
    price determination and   17–20, 27–8
    price-elasticity of   35–8
    schedule   18–19, 35
    small firms   57
demand curves   76–8, 116
demand management   280–2, 288
demand-pull inflation   270
department stores   64
deposits, bank   219–20
depreciation   238, 243, 253–4
    exchange rate   354–7, 374
derived demands   90–1
desk research   44
DETR (Department of Environment,
    Transport and the Regions)   297
devaluation   355
diminishing marginal propensity to
    consume   256
diminishing returns   68–70, 90–1
direct taxes   265, 309–14, 317
Directive on Works Councils (EU)   105
discount houses   205, 206, 207, 228
discount market   203–4, 207
discrimination
    price   147–9, 160, 161
    social   102–3, 111
dispute settlement   105–6
distribution of goods   60–6
dividends
    co-operative societies   48
    investment trusts   210
    shares   49
division of labour   52–3, 54–5
double-counting   113, 238, 240
Driving and Vehicle Licensing Centre   295
dumping   336, 338, 367–8

EAGGF   see Agricultural Guidance and
    Guarantee Fund, European
earnings   98–9, 117–19
    expenditure and   252
    see also wages
ECB see European Central Bank
Economic and Monetary Union (EMU)
    227, 266, 358, 371–5
    Treaty of Maastricht   371–2, 373
economic goods   4, 175
economic growth   see growth
economic policy   138, 231–5, 246, 280–1
economic problem   3–4
economic rent   119–21
economic systems   4–5, 234
    see also command economy; market
        economy; mixed economy (Britain)

economics
  limitations   9–10
  role   10, 175–6
  supply-side   284–6
ECSC   *see* Coal and Steel Community,
  European
ECU   *see* European Currency Unit
EEC (European Economic Community)
  360–1
efficiency
  in allocation of resources   133–4, 151,
    171
  economic   134, 142, 157–8
  exchange   133
  firms   125–6, 314, 330, 366
  technical   133–4
effort   313, 314
EFTA (European Free Trade Area)   361
EIB   *see* European Investment Bank
elasticity
  of demand   35–9, 85, 110, 320, 322, 355–6
  of supply   82–6, 109–10, 120–1, 321, 356
employment
  full   264–7, 268
  opportunities   98
  overfull   281
  self-employment   95, 96
  of women   65, 95, 97–8, 102
  see also occupations; unemployment;
    wages
Employment, Department of   105–6
Employment Transfer Scheme   294
EMU   *see* Economic and Monetary Union
English Partnerships (EP)   297
enterprise   122, 313
  as factor of production   89–90
Enterprise Zones   296
entrepreneurs   49, 91, 98, 122–3, 124
entrepreneurship   122–3
environment   181–2, 186–7, 196
  conservation   176–82
  economic aspects   175–6, 302
  externalities   169–73
  pollution   182–7
  preservation   179–82
  road traffic   187–95
Environment, Transport and the Regions,
  Department of (DETR)   297
Environment Agency   185
EP (English Partnerships)   297
Equal Pay Act (1970)   98
equilibrium
  condition (marginal utility)   32–5
  output   79, 141–2
ERDF   *see* Regional Development Fund,
  European
ERM   *see* Exchange Rate Mechanism
ESF   *see* Social Fund, European
EURATOM (Atomic Energy Authority)   360
Euro   371, 372–3
Eurobond market   208

Eurocurrency market   208
European Central Bank (ECB)   371, 372,
  373–5
European Currency Unit (ECU)   370
  see also Euro
European Economic Community (EEC)
  360–1
European Free Trade Area (EFTA)   361
European Investment Bank (EIB)   298, 362
European Parliament   362
European Union (EU)   291, 293, 297
  background   360–1
  budget   368
  Commission   361
  common market   362–4
  Council of Ministers   361–2, 369
  court of justice   362
  customs union   363
  harmonisation measures   363–4
  institutions   361–2
  law   144, 369
  Parliament   362
  Presidency   362
  problems   366–9
  regional policy and   297–8
  Single Market (1993)   364–5
  subsidiarity   369
  UK membership   365–9
  UK trade with   335
  see also Economic and Monetary Union;
    Exchange Rate Mechanism
exchange controls   212, 223, 336, 353
Exchange Equalisation Account   226, 357–8
Exchange Rate Mechanism (ERM)   283,
  286, 357, 358, 363
  UK membership   369–71
exchange rates (currency)   331
  depreciation   354–7, 374
  determination   342–3
  economic influences on   343–5
  stabilising   357–8, 370–1
  see also Economic and Monetary Union;
    Exchange Rate Mechanism
exchange rates (trade)   *see* terms of trade
excise duties   311
executive agencies   158
expansion (finance)   51, 55, 125, 368
expenditure
  consumption   256–9, 273
  government   266, 305–8, 344
  income and   252–4
  investment   259–61, 262–3
  national   *see* aggregate demand; national
    income (calculation)
  production and   252–4
explicit costs   71
exports   263–4, 280
  dumping   336, 338, 367–8
  free trade   336–40
  invisible   16, 348
  pattern of UK trade   333–5

exports *(continued)*
  visible 348
  see also balance of payments;
    international trade; terms of trade
external costs/benefits 6, 169–70, 179
external economies 55
externalities 6, 169–71
  cost–benefit analysis and 171–3

factor earnings 7
factor houses 48
factors of production 23
  capital 89, 113, 114
  classification 89–90
  combining 68–71
  cost of attracting 84–5
  direction of 8
  earnings 117–19
  enterprise 89–90
  fixed/variable 72–6, 80
  growth and 300–1
  labour as 89, 90–3, 96–7
  land as 59–60, 89, 117–19
  mobility/immobility 6, 78, 137–8
  organisation of 131
  and price 28–9
  returns 117–19
  rewards 90–3
  see also capital; labour; land
Fair Trading Act (1973) 144
Family Expenditure Survey 242, 278
fashion/taste 20
finance 204
  capital 208–11
  expansion 51, 55, 125, 368
  liquid capital 48–9, 113, 115–16, 203
  money 201–2
  money markets 203–8
  public 305–22
  securities markets 211–14
finance corporations 211
finance houses 208, 211
financial account (balance of payments)
    350–1
financial economies 55
financial services 224
Financial Services Authority (FSA) 227
firms 4–5
  decisions 43
  demand curve 91, 92
  development of 142
  efficiency 125–6, 314, 330, 366
  financing expansion 51, 55, 368
  income flow 252–3, 255–6, 263–4
  investment 260–1
  large 65
  legal form 44–8
  location 58–60, 294–7
  objectives 42–3
  output 76–81
  role 41–3
  size 56–8

small 56–8, 368
  see also production
fiscal policy 20, 23, 57, 264–6, 281–2, 288,
    374
fish stocks 177–9
fixed commissions 212
fixed costs 72–3, 80
foreign currency exchange rates *see*
    exchange rates (currency)
foreign currency reserves 226, 342
foreign exchange market 342–3
foreign loans/investments 131–2, 240, 314,
    344, 351, 356–7, 365
franchising 57, 63–4, 145, 146, 164
fraud 214, 368
free goods 4
free market *see* market economy
free trade
  area 363
  protection and 336–40
'free-riders' 156, 170, 180, 181
frictional unemployment 249
Friedman, Milton 272, 273, 281–2
Friends of the Earth 185
FSA (Financial Services Authority) 227
'futures' dealings 16–17

GATT *see* General Agreement on Tariffs
    and Trade
GDP *see* Gross Domestic Product
General Agreement on Tariffs and Trade
    (GATT) 336, 338, 339–40, 368
geographical mobility 101–2, 103, 250
gifts 132
gilts 208, 226, 227, 228
Girobank 210
GNP *see* Gross National Product
gold reserves 226
gold standard 357
goods
  allocation of 9
  collective 7, 156, 157, 159, 160
  community 5–6, 7, 156, 157, 159, 160
  complements 20
  consumer 89, 238, 257, 273, 314
  distribution 60–6
  economic 4, 175
  free 4
  manufactured 334
  merit 7, 157, 159–60
  producer 89
  product differentiation 149–50
  provision of 156–65, 171
  scarce 4, 20, 26–7
  of strategic importance 337
  substitutes 19–20, 37, 38–9
  see also commodities
goodwill 149–50
government
  banking 225–6
  borrowing *see* Public Sector Borrowing
    Requirement

budgetary policy 265–6, 283, 287
debt 114, 241, 266, 281
departments 157
distribution of income 6, 159–60, 234–5, 305
economic policy 138, 231–5, 246, 280–1
environmental policies 181–2, 186–7
expenditure 266, 305–8, 344
fiscal policy 20, 23, 57, 260, 264–6, 281–2, 288, 374
grants 50, 59
growth policy 303–4
inflation control 279–80, 286–7, 357, 370
loans 50
macro objectives 231–2
monetarist policy 282–6
monetary policy 266–7, 281–8, 372
regional policy 293–8
role of 9, 10, 134–5
savings policy 258, 259
services 156–65, 171, 238, 242
wages policy 111–12, 284
see also national income (calculation); taxation
Government Office Regions 297
grants 50, 59
Green Party 185
'greenhouse' effect 185
Greenpeace 170
Gross Domestic Product (GDP) 240, 243, 305, 340, 374
Gross National Product (GNP) 238, 239, 240–3, 244, 299–300
growth
achievement of 300–2
EU and 365
government and 303–4
maximisation 42
nature of 299–300
pollution and 183

Health and Social Security, Department of 295
'highly-geared' companies 50
hire-purchase 257
historic buildings 179–82
holding companies 56
horizontal integration 56
'hot money' 351
households 4–5
income 240, 252–3, 254–8, 262–3
saving 254–6, 256–8, 259, 262–3
housing 238, 294, 311
hypermarkets 64, 65

IBB (Invest in Britain Bureau) 295
IBRD see International Bank for Reconstruction and Development
IMF see International Monetary Fund
imperfect competition 93, 110–11, 136–7, 149–52, 152–3
implicit costs 71–2

imports 62, 263–4, 280
duties 315, 353
free trade 336–40
pattern of UK trade 333–5
quotas 138, 336, 338–9, 353
reduction 352–4
see also balance of payments; international trade; terms of trade
incentives (supply-side) 285–6
income
circular flow 252–3, 254–6, 263–4
distribution 6, 159–60, 234–5, 246–7, 305
effect 34
elasticity of demand 38
government activities 242
household 240, 252–3, 256–8
level (investment changes) 262–3
national 240, 243–5, 254 (see also national income (calculation))
personal disposable 243, 244
real 20
savings and see savings
transfer 240–1
unearned 98
income tax 45, 258, 265, 266, 310, 312–14
independents (retail outlets) 63–4
indirect taxes 86, 266, 309, 311–12, 314–17, 317–18, 320–1
industrial action 111, 112, 248, 249, 284
industry
demand curve 91, 92
infant (protection of) 338
obstacles to labour mobility 102, 250
primary 41
secondary 41
structure 41–66
supply curve 81–2, 92
tertiary 41
see also nationalised industries
Industry, Department of 51
inflation 227
control 279–80, 286, 357, 370
cost-push 271
demand-pull 270
effects 257, 279–80
expectations 273, 274–5, 284
monetarist theory 272–5
process 272
rate 271
recession and recovery 286–7
stagflation 271–2
unemployment and 273–4, 281, 286–7
wages and 106, 271, 272, 273, 274, 284
Inflation Report (Bank of England) 288
information technology 212, 224
inheritance tax 310, 313
Inland Revenue 45, 310
innovation 125, 142, 154, 301–2, 303–4
inquiry (dispute settlement) 105–6
insurance companies 209
integration 56
intercompany deposits 208

interest rates   227, 228, 260–1, 266–7, 273, 284, 344, 373–4
  base rate   287–8
  definition   115–16
internal economies   53–5
International Bank for Reconstruction and Development (IBRD)   226, 358
international indebtedness   240
International Monetary Fund (IMF)   226, 350, 352, 357, 358
international trade   16, 240, 250, 327
  advantages   327–30
  exchange rates   330–1
  free trade and protection   336–40
  multilateral   335
  pattern of UK trade   333–5
  terms of trade   330–3
  see also European Union; General Agreement on Tariffs and Trade
international unemployment   250
Invest in Britain Bureau (IBB)   295
investigation (dispute settlement)   105–6
investment   115–16
  cost   260
  definition   259–60
  foreign   see foreign loans/investments
  government policy and   260
  income level and   262–3
  institutional   209
  private sector   260–1
  public sector   260, 261
  spending   259–61, 262–3
  yield   260
investment trusts   209–10
invisible exports   16, 348
issuing houses   51

jobbers   211
Joint Industrial Councils   104–5
joint stock companies   46–7

Keynes, John Maynard   264, 267, 268, 273, 280–1, 294–5

labour
  availability   59
  costs   110
  demand   90–1, 93, 107
  division of   52–3, 54–5, 115
  as factor of production   89, 90–3, 96–7
  mobility   93, 97, 101–3, 250–1, 292, 293–4, 327
  rewards   98–100
  supply   92–3, 97–8, 101–2, 107, 108, 301
  see also employment; labour force; trade unions; unemployment; wages
labour force
  nature of   96–8, 131
  UK   95–6
Labour government   163, 227, 286

land
  as factor of production   59–60, 89, 117–19
  rent and   116–22
  see also environment
large-scale production   53–5, 57, 330
lateral integration   56
legal tender   201
leisure   114, 244, 302, 312–13
LIBOR (London Inter-Bank Offered Rate)   207
life cycle
  of people   258
  of products   153–4
limited liability   45, 46, 47
liquid capital   48–9, 113, 115–16, 203
liquidity   220, 221, 228
listed buildings   181–2
living standards   327–8
  capital and   114–15
  consumption spending and   256–8
  determination of   130–2
  growth and   299–300
  international comparisons   245–6
  national income and   243–5
Loan Guarantee Scheme   51
loans   116
  bank   219–22
  foreign   see foreign loans/investments
  government   50
  long-term   50, 211
  market   221
  see also credit
local authorities   158, 310
  bills   221
  market (money market)   207
location of firms   58–60, 294–7
London Inter-Bank Offered Rate (LIBOR)   207
losses   124, 125, 126

Macmillan, Harold   231
macro-economics   232–3, 234
mail order   65
malpractice (Stock Exchange)   214
managed flexibility   357–8
management   54, 122
managerial economies   54
managers   42
manufactured goods   334
manufacturing   95, 96, 132, 334
marginal cost   73, 78–9
marginal increment   33
marginal physical product   91, 93
marginal product   69–71, 73
marginal revenue   78–9, 139
marginal revenue product   91, 93, 100–1, 106, 107–9, 116
marginal-utility theory   32–5
market economy   5–7, 9
  defects   5–6
  demand and supply   24–5

externalities and 170
further applications 29–31
price determination 17–24, 27–8
price (functions) 25–9
regional depression and 291–2
stabilisation 231–2
market freedom 284–5
market research 44
Marketing Boards 48, 142
market-makers 212, 214
markets
  capital 203, 208–11
  clearing price 23–4
  contestable 138, 145–6
  definition 13–17
  failure 7, 134–5
  foreign-exchange 342–3
  forms 137
  imperfect 15
  mechanism 5–7
  money 203–8
  negotiation 185–6
  organised produce 15–17
  perfect 15, 16
  securities 211–14
  solutions 145–7, 179–81
merchant banks 51, 205, 206, 212
Mercury 146, 163
merit goods 7, 157, 159–60
micro-economics 232, 234
middlemen 66
migration 292
minimum wage 7
mixed economy (Britain) 9
monetarism 272–5, 282–8
monetary control 282
monetary policy 266–7, 281–8, 372
Monetary Policy Committee (MPC) 227, 287–8
money 5, 53, 201, 252–3
  functions 201–2
  markets 203–8
  supply 202, 272–3, 282–3
  value of 257, 276–80
  see also capital
money illusion 273
Monopolies and Mergers Act (1965) 144
Monopolies and Mergers Commission 164
Monopolies and Restrictive Practices Act (1948) 143
Monopolies Commission 143–4
monopolistic competition 137–8
  conditions giving rise to 149–50
  economic and social effects 151–2
  equilibrium of industry under 150–1
  nature of 149
monopoly
  benefits 142, 143, 160–1
  control of 142–7
  costs 139–40, 142
  criterion 144

deliberate 138, 140, 142–3
discriminating 147
imperfect competition 136–54, 149–52
market solutions 145–7
'natural' 138, 163
output 139–40, 141–2
policy 140–7
power 7, 56, 137–8, 143
price 42, 145
profit 124, 126
prohibition 144
regulation 143–4
revenue 139
spontaneous 138, 140, 142–3
'most-favoured-nation' principle 339–40
motor vehicle duties 311
MPC *see* Monetary Policy Committee
multiples (retail outlets) 64
multiplier effect 262, 294–5

'narrow money' 202
National Bus Company 163
national capital 113–14
National Debt 114, 241, 266, 281
National Food Survey 242
national income (calculation)
  factors 130–2, 259–60
  in practice 237–43
  principle of 236–7
  uses of statistics 243–7
national income (distribution) 234–5
National Insurance
  contributions 311
  Fund 226
National Loans Fund 225
National Parks Commission 158
National Savings Bank 113–14, 210, 226, 258, 308
National Savings Certificates 210, 308, 310
National Trust 171, 176, 180
nationalised industries 157–8, 161–2
  and privatisation 162–5
  see also public sector
NATO (North Atlantic Treaty Organisation) 360
natural resources 130–1, 301
needs, demand and (public sector) 158–9
negotiable certificates of deposit 207
negotiation
  collective bargaining 104–5
  market 185–6
  private 170
Net Book Agreement 144
Net National Product 243
net profit 253–4
normal profit 72, 124, 125
North Atlantic Treaty Organisation (NATO) 360
North Sea gas 260, 301
North Sea oil 260, 290, 301

occupational mobility   101–2, 102–3, 251,
   294
occupations   100–1, 121
Office for Telecommunications (OFTEL)
   164
Office of Fair Trading   144, 212
Office of Gas Supply (OFGAS)   164
Official List (Stock Exchange)   211, 214
OFGAS (Office of Gas Supply)   164
OFTEL (Office for Telecommunications)
   164
Oil and Gas (Enterprise) Act (1982)   146
oligopoly   137, 152–3
'on tap'   226
opportunity costs   3–4, 117–19, 156, 176,
   187, 329
   profit and   71
'option demand'   179–80
ordinary shares   49
Organisation for European Economic
   Co-operation   360
output
   costs and   73–6
   equilibrium   79, 141–2
   growth and   302
   of monopolists   139–40, 141–2
   national   242–3 (*see also* national
      income, calculation)
   perfect competition and   76–81, 141–2,
      151
   price level and   268–70, 272, 281
   see also productivity
overdrafts   222
overheads   153–4
overtime   98

parallel money markets   207–8
partnerships   45–6
patents   138, 142, 144
Patents Acts   142
PAYE   312
pensions   98, 258
   funds   211
perfect competition
   conditions   76–8, 136
   costs   142
   labour demand   90–1
   output and   76–81, 141–2, 151
   and wage-rate   108
perfect knowledge   78, 135, 180
perfect market   78
perfect mobility   78
personal disposable income   243, 244
Personal Equity Plans   258
personal loans   222
personal saving   256–8, 259, 286
Petroleum Revenue Tax   311
PFI (private finance initiative)   164–5
Phillips, A.W.   271
Phillips curve   271–2, 273–4
piece-rates   99–100

planning controls   171
plc (public limited company)   47
political issues   8, 9, 131, 337, 344, 365,
   372
pollution
   aspects   182–3
   control   183–7
   definition   183
   policies   184–7
population
   age-distribution   258
   demand and   20
   growth   183
   labour supply and   97–8, 301
Post Offices   210
PPC *see* production possibility curve
preference shares   49–50
Premium Bonds   210, 258, 308
preservation   176, 177, 179–82
pressure groups   170
price
   control   145
   demand and   17–20
   determination   17–24, 27–8
   discrimination   147–9, 160, 161
   elasticity of demand   35–8
   factors of production and   28–9
   fluctuations   17
   functions   25–31
   inflation   *see* inflation
   level, output and   268–70, 272, 281
   market-clearing   23–4
   minimum price resale   144
   perfect/imperfect markets   15, 152–3
   regulation (by formula)   147
   shadow   185
   shut-down   80
   spot prices   16
   supply and   17–18, 20–2, 117–19
   system   5–7, 171
   value and   13
price-takers   76
pricing policies   153
   cost-plus   153
   mark-up   153–4
   MC = MR principle   153, 154
   public corporations   157–8
   public sector   159–61
   road traffic   191–4
private companies   47, 51
private costs/benefits   169–70
private finance initiative (PFI)   164–5
private property rights   177–8
private sector   9
   demand   32–9
   investment   260–1
   market economy   13–31
   supply (costs and profitability)   68–86
   supply (structure of industry)   41–66
   wealth   6
   see also firms; industry

privatisation 145, 283
  nature of 162
  problems 163–4
  success of 163
producer co-operatives 48, 66
producer goods 89
product
  allocation of 5–7, 8
  differentiation 149–50
  homogeneous 78
  life-cycle 153–4
  national *see* national income,
    calculation)
production
  calculating value of 237–8
  choice of goods 43–4
  costs 71–6
  definition 41
  division of labour 52–3, 54–5, 115
  large-scale 53–5, 57, 330
  location 58–60
  scope 60–1
  spending and 252–4
  technical efficiency 133–4
production possibility curve (PPC) 129–32,
    299–300
productivity 106
  see also growth; output
professional associations 138
profit
  definitions 123–4
  maximisation 42–3, 76, 78–9
  monopoly 124, 126
  nature of 123
  net 253–4
  normal 72, 124, 125
  retained 50, 258–9
  role 124–6
  super-normal 72, 81, 110–11, 124, 125,
    151
  see also supply (costs and profitability)
profit motive 6
profitability 220
Project Grants 295
PSBR *see* Public Sector Borrowing
    Requirement
PSNCR *see* Public Sector Net Cash
    Requirement
psychological attitudes (to thrift) 258
public accountability 157–8
public companies 47
public corporations 157–8
public finance 305–23
public issues 51
public limited company (plc) 47
public sector 9
  accountability 157–8
  case for 156–7
  demand and needs 158–9
  economic efficiency 157–8
  investment 260, 261

pricing policy 159–61
provision of goods 156–65, 171
quangos 158
risks 122
services 156–65, 171, 238, 242
see also local authorities; nationalised
    industries; private sector
Public Sector Borrowing Requirement
    (PSBR) 159, 163, 165, 210, 266, 281,
    283, 286, 307–8
  EMU and 374
Public Sector Net Cash Requirement
    (PSNCR) 259, 283
public utilities 138

quasi-government bodies (quangos) 158
quasi-rent 121–2, 124
quotas
  agricultural production 368
  imports 138, 336, 338–9, 353

RDA (Regional Development Agencies)
    297
real income 20
real investment 259
recession 286–7
regional depression 290–3
regional development
  EU context 298, 365
  location of firms 294–7
  mobility of labour 293–4
  nature of problem 290–3
  urban regeneration 295–7
  see also regional policy
Regional Development Agencies (RDA)
    297
Regional Development Fund, European
    (ERDF) 298, 365, 373
regional policy
  assistance 295
  EU context 295, 297–8, 363–4
  unemployment and 293–5
Regional Selective Assistance 295
Registrar of Companies 43, 44, 46, 47
Registrar's Department (Bank of England)
    226
regulatory bodies 164
reimbursement credit 205–6
rent 59–60
  of ability 121, 124
  'commercial' 116–17
  economic 119–21
  land and 116–22
  quasi-rent 121–2, 124
repo market 208, 227–8
Resale Prices Act (1964) 144
research and development 52, 125, 126,
    142, 303–4
resources
  allocation of 5–7, 9, 132, 133–4, 169–70,
    171, 314, 316
  combining 68–71

resources *(continued)*
  full employment of   133
  growth of   133
  labour   4, 5
  living standards   130–2
  making most of   129–35
  natural   130–1
  organisation of   131
  scarcity problem   3–4
  state ownership   8
retail banks   216, 217–24
retail co-operatives   48
retail outlets   63–5
Retail Price Index   147, 278, 287, 288, 316
retailers   62–3, 66
retained profits   50, 258–9
retirement   98
revenue
  government expenditure and   305–8
  of monopolists   139–40
Ricardo, David   117–18, 119
rights issues   51
risk capital   49
risk-bearing   55, 99, 122
risks   55, 62, 89–90, 122–3, 209
road traffic
  costs and benefits   187
  parking restriction   190–1
  pricing policies   191–4
  private/public transport   192–4
  road investment   189
  traffic congestion policy   194–5
  traffic flows   189–90
  urban traffic problem   188–95
Rochdale Pioneers   47
Royal Mint   158, 225
Rural Development Commission   45

sales methods   42
savings   203, 314
  by business   258–9
  by household   254–6, 256–8, 259, 262–3
Savings Bonds   210
savings certificates   113–14
scarcity   3–10
SEAQ   *see* Stock Exchange Automated
  Quotation system
seasonal unemployment   249–50
securities   209–11, 221, 225
  markets   211–14
Securities and Investments Board (SIB)
  213
Securities Association Compensation Fund
  214
security (bank)   220
'seepage'   147
self-employment   95, 96
Self-Regulating Organisations (SROs)   213
sellers   76–8
services   4, 41, 95, 96
  invisible exports   348
  public sector   156–65, 171, 238, 242

Sex Discrimination Act (1975)   98
shadow pricing   185
share trading arrangements   213
shares   42, 46–8, 49–50, 51, 113–14, 212,
  310
shut-down price   80
Shute, Nevil   262
SIB (Securities and Investments Board)
  213
single capacity requirement   211, 212
single currency   227, 266, 358, 371–5
Single European Act (1987)   361–2
Single European Act (1993)   364–5
Single Market (1993)   364–5
Single Regional Budget (SRB)   297
Smith, Adam   41, 308
social capital   114
Social Chapter   364
social costs/benefits   169–70
social environment (and thrift)   258
Social Fund, European (ESF)   298, 365, 373
social policies   258, 337
Social Trends (1998)   305
sole proprietors   45
sovereignty   374–5
specialisation   334
  benefits   52, 327–30
  disadvantages   52–3
  EU and   365, 373
speculators   51
spillover costs/benefits   169–71
spot prices/transactions   16
SRB (Single Regional Budget)   297
SROs (Self-Regulating Organisations)   213
stagflation   271–2
'stags'   51
stamp duties   212, 311
standing charges   161
state ownership   143
  see also nationalised industries; public
  sector
sterling interbank market   207
stock appreciation   240
Stock Exchange   15, 47, 51, 211–14, 286
Stock Exchange Automated Quotation
  system (SEAQ)   213, 214
Stock Exchange Council   214
strike activity   111, 112, 248, 249, 284
structural unemployment   250–1
subjectivity   10
subsidies   161, 171, 323, 336
subsistence economies   4
substitution   35, 37, 38–9, 108–9, 110,
  149–50
supermarkets   64, 65
super-normal profit   72, 81, 110–11, 124,
  125, 151
superstores   64
supply
  conditions of   22–3, 24–5, 28, 251
  control of source of   138
  costs and profitability   68–86

elasticity of   82–6, 109–10, 120–1, 321, 356
joint   22, 29–30
labour   92–3, 97–8, 101–2, 107, 108, 301
money   202, 272–3, 282–3
and price determination   17–18, 20–2, 117–19
schedule   21–2
small firms   57–8
structure of industry   41–66
supply curve   76–7, 98
aggregate   84
long-period   81–2, 92
short-period   80–1, 98
supply-side economics   284–6
supranational organisations   360

takeovers   56, 138
tariffs
CET   363, 364, 366
GATT   336, 338, 339–40, 368
import duties   315, 353
protection   143
retaliatory   338
taxation   264–6
ad valorem   265, 311, 316
avoidance   314
capital gains   47, 310
corporation   45, 50, 57, 265, 310, 312, 314
council   310
customs and excise   311, 336
direct   265, 310–11, 312–14, 317
effects of   316–23
elasticity of supply   86
externalities and   171
incidence of   316–23
income   45, 258, 265, 266, 310, 312–14
income flow and   263–4
indirect   86, 266, 309, 311–12, 314–17, 317–18, 320–1
inheritance   310, 312
modern approach   308–10
of pollution   186–7
progressive   309, 312, 313
proportional   309
provision of goods and   156, 157, 159–60
regressive   309, 315, 316
specific   311
structure   265, 310–12
VAT   45, 311, 316, 317
see also Inland Revenue
technical economies   54
technical knowledge   131
technology
growth and   301–2, 303
information   212, 224
investment and   260
pollution control   183
'tender'   226
Terms and Conditions of Employment Act (1959)   105
terms of trade   132, 330–3, 337–8

test marketing   44
Thatcher government   162, 163, 164, 282–6
thrift   258
time and motion   52
time periods (elasticity of supply)   73, 84
time-preferences   180
time-rates   99, 100
trade   *see* international trade
Trade, Board of   144
Trade and Industry, Department of   213, 295
trade bills   205, 221
trade unions   138
collective bargaining   104–11
function   104
funds   211
monetarist policy and   283–4
power   103, 111–12, 284
wages and   100, 104–11
tradeable permits   187
trademarks   138
training   97, 300, 302
Training and Enterprise Councils   294
transport costs   14, 58–9
see also road traffic
Treasury Bills   113–14, 206, 207, 221, 223, 225, 283
Treaty of Maastricht (1991)   371–2, 373
Treaty of Rome (1957)   360, 361, 362, 364
trust funds   211

uncertainty   55, 123, 124, 125
underwriting   51
unearned income   98
unemployment   6, 8, 97
benefit   240–1, 249, 265, 294
causes   52–3, 249–51
cyclical   251
deflation and   354
figures   249
frictional   249
immobility and   293–4
inflation and   273–4, 281, 286–7
international   250
natural rate   274, 284
nature of   248–9
rate   271
regional   290–3
seasonal   249–50
stagflation   271–2
structural   250–1
UK   95
Uniform Business Rate   311
unit trusts   210
United Kingdom National Accounts (The Blue Book)   236
Urban Development Corporations   296
urban regeneration   295–7
Uruguay Round   340, 368
user-charges   160–1
utility   41
maximisation   33

value
  calculating   236–8
  price and   13
Value Added Tax (VAT)   45, 311, 316, 317
variable costs   72–3, 80
variable factors   48, 80
VAT   *see* Value Added Tax
venture capital   50, 51
vertical integration   56, 61
visible balance (balance of payments)   349
visible exports   348
voluntary chains   63, 66
voluntary export restraints   336, 337
voluntary negotiation (collective bargaining)
  104

wages
  collective bargaining   104–11
  determination   111
  differentials   106
  government and   111–12, 284
  inflation and   106, 271, 272, 273, 274,
   284
  minimum   7

piece-rates   99–100
time-rates   99, 100
trade unions and   100, 104–11
wage-rates   92–3, 98–103, 106, 107–11
Wages Councils   105
wants   3, 7, 27, 41
waste   176, 182–3, 183, 185
'Ways and Means'   225
wealth   9–10, 113–14, 202, 243, 257
  distribution   6, 7, 20, 234–5
Wealth of Nations   41
welfare   9–10, 243, 302
welfare state   281
Western European Union   360
wholesalers   61–2, 66
women (at work)   65, 95, 97–8, 102
'work to the workers' policy   294–7
'workers to the work' policy   293–4
World Bank   226, 358
world markets   14–15
  see also international trade
World Trade Organisation (WTO)   340
Worldwide Fund for Nature   170, 180
WTO (World Trade Organisation)   340